The Emerging System of International Criminal Law

Cover Photo Credits

- Detonation of car bomb loaded with 500 kg of explosives leaves 15 dead and 80 injured, Lima, Peru, 17 July 1992. © ANP photo.

- Rwandan Patriotic Front soldiers walk past the corpse of a woman killed during the 1994 civil war and genocide, Gitarama, Rwanda, 14 July 1994. © ANP photo.

- Fire-fighters from the Canadian team "Safety Boss" work on one of the last blown-out oil wells, damaged by Iraqi soldiers after nearly 200 wells were capped, Ramadatyn Fields, Kuwait, 2 November 1991. © ANP photo.

- Customs officers' display of cocaine after French police seizure of a record 1.2 tonnes with a street value of some US$ 2 million, Toulouse, France, 21 January 1993. © ANP photo.

- Moslem Bosnian woman prays on her son's grave, Cerckici, 13 August 1993. © ANP photo.

- International Criminal Tribunal for the Former Yugoslavia, proceedings to indict Bosnian Serb leader Radovan Karadzic and top Commander Ratko Mladic, the Hague, the Netherlands, 27 June 1996. © ANP photo.

- United Nations investigators, including the author (third on the right), with skulls of infants murdered in the 1994 genocide, Ntarama, Rwanda, 2 November 1994. Courtesy of José L. Gomez del Prado, Geneva.

- Syrian tank in the streets of Beirut, Lebanon, 1977. © International Committee of the Red Cross, Geneva.

* * * *

Lyal S. Sunga

The Emerging System of International Criminal Law
Developments in Codification and Implementation

KLUWER LAW INTERNATIONAL
THE HAGUE / LONDON / BOSTON

A C.I.P. Catalogue record for this book is available from the Library of Congress.

ISBN 90-411-0472-0

Published by Kluwer Law International,
P.O. Box 85889, 2508 CN The Hague, The Netherlands.

Sold and distributed in the U.S.A. and Canada
by Kluwer Law International,
675 Massachusetts Avenue, Cambridge, MA 02139, U.S.A.

In all other countries, sold and distributed
by Kluwer Law International, Distribution Centre,
P.O. Box 322, 3300 AH Dordrecht, The Netherlands.

Printed on acid-free paper

Printed in the Netherlands

To my dear Ilaria

TABLE OF CONTENTS

ACKNOWLEDGEMENTS

The present work, written in Ottawa, Rome and Geneva, identifies and evaluates prospects for the emergence of a unified system of international criminal law, characterized by broad and coherent material coverage, as well as fair and effective institutional implementation. I have tried to take account of all major relevant developments up to 31 December 1996.

I wish to extend my warmest thanks to Professor Georges Abi-Saab of the Graduate Institute of International Studies, Geneva, who has served as Appeals Chamber Judge of the International Criminal Tribunals for the Former Yugoslavia and Rwanda, for his comments on one of the later drafts which helped me to clarify numerous points of substance and structure. I am deeply indebted to Ilaria Bottigliero, who not only invigorated me to complete the book, but breathed life into it. Her constant encouragement and suggestions over the last two years have vastly benefitted the logical structure and coherence of the enquiry. All remaining defects, errors and omissions, however, remain my sole responsibility.

Finally, I wish to state that the ideas and views expressed in this book, unless explicitly indicated otherwise, are advanced in my personal capacity only and do not represent those of any United Nations organ or body, or those of any other organization, office or person.

Lyal S. Sunga
1 January 1997
Geneva, Switzerland

TABLE OF TREATIES

TABLE OF CASES

INTRODUCTION

AIM AND PLAN OF THE PRESENT ENQUIRY IN LIGHT OF THE COMPLEXITY OF INTERNATIONAL CRIMINAL LAW

1. AIM OF THE ENQUIRY

The last few years have brought about a number of remarkable developments in the field of international criminal law. In the summer of 1991, the International Law Commission (ILC) adopted an expanded draft Code of Crimes against the Peace and Security of Mankind (referred to hereinafter as the "1991 draft Code") that extended far beyond the scope of the initial draft Code, first adopted in 1951, indicating that the time was ripe for the international community to develop broad and coherent norms in this field. More spectacularly, in May 1993, the UN Security Council took decisive action to create the International Criminal Tribunal for the Former Yugoslavia, and in November 1994, established the International Criminal Tribunal for Rwanda. The Statutes for these *ad hoc* Tribunals impose individual criminal responsibility essentially for the most serious violations of international human rights and humanitarian law that were committed in those countries on a systematic and massive scale during recent armed conflicts. In 1994, the ILC adopted a draft statute for a permanent international criminal court. On 11 December 1995, the General Assembly created a Preparatory Committee on the Establishment of a Permanent International Criminal Court "to draft texts, with a view to preparing a widely acceptable consolidated text of a convention for an international criminal court as a next step towards consideration by a conference of plenipotentiaries".[1] In July 1996, the International Law Commission introduced radical revisions to the 1991 draft Code.

All these developments signal the international community's increasing interest in the establishment of an effective system of

---

[1]   A/Res/50/46 of 11 December 1995.

international criminal law. In the contemporary post-Cold War climate, there appear to be greater opportunities for closer political cooperation in this regard, as increasing international attention is focused on the need to suppress, punish and deter the individual from committing or ordering to be committed crimes under international law.

The aim of the present enquiry is to identify and evaluate prospects for the emergence of a unified system of international criminal law, characterized by broad and coherent material coverage, as well as fair and effective institutional implementation.

The present enquiry has three main parts. Part 1 (comprising Chapters I, II and III) uncovers the normative field of international criminal law by examining the relevant UN efforts in codification and progressive development. As explained below, the 1991 draft Code of Crimes against the Peace and Security of Mankind forms an ideal point of departure for this discussion. Part 2 (comprising Chapters IV, V and VI), takes account of increasing recognition of normative hierarchy in international law and then indicates patterns in existing means of international criminal law implementation at both the inter-State and international levels. Finally, Part 3 (Chapter VII) synthesizes these developments in codification and implementation in order to ascertain prospects for the future development of a good system of international criminal law.

However, in order to appreciate the significance of these developments to the prospects for an enhanced system of international criminal law, it is essential first to recognize the perplexing character of this field as it currently exists.

2. THE COMPLEXITY OF INTERNATIONAL CRIMINAL LAW

International criminal law has expanded more in the last fifty years than in the previous five hundred. However, international criminal law norms have originated in diverse sources and developed unsystematically over time. The content and mode of implementation of each norm reflect the immediate historical context of the period in which the norm emerged and the way in which legal recognition came about. International criminal law norms are neither uniform nor

.consistent in application and often vary greatly as regards source of law, form and legal status.

Five centuries ago, the few established norms on crimes under international law were limited in scope and exceptional in application. Ancient customary laws of war provide for individual criminal responsibility only for very narrowly defined breaches of medieval law, such as use of the crossbow, poisoning of wells, or wanton attacks on the civilian population. Generally, such norms, deriving from the ancient *jus militare* and knightly code of honour, have been enforced in few instances and today, are considered arcane or irrelevant. Aside from norms specifically providing for individual criminal responsibility for slave-trading and piracy, developed within the context of the Congress of Vienna, held in 1815, the normative material of international criminal law remained almost completely deficient until five decades ago.

Five decades ago, the Allies staged the spectacular Nuremberg and Tokyo trials in order to prosecute and punish enemy war criminals of the Second World War. The Nuremberg and Tokyo Judgements established definitively the principle that the individual shall be held responsible for crimes against peace and crimes against humanity and eventually brought about general recognition for a more expansive definition of 'war crime' as well. These dramatic developments were followed by efforts through the United Nations to ensure war crimes, crimes against peace, and crimes against humanity, would be deterred systematically and universally in future. In this spirit, the UN General Assembly requested the ILC[2] in 1947 to formulate the Nuremberg Principles and to prepare a draft international criminal code to ensure

---

[2]   Pursuant to Article 13(a) of the UN Charter, the ILC was created to work towards the 'progressive development of international law and its codification'. Art. 15 of the Statute of the International Law Commission defines 'progressive development' as "the preparation of draft conventions on subjects which have not yet been regulated by international law or in regard to which the law has not yet been sufficiently developed in the practice of states" and 'codification' to mean "the more precise formulation and systematisation of rules of international law in fields where there already has been extensive state practice". UN Doc. A/CN.4/Rev.2.

that the lessons provided by the Judgements of Nuremberg and Tokyo would not be forgotten.[3]

Early on in the codification effort, the ILC decided to exclude from its consideration criminal acts which did not have a political element and to include only those matters concerning the maintenance of international peace and security. On this basis, the ILC excluded piracy, traffic in dangerous drugs, traffic in women and children, slavery, counterfeiting of monetary currency, damage to submarine cables and other such matters, from the scope of 'crimes against the peace and security of mankind'. Some matters, such as counterfeiting of monetary currency, have become subject to international conventional regulation on account of their transboundary implications, in regard to which States have a mutual interest in coordinating domestic criminal enforcement, rather than on some connection to issues of international peace and security *per se*.

In 1991, for the first time, the ILC adopted a comprehensive draft Code that reaches far beyond the traditional Nuremberg and Tokyo Charter categories of crimes, as well as the scope of the previous version of the draft Code adopted in 1954.[4] The 1991 draft Code is particularly expansive comprising *inter alia* individual criminal responsibility for such widely divergent matters as the threat of aggression, colonial or alien domination, intervention, drug-trafficking and particularly serious cases of damage to the natural environment. In 1996, the ILC dropped from the draft Code a number of provisions in response to the comments and observations provided by several Governments.[5] Over the years, fluctuations in the draft Code's scope appear to indicate that no particular intrinsic element determines whether a given act is connected to 'maintenance of international peace and security'. Ultimately, whether particular acts are considered to constitute crimes under international law, or even potential threats to international peace and security, depends upon the extent

---

[3]   General Assembly resolution 177 (II) of 21 Nov. 1947.
[4]   *Adopted on* 28 July 1954; UN Doc. A/2693 (1954).
[5]   *See* Comments and Observations of Governments on the Draft Code of Crimes against the Peace and Security of Mankind adopted on First Reading by the International Law Commission at its 43rd Session, A/CN.4/448 of 1 March 1993.

of State recognition to this effect.[6] Certain miscellaneous matters, namely international traffic in obscene publications, unlawful use of the mails, interference with submarine cables, falsification and counterfeiting, and bribery of foreign public officials, currently are viewed as having an indirect relation only to international peace and security. Similarly, they are of peripheral relevance only to the emerging system of international criminal law or to the present enquiry.[7]

On 25 May 1993, the Security Council took a landmark decision to establish the *ad hoc* International Criminal Tribunal for the Former Yugoslavia:[8] the first tangible measure taken by the international community since the Nuremberg and Tokyo Tribunals to enforce international criminal law. In November 1994, the Security Council created another *ad hoc* court: the International Criminal Tribunal for Rwanda.[9]

The Security Council's decisiveness in creating these two *ad hoc* international criminal tribunals indicates that pragmatic action to create implementation mechanisms could yield concrete results more quickly than ILC efforts to codify the field comprehensively. Creation of the two tribunals, though not a smooth or easy process, took some months, whereas the seemingly interminable ILC work on a code and court remains incomplete after half a century. Moreover, the fact that decisions rendered by the two functioning tribunals exert a direct and

---

[6] To take an example, small-scale drug-trafficking appears wholly irrelevant to concerns for international peace and security. On the other hand, systematic or large-scale drug-trafficking may be viewed as a genuine threat to the political stability and sovereign independence of a State and to regional international peace and security, especially where such activity is interlinked with widespread or particularly intensive terrorist acts that threaten law and order or the integrity of the State apparatus. States have not reached a consensus as to whether and what level of drug-trafficking should be regarded as a threat to the peace and security of mankind.

[7] In A Draft International Criminal Code and Draft Statute for an International Criminal Tribunal (1987) at 28-29, Cherif Bassiouni identifies 312 multilateral conventions and 22 categories of crimes that pertain to international criminal law.

[8] *See* Security Council resolution 827, *adopted unanimously* on 25 May 1993.

[9] *See* Security Council resolution 955, *adopted* with 13 votes for, China *abstaining*, and Rwanda *against*, on 8 Nov. 1994.

immediate legal effect on the accused, as well as influence future adjudication, lends the tribunals a much higher profile compared to the slow process of ILC codification. Without having completed an international criminal code or statute for a permanent international criminal court after fifty years, the ILC work may appear to many as relatively abstract and sterile in comparison to that of the *ad hoc* tribunals, or perhaps even totally irrelevant to the quick pace of change in international law and relations.

However, the practical import of the two *ad hoc* tribunals for the more coherent implementation of international criminal law should not be overestimated. Historically, the accretion of international legal norms on individual criminal responsibility lacked preconceived plan, logical interrelation or ordered design, especially as regards pro-cedures of implementation. The agglomeration of the rules therefore remains haphazard, chaotic and complex, and as a result, norms of international criminal law form neither a coherent nor integrated system. The tribunals do not provide a panacea by which the lack of coherence in norms of international criminal law, or the ineffectiveness in its implementation, can be fixed, for the following reasons.

First, the statutes of the established tribunals do not cover the entire normative field of international criminal law, nor were they intended to do so. As such, they neither 'fill in the gaps', nor create broad, generalized norms on individual criminal responsibility in a way that could substantially reduce the perplexing and irregular character of the *lex lata*. Codification and progressive development, on the other hand, aim to bring clarity, comprehensiveness and coherence to the field of international criminal law.

Second, each *ad hoc* tribunal was designed to address the specific factual situation of the country coming within its particular competence. Thus, the judgements of these tribunals, however broadly construed, cannot but reflect the particularities of the subject matter being adjudicated upon and the specific circumstances involved. As such, these judgements will not substitute for a compre-hensive codification and progressive development of the broad principles of international criminal law.

Third, it is certain that, similar to adjudication in domestic criminal courts, cases will continue to come before the international tribunals in a rather unsystematic manner. Given that resources are finite, many practical considerations in the labour and time-intensive prosecution process, such as the availability of evidence, the Prosecutor's success in acquiring custody, as well as decisions whether or not to plea-bargain in order to gain inculpatory information on other suspects, govern the selection of suspects for indictment. Also, various political considerations, such as the position of a soldier suspected of having committed atrocities while acting under a responsible superior in the chain of command, may influence the Prosecutor's choice as to whom to indict and when. Similarly, in high profile cases involving the criminal responsibility of a top leader or military commander, media reports may intensify pressure on the Prosecutor to select that particular individual for indictment over others and to deploy scarce resources to meet that goal. Only very rarely do cases arise in a fashion convenient or conducive to systematic and comprehensive interpretation and adjudication. Although the induction of general principles of international criminal law from specific judgements of the *ad hoc* international criminal tribunals will help the law advance and develop, this cannot provide a substitute for the more comprehensive and deductive approach of a codification effort, whether carried out by the ILC or by some other officially recognized body.

Given the present state of the *lex lata*, the term 'international criminal law' is accurate only if used in any one of three senses: 1) to refer to the accumulation of international legal norms on individual criminal responsibility (without implying that they form a coherent system); 2) to refer to international criminal law as an incipient field of international law currently in a stage of emergence (without implying that it already exists as a relatively self-sufficient or autonomous system); or 3) to refer to the decisions, law and procedure of a permanent international criminal court, which does not yet exist, or those of the *ad hoc* international criminal tribunals, authorized to prosecute individuals for certain crimes under international law, such as those of Nuremberg or Tokyo, or those now currently in existence, namely, the International Criminal Tribunal for the Former Yugoslavia or the International Criminal Tribunal for Rwanda, which may clarify and develop the meaning and application of international criminal law norms.

With all these considerations in mind, it is valuable to bring into the picture an overview of the ILC work on the draft Code of Crimes against the Peace and Security of Mankind, and on a draft statute for a permanent international criminal court.

3. ILC WORK ON THE CODE OF CRIMES AGAINST THE PEACE AND SECURITY OF MANKIND AND STATUTE FOR A PERMANENT INTERNATIONAL CRIMINAL COURT

i) The Draft Code 1946 - 1996

Despite its seeming interminability, and regardless as to whether the draft Code provisions are eventually folded into the competence *ratione materiae* of the draft Statute for a permanent international criminal court, or merely used for guidance, the ILC work on the draft Code remains the most important 'legislative' effort to date on individual criminal responsibility in international law.

In 1946, the General Assembly adopted resolution 94(I) requesting the Committee on the Codification of International Law to begin work on "a general codification of offenses against the peace and security of mankind, or of an International Criminal Code" embodying the principles enunciated by the Nuremberg and Tokyo Tribunals. As mentioned above, on 21 November 1947, the General Assembly adopted resolution 174(II) establishing the International Law Commission and in resolution 177 (II) requested it to "formulate the principles of international law recognized in the Charter of the Nuremberg Tribunal and in the name of the Tribunal" and to "prepare a draft code of offenses against the peace and security of mankind".

In 1951, the ILC prepared a first text of the draft Code,[10] followed by a revised version in 1954. The 1954 draft Code basically comprises 'crimes against peace', 'war crimes', 'crimes against humanity' more or less as formulated in the Nuremberg Charter, 'genocide' as defined in the Convention on the Prevention and Punishment of the Crime of Genocide, 1948,[11] and 'terrorist activities'

---

[10]   The text of the 1951 draft Code is UN Doc. A/1858, paras. 57-58.

[11]   *Adopted unanimously* 9 Dec. 1948; *entered into force* 12 Jan. 1951, 78 UNTS 277. *See* [1954] 2 Yearbook of the ILC, Part II, UN. Doc. A/2693, 151-152, para. 54.

following the Convention for the Prevention and Punishment of Terrorism, 1937 (which has never entered into force).

By the end of 1954, the General Assembly decided that the ILC should postpone further work on the draft Code and draft Statute for a permanent international criminal court until a clear definition of 'aggression' in international law could be developed through the United Nations. Although aggression has long been recognized as one of the most serious breaches of international law, it was considered unwise to create an international court with criminal jurisdiction over aggression unless and until 'aggression' were defined in legal terms. It was not until 1974 that the General Assembly adopted resolution 3314 defining 'aggression'. As Ferencz recounts, in 1977:

> ... several states requested that the draft code again be placed on the UN agenda. By 1978, the topic was being debated in the Sixth Committee. In 1980, it was clear from the statements of the 61 delegates that took the floor that the overwhelming majority were in favour of codifying international criminal law - despite the opposition or scepticism of many Western nations. For the reluctant minority on the Sixth Committee, unable to kill the code idea completely, the next best policy was to stall as long as possible and then refer the topic back to a somnolent ILC where it had rested peacefully since 1954.[12]

On 10 December 1981, the UN General Assembly adopted resolution 36/106, which invites the ILC to resume work on the draft Code and to take into account developments in international law which had taken place since the draft Code was first adopted in 1954.

On the appointment of a Special Rapporteur on the draft Code of Crimes against the Peace and Security of Mankind, Ferencz comments that in 1982:

---

[12]   Benjamin Ferencz, *An International Criminal Code and Court: Where They Stand and Where They're Going* Columbia 30(2) Journal of Transnational Law (1992) at 378.

... the ILC appointed Mr. Doudou Thiam, a former
Minister of Senegal with no special expertise in international criminal law, as Special Rapporteur for the draft
code. Each year thereafter he issued reports describ-
ing problems or offering drafts of the provisions being
debated by members of the Commission. As might
have been expected, the Code was going practically
nowhere.[13]

In the early 1990's, major world events threatened to overtake
completely the ILC's work on the draft Code. In particular, Iraq's
invasion of Kuwait in 1990 became the first serious test of Security
Council solidarity since the end of the Cold War. Not only did the
Security Council demonstrate an ability to act decisively so as to
deprive the aggressor of the fruits of this supreme international crime,
but generally, it renewed the sense of urgency to promote respect for
the rule of law at the international level. This revitalized concern
naturally led to calls for the establishment of an international criminal
court with power and authority to try Saddam Hussein and his
collaborators for crimes under international law. This new sense of
urgency must have encouraged the members of the ILC, including
Special Rapporteur Thiam, to consolidate the results of the ILC's
decades long work on the draft Code.

As it turned out, however, there was far less real support
among key members of the international community to subject
Saddam Hussein to war crimes trials than it first had seemed. Many
commentators too, remained wary of the possible establishment of an
international criminal court.[14] Ultimately, calls to prosecute Saddam

---

[13]   *Ibid.* at 378-9.

[14]   *See e.g.* William O'Brien, *The Nuremberg Precedent and the Gulf
War*, 31(3) Virginia Journal of International Law (1991) at 400 who cautioned
that: "If there are extensive war crimes trials of Iraqis, the charges and trials
will not end there. The first victim will be Israel. There will be widespread
demands to punish the Israelis for violation of UN resolutions and for their
conduct in wars and occupations of the West Bank and Gaza. The difference
between Israeli actions in literal defense of their national existence and Iraqi
actions of gratuitous aggression and cruelty against a peaceful Arab
neighbour will not be recognized by the majority of the world community. ...

Hussein through an international criminal court disappeared once the dust settled from Operation Desert Storm and it became clear that no prosecutor could acquire custody over Saddam as long as he remained securely in power.

On 12 July 1991, the International Law Commission adopted[15] a comprehensive catalogue of 'crimes against the peace and security of mankind' the scope of which extends far beyond the 1954 draft Code catalogue of violations, as mentioned above.[16] Articles 15 to 26 of the 1991 draft Code of Crimes against the Peace and Security of Mankind[17] set out the competence *ratione materiae* for a proposed international criminal court. The 1991 draft Code employs broad categories of crimes in the draft Code, rather than neat, airtight compartments. The ILC considered that excessive compartmentalization would risk producing gaps in the coverage of criminal acts. On the other hand, incorporation of broad categories would produce overlap in the normative content of the crimes enumerated.

Close behind the demands for trials of Israelis will be demands for trials for Americans. There will be calls for trials of Reagan, for his role in Grenada and for the 1982-83 intervention in Lebanon, and Bush, for his role in the 1989 invasion of Panama, as well as of US military personnel for their participation in the actions. ... Where would it end? It is not only Israelis and Americans that might be accused as war criminals. There are charges for acts of aggression, war crimes and crimes against humanity in most modern conflicts - and they are still bitterly remembered."

[15]   Where the ILC as a whole adopts a set of draft articles submitted to it by the Special Rapporteur, it signifies that the draft articles have been approved on a provisional basis. The draft articles may then be submitted to Governments for comments. Governments are usually given one year to reply. *See* Art. 16 of the Statute of the ILC A/CN.4/4/Rev.2. *See further* Ian Sinclair, The International Law Commission (1987) at 33.

[16]   The 1954 draft Code comprises the classic Nuremberg and Tokyo Charter violations (crimes against peace, war crimes and crimes against humanity), as well as the crimes of genocide and intervention.

[17]   Draft Code of Crimes against the Peace and Security of Mankind: Titles and texts of articles adopted by the Drafting Committee, UN Doc. A/CN.4/L.459/Add.1, 5 July 1991, at the ILC 43rd session, 29 Apr.- 19 July 1991. The revised version is A/CN.4/L.464/Add.4, 15 July 1991. *See* Annex 1 to the present book.

Article 3(1) of the 1991 draft Code provides that an "individual who commits a crime against the peace and security of mankind is responsible therefor and is liable to punishment". Article 4 provides that "motives invoked by the accused which are not covered by the definition of the crime" do not affect responsibility. Article 5 provides that "[p]rosecution of an individual for a crime against the peace and security of mankind does not relieve a State of any responsibility under international law for an act or omission attributable to it". Article 6 provides that a State in which an individual alleged to have committed a crime against the peace and security of mankind is present, is obliged to either try or extradite him or her.

The 1991 draft Code also covers the principles of 'non-applicability of statutory limitations to crimes against the peace and security of mankind',[18] the right to a fair trial (including the right to be presumed innocent until proven guilty, and the right to counsel),[19] protection against double jeopardy[20] and non-retroactivity of the draft Code to acts committed before its entry into force.[21]

Articles 11 through 14 establish general principles on individual responsibility relative to the question of superior orders, criminal conduct of subordinates and official rank. Article 14 provides that the court "shall determine the admissibility of defenses under the general principles of law, in the light of the character of each crime" and that it shall, where appropriate, take extenuating circumstances into account when passing sentence.

Some delegations to the UN General Assembly Sixth Committee contended that the court's competence *ratione materiae* should be exhaustive, covering only specific crimes listed in the Code, to ensure respect for the principle *nullum crimen sine lege*.[22] However, other representatives argued that the Code should incorporate an illustrative, non-exhaustive approach to allow flexibility and expansion in

---

[18]   Art. 7.

[19]   Art. 8(a) - 8 (h).

[20]   Art. 9.

[21]   Art. 10.

[22]   Topical Summary of the discussion held in the Sixth Committee of the General Assembly during its forty-fifth session, 6 Feb. 1991, 43rd ILC session (Apr. 29 - 19 July 1991), UN Doc. A/CN.4/L.456 at para. 24.

coverage over time.[23] Another proposition was to include an exhaustive definition of 'crimes against the peace and security of mankind' in the Code but to incorporate other crimes, as defined in other international instruments, in the jurisdiction of the court by way of the court's statute. In this way, new crimes could be added freshly to the criminal court statute as international criminal law evolves over time, thus preserving flexibility in the law without offending the principles *nullum crimen sine lege* and *nulla poena sine lege*.

As regards competence *ratione personae*, the wording of Articles 15 through 26 indicates that the draft Code envisages, depending on the crime, three classes of individual perpetrators:[24] first, State leaders or organizers; second, State agents or representatives; and third, any individual. For example, draft Code provisions on aggression and threat of aggression contemplate criminal responsibility only for State leaders or organizers, while any State agent or representative may be charged for international terrorism, and any individual for a serious human rights violation. The ILC then requested Governments to provide comments on the draft Code it had prepared.

In 1996, in the light of comments received from Governments on the 1991 draft Code, the ILC draft Code Special Rapporteur put forward a severely truncated version. The 1996 draft Code eliminates the following categories of violations from the Code's coverage: threat of aggression; intervention; colonial domination and other forms of alien domination; apartheid; mercenary activity; terrorism; drug-

---

[23]   *See* Ninth Report on the Draft Code of Crimes against the Peace and Security of Mankind, UN Doc. A/CN.4/435/Add.1, 15 Mar. 1991, ILC 43rd session, (29 Apr.-19 July 1991), in which Special Rapporteur Doudou Thiam put forward two versions for delimitation of competence *ratione materiae*.

[24]   The Special Rapporteur noted that in the General Assembly's Sixth Committee, there was a consensus that the draft Code should cover offenses committed by individuals only rather than by corporate entities. *See* [1985] 2 ILC Yearbook, Part 1, 70-71. para. 64; UN Doc./ CN.4/ Ser.A/ 1985/ Add.1 (Part 1). As early as 1981, the German Democratic Republic proposed that individual criminal responsibility should be a basic principle of the draft Code, that it should not affect State responsibility and that an express provision to this effect should be included in the Code. *See* [1982] 2 ILC Yearbook Part 1, 277 para. 8, UN Doc. A/ CN.4/ Ser.A/ 1982/ Add.1 (Part 1).

trafficking; and wilful and severe damage to the environment, leaving only the crime of aggression, genocide and war crimes, adding 'crimes against United Nations and associated personnel' and 'crimes against humanity', and incorporating specific references to rape in provisions prohibiting crimes against humanity and war crimes.[25]

Thus, in the ILC's work on the draft code, a 'hard core' of relatively well-established international criminal law norms can be discerned from a 'softer' normative periphery. These 'soft core' norms are not as well-established or recognized to entail individual criminal responsibility and it appears that many States oppose their inclusion in an international penal code.

In some instances, the deletions appear only to strengthen the draft Code by removing provisions too imprecisely formulated to allow for effective implementation. In other cases, it appears that the singling out of certain norms for elimination from the draft Code was likely motivated more by political and ideological considerations rather than by the concern to meet a certain standard of legal precision.

It is remarkable that the crimes eliminated were those traditionally advocated by developing countries, with the ideological support of the Soviet Union and Eastern Bloc countries, often in clear opposition to western States. Over the years, some western States have consistently opposed the extension of norms of international criminal law beyond the 'hard core', in particular, those covering crimes against peace, war crimes, crimes against humanity (in its narrow Nuremberg Charter sense), grave breaches of the Geneva Conventions, 1949, genocide, torture and slavery. For good or ill, the collapse of the Soviet Union may have weakened the drive of many developing nations for a more comprehensive set of norms in an international criminal code.

A more restrictive and precise international criminal code would promote greater objectivity, fairness and predictability in implementation, which in turn, could enhance prospects for the emergence of an effective system of international criminal law. On the other hand, an

---

[25] *See* Draft Code of Crimes against the Peace and Security of Mankind: Titles and Texts of Draft Articles, *adopted* by the Drafting Committee on second reading at its 47th and 48th sessions; A/CN.4/L.522 of 31 May 1996; and Draft Report of the ILC on the Work of its 48th Session, A/CN.4/L.527/ Add.10 of 16 July 1996, *see* Annex 6 of this book.

overly narrow or restrictive material coverage could put international criminal law into a normative straitjacket, thereby reducing its flexibility and responsiveness to new challenges arising from crime in the perennially turbulent international panorama.

ii) The Draft Statute

As discussed above, the General Assembly decided in 1954 that further consideration of the establishment of an international criminal court should be deferred until aggression were defined with legal precision. Little further work was done on the draft Code until 1989 when, as Ferencz recounts:

> Trinidad and Tobago, ravaged by drug traders who terrorized local judges ... and inspired by its Harvard-educated Prime Minister A.N.R. Robinson, a long-time advocate of international criminal jurisdiction, led a coalition of Caribbean states in calling for an international court to deal with drug trafficking and other international crimes.[26]

On 25 November 1992, the General Assembly adopted resolution 47/33, requesting the ILC to elaborate a draft statute for an international criminal court, and on 9 December 1993, adopted another resolution[27] requesting the International Law Commission not only to continue its work on the draft statute, but if possible, to have it completed by the ILC's next session in 1994.

The ILC then created a 15-member working group, chaired by Mr. Abdul G. Koroma of Sierra Leone, to elaborate specific recommendations on an international criminal court.[28]

In its forty-fifth session, held in 1993, the International Law Commission took note of the report of the Working Group, which contained concrete recommendations for the establishment of an international criminal court, and transmitted the report to the General

---

[26]   Ferencz, *supra* note 12 at 384-85.
[27]   A/Res/48/31 of 9 December 1993.
[28]   Ferencz, *supra* note 12, at 394.

Assembly for comments. The recommendations propose that an international criminal court be: a) created by a statute in the form of a multilateral treaty agreed to by States parties; b) authorized to exercise jurisdiction only over private individuals in its first phase of operation; c) authorized to exercise jurisdiction only over criminal acts of an international character as defined in specific international conventions in force, including, but not limited to, the crimes defined in the draft Code of Crimes against the Peace and Security of Mankind, once adopted and entered into force; d) set up in such a way that a State could become a party to the statute of the court without necessarily having to become a party to the Code; e) permanent rather than *ad hoc*, but amenable to being summoned into operation by States parties to its statute when required, at least, during its first phase of operation; and f) characterized by due process, independence and impartiality in its procedures.[29]

At its forty-sixth session held in 1994, the ILC adopted the draft Statute for an International Criminal Court, after having taken into account written comments received from States, non-governmental organizations and a number of experts.[30] In this session, a consensus emerged among ILC members that the establishment of an international criminal jurisdiction was needed and that this should be instituted as part of the United Nations Organization. The ILC recommended that a conference of plenipotentiaries be convened.

In response, the General Assembly adopted resolution 49/53 of 9 December 1994, creating an *Ad Hoc* Committee on the Establishment of an International Criminal Court, and requested it "to review the major substantive and administrative issues arising out of the draft statute prepared by the International Law Commission and, in light of that review, to consider arrangements for the convening of an international conference of plenipotentiaries". It also decided to place

---

[29] *See* Report of the International Law Commission on the work of its forty-sixth session: 2 May-22 July 1994, UN Doc. A/49/10 Supp. 10, UN General Assembly, 1994.

[30] *See* UN Doc. A/CN.4/L.491/Rev.2/Adds.1&2 (1994).

on the provisional agenda of the Assembly's fiftieth session an item entitled 'Establishment of an International Criminal Court'.[31]

The Report of the *Ad Hoc* Committee on the Establishment of an International Criminal Court[32] proposes guidelines for consideration of the question of the relationship between States parties, non-States parties and the proposed international criminal court. It also considers some major principles of criminal law[33] as set out briefly below.[34]

The *Ad Hoc* Committee took note of broad consensus that a multilateral treaty would be the optimum means by which to create the court as an independent judicial organ, a means interfering least with the principle of State sovereignty. Another possible option was to proceed by way of amending the Charter of the United Nations. However, there was little consensus on this approach: some delegations viewed it as too problematic, while others maintained it could be a viable option, particularly in light of the fact that other more radical efforts to amend the Charter were under consideration, most notably those relative to Security Council restructuring. Generally, it was thought a close relationship with the United Nations would enhance the court's universality and moral authority.[35]

---

[31] On 11 Dec. 1995, the General Assembly adopted resolution 50/46 creating a Preparatory Committee to provide a consolidated convention on a permanent international criminal court with a view to consideration by a conference of plenipotentiaries. *See* Annex 5 of this book. This Preparatory Committee held its first session on 25 Mar. 1996. Ferencz notes that the United States took a negative position on both the code and court and that the US representative argued against both in the Sixth Committee of the General Assembly. *See* Ferencz, *supra* note 12 at 385.

[32] UN Doc. A/50/22 Supp.22, General Assembly, 1995.

[33] *See* Annexes I and II to Report of the Ad Hoc Committee on the Establishment of an International Criminal Court: UN Doc. A/50/22 Supp.22, General Assembly, 1995.

[34] *See also* James Crawford, *The ILC's Draft Statute for an International Criminal Tribunal*, 88(1) American Journal of International Law (1994) and James Crawford, *The ILC Adopts a Statute for an International Criminal Court*, 89 American Journal of International Law (1995).

[35] Report of the Ad Hoc Committee on the Establishment of an International Criminal Court: UN Doc. A/50/22 Supp.22, General Assembly, 1995 at para. 17.

The Working Group recommended that the proposed court should be a permanent institution, amenable to being called into operation according to need, so as to enhance both its flexibility and cost-effectiveness. To ensure a minimum measure of permanence, stability and independence, some delegations thought that a certain number of officials, in particular the judges, the President, Registrar and Prosecutor, should hold office on a full-time basis.[36]
Article 6(1) of the draft Statute provides that:

> The judges of the Court shall be persons of high moral character, impartiality and integrity who possess the qualifications required in their respective countries for appointment to the highest judicial offices, and have, in addition:
> a) criminal trial experience;
> b) recognized competence in international law.

Article 6(1) seeks to ensure a balance between, on the one hand, judges with practical trial experience and, on the other, judges with expertise in international humanitarian law and international human rights law (the two main sources of international norms on individual criminal responsibility). Articles 6(2-5) provide for an election procedure whereby nominating States shall specify whether the nominee is being put forward for election on the basis of trial experience, international law expertise, or both, and take account of the need to ensure that the principal legal systems of the world are represented. The initial recommendation that eighteen judges be appointed for a period of twelve years was countered with a proposal by a number of States to reduce the period of appointment to nine years (the same duration of office for judges of the International Court of Justice). Procedures for dealing with the questions of judicial vacancies and the roles of the President and Vice-Presidents of the court are provided for in Articles 7 and 8 of the draft Statute.
Provision for an appeal chambers consisting of 7 judges is made in Article 9. Article 9(7) prevents a judge who is a national of

---

[36]   *Ibid.* at paras. 18-19.

.either a State bringing a complaint or of a State of which the accused
is a national, of being a member of a chamber seized of the case.

Articles 10 and 11 concern the independence of judges and
procedures for excusing a judge from the exercise of a particular
function of the court and for disqualification. Article 10 stipulates that
judges:

> shall not engage in any activity which is likely to
> interfere with their judicial functions or to affect confi-
> dence in their independence. In particular, they shall
> not while holding the office of a judge be a member of
> the legislative or executive branches of the Government
> of a State, or of a body responsible for the investigation
> or prosecution of crimes.

Article 10 also provides that States parties to the Statute may take a
decision, by two-thirds majority, to require judges to work on a full-
time basis if the work-load of the Court should require it. In that case,
judges shall not hold any other office or employment.

Article 11 authorizes the President of the court, upon request
of a judge, to step down from a particular function otherwise required
by the Statute. Under Articles 11(2) and (3) the Prosecutor or the
accused may request that a judge be disqualified from participating in
a case in which he or she previously has been involved in any
capacity that might lead to doubts of his or her impartiality or in which
he or she had a potential or actual conflict of interest. The disqualification of a judge is to be decided by the judges' peers. Such a
decision is to be made "by an absolute majority of the members of the
Chamber concerned" without the participation of the challenged judge.

The independence of the Procuracy of the proposed court is
provided for in Article 12 which requires that: "A member of the
Procuracy shall not seek or act on instructions from any external
source." The Prosecutor and Deputy Prosecutors are required to be
of high moral character and competence and would be elected by
secret ballot from among candidates nominated by States parties by
an absolute majority of those parties for a period of five years. Similar
to the rule applicable to judges, the Prosecutor and Deputy Prosecutors would be barred from participating in cases that involve a person
of their own nationality. Interestingly, Article 12(6) authorizes the

Presidency to "excuse the Prosecutor or a Deputy Prosecutor at their request from acting in a particular case, and shall decide any question raised in a particular case as to the disqualification of the Prosecutor or a Deputy Prosecutor". Some ILC members felt this disqualification procedure to be unnecessary arguing that it could infringe the independence of the Procuracy vis-à-vis the court's judges.[37]

Articles 13 to 18 concern the registry (principal administrative organ of the proposed court), a mandatory undertaking of impartiality and conscientiousness to be taken by judges and other officers of the court, loss of office, privileges and immunities, allowances and expenses and the working languages of the court (English and French). Article 19 authorizes the judges to make rules for the functioning of the Court to be submitted to States parties for approval.

Part 3 of the draft Statute defines the competence *ratione materiae* of the proposed international criminal court. Initially, the Working Group proposed that the Court should exercise jurisdiction only over those crimes of an international character defined in existing treaties and that States should have the option "between participation and support for the structure and operation of the court on the one hand and acceptance of substantive jurisdiction in a particular case on the other",[38] with separate procedures as in Article 36 of the Statute of the International Court of Justice.

Subsequently, the ILC modified this approach such that the proposed court's competence *ratione materiae* would cover crimes as defined in international conventions as well as 'crimes under general international law' not defined in international conventions. However, reference to 'crimes under general international law' was criticized by some States as too vague. As such, it would end up conferring ill-defined jurisdiction upon the proposed court. In response, the ILC decided to delimit jurisdiction in respect of 'crimes under general international law' to specific instances.[39] A second modification attempted to demarcate the scope of inherent jurisdiction that the proposed court might have over certain categories of acts, specifically,

---

[37]   *See* Report of the International Law Commission on the work of its forty-sixth session: 2 May-22 July 1994, UN Doc. A/49/10 Supp. 10, General Assembly, 1994 Commentary to Article 11 at 58.

[38]   *Ibid.* at 66.

[39]   *Ibid.* at 66-7.

over those universally recognized to constitute crimes under international law, such as genocide as defined in Article II of the Convention
on Genocide.[40]

The discussions also focused on another important issue,
namely what if any distinction should be drawn "between treaties
which define crimes as international crimes and treaties which merely
provide for the suppression of undesirable conduct constituting crimes
under national law". Arguably, the proposed international criminal
court should not be authorized to exercise jurisdiction over any act
which, although defined as a crime in an international convention,
would be prosecuted more appropriately by domestic courts. Certain
matters, such as drug-trafficking, may be outlawed by multilateral
conventions to ensure better international cooperation in their
suppression, notwithstanding the fact that isolated instances do not
entail sufficient gravity as to concern the international community as
a whole. On the other hand, exclusion of the crime of drug-trafficking
altogether from the competence *ratione materiae* of the proposed
court would mean that a highly undesirable activity, that in some
cases might be perpetrated on such a scale as to pose a significant
threat even to the political independence of a State, would lie beyond
the pale of effective deterrence. To solve this dilemma, the Commission decided to leave 'suppression conventions' within the coverage
of the proposed court, but to consider ways to ensure that only acts
of sufficiently grave concern to the international community would be
covered.

With the benefit of the Statute of the International Criminal
Tribunal for the Former Yugoslavia at hand, the ILC put forward a
number of substantive provisions specifying the proposed court's
competence *ratione materiae*. Article 20 of the draft Statute, entitled
'Crimes within the jurisdiction of the Court', provides:

---

[40]   The Convention on the Prevention and Punishment of the Crime of
Genocide was *adopted* on 9 Dec. 1948 by the General Assembly, and
entered into force on 12 Jan. 1951 pursuant to Article XIII.

The Court has competence in accordance with this
Statute with respect to the following crimes:
a) the crime of genocide;
b) the crime of aggression;
c) serious violations of the laws and customs applicable
in armed conflict;
d) crimes against humanity;
e) crimes, established under or pursuant to the treaty
provisions listed in the Annex, which, having regard to
the conduct alleged, constitute exceptionally serious
crimes of international concern.

The Commission noted in the Commentary to Article 20[41] that it was
guided in its selection of these crimes by the fact that genocide,
serious violations of the laws and customs applicable in armed conflict
and crimes against humanity were appear in the Statute of the
International Criminal Tribunal for the Former Yugoslavia, and that the
crime of aggression was of such great importance that it could not be
left out.

The inclusion of these four crimes represented a
common core of agreement in the Commission, and is
without prejudice to the identification and application of
the concept of crimes under general international law
for other purposes.[42]

Article 20 is exhaustive rather than illustrative. It would therefore limit
the capacity of the proposed court to enlarge its own competence
through expansive interpretation of the norms. On the other hand, the

---

[41]   Art. 20 of the Statute of the International Law Commission, UN Doc.
A/CN.4/Rev.2, states that the ILC "... shall prepare its drafts in the form of
articles and shall submit them to the General Assembly together with a
commentary...".   The Sixth Committee of the General Assembly is a
functional committee of the General Assembly that considers proposals for
resolutions on legal matters.
[42]   Report of the Ad Hoc Committee on the Establishment of an International Criminal Court: UN Doc. A/50/22 Supp.22, General Assembly, 1995 at
71.

Commission was careful to point out that Article 20 is exhaustive in the sense that it covers all crimes which ought to fall within the competence of the proposed court, not necessarily all those crimes which come within the category 'crimes under general international law.'[43] In other words, the proposed court's competence, if limited in this way, would not necessarily limit the general normative development of international criminal law.

As the Commentary to Article 20 states, the first four subparagraphs of Article 20 refer to crimes under general international law, while the last focuses on crimes as defined in specific treaties listed in the Annex, thus providing for overlapping categories rather than airtight compartments, except for 'the crime of genocide'. The definition of genocide and the principle of individual criminal responsibility therefor, derive from Article II of the Genocide Convention, 1948, but it has undoubtedly entered into 'general international law' also. Moreover, genocide, states the Commentary, should be considered to fall within the inherent jurisdiction of the court, applicable to all States parties to the Statute by virtue of Article VI of the Genocide Convention.[44] In contrast, the definition of the crime of aggression does not derive from any comprehensive multilateral treaty designed specifically for this purpose.[45]

'Serious violations of the laws and customs applicable in armed conflict' attempts to incorporate elements of Article 3 of the Statute of

---

[43]   *Ibid.* at 77.

[44]   Article VI of the Convention provides: "Persons charged with genocide or any of the other acts enumerated in Article III shall be tried by a competent tribunal of the State in the territory of which the act was committed, or by such international penal tribunal as may have jurisdiction with respect to those Contracting Parties which shall have accepted its jurisdiction."

[45]   Article 6(a) of the Nuremberg Charter providing for individual responsibility for crimes against peace "namely, planning, preparation, initiation or waging of a war of aggression or a war in violation of international treaties, agreements, or assurances, or participation in a common plan or conspiracy" made clear that planning etc. of a 'war of aggression' is a criminal act but did not define it. The main instrument in this regard is the "Definition of Aggression" annexed to General Assembly resolution 3314 (XXIX) of 14 Dec. 1974.

the International Criminal Tribunal for the Former Yugoslavia as well as Article 22 of the 1991 draft Code. Article 3 of the Yugoslavia Tribunal Statute is based on 1907 Hague Convention No. IV respecting the Laws and Customs of War on Land and the Regulations annexed thereto, which are declaratory of customary international law. Article 22 of the draft Code is based primarily on the grave breach provisions of the four Geneva Conventions, 1949, and the two 1977 Protocols additional thereto.

The 1991 draft Code on Crimes against the Peace and Security of Mankind does not include 'crimes against humanity', whereas the draft Statute for an international criminal court, following Article 5 of the Statute of the International Criminal Tribunal for the Former Yugoslavia does. Article 5 lists murder, extermination, enslavement, deportation, imprisonment, torture, rape, persecutions on political, racial and religious grounds and 'other inhumane acts' as 'crimes against humanity' when directed against any civilian population.

In respect of subparagraph Article 20(e) of the 1994 draft Statute, the Annex lists the following: grave breaches as provided for in the four Geneva Conventions of 12 August 1949, and the two Protocols additional thereto of 8 June 1977; the unlawful seizure of aircraft as defined in Article 1 of the Hague Convention for the Suppression of Unlawful Seizure of Aircraft of 16 December 1970; the crimes defined in Article 1 of the Montreal Convention for the Suppression of Unlawful Acts against the Safety of Civil Aviation of 23 September 1971; apartheid as defined in Article II of the International Convention on the Suppression and Punishment of the Crime of Apartheid of 30 November 1973; the crimes defined in Article 2 of the Convention on the Prevention and Punishment of Crimes against Internationally Protected Persons, including Diplomatic Agents of 14 December 1973; hostage-taking and related crimes as defined in Article 1 of the Convention against Torture and Other Cruel, Inhuman or Degrading Treatment or Punishment of 10 December 1984; the crimes defined in Article 3 of the Convention for the Suppression of Unlawful Acts against the Safety of Maritime Navigation of 10 March 1988, and by Article 2 of the Protocol for the Suppression of Unlawful Acts against the Safety of Fixed Platforms Located on the Continental Shelf of 10 March 1988; crimes involving illicit traffic in narcotic drugs as provided for in Article 3(1) of the UN Convention against Illicit

Traffic in Narcotic Drugs and Psychotropic Substances of 20 December 1988 "which, having regard to Article 2 of the Convention, are crimes with an international dimension".[46]

Articles 21 and 22 specify certain preconditions according to which the court may seize jurisdiction namely, a complaints procedure and a declaration of consent by States accepting the jurisdiction of the court. With respect to the crime of aggression, Article 23(2) of the draft Statute makes the court's jurisdiction contingent upon a prior determination of the Security Council "that a State has committed the act of aggression which is the subject of the complaint". By Article 23(3): "No prosecution may be commenced under this Statute arising from a situation which is being dealt with by the Security Council as a threat to or breach of the peace or an act of aggression under Chapter VII of the Charter, unless the Security Council otherwise decides".

Parts 4 to 8 of the draft Statute relate to certain possible institutional aspects of a permanent international criminal court, acquisition of custody over the offender and enforcement. Specifically, Part 4 of the draft Statute concerns investigation and prosecution and Part 5 concerns, *inter alia*, the place, applicable law, issues of admissibility, fair trial guarantees, evidence, sentencing and applicable penalties of the trial. Part 6 concerns appeal and review. Part 7 contains provisions relating to international cooperation and judicial assistance. Part 8 covers implementation issues namely, recognition of judgements, enforcement of sentences and pardon, parole and commutation of sentences.

In addition to the Annex, which has been discussed above, there are three appendices: Appendix I on the possible clauses of a treaty to accompany the draft statute; Appendix II on relevant provisions mentioned in the Annex; and Appendix III outlining possible ways whereby a permanent international criminal court may enter into relationship with the United Nations.

---

[46] Report of the International Law Commission on the work of its forty-sixth session: 2 May-22 July 1994, UN Doc. A/49/10 Supp. 10, UN General Assembly, 1994 at 142.

4. PLAN OF THE ENQUIRY

In order to identify the prospects for the emergence of a unified system of international criminal law, characterized by broad and coherent material coverage, as well as fair and effective institutional implementation, it is necessary to evaluate:

- the extent to which the content and legal status of the main substantive norms of international criminal law are sufficiently clear and precise; and
- institutional avenues for more effective implementation.

Part 1 of the present enquiry evaluates the provisions of the 1991 draft Code, taking into account the changes introduced in the 1996 draft Code. In this connection, whether or not the International Law Commission's work eventually leads to a multilateral convention which, once adopted and ratified, provides the world with a viable code and court, the 1991 draft Code at least provides a highly useful framework for the debate, as well as an ideal reference point for Part 1 of the present enquiry. The 1991 draft Code's attempt at sheer comprehensiveness supplies a useful measuring stick by which to gauge the extent the various elements in the material scope of international criminal law are recognized at the international level. As explained above, as a result of the ILC having radically cleaved many provisions from the 1991 draft Code, the 1996 draft Code comes much closer to the competence *ratione materiae* set out in the 1994 draft Statute, and indeed, to the scope of the 1954 version of the draft Code. Because the 1991 draft Code was severely chopped in reaction to the responses received from Governments, revealing the will of the international community at least to some extent, the 1996 draft Code makes it possible to distinguish clearly the normative 'hard core' of international criminal law from its softer periphery, not only in the context of the codification effort itself, but more significantly, in international criminal law at its present phase of emergence.

However, while the 1991 draft Code is generally valuable from a heuristic point of view for its comprehensiveness, it omitted two major categories of crimes, namely, mass rape and crimes against UN and associated personnel. These two matters, which were included in the 1996 draft Code, are treated in Chapters II(5) and III(3) below.

Part 2 takes account of developments in the institutionalized implementation of international criminal law. In this regard, Chapter IV highlights the relevance to the evolving character of international criminal responsibility of increasing normative hierarchy in international law, as evidenced by the international community's recognition of norms of a *jus cogens* character, obligations *erga omnes* and the concept of 'international crimes of State'. Chapter V then delves into institutional aspects of inter-State criminal jurisdiction, taking note of patterns in municipal implementation and the problem of acquiring custody over the offender. Chapter VI outlines the trend towards centralized international criminal law implementation through the technique of international criminal tribunals, discusses a number of procedural and institutional issues pertaining to the creation of a permanent international criminal court, as well as the right to fair trial, and then makes a proposal to enhance prospects for such a court to acquire custody over the alleged offender.

Part 3 views the myriad elements and aspects of international criminal law and leads, from the analysis of norms and implementation presented in Parts 1 and 2, to a synthetic evaluation of the prospects for a unified, comprehensive, coherent, fair and effective system of international criminal law. It must also be said that international criminal law is not emerging in a vacuum: its possible material coverage and prospects for better implementation reflect political, economic and social elements of the contemporary human experience. The final Part therefore revisits the imperatives to create an effective and coherent system of international criminal law, the rationale for international criminal law as a body of norms as well as the need for a permanent international criminal court, in light of the main dynamics of international legal cooperation.

PART I

DEVELOPMENTS IN CODIFICATION

CHAPTER I

AGGRESSION, THREAT OF AGGRESSION, INTERVENTION AND COLONIAL DOMINATION

Among acts for which the 1991 draft Code contemplates individual criminal responsibility are aggression, threat of aggression, intervention and colonial domination. These four violations of international law are treated in the same chapter of the present enquiry for two main reasons.

First, each of the four violations, of extreme gravity, entails a very direct breach of the peace by one State against another. Indeed, the launching of a war of aggression remains the supreme international offense. Over the centuries, the deployment of aggressive armed force by a State against another, time and time again, has brought immeasurable misery to the world. Indeed, the primary purpose of the United Nations Organization, successor to the League of Nations, is 'to save succeeding generations from the scourge of war, which twice in our lifetime has brought untold sorrow to mankind'. The international community attaches almost the same importance to threats of aggression, intervention and colonial domination. More specifically, the four kinds of violations relate, in a general sense, to 'crimes against peace' as defined in Article 6(a) of the Charter of the Nuremberg Tribunal, which in turn, relate more to violations of the *jus ad bellum*, rather than to violations of the *jus in bello*. In other words, the four violations concern action by one State against another in breach of international peace, rather than violations within the territory of a single State, or violations carried out during armed conflict once war has started.

Second, the four kinds of violations may be considered similar to each other in that each characteristically involves an act carried out by agents of the State pursuing a national policy (even if covertly, or executed by an unauthorized arm of the government apparatus). In other words, aggression, threat of aggression, intervention and colonial domination are major crimes involving responsibility of top Government leaders, and in particular, those with policy-making competence.   In contrast, commission of serious human rights violations or war crimes, for example, typically involve individual criminal responsibility at any or all levels of public authority from Government leader to commander to individual soldier.

At first glance, it may appear that the crime of apartheid should be considered along with these four crimes.   However, individual criminal responsibility for apartheid is considered in the next chapter for two reasons. First, apartheid is a policy perpetrated by the organs of a State within its own territory against a portion of its own national population. It thus constitutes a human rights violation in the classic sense of a violation of fundamental rights and freedoms by a government against persons normally subject to its jurisdiction, such as nationals or permanent residents.   Second, apartheid has been recognized as a crime through multilateral human rights conventions and declarations, which apply primarily in time of peace, whereas this Chapter covers the kinds of acts by one State against another more directly related to the threat or breach of the peace.

1. AGGRESSION

The question of individual criminal responsibility for aggression must be considered against the broader issue as to whether aggression is prohibited in international law, and if so, what kinds of entities may be held responsible.   The lawfulness of the resort to force in international relations is especially important given that traditionally, the use of force, under certain circumstances, has been considered an inherent right of sovereign nations.

i) Prior to the Nuremberg and Tokyo Trials

Prior to the First World War, war was not generally prohibited in any practical way. In the essentially anarchic system of Westphalia, the right to resort to force (or the *jus ad bellum*) was limited only by the doctrine of the 'just war'. Natural Law theory, as expounded by the Spanish theologians[1] and Grotius,[2] maintained that lawfulness of the use of force derived from the justness of its cause. Violations of Natural Law could be vindicated with force to the extent that Justice permitted. However, as the State became supremely powerful in the Age of Absolutism, the demands of *realpolitik*, buttressed by legal positivist theories of State sovereignty, brushed aside Natural Law doctrines. The rise of State sovereignty and power made ideas of divine justice, and its related set of criteria distinguishing lawful from unlawful war, irrelevant. By the 19th century, *raison d'état* reigned supreme, as symbolized in the doctrines of Carl von Clausewitz.[3]

The essentially bilateral character of international rights and obligations meant States incurred little risk of collective sanction for launching an aggressive war. However, the lack of collective sanctions and the intensified technical capacity of States to inflict widespread destruction against an enemy magnified the need for open avenues of peaceful dispute resolution so that opportunities to avoid war at least could be available. The Hague Peace Conferences of 1899 and 1907, through a number of rules on the means and methods of warfare, established regular means for the pacific settlement of disputes to allow parties to step back from the brink of war, applicable if and when war broke out.[4]

The First World War, especially brutal in view of the use of trench warfare and poison gas, confirmed the fears of those who had campaigned for effective pacific resolution of disputes, and impelled

---

[1]   *See* the works of Franciscus de Vitoria in Reflections in Moral Theology of the Very Celebrated Spanish Theologian: Franciscus de Vitoria, The Classics of International Law (1917); *see also* B. Ayala, De Jure et officiis et disciplina miltari libri tres, Douai (1582) Bk.I 5-24; Peter Haggenmacher, Grotius et la doctrine de la guerre juste (1983); *see further* Scott, The Spanish Conception of International Law and of Sanctions Washington (1934), and Scott, The Spanish Origin of International Law (1928).

[2]   Hugo Grotius, De Jure Belli ac Pacis Bk.II, ch.II (1625).

[3]   The Prussian General von Clausewitz (1780-1831) wrote *Vom Kriege* (On War) between 1816 and 1830, advocating 'absolute war'. To Clausewitz, war was a natural expression of the competition between States and its value lay in sorting out the weak from the strong.

[4]   *See* the Hague Conventions of 1899 and 1907 on the Pacific Settlement of Disputes.

the international community to create centralized international mechanisms to avoid such carnage in future. The development of pacific avenues for the resolution of disputes figured as a key element of the League of Nations, created after the end of World War I. The Covenant of the League of Nations was incorporated in the Treaty of Versailles, adopted on 28 June 1919.

The primary purpose of the League of Nations was to maintain international peace and security. Articles 11, 12, 13 and 15 of the League of Nations Covenant imposed certain limitations on the right of a State to wage war. Before launching a war, the parties were obliged to refer the dispute to the League for arbitration, judicial settlement, or to the League Council. Once one of these methods had been tried, Members of the League were required not to go to war until three months after one of these adjudicative bodies submitted their report. The idea was to provide the parties an opportunity to resort to other means of solving the dispute between them according to pacific means. Where one or other party violated one of these provisions, that State "shall *ipso facto* be deemed to have committed an act of war against all other members of the League". The offending State could then be made subject to economic or even military sanctions from the other Members pursuant to Article 16.

Article 10 of the Covenant enjoined Members of the League from according recognition to the ill-gotten gains of aggression. However, under the League of Nations Covenant, war was not prohibited. It was only subject to certain procedural restrictions - the three months delay. These defects of the League of Nations Covenant, against the backdrop of advances in the technical capability to inflict mass suffering, made it seem all the more imperative to outlaw war in international relations.

On 27 September 1922, the Third Assembly of the League of Nations requested the Permanent Advisory Commission to examine the question of aggression and to propose a draft treaty on the matter. The culmination of the Commission's work was its Draft Treaty of Mutual Assistance, completed on 8 June 1923.[5] Article 1 of the Draft Treaty of Mutual Assistance stated: "The High Contracting Parties

---

[5]   Ahmed M. Rifaat, International Aggression: A Study of the Legal Concept - Its Development and Definition in International Law (1979) at 50.

affirm that war of aggression constitutes an international crime and assume a solemn obligation not to commit this crime." The draft put the spotlight on the question of the definition of aggression at the international level, although it was never adopted, owing to a lack of consensus on its content.

Another attempt to elucidate the question was made in connection with efforts to consolidate international obligations to resolve disputes peacefully. The preamble of the Geneva Protocol for the Pacific Settlement of International Disputes[6] was adopted unanimously by the Assembly of the League of Nations and signed by 19 States in 1924. It declares that the signatory States were:

> Animated by the firm desire to ensure the maintenance
> of general peace and the security of nations whose
> existence, independence or territories may be thre-
> atened;
> Recognizing the solidarity of the members of the
> international community;
> Asserting that a war of aggression constitutes a viol-
> ation of this solidarity and an international crime;
> Desirous of facilitating the complete application of the
> system provided in the Covenant of the League of
> Nations for the pacific settlement of disputes between
> States and of ensuring the repression of international
> crimes; ...

However, the Protocol never received the ratifications necessary to enter into force.

In 1927, the League of Nations unanimously adopted the Declaration on Aggressive Wars. It states that aggressive war constitutes an international crime and that pacific means of dispute settlement shall be implemented. At the League of Nations Eighth Assembly, the legal prohibition of aggression was raised. On 9 September 1927, the delegate of Poland submitted that aggressive war should be outlawed and argued that effective prohibition of aggression could not be carried out unless it was first clearly defined.

---

[6]   *See* League of Nations Official Journal, Special Supp. No. 23 at 498.

In this connection, the following resolution of the Assembly was introduced:[7]

> The Assembly ...
>> Being convinced that a war of aggression can never serve as a means of settling international disputes and is, in consequence, an international crime;
>> Considering that a solemn renunciation of all wars of aggression would tend to create an atmosphere of general confidence calculated to facilitate the progress of the work undertaken with a view to disarmament;
>> Declares:
>
> 1)   That all wars of aggression are, and shall always be, prohibited.
> 2)   That every pacific means must be employed to settle disputes, of every description, which may arise between States.

This resolution, although not legally binding, was an important step towards the prohibition of war formalized less than a year later in the 1928 Paris Pact. It was hoped that the Paris Pact, discussed below, would correct some of the defects in the League of Nations Covenant provisions on the settlement of disputes.

The Paris Pact (International Treaty for the Renunciation of War as an Instrument of National Policy), also known as the Kellogg-Briand Pact, had been signed by sixty-three States by the time World War II broke out.[8] It provides that:

> The Signatory States:
> [P]ersuaded that the time has come when a frank renunciation of war as an instrument of national policy

---

[7]   *Unanimously approved*, 24 Sept. 1927.

[8]   *Signed* initially on 27 Aug. 1928 by the representatives of 15 States, *entered into force* 24 July 1929, 94 L.N.T.S. 57, 46 Stat. 2343, T.S. No.796.

should be made to the end that the peaceful and
friendly relations now existing between their peoples
may be perpetuated;
Convinced that all changes in their relations with one
another should be sought only by pacific means and be
the result of a peaceful and orderly process, and that
any signatory Power which shall hereafter seek to
promote its national interests by resort to war should
be denied the benefits furnished by this Treaty ...
Have decided to conclude a Treaty;
Article I: The High Contracting Parties solemnly
declare in the names of their respective peoples that
they condemn recourse to war for the solution of
international controversies, and renounce it as an
instrument of national policy in their relations with one
another.
Article II: The High Contracting Parties agree that
the statement or solution of all disputes or conflicts of
whatever nature or of whatever origin they may be,
which may arise among them, shall never be sought
except by pacific means.

The Kellogg-Briand Pact signalled that the international community
considered war to be an unacceptable means by which to further
domestic priorities.

However, the Pact proved ineffective with respect to Italian
aggression against Ethiopia, and Japanese aggression against
Manchuria. Neither could it prevent Nazi aggression or the outbreak
of World War II. Several serious shortcomings in the Pact weakened
its effectiveness. It has never been clear as to whether or not the
Pact prohibits resort to the use of force short of war, particularly since
the term 'war', as construed in its classic sense, denotes a traditional
situation of inter-State armed belligerency. Moreover, the absence of
any mention of the right to self-defense leaves the scope of the
legitimate use of force ambiguous. Furthermore, there is no sanction
in the Treaty, over and above that the parties that resort to war 'shall
be denied the benefits furnished by the Treaty'. This phrase is in itself
probably circular and seems to entail no legal consequences for a
State that breaches the Treaty. Despite its shortcomings as a legal

instrument, the Kellogg-Briand Pact represents a symbolic step taken by the international community to prohibit the illegitimate use of force in international relations and was accorded great importance by the Nuremberg and Tokyo Tribunals, indeed, as discussed below, much more than it warranted.

Other instruments, adopted in the inter-war years, declare 'aggression' an international crime. Significantly, many of these instruments employ the term 'aggression' rather than 'war', thereby sidestepping one of the important pitfalls of the Kellogg-Briand Pact. For example, in February 1928, the Sixth Pan-American Conference adopted a resolution which declared that: "war of aggression constitutes an international crime against the human species ... all aggression is illicit and as such is declared prohibited." Also, the Treaty of Non-Aggression and Conciliation of 1933, a regional instrument for the Americas, condemns 'wars of aggression'. This provision is also reflected in the Buenos Aires Convention of 1936, which was ratified by many States of Latin America and by the United States.[9]

The meaning and scope of 'aggression' was raised in the context of the 1933 Disarmament Conference, by the Soviet representative thereto, Mr. Litvinoff, who argued that a clear distinction had to be drawn between the defensive and offensive use of force in international relations. In this connection, the Soviet Union submitted a comprehensive draft proposal to the General Commission of the Disarmament Conference which offered a definition of aggression.[10]

A lack of consensus prevented the draft Soviet definition from being adopted by the Disarmament Conference in 1934. Nonetheless, its provisions were to exert some influence as subsequently incorporated in several treaties between the Soviet Union and a number of satellite and neighbouring States.[11]

---

[9]   *See* Igor Lukashuk, *International Illegality and Criminality of Aggression*, in (ed. Ginsburgs and Kudriavtsev) The Nuremberg Trial and International Law (1990) at 127.

[10]   The definition is included in the Report of the Secretary-General on the Question of Defining Aggression, UN. Doc. A/2211, GAOR, VII, Annexes, Agenda item 54 at 17 *et seq*.

[11]   Rifaat, *supra* note 5 at 91.

Perhaps the most important element in the Soviet draft, is that it equates aggression with the first use of armed force in a specific instance.[12] The Soviet draft Definition of Aggression appears to facilitate identification of the aggressor because in principle the first use of armed force is unambiguous. However, in practice, it may be very difficult to determine which State first resorted to armed force, particularly in situations where relations between States have deteriorated to the point that armed force has been used. In such cases, it can not be assumed that either side can be trusted to report the facts faithfully. It was for this reason that the Government of Great Britain, as well as a number of other Governments, opposed the Soviet draft, arguing that in many cases, a rigid definition whose principal criterion was the first use of armed force, could lead to an unrealistic and unfair appreciation of which State is in fact the aggressor, i.e. which State intended to take offensive armed or invasive action, coupled with the actual use of armed force.

In the midst of the Second World War, the Allied Powers decided to ensure that the main instigators responsible for the Nazi aggression would be prosecuted and punished, as reflected in the 1942 Declaration of St. James,[13] which:

> resolves to see to it in a spirit of international solidarity that (a) those guilty or responsible, whatever their nationality, are sought out, handed over to justice and judged, (b) that the sentences pronounced are carried out.

This Declaration was supplemented by other official statements of President Roosevelt, Prime Minister Churchill, representatives of the Soviet Union, and other Allied Governments, indicating their intention to prosecute and punish authors of war crimes, crimes against humanity and crimes against peace.

---

[12] *See* the chapeau to Article 1 of the Soviet Draft.
[13] Punishment for War Crimes - the Inter-Allied Declaration, *signed* 13 Jan. 1942 by representatives of the Governments of Belgium, Czechoslovakia, France, Greece, Luxembourg, Norway, The Netherlands, Poland and Yugoslavia. *See* History of the UN War Crimes Commission (1948) at 89-92.

However, the most important development for the implementation of individual criminal responsibility for aggression came with the
Nuremberg and Tokyo Charters and Judgements.

ii) Nuremberg and Tokyo Charters and Judgments

In October 1943, representatives of the Allied Powers
convened in London and established the United Nations War Crimes
Commission, empowering it with advisory and investigatory functions,
including the preparation of lists of war criminal suspects and
examination of procedures by which prosecution and punishment
could be enforced.[14]
The United States Government took the position that "the
United Nations would, in the first instance, bring before an International Tribunal created by Executive Agreement, the highest ranking
German leaders to a number fairly representative of the groups and
organizations charged with complicity in the basic criminal plan."[15]
Representatives of the four major Allied Powers (Great Britain, France,
the Soviet Union and the United States) met in London on 26 June
1945 to further amplify the law and procedures according to which the
Nazi leaders ought to be prosecuted, tried and punished.
By 1945, no consensus was attained on the question as to
what acts fall within the scope of a 'crime against peace' or an act of
'aggression'. Indeed, the legal category of 'crimes against peace' was
new law. Consequently, criminal responsibility for 'crimes against
peace' was considered to be much more controversial than criminal
responsibility for war crimes, the roots of which extend back to the
Middle Ages. Lack of consensus over the meaning of 'crimes against
peace' meant prosecution and punishment therefor risked appearing
highly subjective and arbitrary. This risk was exacerbated by the fact
that the putative norm prohibiting 'crimes against peace' was enforced
only by the Allied Powers, rather than by neutral Powers or represen-

---

[14]   *See* Bradley Smith, Reaching Judgment at Nuremberg (1977) for a
history of the political events leading up to the Nuremberg Trial.
[15]   Memorandum to President Roosevelt from the Secretaries of State
and War and the Attorney-General, dated 22 Jan. 1945 in Report of Robert
H. Jackson, United States Representative to the International Conference on
Military Trials at 7.

tatives, and only against Axis Power defendants. For these reasons, there was considerable disagreement among the Allies during the drafting of the Nuremberg Charter as to whether 'crimes against peace' should be prosecuted at all. However, upon the insistence of the United States delegation, the Conference decided that individuals should also be tried for 'crimes against peace', in addition to war crimes and crimes against humanity.

The Allies recognized that their collective decision to prosecute 'crimes against peace' was insufficient, in and of itself, to lend 'crimes against peace' or 'aggression' clear and precise legal meaning. To remedy this problem, the US representative proposed that 'the launching of aggressive war' should be inserted in the Charter as a separate crime, distinct from war crimes and crimes against humanity, and that it should be clearly defined in the Charter. The US representative felt that with a clear Charter definition of 'aggression', the defense would be deprived of the argument that 'crimes against peace' lacked precise normative content and therefore could not be enforced. It would also prevent the defense from making purely semantic arguments that might lead the prosecution astray.

Moreover, the US and UK representatives sought to foreclose a possible defense argument that resort to the use of force by the Nazi Government constituted a legitimate act of self-defense, thus equating the moral and legal responsibility of the Axis Powers with that of the Allies. For example, the Soviet Union had signed a mutual non-aggression pact[16] with Nazi Germany, which in effect assured Hitler that his forces could invade Poland unimpeded by interference from the Soviet Union. Even worse, secret supplementary provisions to the pact established the respective spheres of influence of the two parties.

> Once the secret clauses of that pact appeared in evidence, even in summary form, it was difficult not to reach the conclusion that Stalin, like some of the defendants in the dock, had continued to 'cooperate' with Hitler after he knew of the Nazi attack plans. If this kind of conduct would earn defendants such as

---

[16]   *Signed* on 23 Aug. 1939 in Moscow.

Wilhelm Frick prison sentences or death, what was the
Court to say about the actions of the Soviet Union?
The difficulty was compounded by the fact that, when
it was Russia's turn to be an invasion victim in 1941,
the Germans justified their assault on the grounds
Stalin was preparing to tear up the Nazi-Soviet agreement and was about to launch his own attack on
them.[17]

As Smith chronicles in *Reaching Judgement at Nuremberg*, the
position of the United Kingdom was also problematic with regard to its
plans to invade Norway (officially neutral), which had been elaborated
even before the Nazis invaded Norway in 1940.

The Soviet Union strongly resisted the proposal to insert a
definition of aggression in the Charter, citing the grounds that the
question of the meaning of aggression in international law lay beyond
the competence of the Conference, which had been convened to
devote its attention to an enumeration of the acts for which the
European Axis leaders were to be held criminally responsible.[18]

This position was to find support from the French representative, who doubted whether any established norm of international law
prescribed individual criminal responsibility for aggressive war. The
French representative argued that the prosecution of war through
unlawful means and methods of warfare did not necessarily mean that
the launching of war itself was unlawful, or that its initiation necessarily
gave rise to individual criminal responsibility for it.[19] According to the
French representative, violations of the *jus in bello* might involve State
responsibility for the breach of treaty obligations or individual responsibility for war crimes, but the planners and instigators of the war could
not be held criminally responsible for having started the war itself.

---

[17]   Smith, *supra* note 14 at 147-148.
[18]   Rifaat, *supra* note 5 at 148.
[19]   *Ibid.* at 145.

Ultimately, no definition on aggression was inserted in the Nuremberg Charter. Article 6(a) of the Nuremberg Charter[20] provides that:

> The following acts or any of them, are crimes coming within the jurisdiction of the Tribunal for which there shall be individual responsibility:
> a) CRIMES AGAINST PEACE: namely, planning, preparation, initiation or waging of a war of aggression or a war in violation of international treaties, agreements, or assurances, or participation in a common plan or conspiracy for any of the foregoing ...[21]

The concept of 'crimes against peace' is thus broader than the concept of 'war of aggression', the latter being only one element of 'crimes against peace'. In this way, the Allies could maintain the principle of individual criminal responsibility for the planning and starting of war, without actually having to define 'war of aggression' in categorical terms - a difficult and highly political task that was to take many years of negotiation and drafting in the United Nations General Assembly.

---

[20] On 8 Aug. 1945, Great Britain, France, the United States and the Soviet Union signed the London Agreement, Cmd. Paper 6903. H.M.S.O. (1945) which provides that "there shall be established after consultation with the Control Council for Germany an international military tribunal for the trial of war criminals whose offenses have no particular geographical location." The Nuremberg Charter is annexed to the London Agreement.

[21] Articles (b) and (c) define 'war crimes' and 'crimes against humanity'. If Article 6(a) of the Nuremberg Charter had been interpreted broadly, it could have been used to indict a large portion of the German population on the ground that the German population participated, however slightly, in a common plan or conspiracy to commit war crimes or crimes against humanity. *See* Yoram Dinstein, *International Criminal Law* 20 Israel Law Review (1985) at 210, arguing along these lines. However, in the 1948 cases of *German High Command Trial*, 15 International Legal Materials (1948) 376, and *I.G. Farben Trial*, *ibid.* 668, the US Military Tribunal at Nuremberg limited culpability to officers at levels of responsibility for the setting and enforcement of policy.

Twenty-two German nationals were brought before the International Military Tribunal at Nuremberg, which began on 20 November 1945. According to the sentences rendered by the Tribunal on 1 October 1946, in accordance with the Judgement delivered the previous day, twelve of the defendants were sentenced to be hanged, seven to be imprisoned and three acquitted of the charges against them.

The lack of a definition of 'crimes against peace' threatened to undermine the legitimacy of the Nuremberg proceedings:

> The Prosecution in the Nuremberg Trial dealt with four counts of indictment. Defendants accused of crimes against peace were presented under Counts One and Two. Count One of the Indictment charges the defend-ants with conspiring or having a common plan to commit crimes against peace. Count Two of the Indictment charges the defendants with committing specific crimes against peace by planning, initiating, and waging war or aggression against a number of other States.[22]

Relying on the Kellogg-Briand Pact, the prosecution argued that the use of war as an instrument of national policy had been outlawed in 1928 and that this meant the individuals who planned and instigated the launching of aggressive war were criminally responsible under the rules of international law. The prosecution could not deny that the lack of any definition of 'crimes against peace' was a serious defect in the Charter and it had to acknowledge this in the opening spee-ches.[23] However, it was argued that the 1933 Convention on

---

[22] Rifaat, *supra* note 5 at 150.

[23] Mr. Justice Jackson, Chief Prosecutor for the United States stated that: "It is perhaps a weakness in this Charter that it fails to define a war of aggression. Abstractly, the subject is full of difficulty, and all kinds of troublesome hypothetical cases can be conjured up. It is a subject which if the defence should be permitted to go afield beyond the very narrow charge in the Indictment, would prolong the trial and involve the Tribunal in insoluble political issues." *See* Opening Speeches of 21 Nov. 194 of the Nuremberg Trial at 40.

Aggression, which was never adopted by the League of Nations and therefore did not create legal obligations, was nonetheless a valuable aid by which to interpret 'crimes against peace'.[24]

The Chief Prosecutor for the United Kingdom, Sir Hartley Shawcross, in presenting Count Two of the indictment, argued that the Nuremberg Charter did not offend the principle of *nullum crimen sine lege, nulla poena sine lege*, claiming that international law had long ago recognized aggressive war to be a crime, which also meant that individuals could be held criminally responsible for 'crimes against peace' at the international level.[25]

The defense answered that nowhere in the provisions of the Kellogg-Briand Pact is it stated that a war of aggression is a crime. Moreover, the Pact does not confer authority upon any State or tribunal to try individuals. The defense attacked the competence of the Nuremberg Tribunal on the grounds that the entire category 'crimes against peace' was not established law and that, in breach of fundamental principles of justice, it was being applied retroactively by an organ without any jurisdiction to do so.

The defense arguments on aggression were rejected. The Tribunal stated that the:

> ... Charter makes the planning of waging of a war of aggression or a war in violation of international treaties a crime; and it is therefore not strictly necessary to consider whether and to what extent aggressive war was a crime before the execution of the London Agreement.[26]

However, the Tribunal, taking account of its importance, nevertheless went on to consider this question. It held that:

> To initiate a war of aggression ... is not only an international crime; it is the supreme international crime

---

[24] Rifaat, *supra* note 5 at 151.
[25] Opening Speech of 4 Dec. 1945 at 47.
[26] International Military Tribunal (Nuremberg): Judgment and Sentences, 1 Oct. 1946, 41 American Journal of International Law (1947) at 217.

differing only from other war crimes in that it contains within itself the accumulated evil of the whole.

The first acts of aggression referred to in the Indictment are the seizure of Austria and Czechoslovakia; and the first war of aggression charged in the Indictment is the war against Poland begun on 1 September 1939.[27]

The Tribunal acknowledged that neither the Kellogg-Briand Pact nor the 1907 Hague Conventions provide expressly for individual criminal responsibility, but then held that:

> In the opinion of the Tribunal, the solemn renunciation of war as an instrument of national policy necessarily involves the proposition that such a war is illegal in international law; and that those who plan and wage such a war, with its inevitable and terrible consequences, are committing a crime in so doing.[28]

The Tribunal thereby dismissed the defense argument that the Tribunal was applying criminal law retroactively and held that to apply standards of individual criminal responsibility did not breach the principles of *nullum crimen sine lege, nulla poena sine lege*.

The Nuremberg Judgment remains controversial not only because it failed to establish that norms prohibiting 'aggression' were grounded in the *lex lata*, but it also construed norms providing for individual criminal responsibility from instruments that made no mention at all of it, in fact offending the principles of *nullum crimen sine lege, nulla poena sine lege*. At the same time, the Tribunal asserted that the principles of *nullum crimen sine lege, nulla poena sine lege* were at any rate general principles of justice which should not apply where the defendants ought to have known that the acts they committed, or ordered to be committed, were wrong.[29]

---

[27]   *Ibid.* at 186.
[28]   *Ibid.* at 218.
[29]   *Ibid.* at 217.

The question of the meaning of 'aggression' was also raised before the International Military Tribunal for the Far East.[30] The Tokyo Charter was almost identical to that of the Nuremberg Charter, except for a few variations. Article 5(a) of the Tokyo Charter defines 'crimes against peace' as:

> ... the planning, preparation, initiation or waging of declared or undeclared war of aggression or war in violation of international law, treaties, agreements or assurances, or participation in a common plan or conspiracy for the accomplishment of any of the foregoing.

This varies slightly from the Article 6(a) definition of 'crimes against peace' in the Nuremberg Charter because of the insertion of the words 'declared or undeclared' before the words 'war of aggression', thereby foreclosing possible defense arguments that Japan was not technically at war because it had not made any formal declaration to that effect.

The defense arguments raised before the Tokyo Tribunal were similar to those made before the Nuremberg Tribunal. However, the Tokyo Judgement is particularly interesting because several judges filed dissenting judgements, most notably, Mr. Justice Pal of India. Mr. Justice Pal agreed with the defense argument that aggression had never been outlawed in international law, and moreover, that it was not clear what acts constituted 'aggression'.

Mr. Justice Pal also assailed the majority Judgment of the Tribunal for applying one standard to Japan and another to the Allies. In particular, he argued that the Allied action against Japan in connection with Japan's attack on Manchuria violated laws of neutrality and therefore that Allied action immediately preceding the opening of hostilities, directly between the Allies and Japan, could not be ignored. Mr. Justice Pal further called into question the objectivity of the Majority Judgement, arguing that it confused moral wrong with legal wrong. Moral wrongfulness does not necessarily give rise to

---

[30]   Established on 9 Jan. 1946 in Tokyo to bring to trial, sentence and punish the major Japanese war criminals.

legal responsibility or criminal responsibility, even where there may exist a general consensus on what is morally wrong.

> One of the most essential attributes of law is its pre-dictability. It is perhaps this predictability which makes justice according to law preferable to justice without law, legislative or executive justice. The excellence of justice according to law rests upon the fact that judges are not free to render decision based purely on their personal predilections and peculiar dispositions, no matter how good or wise they may be. To leave the aggressive character of war to be determined according to 'the popular sense' or 'the general moral sense of humanity' is to rob the law of its predicability.[31]

Again, neither the Kellogg-Briand Pact nor other pre-Nuremberg Charter sources of international law provide for individual criminal responsibility with regard to 'crimes against peace'.

iii) Content and Legal Status of the Norms on Aggression Since 1945 and the 1991 Draft Code Provisions on Aggression

A retroactive application of international legal norms prohibiting aggression is less likely to arise in future international prosecutions for two reasons. First, the norms on aggression have developed subsequent to the Nuremberg Judgment, largely through: the UN Charter's comprehensive prohibition of the use of force in international relations which admits only self-defense as an exception;[32] the

---

[31] From Justice Pal's dissent, quoted in Elizabeth S. Kopelman, *Ideology and International Law: the Dissent of the Indian Justice at the Tokyo War Crimes Trial*, 23(2) New York University Journal of International Law and Politics (1991) at 413.

[32] Article 2(4) of the UN Charter enjoins members from the threat or use of force against the territorial integrity or political independence of any State, or in any other manner inconsistent with the purposes of the United Nations. Article 39 authorizes the UN Security Council to determine the existence of any threat to the peace, or of an act of aggression, and to make recommen-

Judgement of the Nuremberg Tribunal itself; United Nations codification;[33] as well as resolutions of the General Assembly,[34] most notably, General Assembly resolution 3314 (XXIX) of 14 December 1974. Article 5(2) of resolution 3314 states that: "A war of aggression is a crime against international peace. Aggression gives rise to international responsibility".[35] Second, the Nuremberg and Tòkyo Tribunals' retroactive application of new legal norms seriously undermined the legitimacy of these tribunals. Hopefully, the severe criticisms that the tribunals violated the principles of *nullum crimen sine lege, nulla poena sine lege* provide a lesson to drafters of future tribunal charters not to underestimate the weight of this issue. Interestingly, neither the Statute of the International Criminal Tribunal for the Former Yugoslavia nor that of the International Criminal Tribunal for Rwanda mention responsibility for the opening of hostilities itself.

At this point, it is valuable to turn directly to the 1991 draft Code provisions on aggression and to compare them with the contents of General Assembly resolution 3314, rather than to treat them

---

dations or decisions for the maintenance of international peace and security. Article 51 preserves the customary right of individual or collective self-defense if an armed attack occurs.

[33]   In 1946, the General Assembly affirmed 'the principles of international law as recognized by the Charter of the Nuremberg Tribunal and the judgment of the Tribunal.' The International Law Commission was authorized by the United Nations to further formulate these principles. *See* General Assembly resolution 95(1), GAOR First Session, Part. II, 188 (11 Dec. 1946).

[34]   *See* General Assembly resolution 2131 Declaration on the Inadmissibility of the Intervention in the Domestic Affairs of States and the Protection of their Independence and Sovereignty 1965, General Assembly resolution 2131 (XX), GAOR, 20th Session, Supp.14 at 11, *adopted* 109 to 0, with only the United Kingdom *abstaining*, General Assembly resolution 2625 which states that "[a] war of aggression constitutes a crime against the peace for which there is responsibility under international law" and General Assembly resolution 2625 (XXV), entitled Declaration on Principles of International Law Concerning Friendly Relations and Cooperation among States in Accordance with the Charter of the United Nations, 1970 *adopted without a vote,* 24 Oct. 1970.

[35]   Article 5(2) of General Assembly resolution 3314 [(XXIX), UN GAOR 29th Session, Supp. No.31].

separately, because the 1991 draft Code provisions substantially incorporate elements from the resolution.[36]

Much of Article 15 of the draft Code has been taken from resolution 3314 and it has therefore carried over weaknesses in the resolution's content.[37] It is not clear, for example, whether economic pressure could be considered a 'relevant circumstance' in the determination of aggression by the Security Council within the meaning of Article 15(3) of the draft Code. If it may, might the first use of armed force be excusable were it resorted to in response to extreme economic aggression?

This issue has been left open under the 1991 draft Code. Article 5 of resolution 3314, which reads: "No consideration of whatever nature, whether political, economic, military or otherwise, may serve as a justification for aggression", has been left out of the 1991 draft Code. The absence of a similar clause in the 1991 draft Code might be taken to suggest that the first use of force by a State in response to extreme economic or political provocation from any other State (not covered in the Article 15 definition of 'aggression') is permitted under the draft Code.

Since underdeveloped States and smaller States are more prone to economic aggression directed against them by the immensely stronger industrialized nations, there may be instances where economic pressure, such as blockage of the supply of food during famine or drought, causes sufficiently acute suffering that the human rights of the people, as well as the political independence of the injured State, are threatened. Suppose a State exercised its right to respond to extreme economic pressure under Article 15(3) with the first use of force. The acute question would then become: who is to judge when there exists economic pressure of sufficient extremity to justify the first use of force? The right of a State to resort to force in response to extreme economic provocation would be conditional upon

---

[36] The text of Article 15 of the 1991 draft Code is too lengthy to be reproduced here. *See* Annex 1 of this book.

[37] *See generally* Julius Stone, *Hopes and Loopholes in the 1974 Definition of Aggression*, 71 American Journal of International Law (1977) for a critique of resolution 3314. *See also* Nicolas Nyiri, The United Nations' Search for a Definition of Aggression (1989), and *further*, Rifaat, *supra* note 5.

Security Council review conducted 'in conformity with the Charter'. As a collective body authorized by the United Nations to determine aggression, the Security Council would have critical responsibility to determine which party to the conflict was the 'real aggressor'.

iv) Special Role of the Security Council vis-à-vis Aggression in the 1991 Draft Code

Under the 1991 draft Code, consideration by the proposed international criminal court of individual criminal responsibility for aggression would be subject to the determination of the Security Council that aggression has been committed in a particular instance. The wording of Article 15 of the draft Code thus preserves the role of the UN Security Council, as provided for in the UN Charter, to determine cases of aggression. The Article 15(2) definition of 'aggression' follows Article 1 of General Assembly resolution 3314, which itself is based on Article 2(4) of the UN Charter.[38] In order for there to be aggression under Article 15, there must be actual deployment of armed forces. Other forms of pressure or interference, such as belligerent declarations or economic or other such measures, are not covered.[39]

Preservation of the Security Council's pivotal role serves a vital interest of the international community. Aggression needs to be dealt with in a manner allowing for the greatest degree of negotiation, diplomacy and mediation. Judicial proceedings, in contrast, are adversarial by nature. Suppose aggression is committed, and the international criminal court promptly decided that the aggression was unlawful, and further, it determined that the Head of State was criminally responsible. In such a case, the court's decision might only harden the resolve of the country's leaders to 'fight to the finish', rather than to seek a graceful way to back down. By preserving the political role of UN organs more suited to negotiation, chances for the pacific settlement of disputes arising from unlawful aggression are

---

[38] General Assembly resolution 3314 (XXIX), GAOR 29th Session, Supp. 21, *adopted without a vote* 14 Dec. 1974.

[39] Tom Farer, *Political and Economic Aggression in Contemporary International Law*, in The New Humanitarian Law of Armed Conflict (ed. Cassese) (1986).

enhanced rather than diminished. On a point of more immediate practical importance, permanent Members of the Security Council (and their allies) are not likely to lend their support to a Code on Crimes against the Peace and Security of Mankind that diminishes their prerogative under the UN Charter to determine breaches of international peace and security.

However, Article 15 does not clarify sufficiently the role of the international criminal court in the determination of aggression. If the international criminal court were conferred concurrent jurisdiction to determine whether aggression has been committed, the UN's capability to respond to breaches of international peace and security could be seriously hindered where the Security Council's determination conflicted with the finding of the international criminal court. The Security Council might find there was aggression, but the international criminal court might determine aggression had not been perpetrated, or vice versa. In such cases, the legitimacy of the United Nations to maintain international peace and security on a collective basis would likely be undermined, since decisions even of UN organs would be inconsistent or even contradictory.

Article 15 may mean that it confers authority upon the international criminal court to determine whether there has been aggression, but that the UN Security Council has higher authority to make such a ruling. Even if this were the case, the legitimacy of the international criminal court would be undermined: its authority to make a legal determination on a critical matter of fact - whether aggression had been committed - would be subordinate to the Security Council's political judgement.

This problem is not unique to the relationship between the Security Council and the proposed international criminal court. There is already some ambiguity in the role of the International Court of Justice relative to that of the Security Council. As Gowlland-Debbas observes:

> In fact, concurrent jurisdiction of political and judicial organs is made possible by the constituent instruments themselves. For the Charter provides in Article 35(1) that any member of the United Nations may bring to the attention of the Security Council any dispute, or any situation, likely to endanger the maintenance of interna-

tional peace and security; at the same time, Article 36(1) of the Court's Statute states that 'the jurisdiction of the Court comprises all cases which the parties refer to it and all matters specially provided for in the Charter of the United Nations or in treaties and conventions in force'.[40]

In the *Lockerbie Case*,[41] the International Court of Justice followed the *Nicaragua Case* in opining that:

The Council has functions of a political nature assigned to it, whereas the Court exercises purely judicial functions. Both organs can therefore perform their separate but complementary functions with respect to the same events.[42]

---

[40] Vera Gowlland-Debbas, *The Relationship between the International Court of Justice and the Security Council in the Light of the Lockerbie Case*, 88(4) American Journal of International Law (1994) at 643.

[41] (Libya v. UK) 1992 ICJ Reports 3.

[42] 1992 ICJ Reports at 22, quoting the *dicta* of the *Nicaragua Case* 1984 ICJ Reports 27 at 434-435, cited in Vera Gowlland-Debbas, *supra* note 40 at 648. *See also* Francisco Orrego Vicuña, *The Settlement of Disputes and Conflict Resolution in the Context of the Revitalized Role for the United Nations Security Council*, in Peace-Keeping and Peace-Building: The Development of the Role of the Security Council (ed. Dupuy) (1993) at 47, who states: "A possible approach regarding the harmonization of these colliding jurisdictions would be that within the overall framework of coordination for a new security system under the United Nations, both the Security Council and the International Court of Justice might be empowered to refer to each other such matters that can be considered strictly political or strictly legal within the process of preventive action. This approach would be of particular interest in cases such as this, in which each organ was seized by an opposite party to the same dispute, a situation which was arisen often between regional organizations and the Security Council. However, besides the necessary coordination there would be a need for both organs to proceed to the same time limit in order that their respective decisions might be integrated into the same process of settlement of dispute and conflict prevention."

This implies that the relationship between the International Court of Justice and the Security Council is not characterized by hierarchy, a position the ICJ had already enunciated clearly in the *United States Diplomatic and Consular Staff in Tehran Case*,[43] and cited with approval by Judge Ni in his Separate Opinion in the *Lockerbie Case*. A similar approach might be taken with regard to the relationship between the Security Council and a permanent international criminal court. This question is bound to become more critical as the Security Council's role expands in the post-Cold War world.[44]

Article 15 of the draft Code could preserve weaknesses inherent in the Security Council's role in its determination of particular instances as cases of aggression. For decades, the Security Council's responsibility to coordinate an effective response by the international community upon the outbreak of a breach of international peace was stymied by frequent use of the veto by permanent Members. The record of the Security Council from 1945 until the enforcement action taken against Iraq has been disappointing. Unfortunately, the Council's approach against Iraq is cause for ambivalence or even scepticism about future practice. As Gowlland-Debbas states, the Security Council:

> ... has appeared to show unwillingness to attribute guilt
> in the determinations it has made under Article 39, for
> it has curiously never formally made a finding of an act
> of aggression, preferring to remain within the more
> neutral terminology of a threat to, or breach of the
> peace, not even in blatant cases such as that of the
> invasion of Kuwait by Iraq.[45]

---

[43]   *United States Diplomatic and Consular Staff in Tehran Case*, (US v. Iran), 1980 ICJ Reports 3 at 22.

[44]   *See generally* Peter Wallensteen, *Representing the World: A Security Council for the 21st Century*, 25(1) Security Dialogue (1994) on the expanded role of the Security Council and *also* Matthias J. Herdegen, *The "Constitution-alization" of the UN Security System,* 27(1) Vanderbilt Journal of Trans-national Law (1994).

[45]   Vera Gowlland-Debbas, *Security Council Enforcement Action and Issues of State Responsibility*, 43(1) International and Comparative Law Quarterly (1994) at 63.

Almost every State has a close ally in the Security Council willing to veto Security Council resolutions on its behalf. While the Cold War may have ended, it is not clear that the Security Council will function more effectively to deal with the outbreak of war. Even in the case of Iraq's invasion of Kuwait and the menace this posed to the oil supply of the highly industrialized nations and the direct interests of Security Council permanent Members, the results of the Council's response remain equivocal.[46]

The political role of the Security Council would be very likely to undermine the court's fairness and impartiality and perhaps its legitimacy in general. According to Article 15, the only cases the court could try in respect of aggression would be those in which no Security Council permanent Member exercised its right of veto. In effect, nationals of permanent Member countries might be relatively immune from international criminal prosecution for aggression by the international criminal court. This measure of privilege for the permanent Members (the Republic of China, France, Russia, the United Kingdom of Great Britain and Northern Ireland, and the United States of America) has become increasingly regarded as anachronistic in the post-Cold War world.[47]

What would be the international criminal court's role were the Security Council to do nothing at all in respect of a possible case of

---

[46]   *See* Philip Alston, *The Security Council and Human Rights: Lessons to be Learned from the Iraq-Kuwait Crisis and Its Aftermath*, 13 Australian Yearbook of International Law (1992) where the author takes an in-depth look at the United Nations action against Iraq. For further discussion of the legal basis of Security Council action on the Iraqi invasion of Kuwait, *see* Serge Sur, *Sécurité collective et rétablissement de la paix: la résolution 687 (3 avril 1991) dans l'Affaire du Golfe*, in Peace-Keeping and Peace-Building: The Development of the Role of the Security Council (ed. Dupuy) (1993).

[47]   *See* Mohammed Bedjaoui, The New World Order and the Security Council: Testing the Legality of Its Acts (1994); Benjamin Ferencz, New Legal Foundations for Global Survival: Security through the Security Council (1994); Walter Hoffmann, United Nations Security Council Reform and Restructuring (1994); Joachim W. Muller, The Reform of the United Nations (2 volumes.) (1992); Harris O. Schoenberg, War No More!: A Concrete Action Plan to Revitalize the United Nations Security Council (1995); and Brian Urquhart and Erskine Childers, Towards a More Effective United Nations (1992).

aggression? Would the court be barred from trying a national leader who allegedly had perpetrated aggression where the Security Council had taken no action at all on the matter? Were the court authorized to seize jurisdiction over the matter where the Security Council took no action, at precisely what point in time would it be clear that the Security Council did not act?

One solution would be to authorize the court to seize jurisdiction once a complaint alleging individual criminal responsibility for aggression has been lodged, even where the Security Council has taken no decision on whether aggression in fact had been committed, as long as the Security Council is no longer giving active consideration to the matter by the time the complaint is lodged. Were this solution adopted, it would be necessary to develop clear criteria that indicate the precise point in time at which active Security Council consideration has ceased in cases where the Council failed to so indicate. Future sessions of the ILC must clarify the role of the Security Council in relations to an international criminal court.

Moreover, the relationship between the proposed international criminal court and domestic courts must also be clarified. Article 15(5) of the draft Code addresses only the relationship between the Security Council and domestic courts. In effect, Article 15(5) makes clear in advance that domestic judicial decisions that conflict with the Security Council's determination as to whether aggression has occurred, have no force or effect on the international plane. In other words, a State may not invoke a ruling of its domestic courts that aggression has not been committed, as justification for its failure to abide by its international obligations.

Were the Security Council to function in the way the drafters of the United Nations Charter had intended, it could utilize its unique position to determine aggression on a more fair and impartial basis than could any domestic court, because in most domestic jurisdictions, the judiciary is not constitutionally authorized to rule on such matters of high policy as the legality of the State's use of force on the international plane. The ILC put forward for consideration Article 15(5) which provides that determination by the Security Council on aggression is binding on national courts. Article 15(5) would diminish in advance the force of a government's claim that its country's courts determined that the use of force was legally authorized where in fact it constituted an act of aggression.

The areas of conflict that are bound to involve a question of conflicting or overlapping jurisdiction between the Security Council and international judicial organs (including the International Court of Justice, the International Tribunals for the former Yugoslavia and Rwanda, or the proposed international criminal court) may be growing because the end of the Cold War has made possible an expanded Security Council role. As the Security Council takes on the purposes for which it was designed, as well as some which may not have been originally contemplated at the inception of the United Nations in 1945, its competence relative to other UN organs is bound to require clearer demarcation, in particular between the 'judicial' functions of international criminal tribunals as against the 'executive' functions of the Security Council.

Perhaps it would be better if Article 15(5) were to provide that a State may not invoke a judicial decision of its domestic court as justification for its failure to observe the ruling of the *international criminal court*. This formula would have the merit of establishing the relative authority of a ruling of the international criminal court over that of a domestic court on aggression, rather than relating the determination of the Security Council (a political body of the UN) to a ruling of a domestic court (a judicial body in a State).

v) 1996 Draft Code

Article 16 of the 1996 draft Code concerning the crime of aggression provides that:

> An individual, who, as leader or organizer, actively
> participates in or orders the planning, preparation,
> initiation or waging of aggression committed by a State,
> shall be responsible for a crime of aggression.

Article 16 basically deletes the entire body of Article 15 of the 1991 draft Code, replacing it with a formulation drawn from Article 6(a) of the Nuremberg Charter.

First, the advantage of this approach is that an international criminal court would not be bound to interpret the lengthy provisions drawn from the General Assembly resolution on Aggression of 1974.[48] It must be recalled that resolution 3314 had been drafted for political purposes and not specifically for the purpose of enforcing individual criminal responsibility.[49]   This does not mean, however, that an international criminal court could avoid the issue as to whether aggression had been committed within the meaning of Article 2(4) of the UN Charter.

Second, the resemblance between Article 16 of the 1996 draft Code and the relevant provisions of the Nuremberg and Tokyo Charters would render the jurisprudence arising from these Tribunals, as well as that arising from cases decided pursuant to Control Council Law No. 10, more valuable as guidance for an international criminal court.

Third, Article 16 of the 1996 draft Code introduces an improvement over the corresponding provisions of the 1991 draft Code by including specific reference to individual responsibility for 'aggression committed by a State'.   Thus, individual criminal responsibility for aggression would not be incurred unless the international legal norm that prohibits States from committing aggression were first breached.

Fourth, the wording of Article 16, like Article 15 of the 1991 draft Code and Article 6 of the Nuremberg Charter, focuses on those individuals in the top level of the command structure i.e. leaders and organizers.   However, it must be noted that Article 16 extends beyond the ambit *ratione personae* of Article 15 of the 1991 draft Code through its inclusion of those who have 'actively participated' in the crime of aggression.   How an international criminal court would interpret the scope of this term is unclear.   'Active participation' does not connote a specific level of participation and would have to be decided on a case-by-case basis by the proposed court.   As the

---

[48]   General Assembly resolution 3314 of 14 Dec. 1974.

[49]   The Governments of Switzerland, the United Kingdom and the United States were of the view that resolution 3314 should not form the basis of the draft Code provisions on aggression since it was not designed for the purposes of international criminal law. *See* Comments and Observations of Governments on the Draft Code of Crimes against the Peace and Security of Mankind adopted on First Reading by the International Law Commission at its 43rd Session, A/CN.4/448 of 1 March 1993.

Commentary to Article 16 points out,[50] the provision should be interpreted narrowly to apply to persons having the authority to make decisions at a policy level, rather than persons at lower echelons of authority, such as lower-ranking army officers or soldiers.

2. THREAT OF AGGRESSION

i) Background

In principle, a 'threat of aggression' could be considered as a breach of international law that should give rise to individual criminal responsibility. The seriousness of a threat of aggression should not be underestimated nor can it be doubted that it qualifies as a violation of international law.

Powerful States may make ostentatious display of military strength to intimidate smaller, more vulnerable members of the international community. In some cases, a threat by a State to use armed force unlawfully against another State may be tantamount to actual aggression in effect. Moreover, the use of threats as a form of coercion clearly runs counter to the maintenance of international peace and security since threats have a tendency to escalate into the actual use of force. In some cases, threats may be employed to provoke an armed response, which may then be used as a pretext for aggression under the guise of self-defense. That these dangers were understood by the drafters of the United Nations Charter is evident in Article 2(4) which prohibits 'the threat or use of force' in international relations.

Violations of international law that seriously threaten or impair international peace and security ought to be effectively deterred. The need for effective deterrence militates in favour of increased recognition of norms providing for individual criminal responsibility for such acts, including 'threat of aggression'.

However, norms providing for individual criminal responsibility must be clear and specific. To hold the individual criminally responsible for a crime that is poorly or unclearly defined would in itself

---

[50]   A/CN.4/L.527/Add.7 of 18 July 1996 at 2.

violate cardinal principles of criminal justice. For criminal law to serve as a deterrent, potential perpetrators need to know, within some margin of certainty, what acts constitute crimes. 'Threat of aggression' is difficult to define because a threat of any kind, unlike the actual use of force, may be very subtle. The essence of a threat lies in the appreciation of the subject of a state of possible danger. Moreover, it may prove difficult to establish: first, that the perpetrator had the requisite criminal intent to make the threat; second, that the acts in question were such as to constitute a threat to the Government and that the Government under threat was not unreasonable in its appreciation of the situation it claimed constituted a threat; and third, that the State against which the threat was directed, actually felt threatened by the acts in question.

For example, military manoeuvres by one State in its territory bordering the territory of another State, at a time the two are engaged in a heated dispute, may be interpreted by authorities in the neighbouring State as a sign portending imminent attack. Such manoeuvres may raise the risk of misinterpretation by one State of the other State's intentions, resulting in an outbreak of hostilities. It may also increase tension in both countries to the point that ordinary civilians assume they have license to perpetrate acts of violence against members of ethnic, religious or cultural minority groups whose origins or sympathies may appear to lie across the border. Despite these and other perils, it is unlikely that State recognition of a rule of international law prohibiting military manoeuvres would come about. Equally, it is unlikely that such manoeuvres would be seen to constitute a 'threat of aggression' unless they were carried out along with acts and statements that, taken together, indicate belligerent intentions.

What about the testing of armaments? Customarily, States have recognized for themselves an almost unlimited right to test armaments as long as such testing does not directly affect any other State and is not specifically prohibited by any international agreement. Nevertheless, ostentatious displays of military potency, especially those showing off weapons of highly advanced technical sophistication or of mass destruction, may cause certain other States to fear aggressive war is being contemplated against them. In some cases, weapons testing itself may be seen by other States as deliberate provocation or as a breach of international law for other reasons (such as harm to the indigenous population or damage to the natural environment as in the case of the French nuclear tests).[51] Such fears may be intensified if extensive weapons testing is conducted in a deliberately provocative manner and accompanied by other aggressive actions or statements. However, mere weapons testing by itself is unlikely to be recognized to qualify as a 'threat of aggression' because States are likely to continue to consider this kind of activity as falling legitimately within their respective spheres of national sovereignty.

These and other kinds of ambiguities have led to very sparse Security Council practice in regard to threats of aggression (or threats to the peace). As Kooijmans points out: "Apart from the case of Southern Rhodesia and the rather atypical case of Libya, until now the Security Council has only determined the existence of a threat to the peace *after* fighting had broken out."[52]

In this connection, it is worth considering that expansion in the Security Council role pursuant to Chapter VII of the UN Charter may generate further increased recognition for a somewhat broader construction as to what kinds of occurrences shall be considered to constitute a threat to or breach of international peace and security. This development would undoubtedly narrow the relative autonomy of individuals, who may enjoy the approval or acquiescence of the State, to engage in the use of force. In other words, the interpretation of 'threat or breach of international peace and security' may depend, at least partially, on the capacity of collective security organs to successfully engage in preventive diplomacy, peace-building and peace-enforcement in practice.

ii) 1991 Draft Code Provisions on Threat of Aggression

Article 16 of the 1991 draft Code provides that:

> 1. An individual who as leader or organizer commits or orders the commission of a threat of aggression shall, on conviction thereof, be sentenced [to ...].

---

[51] *See Nuclear Tests Cases* (Australia v. France); (New Zealand v. France) ICJ Reports 1974.

[52] *See further* Peter H. Kooijmans, *The Enlargement of the Concept "Threat to the Peace"*, in Peace-Keeping and Peace-Building: The Development of the Role of the Security Council (ed. Dupuy) (1993) at 120.

2.   Threat of aggression consists of declarations, communications, demonstrations of force or any other measures which would give good reason to the Government of a State to believe that aggression is being seriously contemplated against that State.

The formula of 'threat of aggression' in Article 16 of the draft Code is quite elastic and as such might be difficult to enforce for several reasons. Article 16(2) could be interpreted as providing for a subjective test for determination of a 'threat of aggression' by the words 'which would give good reason to the Government of a State to believe that aggression is being seriously contemplated'. If it were completely or largely up to the State that claims to be the object of a threat of aggression to determine, on its own, whether it had good reason to believe aggression was seriously contemplated, then the claim that there existed such a threat, would be more likely to be used as a tool of political rhetoric.

On the other hand, an international criminal court could apply a set of more objective criteria to evaluate whether a State could maintain its claim that it had reasonable grounds ('good reason') to conclude that aggression was being contemplated against it. Precisely what criteria the court were to choose would affect the draft provision's scope. Even 'aggression' may be a difficult legal concept to apply in practice. As discussed above, it is often unclear which State resorted to armed attack first, and further, whether the State was taking preemptive action in response to an imminent armed attack. 'Threat of aggression' is even more elastic, especially if paragraph 2 were interpreted as authorizing every Government to determine unilaterally when a 'threat' exists.

Moreover, difficulties could arise where the international criminal court determined that there was a 'threat of aggression' within the meaning of Article 16, yet the Security Council ruled that the circumstances did not amount to 'aggression' within the meaning of Article 15.   Strictly speaking, there is nothing illogical about the existence of a threat of aggression which falls short of aggression itself. However, in a given instance, were hostilities to break out between two States, incongruous rulings of the Security Council and the international criminal court over the existence of aggression and threat of aggression would serve only to trivialize both the operation and function of a permanent international criminal court as well as the issue of the criminal culpability of individuals brought before it.

iii) 1996 Draft Code

The Governments of Australia, The Netherlands, the United Kingdom, the United States, Switzerland and Paraguay strongly opposed the inclusion of 'threat of aggression' in the draft Code, arguing that it did not convey a sufficiently precise notion amenable to individual criminal responsibility.[53] The Governments of Denmark, Finland, Iceland, Norway and Sweden, proposed that the provision could be redrafted to provide criminal responsibility for 'threat of violent aggression'.

In response to the comments of Governments, the ILC eliminated from the competence of the proposed international criminal court any provision providing for individual criminal responsibility for a 'threat of aggression', and consequently, no such references appear in the 1996 draft Code.

3. INTERVENTION

Although frequently less obvious than full-scale war, intervention may pose a significant threat to State sovereignty and political independence. Norms providing individual criminal responsibility for intervention were therefore included in the 1991 draft Code.

However, the 1991 draft Code provisions on intervention risked being gored by one or the other horn of a logical and practical dilemma, and as a result, they were eliminated from the draft Code in 1996. On the one hand, as a matter of practical implementation, the draft Code could cover only those cases of intervention involving the outright use of force. Lesser forms of intervention would be extremely difficult to prove, and moreover, would seem to pose a less serious

---

[53] *See* Comments and Observations of Governments on the Draft Code of Crimes against the Peace and Security of Mankind adopted on First Reading by the International Law Commission at its 43rd Session, A/CN.4/ 448 of 1 March 1993.

threat.   Furthermore, the difficulty to arrive at a simple and clear definition of intervention naturally would reduce prospects for effective implementation of individual criminal responsibility therefor.   On the other hand, a provision stipulating criminal responsibility only for intervention involving armed force would be superfluous because the draft Code already prohibits the aggressive use of armed force through its norms on aggression.

For the sake of providing a complete picture of international criminal law at its present stage of emergence, it is valuable to explore the political origins and historical development of the principle of non-intervention, and then to consider some possible exceptions to norms prohibiting intervention.

i) Prior to the UN Charter

The doctrine of non-intervention derives from the basic principle of the sovereign independence of States.   Intervention has been defined as the 'dictatorial interference by a State in the affairs of another State for the purpose of maintaining or altering the condition of things.'[54]   'Intervention' and 'dictatorial interference' are broad terms, covering a wide range of possible measures and actions, from the deployment of military force to more subtle forms of pressure by one State against another, such as those of an economic or political character.   It should be kept in mind that intervention involves unlawful acts as opposed to measures that may be merely unfriendly but not unlawful.[55]

The principle of non-intervention can be traced to the origins of the State as a discrete political and legal entity and to the rise of international law that emerged during the Peace of Westphalia, following the end of the Thirty Years War (1618-1648).   The peace treaties that inaugurated the Peace of Westphalia contained political and legal elements formally recognizing States as sovereign entities,

---

[54]   Lassa Oppenheim, International Law: Eighth Ed. (1963) at 306.

[55]   For example, a State may cease provision of economic aid to another State (which may cause that State considerable harm).   However, this interruption in aid would not breach any international legal obligation and would thus normally exemplify 'retorsion' rather than intervention (unless certain measures are taken which extend beyond the bounds of legality).

separate and independent from the Church. The principles of State equality, independence and mutual non-intervention, continue to form the basic pillars of the contemporary international legal system.

The right of States to be free from intervention found new expression almost two centuries after the settlements reached in Westphalia, in the Message of United States President Monroe to Congress on 2 December 1823. The substance of that message, which came to be known as the Monroe Doctrine, declared that interference from European Powers anywhere in the Americas would no longer be tolerated by the United States, and moreover, that an attempt on the part of any European Power to interfere with any part of the American continent would be considered a danger to the 'peace and safety' of the United States. For its own part, the United States declared its intention not to interfere in any existing colony of Europe, the internal affairs of any European country or any European war.

Ironically, the Monroe Doctrine was employed by several successive American Governments to justify their own unilateral intervention in the internal affairs of Latin American countries, while carving out and consolidating the US sphere of influence.[56] The Monroe Doctrine, combined with the traditional view that a State could take forcible measures to protect its nationals or property, provided an excuse for certain European countries and the United States to enforce recovery of debts, owed to their nationals by certain Latin American States, through naval blockade and other military ventures designed to dictate the policy of the target State.

In reaction to the forcible collection of debts by the more powerful countries in the nineteenth century, the Argentinean Minister

---

[56]   President Theodore Roosevelt announced in his 2 December 1904 annual message a corollary principle to the Monroe Doctrine: "If a nation shows that it knows how to act with reasonable efficiency and decency in social and political matters, if it keeps order and pays its obligations, it need fear no interference from the United States. Chronic wrongdoing, or an impotence which results in a general loosening of the ties of civilized society may in America, as elsewhere, ultimately require intervention by some civilized nation, and in the Western Hemisphere, the adherence of the United States to the Monroe Doctrine may force the United States, however reluctantly, in flagrant cases of such wrongdoing or impotence, to the exercise of an international police power."

of Foreign Affairs in 1902 elaborated the Drago Doctrine. This doctrine proclaimed that the use of force by a foreign State to collect debts arising from any State in Latin America would no longer be countenanced.[57]

Following the First World War, United States foreign policy was restored to reflect more the original intent of the Monroe Doctrine, consonant with growing American isolationism and the renewed efforts to foster good relations with neighbouring States. This increased level of mutual respect for State sovereignty on the part of countries of the Americas were eventually reflected in a number of inter-American treaties that provide for collective security guarantees among States in this part of the world.[58]

Examples abound of foreign intervention by way of covert government operations (sometimes accompanied by overt military action) designed to destabilize and overthrow the Government of another State. Covert action by western Powers in the USSR immediately following the Russian Revolution of November 1917, aimed at thwarting consolidation of effective control throughout Russia by the Bolshevik Government, action by Nazi Germany in Czechoslovakia and Austria preceding the outbreak of World War II, by the United States in Cuba (1961 Bay of Pigs invasion), and in Nicaragua in the 1970's and 1980's, are well-known examples of intervention in the 20th century.

---

[57] The 1907 Hague Conference endorsed the Drago Doctrine through adoption of the Hague Convention on Limiting the Employment of Force for the Recovery of Contract Debts. *See generally* Benedetto Conforti, *The Principle of Non-Intervention* in International Law, in Achievements and Prospects, (ed. Bedjaoui) (1991) at 468-469; and J.G. Starke, Introduction to International Law, Tenth ed. (1989) at 303.

[58] *See* the Act of Chapultepect, 1945, the Inter-American Treaty of Reciprocal Assistance of Rio de Janeiro, 1947, and the Bogotá Charter of the Organization of American States, 1948, as referred to in J.G Starke, *Ibid.* at 107-108.

ii) UN Charter Provisions

- Articles 2(1) and 2(7): Matters
Essentially within Domestic Jurisdiction

Article 2(1) of the UN Charter states: "The Organization is based on the principle of the sovereign equality of all its Members." Article 2(7) of the Charter imposes upon the United Nations Organization a duty not "to intervene in matters which are essentially within the domestic jurisdiction of any state".

Article 2(7) implies limitations to the authority of the Organization, and by extension, to that of a State or States, which may intend to take action under UN auspices in a way that may breach the sovereignty and independence of a State. Article 2(7) thus reproduces the effect of Article 15(8) of the League of Nations Covenant[59] by attempting to delineate between matters which, in principle, may be of international concern (therefore subject to international regulation), and matters of exclusively municipal concern (therefore beyond the rubric of international law and jurisdiction). However, it has never been clear *in abstracto* what matters, if any, fall within this reserved domain of domestic jurisdiction. Indeed, as the Permanent Court of International Justice observed in the *Nationality Decrees issued in Tunis and Morocco Case*:

> The question whether a certain matter is or is not solely within the jurisdiction of a state is an essentially relative question; it depends upon the development of international relations.[60]

Generally eager to reap the many benefits that accrue from active participation in the international community, while loathing international scrutiny in areas they consider lie beyond the scope of outside

---

[59]   Article 15(8) of the League of Nations Covenant reads: "If the dispute between the parties is claimed by one of them, and is found by the Council, to arise out of a matter which by international law is solely within the domestic jurisdiction of that party, the Council shall so report, and shall make no recommendations as to its settlement."

[60]   (Advisory Opinion) PCIJ Reports Series B No.4 (1923) at 24.

interference, States can derive little comfort from the Permanent Court's reasoning on the scope of domestic jurisdiction.

During the drafting of the UN Charter, States sought reassurance that the successor to the League of Nations would not radically diminish national sovereignty. This was an especially acute concern because the Charter was to confer upon the Organization, *inter alia*, wide competence "to achieve international co-operation in solving international problems of an economic, social, cultural or humanitarian character, and in promoting and encouraging respect for human rights".[61] Accordingly, Article 2(7) provides that:

> Nothing contained in the present Charter shall authorize the United Nations to intervene in matters which are essentially within the domestic jurisdiction of any state or shall require the Members to submit such matters to settlement under the present Charter; but this principle shall not prejudice the application of enforcement measures under Chapter VII.

The word 'essentially' qualifies 'matters' in favour of a broad interpretation of the scope of domestic jurisdiction, reflecting the intensified concern of States to guard the breadth of their national sovereignty, even in areas where there may exist treaty obligations.[62] In this sense, the wording of Article 2(7) appears to afford States a strong basis upon which to assert the reserved domain of exclusive domestic jurisdiction.

However, in almost all cases United Nations organs, particularly the General Assembly, have rejected the arguments of States which seek to limit UN action on the basis of Article 2(7).[63] Yet this does not mean that Article 2(7) is a dead letter; the sovereign independence and equality of States remain basic to the international legal system. As Conforti states:

---

[61] Article 1(3) of the UN Charter.

[62] *See generally* Conforti, *supra* note 57 at 477.

[63] *Ibid.* at 478. *See generally* Leland M. Goodrich *et al.*, Charter of the United Nations: Third Ed. (1969) at 67-68.

> In fact the only conclusion which can be drawn from
> the practice of the United Nations is the establishment
> of *specific non-written rules which have removed from*
> Article 2(7) a number of specific matters, such as
> colonialism and particular aspects of human rights, in
> which the Organization is from now on free to inter-
> vene, although they come within the domestic jurisdic-
> tion of States.[64]

In other words, United Nations practice has not rendered the distinction between matters of international jurisdiction and matters of
domestic jurisdiction irrelevant. Neither has it done away with the
concept of the exclusive jurisdiction of the State.

However, the rise of human rights (including the right of a
people to self-determination) to the level of international concern,
signifies that the legitimacy of international action in these areas
depends very much on the current 'development of international
relations'. In particular, the legal validity of the multilateral use of
force under United Nations auspices is likely to depend largely on the
current state of international relations and the international balance of
power. This fact is well demonstrated by the action of the Security
Council to force the withdrawal of Iraqi forces from Kuwait in 1991.
The necessary consensus among the permanent Members of the
Security Council to authorize such action would not likely have been
reached during the Cold War.

Article 2(7) expressly states that it does not apply to any
Security Council action taken under Chapter VII of the UN Charter.
What remains ambiguous is the extent to which international relations
have developed as regards collective action conducted under UN
auspices, such as those not falling under Chapter VII, for example,
international action to enforce observance of international humanitarian or human rights law in cases where such action is taken without
the consent of the Government or *de facto* authority of the particular
territory in question. These questions, are examined below under the
headings of 'humanitarian intervention' and 'collective measures by
the United Nations'.

---

[64]   Conforti, *supra* note 57 at 479.

- Right to Resort to Force: Articles 2(4) and 51

Article 2(4) of the Charter provides that:

All Members shall refrain in their international relations from the threat or use of force against the territorial integrity or political independence of any state, or in any other manner inconsistent with the Purposes of the United Nations.

Article 51 of the Charter provides that:

Nothing in the present Charter shall impair the inherent right of individual or collective self-defence if an armed attack occurs against a Member of the United Nations, until the Security Council has taken measures necessary to maintain international peace and security. Measures taken by Members in the exercise of this right of self-defence shall be immediately reported to the Security Council and shall not in any way affect the authority and responsibility of the Security Council under the present Charter to take at any time such action as it deems necessary in order to maintain or restore international peace and security.

The word 'force' is not in itself clear. Does it cover political or economic pressure or does it refer only to armed force? In the past, western States have argued, in opposition to claims of Eastern Bloc and less developed countries, that Article 2(4) does not refer to force of a political or economic character, but only to armed force. Indeed, despite the absence of the word 'armed' just before 'force', it seems Article 2(4) was intended to cover armed force only, and not political and economic coercion.[65]

---

[65]   During the drafting of the UN Charter, a Brazilian amendment to insert in the Charter a provision prohibiting "the threat or use of economic measures in any manner inconsistent with the purposes of the UN" was not adopted. *See* 6 UN Conference on International Organization Doc., at 355.

The words "against the territorial integrity or political independence of any state or in any other manner inconsistent with the Purposes of the United Nations" in Article 2(4) give rise to unclear interpretation. Textual interpretation does not clarify whether these words were inserted to signify that Article 2(4) prohibits force only where it infringes the territorial integrity or political independence of any state or in any other manner inconsistent with the Purposes of the United Nations (including self-defense), or in all cases except for self-defense (with the qualifying phrase intended simply to emphasize the right of every State to its territorial integrity and political independence).[66]

Were these words meant to restrict the prohibition of the use of force, States would have an ample basis upon which to claim that their resort to force in a particular instance did not breach Article 2(4), on grounds it served a purpose of the United Nations, as outlined in Article 1 of the Charter. Article 1 is so broad that States would be provided expansive legal authority to take unilateral forcible action, for example, 'to maintain international peace and security', or to suppress 'acts of aggression or other breaches of the peace', or to take 'measures to strengthen universal peace' or 'to achieve international cooperation in solving international problems of an economic, social, cultural or humanitarian character' or to promote or encourage 'respect for human rights and for fundamental freedoms'.

The evisceration of Article 2(4) would leave the more powerful States the authority to decide, on the basis of their own subjective interpretations of these broad purposes, whether they had a legal right to deploy armed force or not in a given instance. However, such a broad reading of Article 2(4) runs counter to the very raison d'être of the Charter: the maintenance of international peace through an effective system of collective security.

On the other hand, the view that the last part of Article 2(4) is meant to reinforce the general prohibition of force, would mean States were authorized to use force only in cases of self-defence, regardless of other sorts of motives or justifications. This reading of Article 2(4), which seems the more widely accepted view among members of the international community as well as publicists, recognizes that the

---

[66]   *See e.g.* Ian Brownlie, The Use of Force by States (1963) at 268.

maintenance of international peace and security is the prime purpose of the Charter and that the use of force cannot be justified on grounds that may find a basis in other less important Charter purposes.[67]

The principle of non-intervention may be subject to possible exceptions traditionally advanced by States to justify use of force in particular instances. These grounds, some of which remain highly controversial, are discussed below under the headings: Invitation Emanating from the Territorial State; Protection of Nationals; Forcible Reprisals; and Considerations of 'Humanity', 'Human Rights', 'Defense of Democracy' or 'Self-Determination' as Grounds for Military Intervention.

iii) Possible Exceptions to Norms Prohibiting Forcible Intervention

- Invitation Emanating from the Territorial State

Intervention may be particularly difficult to prove where representatives of the intervening State insist that the deployment of armed force had been requested by the legitimate Government of the subject State, perhaps to quell a civil rebellion brewing there. While classic international law recognizes that a sovereign Head may request foreign assistance, in many instances, invitation is simply fabricated as a pretext to justify military invasion.

In 1956, the Soviet Union claimed that military assistance to intervene in Hungary was requested by the Government of Hungary to put down a rebellion. In 1968, the Soviet Union declared that it had received another invitation, this time from the Czechoslovakian Communist Party to intervene in Czechoslovakia. In 1979, a similar pretext was used to invade Afghanistan. In 1983, the United States Government tried to justify its invasion of Grenada on the grounds, *inter alia*, it had been invited to do so from the Organization of Eastern

---

[67]   *See e.g.* Ronald St. John Macdonald, *The Use of Force by States in International Law*, in (ed. Bedjaoui) International Law: Achievements and Prospects (1991) at 720 *et seq.*; Antonio Cassese, International Law in a Divided World, (1986) at 137; and Oscar Schachter, International Law in Theory and Practice (1991) at 113.

Caribbean States and the Governor-General of Grenada.[68] On 2 August 1990, to justify its invasion of Kuwait, the Government of Iraq claimed to have been invited into Kuwait by the 'Provisional Council of Kuwait' - a flimsy pretext - since there seemed to be no evidence that such a Council even existed at the time.

The deployment of force by one State in the territory of another State is *prima facie* a contravention of the territorial State's political independence and territorial sovereignty. However, in principle, where genuine invitation is freely issued by the lawfully competent authorities of the territorial State, the deployment of armed force by the requested State does not necessarily constitute 'intervention'.[69] Moreover, such use of armed force might not infringe 'the territorial integrity or political independence' of the State or be carried out in a 'manner inconsistent with the Purposes of the United Nations'.[70]

However, in such cases consent must be express, rather than construed by the Government of the State which deploys force and it must be issued by the legally competent authority, namely, the Government of the inviting State. Moreover, if collective self-defense is invoked as the grounds for the invitation then, as the ICJ held in the *Nicaragua Case*, at least there had to have been an armed attack:

> There is no rule, in customary international law, permitting another State to exercise the right of collective self-defense on the basis of its own assessment of the situation. Where collective self-defense is invoked, it is to be expected that the State for whose benefit this right is used will have declared itself to be the victim of an armed attack.[71]

It is clear that an invitation fabricated by the State using armed force does not qualify as genuine invitation, especially where the body issuing the invitation has been installed by unlawful means or through

---

   [68]   *See* William C. Gilmore, The Grenada Intervention (1984).

   [69]   *See* Antonio Tanca, Foreign Armed Intervention in Internal Conflict (1993) at 19.

   [70]   *See* Schachter, *supra* note 67 at 114.

   [71]   *Case concerning Military and Paramilitary Activities in and Against Nicaragua*, 1986 ICJ Reports at para. 195.

some form of foreign intervention. Whether such 'invitation' is regarded as valid depends upon recognition of the legitimacy of the Government by the international community, as demonstrated by the unequivocal rejection of the Soviet invasion of Hungary in 1956, and of Afghanistan in 1979, and by considerable opposition to the United States invasion of Grenada in 1983.

In classic international law, States could provide assistance only to the Government of the requesting State, and not to rebels or insurgents. This rule has been reaffirmed by the General Assembly in resolution 2131 (XX)[72] which in Article 2 declares that:

> ... no State shall organize, assist, foment, finance, incite or tolerate subversive, terrorist or armed activities directed at the violent overthrow of the regime of another State.

In the view of some commentators, the rule prohibiting armed assistance extends also to provision of such assistance to a beleaguered government, particularly where it is engaged in civil war. In this situation, the use of military force against the insurgents, especially if actively supported by a foreign State or States (not including the provision of arms), would threaten the political independence of the State in the sense that the people of the State would not be free to determine their own 'political, economic, social and cultural systems, without interference in any form by another state.'[73]

---

[72]   Declaration on the Inadmissibility of the Intervention in the Domestic Affairs of States and the Protection of their Independence and Sovereignty 1965, General Assembly resolution 2131 (XX), GAOR, 20th Session, Supp. 14 at 11, *adopted* 109 to 0, with only the United Kingdom *abstaining*.

[73]   Article 5 of General Assembly resolution 2131. *See* Schachter, *supra* note 67 at 115. *See also* Louise Doswald-Beck, *The Legal Validity of Military Intervention by Invitation of the Government*, 55 British Yearbook of International Law (1985) at 251.

- Protection of Nationals

Some commentators[74] maintain that contemporary customary international law authorizes the State to protect its nationals abroad through the unilateral use of force without the territorial State's consent. This supposed right has been asserted to be based on the inherent right of self-defense or alternatively, as an action that, where conducted genuinely for the narrow purpose of protection and limited by the proportionate use of force, does not encroach upon the sovereignty and political independence of the territorial State. As discussed above, the right to protect nationals and property was asserted by the United States and certain European countries with respect to a number of Latin American States.

The supposed right to protect nationals through unilateral use of force finds some support in the doctrine of the international minimum standard. Proponents of this doctrine, chiefly western States, have maintained that international law obliges every State to observe a certain minimum standard of treatment with respect to an alien admitted to its territory. Breach of this standard, it has been maintained, gives rise to the right of the national State to intervene militarily to protect nationals in the territory of the 'law-breaker' State to the minimum extent necessary.

No doubt, in customary international law, every State has the right to exercise diplomatic protection, as affirmed in the *Mavrommatis Case*.[75] Moreover, many arbitral decisions have affirmed the obligation to respect the international minimum standard, even where the rights of the alien exceed those of nationals.[76] However, the right

---

[74]   *See e.g.* Derek Bowett, *The Use of Force for the Protection of Nationals Abroad*, in The New Humanitarian Law of Armed Conflict (1986) at 49.

[75]   (Greece v. UK) (1924) PCIJ Reports Ser. A, No. 2 at 12.

[76]   *See* the *Hopkins Case* Reports of International Arbitral Awards (1927). *See also* the *Neer Claim* (US v. Mexico), 4 Reports of International Arbitral Awards 60 (1926), in which the US claimed that Mexico failed to exercise due diligence to search and prosecute the murderer of a US national. *See also* the *Roberts Claim*, (US v. Mexico), 4 Reports of International Arbitral Awards (1926) at 77, where it was held that Mexico was responsible under international law for the injury it caused to Harry Roberts

to protect nationals through unilateral use of force was always open
to abuse since the slightest provocation by small States could be used
as an excuse by stronger States to override the sovereignty of the
territorial State.

A second approach, the Calvo Doctrine, arose in reaction to
the doctrine of the international minimum standard. The proponents
of the Calvo Doctrine saw military intervention in the name of
protection of nationals as little more than thinly disguised economic
imperialism. In this vein, the 'Calvo clause' was routinely incorporated
into the contracts in Latin American States, especially those involving
foreign investment.[77] The Calvo Doctrine conflicts with the international minimum standard doctrine in all cases where nationals enjoy
less than the international minimum standard of protection.[78]

It appears quite doubtful that unilateral use of armed force by
a State to protect personal property of nationals in a foreign State,
without the territorial State's consent is, or ought to be, permitted in
international law. A too flexible interpretation of Article 51 of the UN

---

who was detained for 7 months in poor jail conditions and without the benefit
of access to legal counsel. In *Janes Claim* (US v. Mexico), 4 Reports of
International Arbitral Awards 82 (1926), the US claimed against Mexico and
sought $25,000.00 in damages for suffering brought about by the murder of
a US national.

[77]   The 'Calvo clause' stipulates that a foreign national accepts in
advance that judicial remedies may be sought only in the host State; resort
to diplomatic protection from the State of nationality is not an option. Advocated by the Argentinean jurist Calvo, this doctrine was supported by Latin
American countries and was eventually incorporated into several international
agreements, including the Convention on Rights and Duties of States, *signed*
at the Seventh International Conference of American States in Montevideo
in 1933. However, several international tribunals have rejected the Calvo
Doctrine. In the *North American Dredging Co. Case* (US v. Mexico) 4
Reports of International Arbitral Awards (1926) at 26, the Calvo clause was
rejected on the ground that an alien: "cannot deprive the Government of his
nation of its undoubted right of applying international remedies to violations
of international law committed to his damage. ... [A] citizen cannot by
contract in this respect, tie the hands of his Government."

[78]   However, the doctrine of the international minimum standard has
been subject to trenchant criticism in the context of the International Law
Commission's codification efforts on international State responsibility.

Charter may be used by stronger States to use force against weaker States on the basis of relatively minor or inconsequential purposes, such as the right to use force in order to protect property. As Brownlie argues:

> The instances in which states have purported to exercise [forcible intervention], and the terms in which it is delimited, show that it provides infinite opportunities for abuse. Forcible intervention is now unlawful. It is true that the protection of nationals presents particular difficulties and that a Government faced with a deliberate massacre of a considerable number of nationals in a foreign state would have cogent reasons of humanity for acting, and would also be under very great political pressure. The possible risks of denying the legality of action in a case of such urgency, an exceptional circumstance, must be weighed against the more calculable dangers of providing legal pretexts for the commission of breaches of the peace in the pursuit of national rather than humanitarian interests.[79]

Brownlie's position that forcible intervention for protection of nationals abroad without the consent of the territorial State constitutes a breach of international law, probably represents the majority opinion of publicists on this question.[80]

- Forcible Reprisals

Much of the controversy over the content and legal status of legal norms on reprisals (which represent a form of self-help or

---

[79]   Brownlie, *supra* note 66 at 301.

[80]   For example, Ronzitti states that: "The use of force to protect nationals abroad is a breach of international law, even if some authorities have claimed the contrary and international practice is showing a tendency to resurrect the law in existence before the UN Charter came into force." *See* Natalino Ronzitti, *Use of Force, Jus Cogens and State Consent* in The New Humanitarian Law of Armed Conflict, (ed. Cassese) (1986) at 153. *See also* Macdonald, *supra* note 67.

'countermeasure') has arisen over incongruity between the purposes and principles of the United Nations, on the one hand, and the actual functioning of the UN system of collective security on the other. Almost half a century of virtual stalemate in the Security Council, which prevented the effective use of enforcement measures under Chapter VII of the UN Charter, seemed to signal that the Security Council did not provide a reliable means by which to extinguish swiftly the flames of armed conflict.

The following discussion focuses only on forcible reprisals rather than on reprisals or retaliatory measures not involving armed force. Also, 'belligerent reprisals'[81] i.e. retaliatory measures taken once armed conflict has already started, and which therefore concern the *jus in bello*, rather than the *jus ad bellum*, do not relate directly to the principle of non-intervention and therefore are not considered below.

'Reprisal', to be distinguished from 'retorsion' (unfriendly but not unlawful measures), was defined by a mixed arbitral tribunal in the *Naulilaa Case*.[82]

> A reprisal is an act of self-help by the injured State, responding - *after an unsatisfied demand* - to an act contrary to international law committed by the offending State. It has the effect of suspending momentarily, in relation to the States, the observance of the rule of international law in question. It is limited by common human experiences and the rule of good faith, applicable in the relations between the two States. It would be illegal in the absence of a prior act contrary to international law justifying it. Its object is to effect

---

[81] On belligerent reprisals, *see* Frits Kalshoven, Constraints on the Waging of War (1987) at 175; Stanislaw Nahlik, *From Reprisals to Individual Penal Responsibility*, in Humanitarian Law of Armed Conflict: Challenges Ahead, (ed. Delissen and Tanja) (1991); and Bristol, *The Laws of War and Belligerent Reprisals Against Enemy Civilian Populations*, 21 Air Force Law Review (1979).

[82] *The Naulilaa Case* (Portugal v. Germany) 2 Reports of International Arbitral Awards (1928) 1012.

reparation from the offending State for the offense or a
return to legality by the avoidance of further offenses.

The right of a State to take reprisal action is limited by the requirement of proportionality, a point made by the tribunal.

As discussed above, Articles 2(4) and 51 of the UN Charter
read together, appear to prohibit the use of force except in cases of
self-defense, and then only 'if an armed attack occurs'. That the UN
Charter therefore prohibits any reprisal that does not fall within the
scope of the inherent right of self-defense has been affirmed in
numerous resolutions of the Security Council and General Assembly.
Security Council resolution 188 (1964), in which the Council: "*[c]on-
demns* reprisals as incompatible with the purposes and principles of
the United Nations"[83] is illustrative in this regard. Moreover, third
States have condemned the use of reprisals consistently and
outspokenly in Security Council debates whenever the issue has
arisen.

The General Assembly similarly has expressed its clearest
condemnation of the use of forcible reprisals as a form of prohibited
interference in the internal affairs of other States, as for example in
resolution 36/103, which refers to:[84]

> The duty of a State to refrain from armed intervention,
> subversion, military occupation ... or any act of military
> ... interference in the internal affairs of another State,
> including acts of reprisal involving the use of force.

The 1970 General Assembly Declaration on Principles of International
Law Concerning Friendly Relations[85] also affirms that:

> States have a duty to refrain from acts of reprisal
> involving the use of force.

---

[83]   *See e.g.* Roberto Barsotti, *Armed Reprisals,* in The New Humanitarian Law of Armed Conflict (ed. Cassese) (1986) at 80.

[84]   Para. II(c) of the Declaration on the Inadmissibility of Intervention and
Interference in the Internal Affairs of States, *adopted* 9 Dec. 1981.

[85]   General Assembly resolution 2625 XXV, *adopted without a vote* 25
Oct. 1970.

Conversely, the 1974 General Assembly resolution on the Definition of Aggression,[86] states that:

> No consideration of whatever nature, whether political, economic, military or otherwise, may serve as a justification for aggression.

In other words, no form of aggression, including resort to forcible reprisals, can be justified on political, economic, military or other grounds.[87]

The international community continues to move progressively towards a firmer and more categorical prohibition of the use of force. As St. John Macdonald states:

> Today States are obliged to settle their disputes peacefully. Armed force may be used only in circumstances permitted by the Charter of the United Nations, that is, when the use of force is in self-defense, collective self-defense or regional action authorized by the Security Council, though other exceptions are emerging. The old rights of self-help, self-preservation, necessity, reprisals and blockade have been extinguished. Further, the prohibitions on the use of force are being extended to enforce means of coercion beyond armed force to matters such as economic pressure, though these developments are still inchoate.[88]

The fact that the Security Council may not have applied international law prohibiting forcible reprisals consistently in every single case, does not negate the progressive development of international law towards

---

[86]   General Assembly resolution 3314 XXIX; 69 American Journal of International Law (1975).

[87]   Barsotti, *supra* note 83 at 83. Furthermore, as Barsotti notes, the position that reprisals involving the use of force are unlawful, is evidenced in the *opinio juris* of States outside the United Nations context, for example in the Final Act of the Conference on Security and Cooperation in Europe, 1975.

[88]   Macdonald, *supra* note 67 at 735.

a generalized prohibition of the use of force by a State, allowing self-defense as the sole exception. In sum, 'forcible reprisal' no longer affords a State a credible excuse for having committed armed intervention.

- Considerations of 'Humanity', 'Human Rights',
'Defense of Democracy' or 'Self-Determination'
as Grounds for Military Intervention

Unilateral 'humanitarian intervention' has been defined traditionally as military intervention by State 'A' (or States acting collectively) in the territory of State 'B', without the consent of State B, to protect State B's nationals against its own Government's serious violations of human rights.[89] This classic formula implies the right of the intervening State or States to come to a subjective appreciation of the facts and to evaluate whether, in a given instance, norms prohibiting commission of serious violations of human rights or humanitarian law (or the 'laws of humanity' etc.) have been breached, and moreover, whether the breach warrants military intervention.

Protection of nationals differs from humanitarian intervention in a number of important respects. Military intervention to protect nationals is carried out explicitly for that purpose. In contrast, humanitarian intervention involves action in which the nationality of the beneficiaries in principle is irrelevant, because the intervening State is supposed to be acting on an exclusively humanitarian basis, rather than out of any particular self-interest, including any deriving from connections of nationality. Moreover, humanitarian intervention will most likely involve beneficiaries who are permanent residents of the State subject to the intervention, and as Bowett rightly remarks, the "degree of interference with the authority of that State is therefore greater than in the case of the protection of nationals who are aliens *vis-à-vis* the territorial State".[90]

---

[89]   *See* Louis A. Rougier, *La Theorie de l'intervention d'Humanité* 17 Revue generale du droit international (1910) 468; Edwin Borchard, The Diplomatic Protection of Citizens Abroad (1915) and Stowell, International Law (1931) for classic formulations of 'humanitarian intervention'.

[90]   *Ibid.*

The traditional doctrine of humanitarian intervention supposes that in general international law every State has the legal right to intervene militarily in the territory of another State wherever necessary to defend nationals of the State subject to the intervention. In its more recent incarnation, broad human rights or humanitarian considerations are considered grounds for intervention, as discussed below.

As regards broad humanitarian moral grounds for intervention, it is not clear how such grounds, on their own, could possibly support a legal right to intervene militarily. Moral convictions that have not been expressed as a specific legal norm, remain notoriously subjective and may be used to cover the advancement of crude political interests. It must be remembered that States typically find it difficult to risk the lives of soldier and citizen, and to jeopardize domestic public support as well as the good will of other States, for purely humanitarian considerations.

This is not to say that unilateral military intervention on genuine humanitarian grounds is *a priori* invalid as a matter of principle. On the contrary, the use of military intervention for humanitarian purposes may be morally justified or even required, for example to bring a halt to the execution of a programme of genocide by a government in power. The difficulty that naturally arises is to ensure that a permissive legal right on humanitarian grounds is defined with sufficient precision so as to minimize the opportunity for abuse.

On several occasions, the Triple Entente Powers (France, Great Britain and Russia) invoked the term 'laws of humanity' to denounce the Ottoman Porte for its treatment of Christian subjects in the 19th century, and in 1915, the Government of Turkey for its large-scale massacres of Turkish nationals of Armenian origin. However, the terms 'laws of humanity' and 'crimes against humanity and civilization' never acquired precise legal content, nor was the practice of intervention by these Powers clear of political self-interest. Consequently, these terms remained more in the realm of moral and political considerations.[91]

---

[91]   *See however,* History of the UN War Crimes Commission (1948) at 35, and *see generally,* Cherif Bassiouni, *Crimes against Humanity,* in 1 International Criminal Law (ed. Bassiouni) (1986).

.   Some commentators have argued that humanitarian intervention outside the United Nations system or other collective security organization, is authorized by general international law, or that, at least a rule of customary international law is currently in the process of development.[92]

On the other hand, many empirically-based examinations have reached the opposite conclusion i.e. that there is a lack of evidence to justify the notion there exists a customary rule of international law authorizing States to undertake humanitarian intervention.[93]

As regards foreign military support for national liberation movements fighting for self-determination, Schachter says:

> If the legality of foreign military support on behalf of national liberation movements were put to the International Court, I believe the judges would have to conclude that no such exception to the general prohibition has been accepted by the community of States.[94]

On the notion that a State may use armed force to intervene in another country to protect human rights or democracy, Schachter observes that:

> The idea that armed invasions could make the world 'safe for democracy' has had little appeal to governments. Memories of past invasions and seizure of power in the name of self-determination and freedom are still fresh in many parts of the world. 'People's democracies' have been imposed on unwilling peoples.

---

[92]   *See e.g.,* Wil Verwey, *Humanitarian Intervention* in The New Humanitarian Law of Armed Conflict, (ed. Cassese) (1986) at 60-66; and Fernando Teson, Humanitarian Intervention: An Inquiry into Law and Morality (1988) at 272; Jean-Pierre Fonteyne, *The Customary Law Doctrine of Humanitarian Interventions: Its Current Validity Under the United Nations Charter,* 17 Comparative Juridical Review (USA) (1980); and de Schutter, *Humanitarian Intervention: a United Nations Task,* 3 California Western Law Review (1972).

[93]   *See e.g.,* Tanca, *supra* note 69 at 115.

[94]   Schachter, *supra* note 67 at 120.

States deeply committed to democracy have feared the manipulative and tendentious use of self-determination as a ground for foreign intervention. Governments of various shades of opinion have a common interest in rejecting a principle that would encourage their internal opposition movements to seek foreign military support to topple their allegedly non-democratic regimes. Moreover, the world in general has good reason to worry about the risks of escalation resulting from ideological wars, particularly those involving major powers.[95]

Certain others,[96] such as Doswald-Beck, echo this opinion:

It is clear ... that the content of the right to self-determination, that is the right of a people to choose its own government, means in effect the absence of outside interference. It does not appear to mean, in the minds of the majority of States, the right to democratic representation or even that the government should reflect the will of the majority of the people. Rather it requires that the government be drawn from a group of people perceived as entitled to self-determination, even if that government actually represents a minority interest within that group and rules by force.[97]

The International Court of Justice most emphatically voiced similar arguments, holding in the *Nicaragua Case* that:

The use of force could not be the appropriate method to monitor or ensure ... respect for [human rights].

---

[95]   *Ibid.* at 123.

[96]   *See also* Tom Farer, *Human Rights in Law's Empire: the Jurisprudence War*, 85 American Journal of International Law (1991) 117; and James A.R. Nafziger, *Self-Determination and Humanitarian Intervention in a Community of Power*, 20(1) Denver Journal of International Law and Policy (1991).

[97]   Doswald-Beck, *supra* note 73 at 207.

> With regard to the steps actually taken, the protection
> of human rights, a strictly humanitarian objective,
> cannot be compatible with the mining of ports, the
> destruction of oil installations, or again with the training,
> arming and equipping of the *contras*.   The Court
> concludes that the argument derived from the preserva-
> tion of human rights in Nicaragua cannot afford a legal
> justification for the conduct of the United States, and
> cannot in any event be reconciled with the legal strat-
> egy of the respondent State, which is based on the
> right of collective self-defense.[98]

The ICJ went on to hold that:

> The Court therefore finds that no such general right of
> intervention in support of an opposition within another
> State, exists in contemporary international law. The
> Court concludes that acts constituting a breach of the
> customary principle of non-intervention will also, if they
> directly or indirectly involve the use of force, constitute
> a breach of the principle of non-use of force in interna-
> tional relations.[99]

In sum, the unilateral exercise of military intervention on humanitarian
or moral grounds constitutes a breach of Article 2(4) of the UN
Charter.[100]

'Humanitarian intervention' may be taken to refer to military
enforcement action through the United Nations or other competent
inter-governmental organization such as the Organization of Security

---

[98]   *Case concerning Military and Paramilitary Activities in and Against
Nicaragua*, (Nicaragua v. United States) 1986 ICJ Reports.

[99]   *Ibid.* at para. 209.

[100]   *See* Ronzitti, *supra* note 80 at 155, who also concludes, following a
consideration of a number of cases in history that have been put forward as
instances of 'humanitarian intervention', that such interventions were, in fact,
unlawful.   *See also* Franck and Rodley, *After Bangladesh: the Law of
Humanitarian Intervention by Military Force*, 67 American Journal of
International Law (1973).

and Cooperation in Europe, Organization of African Unity or the Organization of American States.

The United Nations has no authority 'to intervene in matters which are essentially within the domestic jurisdiction of any State or [to] require the Members to submit such matters to settlement', as stated in Article 2(7) of the UN Charter. This means that the United Nations can not take action in the territory of a State without the consent of that State's Government in respect of domestic matters.

On the other hand, among the four main purposes of the United Nations Organization are maintenance of international peace and security and promotion of human rights. 'Promotion of human rights' has never been considered sufficient grounds for United Nations military intervention. The question that remains then, is whether a sufficiently strong connection can be found between United Nations intervention on humanitarian or human rights grounds and the maintenance of international peace and security and if so, whether it may justify Security Council action on the basis of Chapter VII of the Charter, in which case, consent of the State subject to intervention would not be required.

The form and legal status of humanitarian intervention, carried out through an organization duly authorized to enforce collective security guarantees, differ substantially from those of humanitarian intervention carried out on a unilateral basis. Unilateral exercise of force remains suspect *ab initio*. That force has been used by only one or a few individual States, without any form of fiat from the international community at large, is *ipso facto prima facie* evidence that only the interests of the intervening State or States are at stake. This aspect negates the requirement that for humanitarian intervention to be genuinely humanitarian, it must not involve any self-interest on the part of the intervenors. In contrast, deployment of armed force through collective organs allows for debate to take place in a plenary forum in which members of the international community have an opportunity to debate the legality, desirability and feasibility of taking armed intervention in a given case and whether the action contemplated is sufficiently supported by the international community.

Numerous factors militate in favour of more frequent use of armed force through the United Nations or other competent international organization for humanitarian purposes.[101]

The end of the Cold War has removed a persistent source of stalemate among permanent Members of the Security Council. Over the last few years, the Security Council, no longer impeded by the overuse of the veto, has been able to take more decisive action to prevent or redress flagrant breaches of international human rights and humanitarian law through deployment of peace-keeping forces.

Moreover, the definition of 'peace-keeping' has developed substantially over the last few years in two respects: first, it has become more closely linked to expanded efforts at preventive diplomacy through the good offices of the Secretary-General; and second, considerations of the human rights and humanitarian situation in some cases have become at least partially integrated in the aims of both peace-keeping and preventive diplomacy.

Thus, the option of using military intervention through the United Nations for humanitarian aims has developed significantly in the last few years, especially in cases where the organs of the State in question have collapsed or disappeared. The need for United Nations humanitarian intervention may increase as ethnic conflicts more frequently threaten international peace and security. In many so-called 'ethnic conflicts', law and order have deteriorated to the point that general anarchy, chaos and violence reign supreme. In such

---

[101] Articles 53(1) and 53(2) of the UN Charter provide that: "The Security Council shall, where appropriate, utilize such regional arrangements or agencies for enforcement action under its authority. But no enforcement action shall be taken under regional arrangements or by regional agencies without the authorization of the Security Council, with the exception of measures against any [state which during the Second World War has been an enemy of any signatory of the UN Charter], provided for pursuant to Article 107 or in regional arrangements directed against renewal of aggressive policy on the part of any such state, until such time as the Organization may, on request of the Governments concerned, be charged with the responsibility for preventing further aggression by such a State." Article 54 provides that: "The Security Council shall at all times be kept fully informed of activities undertaken or in contemplation under regional arrangements or by regional agencies for the maintenance of international peace and security."

cases, it is incumbent upon the Security Council to act decisively to prevent greater loss of life and to ensure that human dignity is safeguarded.

The increasingly strong link between preventive diplomacy and humanitarian intervention is demonstrated by recent UN practice in a number of cases, for example, as regards the breach of or threat to international peace and security and the widespread occurrence of serious human rights and humanitarian law violations in Iraq, Somalia, former Yugoslavia and Rwanda.

iv) 1991 Draft Code Provisions on Intervention

Article 17 of the 1991 draft Code provides that:

1. An individual who as leader or organizer commits or orders the commission of an act of intervention in the internal or external affairs of a State shall, on conviction thereof, be sentenced [to ...].
2. Intervention in the internal or external affairs of a State consists of fomenting [armed] subversive or terrorist activities or by organizing, assisting or financing such activities, or supplying arms for the purpose of such activities, thereby [seriously] undermining the free exercise by that State of its sovereign rights.
3. Nothing in this article shall in any way prejudice the right of peoples to self-determination as enshrined in the Charter of the United Nations.

The formula of Article 17 of the 1991 draft Code borrows wording from the General Assembly Declaration on Principles of International Law concerning Friendly Relations and Co-operation among States in Accordance with the Charter of the United Nations, 1970.[102]

---

[102] Resolution 2625 of 24 Oct. 1970, *adopted without a vote*, 25 GAOR Supp., (No. 28) 121, UN Doc. A/8028 (1970). The statement in the Declaration provides that "no State shall organize, assist, foment, finance, incite or tolerate subversive, terrorist or armed activities towards the violent overthrow of the regime of another State, or interfere in civil strife in another State."

The word 'armed' in square brackets[103] indicates that military, rather than non-military political or economic intervention is covered by the provision. However, the 1991 draft Code concept of 'intervention' is ambiguous since it would import individual criminal responsibility for merely *fomenting* subversive or terrorist activity etc. In other words, a State leader could be held criminally responsible for only having agitated, provoked, incited or goaded, subversion that seriously undermines the free exercise of another State's sovereign rights. Yet 'subversion', being a covert activity, may be perceived or imagined only by the intelligence agencies of the State. Moreover, the concept of 'subversion' in most domestic criminal codes relates to 'national security'. 'National security' is a very broad concept, often used in a highly politicized way to suppress threats to the Government in power. In many countries, 'threat to national security' has been used as a convenient label by which to denounce *any* opposition to the ruling élite. Thus, the 1991 draft Code provisions on intervention are unduly broad and vague.

v) 1996 Draft Code

The Governments of Australia, Belgium, Brazil, The Netherlands, Switzerland, the United Kingdom and the United States argued that established norms on intervention do not provide for individual criminal responsibility. Moreover, the definition of 'intervention' was far too ambiguous for the purposes of international criminal law. They expressed the view that it was unlikely that States would accept such provisions in the draft Code.[104] The Government of Belgium contended that intervention of an economic form was difficult to assess and that it was inappropriate to consider it among the category of particularly serious acts. Consequently, in 1996, the ILC dropped

---

See also General Assembly resolution 2131 (XX), 1965.

[103] This provision was placed in square brackets to indicate that the ILC wishes to receive the comments of the General Assembly's Sixth Committee.

[104] *See* Comments and Observations of Governments on the Draft Code of Crimes against the Peace and Security of Mankind adopted on First Reading by the International Law Commission at its 43rd Session, A/CN.4/448 of 1 March 1993.

provisions stipulating individual criminal responsibility for intervention from the draft Code.

4. COLONIAL DOMINATION AND OTHER FORMS OF ALIEN DOMINATION

In the 1950's and 60's, numerous wars of national liberation were fought by peoples of Africa and Asia to throw off the shackles of colonial oppression and eventually, the greater part of the international community has come to recognize the legitimacy of these struggles. Almost all former colonies have attained independence and few instances of colonialism remain. Today's armed conflicts more frequently involve a people's fight against the hegemony of its own Government, rather than revolt against overseas colonial domination.

In the United Nations era, particularly since the end of the Cold War, there appears to be a proliferation of armed conflict fought *within* national boundaries as compared to inter-State war.[105] As the UN Secretary-General stated in the Supplement to his *Agenda for Peace*:[106]

> Of the five peace-keeping operations that existed in early 1988, four related to inter-State wars and only one (20 per cent of the total) to an intra-State conflict. Of the 21 operations established since then, only 8 have related to inter-State wars, whereas 13 (62 per cent) have related to intra-State conflicts, though some of them, especially those in the former Yugoslavia,

---

[105] According to some estimates, over 80 per cent of armed conflicts that have occurred since 1945 have been non-international in character. *See* Small and Singer, Resort to Arms: International and Civil Wars, 1816-1980 (1982) which applies modern statistical analysis to the frequency, duration, intensity and occurrence of armed conflict. *See also* Ethnicity and War (ed. van Horne and Tonnesen) (1984).

[106] *See* Boutros Boutros-Ghali, Supplement to An Agenda for Peace: Position Paper of the Secretary-General on the Occasion of the Fiftieth Anniversary of the United Nations; UN Doc. A/50/60-S/1995/1 of 3 Jan. 1995, United Nations at para. 11.

have some inter-State dimensions also. Of the 11 operations established since January 1992, all but 2 (82 per cent) relate to intra-State conflicts.

In many of these internal conflicts, the claim of self-determination is loudly proclaimed.

In severe cases of systematic discrimination or persecution by a State against a particular group distinguished from the general population on racial, religious, ethnic or other such grounds, perhaps the right to self-determination may apply to the people suffering persecution. Low intensity conflicts may become particularly bloody when exacerbated or caused by simmering ethnic hatred as indicated in a number of former Soviet Republics, Burundi, Kashmir, Kurdistan, Rwanda, the former Yugoslavia and Zaire, to name only a few cases. Many of these blazes, if not extinguished, risk spreading further flames and igniting even greater conflagration. What may begin as internal unrest can spark full-scale inter-State war, where individuals, groups, or eventually Governments in neighbouring territories or States, become drawn into the conflict. Such situations may be particularly instrumental in causing a serious deterioration in regional peace and security while law and order within the country vanishes. It is therefore incumbent upon the international community not to ignore extreme cases of systematic discrimination and persecution of national minorities by a State.

Does the demise of colonialism imply that the principle of self-determination has served its purpose and is on the verge of slipping quietly into desuetude? In such a case, it would no longer give rise to any legal consequences and the issue of individual criminal responsibility for colonial domination could become moot. On the other hand, if the right to self-determination continues to hold relevance for the contemporary international community, and if it has attained content of sufficient specificity and the status of a legal norm to entail legal obligations, breach of the right to self-determination might possibly give rise to individual criminal responsibility.

To determine the extent of individual criminal responsibility for colonial or alien domination, it is necessary to explore the background, content and legal status of the right to self-determination in international law. In light of this discussion, it will then be instructive to consider the relevant 1991 draft Code provisions and then to consider why they were dropped from the 1996 version.

i) Background

Self-determination was advocated as a right of all nations at the London International Socialist Congress as early as 1886. Some authors[107] trace the etymological origin of the word 'self-determination' to the German word *selbstbestimmungsrecht*.

Vladimir Lenin advocated forcefully the principle of self-determination of peoples in his *Theses on the Socialist Revolution and the Right of Nations to Self-Determination* as an integral plank in the programme of socialist internationalism:

> The right of nations to self-determination implies exclusively the right to independence in the political sense, the right to free political separation from the oppressor nation. Specifically, this demand for political democracy implies complete freedom to agitate for secession and for a referendum on secession by the seceding nation.[108]

In unequivocally advocating the political and legal implications of self-determination as "political self-determination, political independence, the formation of a national state",[109] Lenin called not only for the

---

[107] Umozurike Oji Umozurike, Self-Determination in International Law (1972) at 1.

[108] *See* Vladimir Lenin, *The Significance of the Right to Self-Determination and its Relation to Federation*, 22 Collected Works (Jan.- Feb. 1916) at 143-148. *See also* Vladimir Lenin, *Report of the Commission on the National and the Colonial Questions: Second Congress of the Communist International*, 31 Collected Works (1920). In the 1920's, the USSR inserted self-determination as a principle in treaties concluded between itself and several countries such as Persia, Turkey and China.

[109] Vladimir Lenin, *The Right of Nations to Self-Determination* in Lenin, The Right of Nations to Self-Determination: Selected Writings (1951) at 14, originally published in *Enlightenment* (a Bolshevik monthly journal of St. Petersburg, 1911-1914).

colonies to be liberated, but championed their cause and offered them material support.

The promotion of the right to self-determination thus formed an essential component of Lenin's political philosophy and programme of action and was adopted as official policy by the Soviet Union. However, Stalin's brutal and extensive persecution of certain national minorities of the Soviet Union called into question the Bolshevik Party's commitment to the fair implementation of the right to self-determination domestically and even caused some to dismiss Lenin's contribution to the principle of self-determination altogether.

One may turn instead to the approach of United States President Wilson who advocated the principle of self-determination as one of his famous Fourteen Points at the international level. However, President Wilson's formula, in contrast to that of Lenin's, actually sought to accommodate the colonial system in place. Wilson's fifth point was:

> A free, open-minded, and absolutely impartial adjustment of all colonial claims, based upon a strict observance of the principle that in determining all such questions of sovereignty the interests of the populations concerned must have equal weight with the equitable claims of the government whose title is to be determined.[110]

Wilson's formula sought to *balance* claims of self-determination with the interests of the colonizers and failed to reject colonial domination as a form of oppression.[111]

Point V was later given more precise meaning by way of the following interpretation which was to receive explicit approval from President Wilson:

> It would seem as if the principle involved in this proposition is that a colonial power acts not as owner of its colonies, but as trustee for the natives and for the

---

[110] Woodrow Wilson, Public Papers: War and Peace (1927) at 155-62.
[111] *See also* Cassese, *supra* note 67 at 132.

interests of the society of nations, the terms on which
the colonial administration is conducted as a matter of
international concern and may legitimately be the
subject of international inquiry, and that the Peace
Conference may, therefore, write a code of colonial
conduct binding upon colonial powers.[112]

This interpretation of the principle of self-determination, however tepid,
did seek to introduce the notion that the colonial power, as a kind of
trustee, was obliged to guard the interests of colonial subjects at least
to the extent that it might be subject to the supervision of an international inquiry.

Self-determination was never explicitly enshrined in the League
of Nations Covenant. Consequently, when the issue arose in
connection with the will of the Swedish-speaking minority to reunify
with Sweden upon Finland's declaration of independence from Russia
in 1917, the International Committee of Jurists held in the *Åland
Islands Question* Advisory Opinion that:

Although the principle of self-determination of peoples
plays an important part in modern political thought,
especially since the Great War, it must be pointed out
that there is no mention of it in the Covenant of the
League of Nations. The recognition of this principle in
a certain number of international treaties cannot be
considered as sufficient to put it upon the same footing
as a positive rule of the Law of Nations.[113]

The League's mandates system, however paternalistic in design and
expression, did advance the principle of self-determination in so far as
Mandatory Powers were obliged to safeguard "the well-being and
development of such peoples [which] form a sacred trust of civilization".[114]

---

[112] Whiteman's Digest of International Law (1965), 5 at 604; 1 Foreign
Relations, supp. 1, 407 and 421, *cited* in Umozurike, *supra* note 107 at 30.
[113] *Åland Islands Question*, League of Nations Official Journal Special
Supp. 3 (Oct. 1920) at 5.
[114] *See* Article 22 of the Covenant of the League of Nations.

ii) Content of the Principle of Self-Determination

The principle of self-determination was revitalized by the joint position of President Franklin Roosevelt and Prime Minister Winston Churchill, expressed in the Atlantic Charter[115] setting forth the major pillars of American and British policy for the formation and organization of the postwar world. As regards self-determination, the first three points of the Atlantic Charter stated that:

First, their countries seek no aggrandizement, territorial or other;
Second, they desire to see no territorial changes that do not accord with the freely expressed wishes of the peoples concerned;
Third, they respect the right of all peoples to choose the form of government under which they live, and they wish to see sovereign rights and self-government restored to those who have been forcibly deprived of them ...

The Atlantic Charter was subsequently signed by twenty-two Allied Governments on 2 January 1942.

With respect to the third point, while Roosevelt seems to have envisioned this principle to apply to all peoples,[116] Churchill had made clear in a statement to the House of Commons on 9 September 1941 that he did not consider the Atlantic Charter to apply to the colonies under the British Crown. Referring to the drafting of the Atlantic Charter, Churchill stated:

At the Atlantic meeting, we had in mind, primarily, the restoration of the sovereignty, self-government, and national life of the states and nations of Europe now under the Nazi yoke, and the principles governing any

---

[115]   Issued as a Joint Declaration of Eight Points on 14 Aug. 1941, *later reissued* as the annex to the Declaration by the United Nations of 1 Jan. 1942, 204 L.N.T.S. 382.

[116]   *See* Edward A Laing, *The Norm of Self-Determination, 1941-1991*, 22(2) California Western International Law Journal (1991-92).

alterations in the territorial boundaries which may have
to be made. So that it is quite a separate problem from
the progressive evolution of self-governing institutions
in the regions and peoples which owe allegiance to the
British Crown.[117]

Naturally, the colonized peoples could not be enthusiastic about the
Atlantic Charter. Nehru considered the Atlantic Charter 'a pious and
nebulous expression of hope'.[118] Understandably, the Atlantic Charter
did not alter Gandhi's distrust of Churchill's intentions vis-à-vis
Congress' drive for Indian independence from Britain.[119] On 10
November 1942, Churchill stated publicly: "I have not become the
King's First Minister in order to preside over the liquidation of the
British Empire."[120]

This position stands in stark contrast to official Soviet foreign
policy, established since Lenin's time, to support the principle of self-
determination expressly with regard to the colonies. At the time of the
drafting of the United Nations Charter, with the support of President
Roosevelt, the Soviet Union contended that explicit guarantees of the
right to self-determination should be included. However, the Government of Great Britain, supported by France, opposed the Soviet
initiative. To secure the approval of these recalcitrant Governments,
which sought to retain as much control over territories under their
subjugation, the guarantee of self-determination was diluted to
express only a programmatic goal towards which States should strive
in cooperation with the UN, taking the form of a general principle
rather than an enforceable legal right with specific content.

During formulation of Article 1(2) of the UN Charter, the
question of subjects (i.e. entities conferred rights) and respondents

---

[117] *Quoted in* Edward R. Stettinius, Roosevelt and the Russians: The
Yalta Conference (1950) at 218-219.

[118] *See* Jawaharlal Nehru, *The End of Imperialism* in Beyond Victory at
144, cited in Laing, *supra* note 116 at 26.

[119] *See* H.S.L Polak, H.N. Brailsford, and Lord Pethick-Lawrence,
Mahatma Gandhi (1949) at 249.

[120] For an extensive review of other Asian and African reaction to the
Atlantic Charter, *see* Laing, *supra* note 116 at 209-308.

(i.e. entities having correlative obligations) of the right to self-determination was discussed. It was maintained:

> That what is intended by paragraph 2 is to proclaim the equal rights of people as such, consequently their right to self-determination. Equality of rights, therefore extends in the Charter to states, nations and peoples.[121]

Does this statement imply the right of a people to exercise the right to self-determination against its own State and even a right to secede? Paragraph 2 of General Assembly resolution 1514 (XV), adopted in 1960,[122] declares that:

> All peoples have the right to self-determination; by virtue of that right they freely determine their political status and freely pursue their economic, social and cultural development [.]

However, paragraph 6 of the same resolution states that:

> Any attempt aimed at the partial or total disruption of the national unity and the territorial integrity of a county is incompatible with the Purposes and Principles of the Charter of the United Nations [.]

Paragraph 6 clearly establishes the priority of the principle of territorial integrity over the right to self-determination where the two conflict.

Of even greater significance is the Declaration on Principles of International Law concerning Friendly Relations and Co-operation among States in Accordance with the Charter of the United Nations,

---

[121] Documents of the UN Conference on International Organisation, I/1/17. vol VI at 704, cited in Alexandre Kiss, *The Peoples' Right to Self-Determination,* 7 Human Rights Law Journal (1986).

[122] *Adopted* on 14 Dec. 1960, GAOR Session, Supp. 16 at 66, by 89 votes to 0 with nine abstentions: Australia, Belgium, Dominican Republic, France, Portugal, South Africa, Spain, the United Kingdom and the United States.

1970. The Governments of the United Kingdom and the United States pushed for the following formula to be inserted: "Every State has the duty to respect the principle", but these same Powers also argued that any reference to self-determination as conferring legal rights to a people ought to be omitted. However, Algeria, Cameroon, Czechoslovakia, Ghana, India, Kenya, Madagascar, Nigeria, Poland, Romania, Syria, the United Arab Republic, USSR and Yugoslavia insisted that the phrase: "[a]ll peoples have the inalienable right to self-determination" should be inserted.

In the result, denial of self-determination is declared a denial 'of fundamental human rights' and as contrary to the UN Charter. As finally adopted, this resolution provides that:

> By virtue of the principle of equal rights and self-determination enshrined in the Charter, all peoples have the right freely to determine, without external interference, their political status and to pursue their economic, social and cultural development, and every State has the duty to respect this right in accordance with the provisions of the Charter.

The Declaration on Friendly Relations was adopted by consensus by the UN General Assembly after years of careful drafting taking into consideration all major political and ideological blocs in the international community.[123] In the words of Professor Georges Abi-Saab:

> Thus for the first time the Western Powers as a whole recognized self-determination as a legal right and its denial as a violation of the Charter. This consensus was reached not on a vague general formula, but on a detailed interpretation, making explicit the different legal implications of the principle. It can thus be said that even if self-determination was not universally accepted as a legal principle in 1945, or even in 1960, the practice which has taken place in interstate rela-

---

[123] Georges M. Abi-Saab, *Wars of National Liberation* 165 Hague Recueil (1979) at 370.

tions since the adoption of the Charter, leading to the emergence of almost a hundred new States, as well as the consistent and cumulative practice of the organs of the United Nations, have led in 1970 to the universal recognition of the legally binding nature of the principle of self-determination.

Other respected scholars, such as Conforti[124] and Schachter,[125] support this evaluation of the legal status of the right to self-determination.

The official policy of the UN has been that the right to self-determination does not entail a right to secession. In a press conference on 4 January 1970, UN Secretary General U Thant stated that:

> ... as far as the question of secession of a particular section of a Member State is concerned, the United Nations' attitude is unequivocable. As an international organization, the United Nations has never accepted and does not accept and I do not believe that it will ever accept the principle of secession of a part of its Member State.[126]

This policy guards against the dismemberment of States and the fragmentation of the international community into hundreds of mini-States. Proliferation in the number of States might render international peace and security much more difficult to maintain; each State would tend to pursue even narrower interests which might hinder the pursuit of common objectives among them.

The issue of secession was addressed again in resolution 2625 which proclaims that:

> The establishment of a sovereign and independent State, the free association or integration with an

---

124 Conforti, *supra* note 57 at 470.
125 Schachter, *supra* note 67 at 119.
126 7 United Nations Monthly Chronicle 36 (Feb. 1970).

independent State or the emergence into any other
political status freely determined by a people constitute
modes of implementing the right of self-determination
by that people.[127]

However, a subsequent paragraph of resolution 2625 states that:

Nothing in the foregoing paragraphs shall be construed
as authorizing or encouraging any action which would
dismember or impair, totally or in part, the territorial
integrity or political unity of sovereign and independent
States conducting themselves in compliance with the
principle of equal rights and self-determination of
peoples as described above and thus possessed of a
government representing the whole people belonging
to the territory without distinction as to race, creed or
colour.

The Declaration expresses the position of the international community
that the principle of self-determination does not give rise to a right to
secede. In general, the right to self-determination has been construed
to apply only to cases of decolonization rather than to minority groups
within a State.[128]

However, this position is qualified by the condition that the
State is obliged to honour the principles of equal rights and self-
determination of peoples within its own territory and to represent all
peoples within its territory on a non-discriminatory basis. Thus the
door was never completely closed to secessionist movements. In
cases where the Government of a multi-ethnic State engages in
systematic discrimination against a people, particularly on the basis of
race, creed or colour to the point of the people's denial of their right

---

[127] General Assembly resolution 2625 (XXV), *adopted* without vote 24
Oct. 1970. *See* Johnson, *Toward Self-Determination - A Reappraisal as
Reflected in the Declaration on Friendly Relations*, 3 Georgia Journal of
International and Comparative Law (1973).
[128] *See* James Crawford, *The Rights of Peoples: 'Peoples' or 'Govern-
ments'?* in The Rights of Peoples (ed. Crawford) (1988) at 58.

to determine their own political future, a drive to secede may be tolerated by the international community.

Moreover, the right to self-determination is not cast in stone and will almost certainly be interpreted less narrowly in future to meet the changing needs of the international community. Evidence of this trend is suggested by recent United Nations practise. The international community is likely to be more sympathetic towards secessionist movements where past claims to territorial sovereignty have been overridden (such as in Lithuania or Latvia), where serious human rights violations have been perpetrated against a population of a definable territory (such as the Iraqi repression of the Kurds), where there is the breakup of a federal State made up of distinct nationalities (such as in the former USSR or in Yugoslavia) or where the people seeking secession differ in ethnicity, religion, culture and language and are separated geographically by land or water (such as the case of East Pakistan which seceded from Pakistan to become Bangladesh).

iii) Legal Status of the Principle of Self-Determination

A few former colonial Powers refused, as late as the mid 1970's, to recognize that the principle of self-determination has any legal force whatsoever on grounds its content remains too ambiguous. The Belgian, British and Irish Governments, during the drafting of the 1977 Protocols additional to the Geneva Conventions of 12 August 1949, argued that the principle of self-determination was devoid of legal status.[129] Nonetheless, while certain ambiguities in the precise content of the right to self-determination remain unresolved, there is very widespread recognition of its status as a norm of international law.

Article 1(2) of the UN Charter places development of "friendly relations among nations based on respect for the principle of equal rights and self-determination of peoples" as one of the four central

---

[129]   *See* Abi-Saab, *supra* note 123 at 378 for an interesting account of the controversy over wars of national liberation in the Diplomatic Conference (1974-1977) to develop and reaffirm international humanitarian law through elaboration of the 1977 Protocols additional to the Geneva Conventions, 1949.

purposes of the United Nations Organization. Article 55 of the UN Charter reiterates that international economic and social cooperation shall be promoted by the United Nations on the basis of "respect for the principle of equal rights and self-determination of peoples".[130]

The validity of the right to self-determination as a norm of international law finds further support in resolution 1514 discussed above. Significantly, Article 1 of both the International Covenant on Civil and Political Rights[131] and the International Covenant on Economic, Social and Political Rights[132] provides that:

> All peoples have the right to self-determination. By virtue of that right they freely determine their political status and freely pursue their economic, social and cultural development.

Economic self-determination of peoples is guaranteed in the General Assembly resolution on Permanent Sovereignty over Natural Resources.[133]

Following adoption of the Declaration on Friendly Relations, the international community affirmed its recognition that the use of force in struggles to realize the legitimate right to self-determination is an international matter governed by international humanitarian law.[134] In this connection, 1977 Protocol I additional to the Geneva Conventions, 1949,[135] recognizes wars of national liberation as 'international armed conflicts' within the scope of Article 2 common to the Conventions and further crystallizes the norm prohibiting colonial domination or other

---

[130]   *See also* Arts. 73 and 76 concerning the progressive development toward self-government with regard to non-self-governing territories and the international trusteeship system.

[131]   General Assembly resolution 2200 A (XXI), *adopted* on 16 Dec. 1966, *entered into force* 23 Mar. 1976.

[132]   General Assembly resolution 2200 A (XVI) of 16 Dec. 1966, *entered into force* 3 Jan. 1976.

[133]   *Adopted* on 14 Dec. 1962 by 87 votes to 2 with 12 abstentions. General Assembly resolution 1803 (XVII) GAOR, 17th Session, Supp. 17, 15.

[134]   *See* Abi-Saab, *supra* note 123 at 371.

[135]   Protocol I Additional to the Geneva Conventions of 12 Aug. 1949, and Relating to the Protection of Victims of International Armed Conflicts.

forms of alien domination. In this connection, Article 1(4) of Protocol I refers to "peoples fighting against colonial domination and alien occupation and against racist regimes in the exercise of their right to self-determination".

iv) 1991 Draft Code Provisions on Colonial Domination

Article 18 of the ILC draft Code reads:

An individual who as leader or organizer establishes or maintains by force or orders the establishment or form of maintenance by force of colonial domination or any other alien domination contrary to the right of peoples to self-determination as enshrined in the Charter of the United Nations shall, on conviction thereof, be sentenced [to ...].

Article 18 contemplates prosecution of policy level officials as denoted by the phrase "an individual who as leader or organizer". Article 18 is rather ambiguous because it is not clear whether the employment of economic, political or other coercive methods would qualify as 'force'.

The debate over Article 18 exposed a certain measure of continuing discord in the international community over the principle of self-determination of peoples at the 1991 ILC session. Two main views regarding Article 18 of the draft Code emerged. One ILC member of a former colonial Power argued that reference to 'colonial domination' in Article 18 should be deleted on the grounds that virtually all colonies had already emerged as independent entities and that the system of colonialism no longer existed. However, many ILC members of countries that formerly were colonized, insisted Article 18 be retained. These members argued that because it is not inconceivable that new colonies might be created in future, the draft Code should cover future cases of colonial domination that may arise in addition to those situations still in existence.[136]

v) 1996 Draft Code

The Governments of Australia, Denmark, Finland, Iceland, The Netherlands, Norway, Sweden, Switzerland, the United Kingdom and the United States proposed that the provisions concerning colonial or other forms of alien domination be deleted from the draft Code.

Australia noted that the content of right to self-determination was subject to continuing debate and contended that reference in the 1991 draft Code to 'alien domination' unduly extended the right to self-determination beyond its classic meaning.[137] The Nordic countries did not oppose outright deletion of any provision on colonial or other forms of alien domination, but argued that such provisions had to be made much more precise before they could be retained. The United States argued that the overly broad and vague character of Article 18 of the 1991 draft Code would likely help foster secessionist claims and thereby undermine international peace and security. The Government of Switzerland maintained that if alien domination were understood as some form of neocolonialism, there would be no place for such a term in a Code of Crimes against the Peace and Security of Mankind because, although such domination was not to be condoned, no established international legal norms prohibited it.

Rather than to attempt to make the provisions on individual criminal responsibility for colonial domination in the 1991 draft Code more precise, the ILC took the radical step of deleting them entirely.

---

[136] *See* General Assembly resolutions 45/21 - 45/32 relating to Decolonization on the question of Western Sahara, New Caledonia, Anguilla, Bermuda, British Virgin Islands, Cayman Islands, Montserrat, the Turks and Caicos Islands, Tokelau, American Samoa, United States Virgin Islands and Guam, Resolutions and Decisions Adopted by the General Assembly during the First Part of its Forty-Fifth Session (18 Sept. - 21 Dec. 1990).

[137] *See* Comments and Observations of Governments on the Draft Code of Crimes against the Peace and Security of Mankind adopted on First Reading by the International Law Commission at its 43rd Session, A/CN.4/ 448 of 1 March 1993.

CHAPTER II

SERIOUS VIOLATIONS OF INTERNATIONAL HUMAN RIGHTS AND HUMANITARIAN LAW

1. GENOCIDE

i) Background

The term 'genocide' is of rather recent origin. It is "[b]ased upon a combination of the Greek *genos* (meaning race or tribe) with the Latin *cide* (meaning killing)"[1] made current through the personal efforts of Raphael Lemkin,[2] who in the early 1940's lobbied Member States of the United Nations to outlaw this kind of atrocity.

Prior to adoption of the Genocide Convention in 1948,[3] international law did not specifically prohibit genocide in peace-time. The only relevant international legal norms at the time, namely those on crimes against humanity and war crimes, provided partial coverage by outlawing murder in certain situations. To appreciate fully the function and role of the Genocide Convention, it is essential first to understand the gaps in international criminal law at the moment of the Convention's adoption by reviewing briefly the norms on war crimes and crimes against humanity.

In 1948, norms prohibiting war crimes and crimes against humanity applied only to situations of international armed conflict i.e. classic inter-State war rather than peace-time situations. More recently, a trend towards the application of these norms also to situations of non-international armed conflict has become more pronounced.

---

[1]   Louis René Beres, *International Law: Personhood and the Prevention of Genocide*, 11(1) Loyola of Los Angeles International and Comparative Law Journal (1989) at 25.

[2]   *See* Raphael Lemkin, Axis Rule in Occupied Europe (1944).

[3]   Convention on the Prevention and Punishment of the Crime of Genocide, *adopted unanimously* 9 Dec. 1948, *entered into force* 12 Jan. 1951; 78 UNTS 277.

Norms prohibiting war crimes prohibit the massacre of civilians during war, but are intended to punish and deter enemy soldiers from committing such acts. As such, these norms covered neither atrocities committed by a government against its own civilian population nor acts committed outside the context of war.

During the drafting of the Nuremberg Charter, the United States Government insisted that 'crimes against humanity' be introduced in the Nuremberg Charter as a legal category separate from 'war crimes', in order to cover atrocities committed by a government against its own civilian population.

Article 6(c) of the Nuremberg Charter defines 'crimes against humanity' as:

> murder, extermination, enslavement, deportation, and other inhumane acts committed against any civilian population, before or during the war, or persecutions on political, racial or religious grounds in execution or in connection with any crime within the jurisdiction of the Tribunal whether or not in violation of the domestic law of the country where perpetrated.

Initially, Article 6(c) contained a semicolon following the word 'war' which implied a disjunction between "murder, extermination, enslavement, deportation, and other inhumane acts committed against any civilian population, before or during the war" from "persecutions ... in connection with any crime within the jurisdiction of the Tribunal". Article 6(c), as originally formulated, implied that murder and extermination of civilians (including the Government's own nationals) were prohibited, regardless as to when these violations were committed. Thus, 'crimes against humanity', undoubtedly a new legal category in 1945,[4] was formulated and interpreted very restrictively to apply only to those acts committed in direct connection with the events of the Second World War.

---

[4]   *See further*, Lyal S. Sunga, Individual Responsibility in International Law for Serious Human Rights Violations (1992) Chapter II(4) on crimes against humanity.

However on 6 October 1945, a Protocol was adopted by the Allied Powers replacing the semicolon in Article 6(c) with a comma, thereby ensuring that only those acts connected to the war would qualify as crimes against humanity within the competence of the Nuremberg Tribunal. This link between crimes against humanity and acts directly connected to the war was reconfirmed in the United Nations War Crimes Committee on Facts and Evidence which, in its January 1946 discussions, decided that "... crimes against humanity as referred to in the Four Power Agreement of 8th August, 1945, were war crimes within the jurisdiction of the [United Nations War Crimes] Commission".[5]

Accordingly, in the years immediately following the end of the Second World War, norms prohibiting 'crimes against humanity' were considered not to apply to peace-time situations, in line with the construction and interpretation of Article 6(c) described above and hence, prior to the adoption of the Genocide Convention, 1948, international legal norms covered neither mass murder nor extermination perpetrated in peace-time.

Consequently, prior to the Genocide Convention, genocide i.e. the actual or attempted destruction of a group in whole or in part, where committed by a government against its own population or by any government in situations which did not qualify as 'war' (in the classic sense of 'inter-State armed conflict') were not specifically prohibited by international law.

These gaps in international norms underscored the need for a more comprehensive set of norms prohibiting mass extermination, particularly by a Government against its own civilian population.

General Assembly resolution 96(I), adopted the same day as the Nuremberg Principles,[6] affirms that genocide is a crime under international law and, *inter alia*, requests ECOSOC to prepare the necessary groundwork for drafting a convention against genocide. On 21 November 1947, at its second session, the General Assembly adopted resolution 180 (II), reaffirming resolution 96(I), and requesting

---

5   *See* History of the UN War Crimes Commission (1948) at 35 *et seq.*; and Yoram Dinstein, *International Criminal Law*, 20 Israel Law Review (1985).

6   General Assembly resolution 95(I), *adopted* on 11 Dec. 1946, embodies the main principles of international criminal responsibility *as affirmed by* the Nuremberg Judgement.

ECOSOC to continue its work on the draft convention. On 30 January 1948, ECOSOC appointed an *Ad Hoc* Committee to draft the convention, which met from 5 April to 10 May 1948, composed of representatives of China, France, Lebanon, Poland, USA, USSR and Venezuela. On 26 August 1948, ECOSOC submitted the draft convention to the third session of the General Assembly. The General Assembly then transmitted the *Ad Hoc* Committee's report to the Assembly's Sixth Committee for extensive examination after which an amended text was adopted.

The General Assembly adopted the UN Genocide Convention unanimously on 9 December 1948.[7] In accordance with Article XIII which stipulates that the "Convention shall come into force on the ninetieth day following the date of deposit of the twentieth instrument of ratification or accession", the Convention entered into force on 12 January 1951.

ii) Principal Normative Aspects
of the Genocide Convention, 1948

The Genocide Convention states specifically in Article I that "genocide, whether committed in time of peace or in time of war, is a crime under international law" making clear that norms prohibiting genocide apply at all times. Article II provides that:

> In the present Convention, genocide means any of the following acts committed with intent to destroy, in whole or in part, a national, ethnical, racial, or religious group, as such:
> (a)   Killing members of the group;
> (b)   Causing serious bodily or mental harm
>   to members of the group;
> (c)   Deliberately inflicting on the group conditions of life calculated to bring about its physical destruction in whole or in part;
> (d)   Imposing measures intended to prevent births within the group;

---

[7]   *See* Joseph Kunz, *The United Nations Convention on Genocide*, 43 American Journal of International Law (1949) at 739.

(e)   Forcibly transferring children of the group to another
        group.

Article III provides that:

> ... the following acts shall be punishable:
> (a)   Genocide;
> (b)   Conspiracy to commit genocide;
> (c)   Direct and public incitement to commit genocide;
> (d)   Attempt to commit genocide;
> (e)   Complicity in genocide.

The Convention's use of the words 'killing', 'serious bodily or
mental harm' and 'inflicting on the group conditions of life calculated
to bring about its physical destruction' emphasizes that actual or
attempted destruction of the physical existence of a 'national, ethnical,
racial, or religious group, as such' is covered by the crime of genocide. Measures designed merely to alter or influence the economic,
social or cultural character of the group, such as assimilation policies,
are not covered by the Convention.[8]

As for what kinds of groups are covered by the Genocide
Convention, it is remarkable that resolution 96(I) refers in a pre-

---

[8]   The Lebanese delegate on the *Ad Hoc* Committee had proposed that
the Genocide Convention cover the kinds of measures taken by a government to destroy a group without actually killing any of its members; *see* UN
Doc. E/AC.25/S-R 1-28. The destruction of a people's way of life, through
relocation, lack of support, or actual destruction of the books and monuments
of the community, suppression of a group's education of children in their
native language or other assimilation policies may be termed 'cultural
genocide'. During the drafting of the Genocide Convention, the United States
and Canada were successful in leading the drive to delete any proposed
references to 'cultural genocide' in the Convention. It should be noted that
both Governments at both the federal and State (or provincial) levels have
practised some or all of these and many other kinds of assimilation policies,
directed at their respective North American indigenous populations. *See
further*, Jerry Kammer, The Second Long Walk: The Navajo-Hopi Land
Dispute (1978), and Robert Davis and Mark Zannis, The Genocide Machine
in Canada: The Pacification of the North (1973).

ambular paragraph to "Many instances of such crimes of genocide ... when racial, religious, political and other groups have been destroyed, entirely or in part", and in its first operative paragraph, affirms that "genocide is a crime under international law ... whether the crime is committed on religious, racial, political or any other grounds". The resolution thus envisages a non-exhaustive list of grounds of persecution ('any other grounds') which could qualify acts as 'genocide' and refers specifically to 'political groups' as covered by norms prohibiting genocide. However, Article II of the Convention refers neither to 'political groups' nor to 'any other grounds' and is therefore narrower in scope than resolution 96(I). The attempted destruction of a particular political group does not fall within the scope of Article II. As Webb explains:

> Political groups are conspicuously not on the list
> because some states feared that the inclusion of such
> an arguably unstable category would create an obsta-
> cle to the Convention's ratification. Unfortunately, an
> unscrupulously entity could attempt to avoid application
> of the Convention in cases of discriminate killings by
> labelling the victims as a political group.[9]

On the other hand, the fact that the Genocide Convention does not protect 'political groups' cannot be construed to imply that the attempted destruction of a 'national, ethnical, racial, or religious group' is excluded from the Convention's coverage wherever political motive may be involved in the execution of genocide. To the contrary, it is clear that the Genocide Convention was specifically designed to prohibit a State-sponsored programme of extermination. As Leblanc observes:

> The often expressed concern that the convention does
> not cover politically motivated genocide reflects a
> curious and probably erroneous interpretation of Article

---

[9] John Webb, *Genocide Treaty: Ethnic Cleansing, Substantive and Procedural Hurdles in the Application of the Genocide Convention to Alleged Crimes in the Former Yugoslavia*, 23(2) Georgia Journal of International and Comparative Law (1993) at 391.

II and, more broadly, of the convention as a whole. The critics are preoccupied with motives. According to Article II, however, genocide is defined simply as the commission of certain acts 'with the intent to destroy, in whole or in part, a national, ethnical, racial, or religious group, as such.' Neither Article II nor any other article of the convention refers to the motives that must lie behind the commission of such acts.[10]

In other words, broad motivations behind the instigation and execution of a genocidal programme should not be muddled with the more specific legal issue of criminal intent to commit genocide. In criminal prosecutions, the issue of broad motivations is likely to assume only background importance, perhaps to support the prosecution's case as regards criminal intent. The issue of criminal intent to commit an act of genocide is the more essential element to be established, along with the *actus reus*, to prove individual criminal responsibility in a given case.

As regards the groups specifically protected in Article II, there remains considerable ambiguity in the scope of the terms 'national, ethnical, racial, or religious group'. The intent behind Article II is to prohibit violations against a particularly vulnerable group, more likely to be a minority singled out from the rest of the population, and targeted on the basis of certain recognizable attributes, such as differences in ethnocultural origin or practises, faith or physical traits.[11]

The terms 'ethnical, racial, or religious group', although difficult to define, are not devoid of meaning. The effort to define 'ethnic group' or 'race' or 'religion' *in abstracto* is naturally fraught with difficulty, especially if one aims at a universally applicable or empirically objective set of criteria to support such distinctions.

---

[10]   Lawrence Leblanc, The United States and the Genocide Convention (1991) at 80.

[11]   'National group' in Article II appears to refer to a distinct people who forms a 'nation' or 'people' in the sense that the members of such a group share linguistic, ethnic, religious and cultural similarities (or some of these) which distinguish it from the general population, rather than to any legal criteria concerning citizenship or nationality.

However, in cases on genocide, it seems that the prosecution must prove that the accused acted in conformity with a policy or programme that stigmatized a particular group as inferior on the basis of relatively immutable characteristics through hate propaganda or other means designed to prepare the way for extermination. It would not be logically necessary to postulate the existence of objective and clear-cut distinctions among groups of people to prove that a particular group was stigmatized and targeted. In this sense, the perception of differences is more important than the differences themselves. For example in the case of genocide committed in Rwanda in 1994, in trying to exterminate the minority Tutsi people, the perpetrators consciously stigmatized and targeted persons who were legally and administratively designated as Tutsis by Rwandese law.[12] Given the high rate of intermarriage in Rwanda and a common language, religion and geographic area of habitation over several centuries, it is unlikely that the Hutus and Tutsis can be distinguished from each other on an exclusively anthropological basis, despite distinct origins and histories. In other words, the Genocide Convention can be implemented effectively only if courts recognize that the prosecution should not be expected to prove the unprovable. What matters is the targeting of the group in question, the intention to destroy the group in whole or in part and actual measures taken to carry this intention out.

The difficulty at defining 'nationality', 'ethnicity', 'race' or 'religion' may explain why the drafters of the Convention opted to enumerate rather than substantively define these terms. To enable effective implementation of the Convention, it is important to recognize that the intention of the Convention's drafters was to protect stable groups than to arrive at airtight definitions. As Leblanc argues:

> Because the convention was obviously drafted in response to atrocities committed against the Jews, Poles, Gypsies, and other groups by the Nazis during

---

[12] *See* Preliminary and Final Reports of the Independent Commission of Experts on Rwanda established pursuant to Security Council resolution 935 (1994), Part VIII (A) of UN Doc. S/1994/1125, 4 Oct. 1994; and UN Doc. S/1994/1405 of 9 Dec. 1994. *See also* Rwanda: Accountability for War Crimes and Genocide (1995), a report of the United States Institute of Peace.

World War II, Article II would apply to such a situation whether Jews were considered a religious, ethnic, or even racial or national group. Similarly, the convention would cover the Armenian genocide, and it would probably apply as well to numerous other instances of genocide that have occurred in Africa, Asia and Latin America since World War II.[13]

Thus the Convention aims to protect groups whose identity is more permanent than political allegiance or even legal status.

Article IV provides that "persons committing genocide or any of the other acts enumerated in article III shall be punished, whether they are constitutionally responsible rulers, public officials or private individuals." The principle that any individual, regardless of rank or official position, may be held responsible and punished, was clearly established by Article 8 of the Nuremberg Charter which makes inadmissible any defense to a charge of crime against peace, crime against humanity or war crime which seeks to exculpate the accused on grounds that he or she was following orders from a superior.[14]

However, the specific reference to 'constitutionally responsible rulers' was employed in the Genocide Convention, rather than a broad reference to 'anyone'. This construction was thought necessary because representatives of the Netherlands, Sweden, Thailand and the United Kingdom, all monarchic States, (as well as certain other States), indicated during the drafting of the Convention that, according to their domestic law, they could not subject the sovereign to the criminal trial process.[15] However, inclusion of this phrase seems to have been misguided since the Genocide Convention itself, in Article VI, envisages the creation of an "international penal tribunal as may have jurisdiction" over genocide criminal suspects. Such international tribunal would not be bound by domestic immunities conferred by the constitution of the national State of the monarch.

---

[13]   Leblanc, *supra* note 10 at 60-61.

[14]   Article 8 of the Nuremberg Charter provides that: "The fact that the defendant acted pursuant to order of his Government or of a superior shall not free him from responsibility, but may be considered in mitigation of punishment if the Tribunal determine that justice so requires".

[15]   Leblanc, *supra* note 10 at 29-30.

The roots of the term 'genocide', as well as its use in common parlance, imply that many individuals have to be killed before such killings qualify as a case of genocide. However, the Genocide Convention does not itself establish any such number. In Article II of the Convention, neither a particular number of persons killed, nor even the *actus reus* of killing is essential to the crime of genocide.[16]

A requirement that a high number have to be killed before such slaughter qualified as 'genocide' in the legal sense, would obviously render nugatory international criminal law enforcement as regards genocide. This explains the Convention's emphasis on an intention to destroy the group as such rather than a particular number of persons killed. Moreover, Article II of the Convention states that there must be 'intent to destroy' 'in whole or in part'. Thus, cases which involve an intention to destroy even part of the group come within the meaning of Article II.

Finally, it is important to take note of the peremptory legal status of international norms prohibiting genocide. As the International Court of Justice observed in the *Reservations to the Convention on Genocide Case*:

> The origins of the Convention show that it was the intention of the United Nations to condemn and punish genocide as 'a crime under international law' ... The first consequence arising from this conception is that the principles underlying the Convention are principles which are recognized by civilized nations as binding on States, even without any conventional obligation. A second consequence is the universal character both of the condemnation of genocide and of the cooperation required 'in order to liberate mankind from such an odious scourge' (Preamble to the Convention).[17]

---

[16]   Article III of the Genocide Convention lists as punishable acts genocide, conspiracy to commit genocide, direct and public incitement to commit genocide, attempt to commit genocide and complicity to commit genocide.

[17]   *Reservations to the Convention on Genocide Case* (Advisory Opinion) 1951 ICJ Reports 15 at 23.

In the *Barcelona Traction Case (Second Phase)*[18] the International Court of Justice referred in *obiter dicta* to the prohibition of genocide as an obligation *erga omnes*[19] in which all States have a legal interest. Although the *Barcelona Traction Case* does not explicitly state that genocide is a norm of *jus cogens* character, evidence of *opinio juris* and general State practice, support the conclusion that the rule against genocide is part of customary international law and most probably of *jus cogens* as well.

iii) 1991 Draft Code Provisions on Genocide

Article 2(10) of the 1954 draft Code[20] had incorporated a broader definition of 'genocide' than that of the 1948 Convention by inserting the word 'including', which made the enumeration non-exhaustive.[21] In its 1991 session, the ILC rejected this approach and decided that it would be better to follow the exhaustive Genocide Convention definition of 'genocide' for the sake of clarity in definition.

Thus, Article 19(1) of the 1991 draft Code provides that an individual is criminally responsible for committing or ordering 'an act

---

[18]   *Barcelona Traction Case* (Belgium v. Spain) 1970 ICJ Reports 3 at 32.

[19]   The term 'obligation *erga omnes*' refers to an obligation of each State towards the international community as a whole in respect of a beneficiary. *See further* Chapter IV(2).

[20]   2 ILC Yearbook (1954), Part II, UN Doc. A/2693, 151-152, para. 54.

[21]   *See* the UN Report on the Study of the Question of the Prevention and Punishment of Genocide E/CN.4/Sub.2/416, 4 July 1978. During the drafting of the Genocide Convention it was argued that the definition of 'genocide' should illustrate rather than enumerate acts of genocide to cover any particular way in which genocide might be committed. However, an enumerative approach was adopted on the grounds that since genocide was a new concept, it should be unequivocally defined to meet the defence of *nullum crimen sine lege*.

of genocide'.[22] Article 19(2) of the draft Code follows Article II of the Genocide Convention word for word.

The Commentary to Article 19 of the draft Code emphasizes the distinction between 'physical genocide' and 'biological genocide'. 'Physical genocide', as covered by paragraphs (a), (b) and (c) of Article 19(2), relates to actual or direct physical destruction, while 'biological genocide', as covered by paragraphs (d) and (e), relates to suppression of the natural capacity of the group to reproduce itself.

iv) 1996 Draft Code

In their comments and observations on the 1991 draft Code,[23] the Government of The Netherlands noted that the draft Code provisions on aggression prohibit planning of the crime while those on genocide do not and argued that this was inconsistent. The Netherlands Government suggested that Article 3 of the 1991 draft Code be amended so that the planning of any of the crimes set out in the draft Code would also itself constitute a crime. This approach would have the advantage of placing greater emphasis on prevention and deterrence, although it is unclear how much this amendment would really add to the effectiveness of international criminal law.

Another alternative would be to include in the genocide provisions of the Code the contents of Article III of the Genocide Convention which makes conspiracy, direct and public incitement, attempt and complicity to commit genocide crimes in themselves. However, the contents of Article III of the Genocide Convention, which

---

[22] One ILC member thought reference to genocide as an 'act' under-stated the seriousness of genocide as a crime carried out systematically over a long period of time and that it would be more accurate to refer to genocide, and also apartheid, as 'policies' rather than as 'acts'. Other members countered that responsibility for a policy as such was not legally enforceable. Furthermore, a policy is comprised of acts in any event, such as enactment of legislation or actual implementation of the law. *See* Summary Records of the International Law Commission for July 1991.

[23] *See* Comments and Observations of Governments on the Draft Code of Crimes against the Peace and Security of Mankind adopted on First Reading by the International Law Commission at its 43rd Session, A/CN.4/ 448 of 1 March 1993.

appears in the statutes of both the International Criminal Tribunal for the Former Yugoslavia and the International Criminal Tribunal for Rwanda, will have to be interpreted with care. Imposition of criminal responsibility for mere plans, in cases where such plans are not actually carried out, may risk engulfing an international criminal court in a quagmire of speculative hypotheses.

The United States commented[24] that the 1991 draft Code does not frame the issue of *mens rea* with sufficient precision as to meet the standards of international criminal law. In particular, the US Government wished to see a formulation that linked more clearly the specific intent to commit one of the prohibited acts to the intention to destroy the group in question.

Interestingly, the Government of Belgium commented that Article 19 of the 1991 draft Code could have been drafted in a non-exhaustive manner so as to lend greater flexibility to the provisions on genocide. The Government of Belgium proposed that target groups not covered by the classic definition of genocide could be afforded coverage by a redrafted provision in either of two ways. The definition of genocide could be broadened so as to include other groups, such as political groups. Alternatively, the provision could be supplemented with other clauses that extended criminal responsibility for acts aimed at political or social groups not covered by the provisions directly related to genocide in its classic definition.

Article 17 of the 1996 draft Code reproduces Article II of the Genocide Convention, which as noted above, is considered part of international customary law and of *jus cogens*. It maintains the exhaustive approach, thereby achieving greater clarity and greater predictability in interpretation, at the expense however, of less flexibility.

v) The Statutes of the *Ad Hoc* International Criminal Tribunals and the Draft Statute for an International Criminal Court

Article 4 of the Statute for the International Criminal Tribunal for the Former Yugoslavia and Article 2 of the Statute of the International Criminal Tribunal for Rwanda, respectively, incorporate Articles

---

24   *Ibid.*

II and III of the Genocide Convention without alteration. In fact, the Genocide Convention itself foresees implementation by a tribunal that, at the time of the Convention's adoption, had yet to be created. In this regard, Article VI of the Genocide Convention provides:

> Persons charged with genocide or any of the other acts enumerated in Article III shall be tried by a competent tribunal of the State in the territory of which the act was committed, or by such international penal tribunal as may have jurisdiction with respect to those Contracting Parties which shall have accepted its jurisdiction.

Article VI draws upon territorial rather than universal jurisdiction such that the obligation to try persons charged with genocide rests with the State the territory in which genocide was perpetrated. Incorporation of the Convention definition of genocide in the *ad hoc* Tribunal Statutes thus dove-tails with Article VI of the Genocide Convention.

The International Law Commission's draft Statute for an international criminal court lists 'the crime of genocide' as coming within the competence of the proposed court (Article 20(a)) along with 'the crime of aggression', 'serious violations of the laws and customs applicable in armed conflict', 'crimes against humanity' and crimes established as such by treaty that may be included in the court's jurisdiction by way of the statute's annex. The Commentary to Article 20 states that the Commission was "guided in the choice of these [four categories of crimes] in particular by the fact that three of the four are singled out in the Statute of the International Criminal Tribunal for Former Yugoslavia as crimes under general international law falling within the jurisdiction of the Tribunal ...". By itself, this reasoning sounds rather weak since the ILC is not bound to follow the drafters of the Statute of the International Tribunal. Fortunately, in paragraph 5, the Commentary also states in referring to genocide that:

> It is clearly and authoritatively defined in the 1948 Convention which is widely ratified, and which envis-ages that cases of genocide may be referred to an international criminal court. ... [T]he Commission believes that, exceptionally, the Court should have inherent jurisdiction over the crime of genocide - that is

to say, its jurisdiction should exist as between all States parties to the Statute, and it should be able to be triggered by a complaint brought by any State party to the Genocide Convention, as expressly envisaged in article VI of that Convention.

In Sixth Committee meetings on the draft statute, many delegates echoed the ILC's view that provisions prohibiting genocide should be explicitly included in the proposed court's inherent jurisdiction (if inherent jurisdiction is finally to be conferred) rather than in an annex to the statute, to ensure implementation would not be hindered by technical obstacles.[25]

2. APARTHEID

i) The Apartheid Convention, 1973

Article II of the Apartheid Convention, 1973,[26] refers to apartheid 'as practised in southern Africa',[27] linking the definition of apartheid to that region. In contrast, 'southern Africa' is not mentioned in Article 20 of the 1991 draft Code so that in principle, the prohibition of apartheid in the draft Code could apply to other geographic areas.

The Apartheid Convention has been signed by only slightly more than half the member States of the United Nations, which do not include any of the influential western industrialized States. Even

---

[25] *See* UNGA/L/2880 Sixth Committee of 2 Nov. 1995; Background Press release L/2760 of 22 Mar. 1996; Preparatory Committee on Establishment of International Criminal Court Meetings L/2761 of 25 Mar. 1996, first meeting of the first session; L/2762 of 25 Mar. 1996; L/2763/Rev.1 of 26 Mar. 1996; L/2764 of 26 Mar. 1996 *et seq.*

[26] By resolution 3068 (XXVIII) *adopted* by the General Assembly 30 Nov. 1973, *opened for signature*, as the International Convention on the Suppression and Punishment of the Crime of Apartheid.

[27] Although the Apartheid Convention does not mention the State of South Africa in particular, it is aimed chiefly at the criminalization of South African policies of racial segregation and discrimination, whence came the term 'apartheid'.

several States that have repeatedly condemned apartheid policies have not signed it.

However, many States likely have withheld their support from the Apartheid Convention not because they oppose the Convention's basic condemnation of apartheid policies, but because the Convention's definition of apartheid is overly broad and poorly drafted.

The ILC had considerably refined the definition of 'apartheid' for the purposes of individual criminal responsibility under the 1991 draft Code. However, in 1996, the ILC eliminated any provisions on apartheid from the draft Code.

ii) 1991 Draft Code Provisions on Apartheid

Article 20(2) of the 1991 draft Code defines apartheid to consist:

> ... of any of the following acts based on policies and practices of racial segregation and discrimination committed for the purpose of establishing or maintaining domination by one racial group over any other racial group and systematically oppressing it:
> a) denial to a member or members of a racial group of the right to life and liberty of the person;
> b) deliberate imposition on a racial group of living conditions calculated to cause its physical destruction in whole or in part;
> c) any legislative measures and other measures calculated to prevent a racial group from participating in the political, social, economic and cultural life of the country and the deliberate creation of conditions preventing the full development of such a group;
> d) any measures, including legislative measures, designed to divide the population along racial lines, in particular by the creation of separate reserves and ghettos for the members of a racial group, the prohibition of marriages among members of various racial groups or the expropriation of landed property belonging to a racial group or to members thereof;

e) exploitation of the labour of the members of a racial
group, in particular by submitting them to forced labour;
f) persecution of organizations and persons, by depriving them of fundamental rights and freedoms, because
they oppose apartheid.

This definition of 'apartheid' is less complicated than that incorporated
in the 1973 UN Apartheid Convention. As the ILC observed in the
Commentary to Article 20, the 1991 draft Code definition has captured
only the essential elements of the crime of apartheid by excluding the
illustrative examples set out in the Apartheid Convention.

The chapeau to Article 20 of the 1991 draft Code makes clear
that 'apartheid' refers to 'policies and practises of racial segregation'
rather than to isolated acts of racial discrimination. Moreover, in order
for the policy of apartheid to involve individual criminal responsibility,
it must be committed with "the purpose of establishing or maintaining
domination by one racial group over any other racial group and
systematically oppressing it".

In many instances, the existence of racial segregation policies
is likely to be relatively easy to establish on account of the sheer
volume of law required to enforce them. For example, the laws of
segregationist states of the United States, or those of the Government
of South Africa during the apartheid era, were thoroughly imbued with
distinctions based on race, imposed in all areas of life, from voting
rights, to access to social services and housing and employment, to
marriage etc.

However, situations involving systematically unequal implementation of legislation pose greater difficulties where such legislation is
prima facie equal, but has a discriminatory effect. In cases where the
law is not expressly discriminatory, the application of Article 20 of the
1991 draft Code would likely become mired in overly politicized
rhetoric unconducive to fair and effective criminal law enforcement.

Where the law appears nondiscriminatory but is implemented
in a systematically discriminatory way, the burden of proof would be
on the prosecution to establish an intention on the part of the
Government or its agents to dominate and oppress a particular racial
group. In the absence of expressly discriminatory provisions or
declarations, the prosecution might then have to resort, as a first step,
to social science studies that indicate statistically *de facto* disparities

between or among racial groups in society as regards income, wealth and opportunity. Next, the prosecution would have to establish that such disparity was causally linked to government policy (express or hidden), and in particular, that the intention of such policy was to dominate and oppress a racial group. Given the ambiguity of the terms 'dominate' and 'oppress' in this context as well as the difficulty in establishing causality and intention, it would appear virtually impossible for the prosecution to establish the existence of an apartheid policy beyond a reasonable doubt.

Moreover, while the terms 'domination' and 'oppression' in the chapeau of Article 20 may serve to guide the interpretation of subparagraphs (a) to (f), these words suffer from a lack of precision and leave ample opportunity for defendants to trivialize the charges on the ground that, in every society, some racial groups enjoy greater access to income, wealth and opportunity than others. Further, it could be argued convincingly that since no society is free of domination or oppression, it must follow that the prosecution's choice to prosecute the particular case in question is motivated more by politically biased considerations, rather than by objective requirements of international criminal law.

Subparagraph (a) refers to 'the right to life and liberty of the person', as guaranteed in numerous international human rights instruments, for example, in Articles 6 and 9 respectively of the International Covenant on Civil and Political Rights, 1966. Subparagraph (b) refers to the 'living conditions calculated to cause [the racial group's] physical destruction in whole or in part', echoing Article II of the Genocide Convention.

Subparagraphs (c) and (d) are perhaps the least ambiguous of the 1991 draft Code provisions prohibiting apartheid. The reference in subparagraph (c) to "legislative measures or other measures" clearly prohibits law and policy adopted with an obvious intention to prevent a racial group from participation in the "political, social, economic and cultural life of the country", rather than on legislative measures that may produce unintended discriminatory effects.[28]

---

[28]   Subparagraph (d) prohibits the creation of separate reserves or ghettos and any legislative measures designed to divide the population along racial lines. Subparagraph (d) would very likely apply to the reserve system created in Australia, Canada and the United States in respect of indigenous

Subparagraph (e) should perhaps have made reference only
to a prohibition of 'forced labour' rather than to 'exploitation of the
labour'. Whereas international legal norms prohibiting forced labour,
slavery and servitude are well established in international conventions,
particularly those of the International Labour Organization, the word
'exploitation' is less clear. Arguably, any valid employment contract
involves some exploitation of labour, many forms of which were not
intended to come within the ambit of an international criminal code,
but which are not clearly excluded by Article 20.

Subparagraph (f) prohibits 'persecution' - a rather ambiguous
term - of any individual or movement that opposes apartheid policy
and practises. In the interests of greater specificity in the law,
perhaps it would have been preferable if subparagraph (f) had
reaffirmed specifically the rights of freedom of opinion, expression,
assembly and association.

iii) 1996 Draft Code

Given the lack of precision in the 1991 draft Code provisions
on apartheid, as well as the weak state of the *lex lata* on which it is
based, it should not be surprising that the provisions on apartheid
were dropped from the 1996 draft Code. While terms such as
'domination', 'oppression' and 'exploitation' tend to evoke indignation
and may suit very well General Assembly resolutions urging a
segregationist government to end its discriminatory practises, these
terms are not specific or clear enough for the purposes of international

---

populations. It has been well documented that many indigenous populations
suffer from a chronic cycle of poverty, drug and alcohol dependence and
crime as well as stigmatization and even ostracism on the part of the larger
community. *See* J.R. Martinez Cobo, Study of the Problem of Discrimination
against Indigenous Populations (United Nations) 1987, UN Doc. E/CN.4/
Sub.2/1986/ 7/Add.4; 1957 ILO Convention (No. 107) concerning the
Protection and Integration of Indigenous and Other Tribal and Semi-Tribal
Populations of Independent Countries; and Convention (No.169) concerning
Indigenous and Tribal Populations in Independent Countries, *adopted* on 27
June 1989 by the ILO General Conference at its 77th session, *entered into
force* 5 Sept. 1991.

criminal law. The provision therefore would have to be entirely redrafted to find a rightful place in an international penal code.

This concern was reflected in the comments and observations of Governments on the 1991 draft Code. Austria proposed that the title could refer to 'institutionalized racial discrimination', instead of 'apartheid', to denote the prohibited pattern of acts set out in Article 20.[29] The Governments of Denmark, Finland, Iceland, Norway, The Netherlands, Sweden, the UK and the US, considered the provisions too vague for the purposes of an international criminal code. Furthermore, the Nordic Governments commented that the substance of the acts prohibited in Article 20 was covered in Article 21 on mass violations of human rights, and therefore, that the contents of Article 21 rendered Article 20 superfluous.

3. SYSTEMATIC OR MASS VIOLATIONS OF HUMAN RIGHTS

i) Breadth of Coverage of Article 21 of the 1991 Draft Code

Article 21 of the 1991 draft Code contains a general description of systematic or mass violations of human rights, followed by an enumeration of such acts. It reads:

> An individual who commits or orders the com-
> mission of any of the following violations of human
> rights:
> - murder
> - torture
> - establishing or maintaining over per-
> sons a status of slavery, servitude or
> forced labour

---

[29]   *See* Comments and Observations of Governments on the Draft Code of Crimes against the Peace and Security of Mankind adopted on First Reading by the International Law Commission at its 43rd Session, A/CN.4/ 448 of 1 March 1993.

> - persecution on social, political, racial,
> religious or cultural grounds,
> in a systematic manner or on a mass scale; or
> - deportation or forcible transfer of popu-
> lation shall, on conviction thereof, be
> sentenced [to ...].

The word 'individual' signifies that any individual, not only government officials or agents, may be held liable for crimes enumerated in Article 21. As stated in the Commentary to Article 21:[30]

> It is important to point out that the draft article does not confine possible perpetrators of the crimes to public officials or representatives alone. Admittedly, they would normally be in the best position, in view of their official position, to commit the crimes covered by the draft article, yet the article does not rule out the possibility that private individuals with *de facto* power or organized in criminal gangs or groups might also commit the kind of systematic or mass violations of human rights covered by the article; in that case, their acts would come under the draft Code.

Clearly, under Article 21, a perpetrator may be held criminally responsible even where there is no colour of official capacity.

The 1991 draft Code provides for criminal responsibility only for the most serious human rights violations committed in a systematic manner or on a mass scale. 'Deportation or forcible transfer of population' is listed separately from the other crimes because the reference to 'population' already implies that the offense is committed on a mass scale. It seems that the provision should be read as referring to 'deportation of population or forcible transfer of population' i.e. criminal responsibility would not arise from isolated cases of deportation of single individuals, but only to deportation of population

---

[30] *See* Draft Report of the International Law Commission on the Work of the Forty-Third Session, Draft Code of Crimes against the Peace and Security of Mankind, 43rd session, (29 Apr.- 19 July 1991), UN Doc. A/CN.4/L.464/Add.4, 15 July 1991 at 26 para. 5.

(whether executed *en masse* or as a systematic and arbitrary treatment of the population's members).[31]

The ILC Commentary to Article 21 states that the word 'systematic' refers to 'a constant practice or to a methodical plan'. 'Mass scale' relates 'to the number of people affected by such violations or the entity that has been affected'. The presence of either one of these conditions is sufficient to engage the court's jurisdiction under Article 21.

Article 21 of the 1991 draft Code does not make clear what is meant by 'systematic' basis or 'mass scale', but such terms do not necessarily have to be spelt out in an international criminal code. Whether violations were committed pursuant to an official policy (whether overt or covert), or systematic plan, would go to the question of culpability.[32] These factors would have to be assessed by an international criminal court in light of surrounding circumstances as an evidentiary matter. Thus the threshold of the Court's jurisdiction concerning the systematic manner or mass scale of human rights

---

[31]   Any deportation or forcible transfer of population is in itself sufficiently serious to warrant individual criminal responsibility, since the word 'population' refers to a large number of persons. One ILC member suggested that 'changes to the demographic composition in occupied territories by settlers' should also be included as a serious human rights violation rather than only under the draft Code provision on war crimes since, in fact, such policies may be perpetrated either in time of armed conflict or in time of peace.

[32]   Where the wrongful acts of private persons gain the approval of the State, these private persons may be considered agents of the State and State responsibility in international law may be incurred. For example, it was held in *United States Diplomatic and Consular Staff in Tehran Case*, (US v. Iran), 1980 ICJ Reports 3 at para. 74, following an overview by the Court of the facts of the case which included the seizure of documents and archives of the US Embassy and of Consulates in Iran, occupation of the premises and the taking of 52 US nationals as hostages that: "The approval given to these facts by the Ayatollah Khomeini and other organs of the Iranian State, and the decision to perpetuate them, translated continuing occupation of the Embassy and detention of the hostages into acts of the State. The militants, authors of the invasion and jailers of the hostages, had now become agents of the Iranian State for whose acts the State itself was internationally responsible...".

violations should be left to the proposed court itself to determine on a case-by-case basis.

Although in general international law genocide and apartheid clearly qualify as 'serious human rights violations', the 1991 draft Code places these crimes in separate provisions. Some ILC members felt that since specific UN conventions on genocide and apartheid are more established than legal norms that prohibit murder, torture, slavery or deportation on a mass scale, genocide and apartheid must not be lumped together with the other violations in Article 21.

However, norms prohibiting criminal acts should not necessarily be categorized according to their existing source in international law. Were a Code of Crimes against the Peace and Security of Mankind to enter into force as a widely ratified multilateral convention, it would itself constitute the principal source of criminal responsibility in international law. At that point, little purpose would be served in maintaining categories fashioned so closely to the *lex lata* that the Code would crystallize traditional technical distinctions. The enumeration of crimes in the draft Code should enhance coherence in the content of the norms *de lege ferenda*, rather than to reflect slavishly the source of norms *de lege lata*.

ii) *Lex Lata* on Specific Crimes Under Article 21

- Murder

Since the criminal law of every municipal jurisdiction prohibits ordinary murder, it might be supposed that the prohibition of murder may be counted "among the general principles of law recognized by civilized nations".[33] Strictly speaking however, there is an absence of positive international legal norms specifically stipulating individual criminal responsibility for mass murder, except as regards particular intent or circumstances as discussed below.[34]

---

[33]   *See* Article 38(1)(c) of the Statute of the International Court of Justice.

[34]   As Oscar Schachter argues: "The most important limitation on the use of municipal law principles arises from the requirement that the principle be appropriate for application on the international level. Thus, the universally accepted common crimes - murder, theft, assault, incest - that apply to

On the one hand, the Genocide Convention prohibits murder on a mass scale where killing is perpetrated "with intent to destroy, in whole or in part, a national, ethnical, racial, or religious group, as such".[35] The Genocide Convention does not appear to cover ordinary murder on a mass scale where an intention to destroy the group is absent.

On the other hand, 'murder' figures in the Nuremberg Charter definitions of 'war crimes' and 'crimes against humanity' and is covered in the system designed to repress grave breaches of the Geneva Conventions, 1949.[36] Murder appears also as a crime against humanity in Articles 5(a) and 3(a) of the Statutes of the International Criminal Tribunals for the Former Yugoslavia and Rwanda respectively. However these proscriptions relate to situations of armed conflict and not to peace-time violations.

It may appear that, in order to be more coherent, international criminal law should cover murder committed on a systematic basis or on a mass scale. However, laws against murder evolved within the municipal sphere, not on the international plane. States naturally enforce criminal law to the extent of their jurisdiction without concerning themselves with promoting the legal prohibition of murder at the international level. Prior to 1945, violations of human rights, including State-sponsored murder, were not considered to be of international concern.

States are unlikely simply to surrender their jurisdiction over murder to an international criminal court. If, however, an international criminal court were to have concurrent jurisdiction with States, thus supplementing rather than replacing domestic jurisdiction over this area, it would be difficult to understand what reasonable objection States could have to recognition of mass murder as a serious human

---

individuals are not crimes under international law by virtue of their ubiquity". *See* Schachter *General Course in Public International Law*, 178 Hague Recueil (1982) at 78.

[35]   *See* Article II of the Genocide Convention.

[36]   It is termed 'wilful killing'. *See* Arts. 50 of Geneva Convention I, 51 of II, 130 of III, 147 of IV and Art. 85 of 1977 Protocol I. *See generally,* Yves Sandoz, *Implementing International Humanitarian Law*, in International Dimensions of Humanitarian Law (ed. UNESCO) (1988), and Igor Blishchenko, *Responsibility in Breaches of International Humanitarian Law,* in *ibid.*

rights violation. On the other hand, since the definition of 'murder' in domestic legal systems vary, it would have to be more fully spelt out in an international penal code. The lack of such a definition in international law could prove to be the more serious obstacle to general acceptance of this formulation.

The chapeau to Article 21 of the 1991 draft Code refers to 'anyone' which signifies that mass murder by private individuals would come within the court's jurisdiction. In the case of mass murder perpetrated by someone who has no connection with any public authority, the draft Code's reach would extend beyond human rights violations (which concern the rights of the individual or group against the Government under whose jurisdiction it is subject) into the realm of 'peace and security'.

- Torture

Article 21 of the 1991 draft Code does not define 'torture'. An international criminal court very likely would look therefore to the definition set out in the UN Convention against Torture and Other Cruel, Inhuman or Degrading Treatment or Punishment, 1984,[37] especially if the annex to the proposed court's statute were to incorporate the UN Torture Convention so as to include norms against torture in the court's inherent jurisdiction.

Before examining the main substantive issues raised by the construction of 'torture' in Article 1 of the UN Torture Convention, it is convenient to review the prohibition of torture in international humanitarian law as well as the legal status of norms prohibiting torture in general international law.

Article 3 common to the four Geneva Conventions, 1949,[38] prohibits parties from committing at any time or in any place acts of "violence to life and person, ... mutilation, cruel treatment, and torture" or "outrages against human dignity, in particular humiliating and degrading treatment". Common Article 3 establishes a minimum

---

[37]   *Adopted by consensus* by the General Assembly 10 Dec. 1984, *opened for signature* 4 Feb. 1985, *entered into force* 26 June 1987. As of 31 Dec. 1995, there were 93 States-Parties to the Torture Convention of which 3 had not yet ratified.

[38]   *Adopted* on 12 Aug. 1949.

standard of treatment and applies both in time of international as well as non-international armed conflict. Thus, the prohibition of torture in humanitarian law constitutes a fundamental guarantee.

Articles 5(f) and 3(f) of the Statutes of the International Criminal Tribunals for the Former Yugoslavia and Rwanda respectively prohibit torture as a crime against humanity. Article 2(b) of the Yugoslavia Statute refers to "torture or inhuman treatment, including biological experiments" as a grave breach of the Geneva Conventions, 1949, in line with Articles 50, 51, 130 and 147 of Geneva Conventions I, II, III and IV respectively, and Article 85 of Protocol I. The Statute for the International Criminal Tribunal for Rwanda provides for criminal responsibility for the breach of common Article 3 to the four Geneva Conventions thereby establishing clearly that the principle of individual criminal responsibility applies also to violations committed during situations of non-international armed conflict.

The Universal Declaration of Human Rights, 1948,[39] states in Article 5, that: "No one shall be subjected to torture or to cruel, inhuman or degrading treatment or punishment". The International Covenant on Civil and Political Rights, 1966,[40] in Article 7, reiterates Article 5 of the UN Declaration of Human Rights, but also provides that: "In particular, no one shall be subjected without his free consent to medical or scientific experimentation". In Article 10(1), the same Covenant also provides that "All persons deprived of their liberty shall be treated with humanity and with respect for the inherent dignity of the human person".

At the first UN Congress on the Prevention of Crime and the Treatment of Offenders, held on 30 August 1955 in Geneva, the Standard Minimum Rules for the Treatment of Prisoners were adopted and eventually approved by ECOSOC on 31 July 1957. A Code of Conduct for Law Enforcement Officials was adopted by the General Assembly on 17 December 1979.[41]

Regional human rights instruments also provide guarantees against torture. The American Declaration of the Rights and Duties of

---

[39]   *Adopted* by General Assembly resolution 217 A (III) of 10 Dec. 1948.
[40]   *Adopted* by General Assembly resolution 2200 A (XXI) of 16 Dec. 1966, *entered into force* 23 Mar. 1976.
[41]   *Adopted* by resolution 34/169.

Man, 1948,[42] provides in Article XXV that "Every individual who has been deprived of his liberty has the right ... to humane treatment during the time he is in custody." The American Convention on Human Rights, 1969,[43] provides that "No one shall be subjected to torture or to cruel, inhuman, or degrading punishment or treatment. All persons deprived of their liberty shall be treated with respect for the inherent dignity of the human person".[44] Also, the Inter-American Convention to Prevent and Punish Torture, 1985,[45] contains a definition of torture in Article 2. The African Charter on Human and Peoples' Rights, 1981,[46] in Article 5, provides that: "All forms of exploitation and degradation of man, particularly ... torture, cruel or inhuman or degrading punishment and treatment shall be prohibited". Article 3 of the European Convention on Human Rights, 1950, provides that "No one shall be subjected to torture or to inhuman or degrading treatment or punishment."[47]

---

[42]   The American Declaration of the Rights and Duties of Man, Organization of American States resolution XXX, *adopted* by the Ninth International Conference of American States, Bogota, 1948.

[43]   The American Convention on Human Rights, Art. 5(2), *signed* 22 Nov. 1969, *entered into force* 18 July 1978, OAS Treaty Series No. 36 at 1.

[44]   Art. 5(2).

[45]   *Signed* 9 Dec. 1985.

[46]   *Adopted* in June 1981 by the Organization of African Unity Heads of State, *entered into force* 1986.

[47]   *See* the European Convention on Human Rights cases of Greece v. UK Appl. 176/56 of 7 May 1956, Denmark, Norway, Sweden. and Netherlands v. Greece Appl. 3321, 3322, 3323, 3344/67 of Sept. 1967 (Y.B. 1969 [1972]), Ireland v. UK Appl. 5310/71, 5451/72 (Y.B. 15 [1974]), Cyprus v. Turkey, Application 6780/74, 6950/75 of 19 Sept. 1974 and 2 March 1975 (Y.B.18 [1975]) and Denmark, Norway, Sweden, Netherlands, and France v. Greece, Application 9940 -9944/82 of 15 Sept. 1982. *See* Louise Doswald-Beck, *What Does the Prohibition of 'Torture, Inhuman or Degrading Punishment' Mean? The Interpretation of the European Commission and Court of Human Rights,* 25 Netherlands International Law Review (1978). A significant development concerning implementation of international norms against torture is the recent adoption of the European Convention for the Prevention of Torture and Inhuman or Degrading Treatment or Punishment. *Done* at Strasbourg, 26 Nov. 1987, 27 International Legal Materials, 1152-9 (1988). *See further*, Kellberg, *The Case-Law of the European Commission*

In 1975, the General Assembly adopted the Declaration on the Protection of All Persons from Being Subjected to Torture, Cruel, Inhuman or Degrading Treatment or Punishment.[48] In 1984, following seven years of negotiations, the General Assembly adopted the Convention against Torture and Other Cruel, Inhuman or Degrading Treatment or Punishment.[49]

Article 1 of the United Nations Torture Convention defines 'torture' as:

> ... any act by which severe pain or suffering, whether physical or mental, is intentionally inflicted on a person for such purposes as obtaining from him or a third person information or a confession, punishing him for an act he or a third person has committed or is suspected of having committed, or intimidating or coercing him or a third person, or for any reason based on discrimination of any kind, when such pain or suffering is inflicted by or at the instigation of or with the consent or acquiescence of a public official or other person acting in an official capacity. It does not include pain or suffering arising only from, inherent in or incidental to lawful sanctions.

Article 1 thus refers to three main elements: the character of an act of torture; the intention of the perpetrator; and the category of individual who may qualify as a perpetrator.

An act of torture is defined as "infliction of severe pain or suffering", whether physical or mental. Methods of torture are as numerous as the imaginativeness and capability of the torturer. Over the years, the UN Human Rights Committee has heard numerous cases, such as the following:

---

on Human Rights, in The International Fight against Torture (ed. Cassese) (1991) on Art. 3 of the European Convention on Human Rights, 1950.

[48]   *Adopted by consensus* on 9 Dec. 1975.

[49]   *Adopted by consensus* by the General Assembly 10 Dec. 1984, *opened for signature* 4 Feb. 1985, *entered into force* 26 June 1987.

> In order to extract a confession a detainee was hanged by the wrists for 10 days and was subjected to burnings and repeated 'submarino' - immersing the head of the victim in water fouled by blood, urine and vomit almost to the point of drowning ... Other alleged acts of torture include: physical beatings, 'planton' - being forced to stand, often hooded, for periods of time as long as four days, insertion of bottles or barrels of automatic rifles into the anus, the 'typist' - squeezing of a detainee's fingers after pieces of wood have been placed between them, the use of hallucinogenic substances, 'electric prods', particularly in the genital region, being forced to remain continually naked during interrogation, and threats of further violence and promises of further cruelty.[50]

Mental torture may involve the infliction of severe pain or suffering through threats or the compelling of the victim to watch his or her family members or other persons being tortured.

The UN Torture Convention's definition[51] underlines the *mens rea* element of the offense: severe pain or suffering must be 'intentionally inflicted'. The definition is not meant to apply to accidental acts or breach of a duty of care.

During the drafting of Article 1, some Government representatives argued that the definition should indicate the purposes for which torture may be inflicted, whereas others preferred a more formal definition, without specific references. Enumeration of such purposes would risk unduly narrowing the application of the Torture Convention for technical considerations. In particular, cases of intentional infliction

---

[50]   *See further* Paul R. Williams, Treatment of Detainees: Examination of Issues Relevant to Detention by the United Nations Human Rights Committee (1990) at 32.

[51]   Arguably, Article 1 of the Convention is not sufficiently precise as to define torture, but merely to describe it, because the list of illustrative examples is non-exhaustive. Where an individual is accused of having inflicted severe pain or suffering by means not specifically mentioned in Article 1, defense counsel would likely argue that to apply the Convention to the accused would violate the principle *nullum crimen sine lege*.

of pain or suffering might be excluded from the scope of Article 1 merely because they involved a particular purpose not anticipated by the drafters.

Article 1 represents a compromise between these two positions. It refers to "such purposes as obtaining from him or a third person information or a confession, punishing him for an act he or a third person has committed or is suspected of having committed, or intimidating or coercing him or a third person, or for any reason based on discrimination of any kind". Thus, in order to avoid an undue narrowing of the Convention's scope, Article 1 illustrates rather than enumerates the kinds of acts that constitute torture.[52]

However, a number of commentators as well as those involved in the drafting process, such as Professor Tardu, have expressed strong misgivings about the enumerative approach employed in Article 1 as too narrow:

> It does not include, in particular, the infliction of pain for the purpose of scientific experiment without informed consent. This is a most surprising omission, considering that such experiments in Nazi concentration camps had been met with criminal penalties by several Allied Military Tribunals in 1945 under post-Nuremberg legislation. They were condemned by UN resolutions and prohibited in global terms by Article 7 of the UN Covenant. The alarming impression may be gathered of a retreat from this earlier condemnation. ... The list does not include, either, the infinite range of tortures committed out of jealousy, revenge or other personal motivations not 'based on discrimination'.[53]

---

[52]   *See* Herman Burgers and Hans Danelius, The United Nations Convention against Torture: A Handbook on the Convention against Torture and Other Cruel, Inhuman or Degrading Treatment or Punishment (1988) at 118.

[53]   Maxime E. Tardu, *The United Nations Convention against Torture and Other Cruel and Inhuman or Degrading Treatment or Punishment,* 56(4) Nordic Journal of International Law (1987) at 305.

Burgers and Danelius, both participants in the drafting process, register similar concerns that torture committed by a public official for private motives, such as revenge or sadistic pleasure, conceivably might not be covered by Article 1. However, they suppose that:

> ... even where a sadistic motive is predominating, there is normally also an element of punishment or intimidation which would bring the act under the definition of article 1. Moreover, it can often be assumed that where a public official performs such an act, there is also to some extent a public policy to tolerate or to acquiesce in such acts.[54]

One would hope that an international criminal court would interpret Article 1 broadly in order to overcome this ambiguity.[55] The words 'such as' are intended to be illustrate by way of example. However, the purposes enumerated are not only vague but too different from one another to indicate clearly what kinds of acts are prohibited.

The third element of Article 1 concerns the category of individual that may qualify as perpetrator of torture. During the drafting of the Convention, a number of Government representatives indicated that they considered the prohibition of torture should apply to any individual person regardless of public official rank or capacity. Other States felt that only public officials should be liable, which could mean however that acts perpetrated by agents who were not public officials or by private persons with the tacit support of the Government, would not be covered.

The Torture Convention, as finally drafted, covers acts 'inflicted by or at the instigation of or with the consent or acquiescence of a public official or other person acting in an official capacity'. States felt that they could not be held responsible for acts perpetrated beyond

---

[54]   *See* Burgers and Danelius, *supra* note 52 at 119.

[55]   Article 1 does not imply that the purposes for which torture may be inflicted are necessarily prohibited in themselves. In other words, employing a certain level of coercion or intimidation to obtain information in the pursuit of a criminal investigation is considered not prohibited as long as such methods do not involve the infliction of severe pain or suffering or do not breach other norms of international human rights or humanitarian law.

the public sphere and that privately motivated acts would normally be subject to the regular domestic criminal prosecution process. The Convention is intended to prohibit cases of inhuman treatment perpetrated by public officials or individuals acting with at least a colour of public authority, as in the *Caire Claim*,[56] concerning the case in which a French national in Mexico was murdered by Mexican soldiers after he refused to give in to their attempts to extort money from him. The Arbitral Commission applied the doctrine of objective responsibility in holding that:

> It is generally agreed that acts committed by officials and agents of a State entail the international responsibility of that State, even if the perpetrator did not have specific authorization. ...
> But in order to be able to admit this so-called objective responsibility of the State for acts committed by its officials or organs outside their competence, they must have acted at least to all appearances as competent officials or organs, or they must have used powers or methods appropriate to their official capacity.

Apparent rather than actual competence was sufficient to engage the responsibility of the State in the *Caire Claim*.[57] However, Article 1 of the Torture Convention does not concern acts perpetrated purely in a non-governmental context. The compromise formula adopted by the Convention's drafters sweeps in individuals, such as militia members, who may perpetrate acts of torture with the support or toleration of the government, while maintaining the qualification that there must be at least 'instigation', 'consent' or 'acquiescence' on the part of a public official or person acting in such a capacity that brings the matter into the public realm.

---

[56]   *Caire Claim*, (France v. Mexico) French-Mexican Claims Commission, 5 Reports of International Arbitral Awards (1929) 516.

[57]   *See also Youmans Claim* (US v. Mexico) 4 Reports of International Arbitral Awards (1926) 110, in which compensation was awarded where Mexican troops, ordered to quell a mob riot against three American nationals in Mexico, instead attacked and participated in the killing of the three Americans.

In contrast, the chapeau to Article 21 of the 1991 draft Code refers to 'an individual' which would cover any person regardless as to whether he or she held any position, or possessed any colour of public authority. It would therefore appear that the 1991 draft Code's formula concerning competence *ratione personae* in respect of the prohibition of torture is less problematic than that of Article 1 of the Torture Convention. However, the very fact that States were unwilling to recognize the scope of Article 1 of the Torture Convention, as extending to any individual, may indicate that, at the time of the Convention's adoption, there was insufficient support for broad norms prohibiting torture relative to the class of perpetrator covered. This very same hesitancy on the part of some States could pose an obstacle to the adoption of a prohibition of torture if drafted the same way in an international penal code.

The last sentence of Article 1 of the Convention makes clear that the term 'torture': "does not include pain or suffering arising only from, inherent in or incidental to lawful sanctions". During the drafting of the Convention, it was argued that:

> the Convention was intended to strengthen the already existing prohibition of torture in international law, it was not intended to lead to a reform of the system of penal sanctions in different States and that, if that had been the intention, the Convention would have been unacceptable to a number of countries.[58]

In that case, Article 1 should have referred to standards that limit the validity of lawful sanctions. As Burgers and Danelius recount, the original Swedish draft referred to the Standard Minimum Rules for the Treatment of Prisoners as providing a set of criteria by which to determine the conformity of domestic 'lawful sanctions' to international human rights standards. However, such a reference to the Standard Minimum Rules - a non-binding instrument - was considered by many States to be unacceptable in a binding instrument.[59]

---

[58]   *See* Burgers and Danelius, *supra* note 52 at 121.
[59]   *Ibid.*

The unfortunate result is that the Torture Convention's definition of torture contains a major loophole, which if incorporated in a code of crimes for a permanent international criminal court, would severely weaken the court's effectiveness in regard to this serious human rights violation.[60]

Article 2(2) of the Torture Convention affirms the non-derogability of the Convention's norms prohibiting torture, even in time of war or other public emergency. There are provisions concerning the inadmissibility of superior orders as a defense (Article 2(3)) the inadmissibility in evidence of statements arising out of torture (Article 15) and the right of victims to receive compensation (Article 14).

In addition to a lack of clarity in the UN Torture Convention's definition of 'torture', there remains substantial uncertainty as to the legal status of norms prohibiting torture. At present, many States have not ratified the Torture Convention. By way of comparison, the Convention on the Rights of the Child, adopted only on 20 November 1989, had obtained 190 States Parties as of 31 December 1995 (3 of which had not ratified), whereas by the same date, the Torture Convention had obtained only 93 signatures, 13 of which had not been followed by ratification. With the lack of widespread recognition of the Convention's provisions, it cannot be stated that the norms set out therein have attained the status of customary international law. As discussed above, many widely ratified treaties currently in force prohibit torture, but do not define the term. The effect of these conventional guarantees has always been limited by the absence of a definition in international law of 'torture' - as well as the lack of strong implementation mechanisms - problems left unresolved by Article 1 of the Torture Convention.

Worse, a great many Governments are shockingly and blatantly dishonest about the question of torture in their countries.

---

[60] Former United Nations Special Rapporteur on Torture, Mr. Kooijmans, explains that in response to his having brought to the attention of certain Governments cases of flogging, amputation and other forms of corporal punishment by the authorities, these Governments responded that such punishments were approved by the population, authorized by religious dictates and codified in law. They therefore constituted 'lawful sanctions' in the opinion of such Governments. *See* e.g. E/CN.4/1986/15, 19 Feb. 1986, para. 2.

Despite actual Government toleration or even support of the use of torture by law enforcement officials and indications that torture is perpetrated systematically in a great number of countries around the globe, on a widespread and systematic basis,[61] every Government consistently denounces torture at the international level. Guarantees against torture, cruel and other inhuman treatment are found in the constitutions and legislation of most countries of the world.[62] No government denies that torture is prohibited by international law. However, reports of human rights organs of the United Nations, including those of the UN Special Rapporteur on Torture, Amnesty International as well as many other human rights NGOs,[63] indicate that torture is practised extensively in many countries. A government, particularly those controlled by the military, may ignore, tolerate or support the use of torture, perhaps because it lacks the political determination to effectively suppress it, or as a method by which to brutalize and intimidate the political opposition or the public in general.

In this context, it is necessary to consider whether international legal norms prohibiting torture can be considered part of international customary law, specifically, in terms of the two principal elements of custom: general State practise and *opinio juris sive necessitatis.*[64]

---

[61]   *See e.g.* Amnesty International, Report 1996 and *ibid.*

[62]   For specific legal measures enacted in national laws, *see* Report by the Special Rapporteur, Kooijmans *supra* note 60 at paras. 69-94.

[63]   *See e.g.* Human Rights Watch World Global Report on Prisons 1995 at xviii which states: "The world community must begin to take seriously its responsibilities toward people in prison. Domestic politics and indifference, reinforced by financial stringency, often block any attempt to improve prison conditions, and outside pressure is necessary to produce change. ... Also, though UN standards have been much criticized for vagueness and imprecision, they are widely known and accepted in principle. Yet, many of these standards are clearly violated routinely and systematically throughout the world."

[64]   As Condorelli has put it: "The fact is that custom develops through a process of 'social sedimentation', i.e. one resulting from the accumulation of the patterns of behaviour and convictions of the members of a given society, the international society." *See* Luigi Condorelli, *Custom*, in International Law: Achievements and Prospects (ed. Bedjaoui) (1991) at 181.

In the *North Sea Continental Shelf Cases*,[65] the Court stated that:

> ... although the passage of only a short period of time is not necessarily, or of itself, a bar to the formation of a new rule of customary international law on the basis of what was originally a purely conventional rule, an indispensable requirement would be that within the time period in question, short though it might be, State practice, including that of States whose interests are specially affected, should have been both extensive and virtually uniform in the sense of the provision invoked - and should moreover have occurred in such a way as to show a general recognition that a rule of law or legal obligation is involved.

This pronouncement has been consistently followed in other ICJ cases and in the decisions of other judicial bodies.

It is undeniable that, as regards the prohibition of torture, States have failed to bring their actual practice into conformity with their official statements. As Condorelli remarks:

> If a significant number of States behave in practice differently to how they believe they should act (or to how they declare themselves obliged to act) the fact of the matter is that they do not really believe what they say they believe![66]

This might seem to be rather obvious. However, the point bears emphasis since many human rights advocates frequently insist that norms prohibiting torture constitute customary international law. To be sure, torture is a most horrible evil that must be eradicated. It may

---

[65]   *North Sea Continental Shelf Cases* (Federal Republic of Germany v. Denmark) (Federal Republic of Germany v. The Netherlands) 1969 ICJ Reports 3. The issue was whether rules prescribing delimitation of the continental shelf, according as provided for in Article 6 of the Geneva Convention on the Continental Shelf, 1958, formed customary law.

[66]   Condorelli, *supra* note 64 at 188.

even appear to some that not to assert the customary status of international norms against torture is tantamount in some way to condoning this odious practise.

However, an unsupported pronouncement to the effect that international legal norms prohibiting torture constitute customary law represents a classic case of wishful thinking. It certainly ought to be the case that States recognize the meaning and validity of the legal prohibition of torture, along with every other serious human rights violation, not only in their statements but in practise. Yet the reality is that 'extensive and virtually uniform' practise against torture simply does not exist at present. An unwarranted insistence that norms prohibiting torture constitute customary international law may even play into the hands of recalcitrant governments by lending the erroneous impression of substantially uniform and extensive practise respecting such norms when the very contrary is actually the case.

As Simma and Alston argue forcefully, there is an increasing tendency to shortcut the issue of the legal status of a norm by reverting to custom as its source:

> In particular, if customary law can be construed or approached in such a way as to supply a relatively comprehensive package of norms which are applicable to all States, then the debate over the sources of international human rights law can be resolved without much further ado. Given the fundamental importance of the human rights component of a just world order, the temptation to adapt or reinterpret the concept of customary law in such a way as to ensure that it provides the 'right' answers is strong, and at least to some, irresistible.[67]

As the authors argue, the International Court of Justice's reminder in the *Nicaragua Case*[68] that breach of a legal norm must be considered

---

[67]   Bruno Simma and Philip Alston, *The Sources of Human Rights Law: Custom, Jus Cogens, and General Principles*, 12 Australian Yearbook of International Law (1992) at 83.

[68]   *Case concerning Military and Paramilitary Activities in and against Nicaragua* (Nicaragua v. United States) (Merits) 1986 ICJ Reports 3.

as a breach rather than as proof of a new norm *de lege ferenda*, only makes sense "in those cases in which State practice and *opinio juris* have had a chance to establish themselves solidly in an initial, formative stage".[69] In other words, in the case of a customary rule of international law, there must first be an established rule, and this requires more than statements, namely settled practise in conformity with the sense of legal obligation.

- Slavery, Servitude or Forced Labour

Slavery and slavery-like practises have not been substantially eradicated as one might suppose. They continue not only to be very widespread but pervasive. Such practises comprise many different forms,[70] including chattel-slavery, apartheid, colonialism, involuntary marriage, traffic in women and children, exploitation for the purposes of forced prostitution, sale of women, killings for reasons of dowry, debt bondage, exploitation of child labour, forced labour, exploitation of hard-drug addicts, illicit traffic in migrant workers as well as traditional forms of slavery.[71]

---

[69]   Simma and Alston, *supra* note 67 at 97.

[70]   *See generally* Updating of the Report on Slavery Submitted to the Sub-Commission in 1966: Report by Benjamin Whitaker, Special Rapporteur; E/CN.4/Sub.2/1982/20 of 5 July 1982, which employs these categories in the structure of Part 1 of the report entitled 'General Observations: the Scope of the Problem'.

[71]   Arguably, genital mutilation of female children, represents a slavery-like practice in so far as it constitutes an extreme form of the subjugation of women. This widespread practice, deeply rooted in the cultural norms of numerous countries, is frequently defended as a legitimate expression of cultural norms rather than as an attempt to disfigure or to control female sexuality. *See further* Female Circumcision, Excision and Infibulation: Facts and Proposals for Change: Report of Minority Rights Group (1980). *See further* Kirsten Lee, *Female Genital Mutilation: Medical Aspects and the Rights of Children,* in 2 International Journal of Children's Rights (1994); William J. House, *The Status of Women in the Sudan*, 26(2) The Journal of Modern African Studies (1988); and Efua Dorkenoo and Scilla Elworthy, *Female Genital Mutilation: Proposals for Change*, (Report of Minority Rights Group International) (1992) which explains the main motives for and functions of female genital mutilation.

In his report on slavery, the Special Rapporteur on Slavery to the Sub-commission on Prevention of Discrimination and Protection of Minorities, Mr. Benjamin Whitaker, cites a number of examples to indicate the extent of slavery in various periods, such as the transport of some 29 million slaves from Africa between the tenth and nineteenth centuries, the use of slave camps by the Nazi Government from 1942 to 1945, the use of slave labour by the Soviet Union, as well as Japan during the Second World War, and the extensive use of indentured and bonded labour by imperial Great Britain. The Special Rapporteur suggests that these, and a plethora of other examples, evidence:

> (a) the near universality of such phenomena; (b) the
> recentness of some of the most grave instances, both
> in terms of numbers and of atrocity; and (c) the failure
> of people - including of so-called developed nations -
> always to recognize the fact of such events happening
> within their own borders, even in countries which
> possess the benefit of considerable press and aca-
> demic resources.[72]

Moreover, one of the lasting effects of slavery is the persistence of a sense of inferiority, perhaps many generations following abolition of the practise in question.[73]

International legal norms for the suppression of slave-trading date back to 1815, when the Major Powers condemned the slave trade and endeavoured to outlaw slavery on moral grounds, at the Congress of Vienna. Responding to British public opinion, Castlereagh urged condemnation of slavery and the slave trade at the Congress. A declaration condemning the slave trade was annexed to the Final Act of the Congress. Slaves that fell into the hands of the

---

[72] Updating of the Report on Slavery Submitted to the Sub-Commission in 1966: Report by Benjamin Whitaker, Special Rapporteur; E/CN.4/Sub.2/1982/20 of 5 July 1982 at para. 28.

[73] *Ibid.* at para.19. *See further* the reports of the Anti-Slavery Society or the reports of Human Rights Watch / Africa, such as Children of Sudan: Slaves, Street Children and Child Soldiers (1995).

signatory Powers were to be considered free persons. Cassese[74]
cites other forces as more important in the outlawing of slavery,
namely, the rise of the Quaker movement, growing commercial
competition from newly independent American slave States, the new
supply of cheap labour for British interests in India, which eliminated
British reliance on slavery, and also Legislative Union in Ireland (1800)
that brought Irish representatives, with no financial stake in the slave-
trade, to the British Parliament where they could freely voice abolition-
ist sentiments.

Whatever the precise economic and political motivations to
outlaw slavery, the right not to be subjected to slavery antedates most
other human rights guarantees in international law by almost a century
and a half.

Since the Congress of Vienna, several international agreements have affirmed and reiterated the duty of States to prosecute
slave-traders. These agreements were developed through the final
acts adopted upon conclusion of a number of international conferences, held under the auspices of the Concert of Europe system and
beyond, namely the 1822 Declaration Respecting the Abolition of the
Slave Trade, adopted at the Congress of Verona, the 1841 Treaty for
the Suppression of the African Slave Trade adopted in London, the
1885 General Act of the Conference Respecting the Congo adopted
in Berlin, the 1890 Convention relative to the Slave Trade and
Importation into Africa of Firearms, Ammunition, Spirituous Liquors
and the 1890 Treaty between Great Britain and Spain for the
Suppression of the African Slave Trade, both adopted in Brussels, the
1910 International Convention for the Suppression of the White Slave
Traffic adopted in Paris, and the 1921 Convention International
Convention for the Suppression of the Traffic in Women and Children
adopted in Geneva.[75]

---

[74]   *See* Antonio Cassese, International Law in a Divided World (1986) at
52-53.
[75]   *See* Cherif Bassiouni, *Enslavement as an International Crime*, 23(2)
New York University Journal of International Law and Politics (1991) which
provides a useful summary of each of these and other conventions relating
to the prohibition of slavery and slavery-like practises. *See also* Nina Lassen,
*Slavery and Slavery-Like Practices: United Nations Standards and Implemen-
tation*, 57(2) Nordic Journal of International Law (1988); Arjuna Naidu, *The*

The International Slavery Convention of 1926,[76] the first comprehensive multilateral convention to define slavery, defines it as "... the status or condition of a person over whom any or all of the powers attaching to the right of ownership are exercised."[77] The Convention obliges states to prohibit slavery through domestic law. Specifically, the High Contracting Parties are obliged "... to take all necessary measures to prevent compulsory or forced labour from developing into conditions analogous to slavery."[78] The Convention tries to ensure that the exaction of compulsory or forced labour is permitted only under narrowly specified conditions and does not degenerate into slavery.[79] For example, forced labour is allowable only under certain circumstances and only where administered by a government organ, rather than executed by private interests. Parties to the Convention are obliged to impose severe penalties for violations of national laws implementing the Convention.[80]

Thirty years after its adoption, the 1926 Slavery Convention was augmented by the Supplementary Convention on the Abolition of Slavery, the Slave Trade, and Institutions and Practices Similar to Slavery.[81] In the 1956 Supplementary Convention, the act of

---

Right to be Free from Slavery, Servitude and Forced Labour, 20(1) Comparative and International Law Journal of Southern Africa (1987); and Kathryn Zoglin, *United Nations Action against Slavery: A Critical Evaluation*, 8(2) Human Rights Quarterly (1986).

[76] *Adopted* by the League of Nations 25 Sept. 1926, *entered into force*, 9 Mar. 1927, *amended* by a Protocol of 7 Dec. 1953 in New York. The Convention *entered into force as amended* on 7 July 1955.

[77] Art. 1(1).

[78] Art. 5.

[79] Article 5(3) of the 1926 Slavery Convention provides that: "In all cases, the responsibility for any recourse to compulsory or forced labour shall rest with the competent central authorities of the territory concerned."

[80] Art. 6.

[81] *Adopted* by a Conference of Plenipotentiaries convened by ECOSOC resolution 608 (XXI) of 30 Apr. 1956, *done* at Geneva, 7 Sept. 1956, *entered into force*, 30 Apr. 1957. The Supplementary Convention obliges State Parties to bring about progressively and as soon as possible the complete abolition or abandonment of institutions and practices similar to slavery, including such practices as debt bondage, serfdom, the promise or gift of a woman in marriage without her consent in exchange for payment, liability of

conveying slaves "... shall be a criminal offence under the laws of the States Parties to this Convention and persons convicted thereof shall be liable to very severe penalties."[82]

The International Labour Organisation, which has as its special mandate the improvement of conditions of work everywhere, has assumed a distinct role in international efforts for the elimination of slavery. In 1930, the ILO adopted the Forced Labour Convention (No.29) which defines 'forced labour' as all work or service "exacted from any person under the menace of any penalty and for which the said person has not offered himself voluntarily."[83] The Abolition of Forced Labour Convention (No.105) was adopted in 1957, obliging Members of the ILO to suppress, and not to make use of, any form of forced or compulsory labour, as a means of political coercion, discipline, or punishment for having participated in strikes, or to mobilize labour for purposes of economic development, or as a means of racial, social, national or religious discrimination.

Since 1945, the prohibition against slavery has been reiterated and reaffirmed in several international human rights instruments.[84] In most of these instruments, the right not to be subjected to slavery is expressly non-derogable.[85]

The white-slave traffic (i.e. the transboundary movement of persons entrapped and forced into prostitution), represents a contem-

---

a woman to be inherited upon the death of her husband to another person, and various kinds of exploitation of child labour.

[82]   *See* Arts. 3, 5 and 6.

[83]   Art. 2. *See also* the Forced Labour (Indirect Compulsion) Recommendation, 1930, No.35.

[84]   Article 5 of the Universal Declaration of Human Rights, 1948, provides that: "No one shall be held in slavery or servitude; slavery and the slave trade shall be prohibited in all their forms." *See also* Art. 8 of the International Covenant on Civil and Political Rights, 1966, Art. XXXIV of the American Declaration of the Rights and Duties of Man, 1948; Art. 4 of the European Convention on Human Rights, 1950; Art. 6 of the American Convention on Human Rights, 1969; and Art. 5 of the African Charter on Human and Peoples' Rights, 1981.

[85]   *See* Arts. 4(2) of the International Covenant on Civil and Political Rights, 15(2) of the European Convention on Human Rights and 27(2) of the American Convention on Human Rights, 1969.

porary form of slavery of international concern.[86] Norms specifically addressing the problem of child labour are contained in the UN Convention on the Rights of the Child, 1989[87] including Article 11, which obliges States to "take measures to combat the illicit transfer and non-return of children abroad." Article 32 prohibits economic exploitation of the child,[88] and Articles 34 to 36, prohibit sexual exploitation, abuse and traffic for such purposes.[89]

The multitude of conventions and evidence of *opinio juris* and general State practice, indicate that the prohibition against slavery, slavery-like practices and slave-trading, forms part of customary law. The peremptory status of norms against slavery was alluded to in the *dictum* of the *Barcelona Traction Case*[90] in which it was held that all States have a legal interest in their safeguard. Moreover, in view of the relatively consistent formulation of the right not to be subjected to

---

[86]   *See* the Convention for the Suppression of the Traffic in Persons and the Exploitation of the Prostitution of Others, *approved* by General Assembly resolution 317(IV) of 2 Dec. 1949, *entered into force*, 25 July 1951 and the International Agreement of 18 May 1904 for the Suppression of the White Slave Traffic, *as amended* by the Protocol, *approved* by the General Assembly on 3 Dec. 1948. *See also* George Hicks, The Comfort Women: Sex Slaves of the Japanese Imperial Forces (1995); Ustinia Dolgopol and Snehal Paranjape, *Comfort Women: an Unfinished Ordeal*, International Commission of Jurists (1994); The Flesh Trade: the Trafficking of Women and Children in Pakistan: Lawyers for Human Rights and Legal Aid (1993).
[87]   *Adopted unanimously* 20 Nov. 1989, *opened for signature* 26 Jan. 1990, *entered into force* 2 Sept. 1990.
[88]   Article 32 affirms that: "States recognize the right of the child to be protected from economic exploitation and from performing any work that is likely to be hazardous or to interfere with the child's education, or to be harmful to the child's health or physical, mental, spiritual, moral or social development."
[89]   *See* Commission on Human Rights resolution 1992/74 of 5 Mar. 1992 on the Programme of Action for the Prevention of the Sale of Children, Child Prostitution and Child Pornography. *See generally* the Reports of the Working Group on Contemporary Forms of Slavery and E/CN.4/Sub.2/1995/ 28/Add.1 of 13 June 1995 on the traffic on the draft programme of action on the traffic in persons and the exploitation of the prostitution of others.
[90]   *Barcelona Traction Power & Light Co. Case*, (Belgium v. Spain) 1970 ICJ Reports at paras. 33-34.

slavery and concerted efforts to eradicate slavery, it seems that international norms against slave-trading and slavery constitute *jus cogens.* Thus, the 1991 draft Code's provision on individual criminal responsibility for slavery is strongly supported by the *lex lata* and represents codification rather than progressive development of the law.

It is therefore sufficient that Article 21 of the 1991 draft Code refers simply to "establishing or maintaining over persons a status of slavery, servitude or forced labour", rather than to spell out the prescriptive content of the norm in detail, which is done in a number of the conventions as discussed above.

Article 21 refers to *maintenance* of a person in the status of slavery. Thus, the provision could be applied to practices of slavery which began prior to Article 21 having gained the force of law without offending the principle of *nullum crimen sine lege.* Practices of slavery already in existence would therefore come within the competence *ratione temporis* of an international criminal court with jurisdiction over crimes against the peace and security of mankind.

- Persecution on Social, Political, Racial, Religious or Cultural Grounds

Article 21 of the 1991 draft Code is broader than Article 6(c) of the Nuremberg Charter[91] (which covers only political, racial and religious grounds), adding cultural and social grounds of persecution.

The principal element of persecution is not a particular degree of oppression, subjugation or tyranny, but the presence of discrimination according to a prohibited ground. However, Article 21's prohibition of 'persecution on social, political, racial, religious or cultural grounds' does not make clear what kinds and what degree of seriousness of persecution lead to individual criminal responsibility. Persecution may be extremely serious, or it may be frivolous and insignificant (relative to other crimes against the peace and security of mankind). For example, a broad reading of the provision could make unequal distribution of public financial assistance on the basis of social or cultural grounds qualify as 'persecution' where some such

---

[91]   Command Paper 6903. His Majesty's Stationery Office (1945).

groups did not receive the same level of assistance as others. A narrow reading might cover only very serious kinds of acts, such as murder, torture, genocide or apartheid, in which case the article would not appear to add significantly to provisions in the draft Code that address these specific kinds of violations. Not surprisingly, some ILC members have objected to retention of 'persecution' as a crime in the draft Code on the ground that it is not clearly defined in international law.

The word 'persecution' is ambiguous and elastic, simply because there is no generally recognized definition of what persecution entails in the context of international criminal law. However, the term 'persecution' as used in international refugee law, following that laid down in Article 1(a)(2) Convention relating to the Status of Refugees, 1951,[92] as amended by the Protocol relating to the Status of Refugees, 1967,[93] refers to persecution "for reasons of race, religion, nationality, membership of a particular social group or political opinion". While the term 'persecution' in the context of international refugee law may not necessarily denote the same meaning for the purposes of international criminal law, it is clear that international legal definitions of 'persecution' refers to the effects of discriminatory actions, measures or policies.

The main significance of the principle of non-discrimination, a principle well established in international law, derives from its procedural role in governing the application of international human rights norms in general. Thus, the UN Charter lists, as one of the purposes of the United Nations, the achievement of:

> ... international co-operation in solving international problems of an economic, social, cultural, or humanitarian character, and in promoting and encouraging respect for human rights and for fundamental freedoms

---

[92] Convention relating to the Status of Refugees, 189 UNTS 150, *adopted* 28 July 1951, *entered into force* 22 April 1954.

[93] Protocol relating to the Status of Refugees, 606 UNTS 267, *adopted* 31 Jan. 1967, *entered into force* 4 Oct. 1967.

for all without distinction as to race, sex, language, or religion; ...[94]

Rules on non-discrimination relate to individual criminal responsibility in international law in at least two important ways. First, the principle of non-discrimination forms part of the prescriptive content of a number of international human rights norms; the crimes of slavery, apartheid and genocide, for example, are defined in terms of non-discrimination. Second, the principle of non-discrimination prescribes how human rights norms in general are to be applied.

Numerous instruments guarantee the right not to be subject to discrimination.[95] Because the most serious human rights violations frequently are committed against a particular group, targeted on the basis of certain immutable characteristics, systematic discrimination may provide the international community with a clear signal in advance that particularly serious violations are about to follow. Thus,

---

[94]   Art. 1(3).   *See also* the preamble and Arts. 13(1)(b), 55(c), 76(c), 62(2), and 68.

[95]   *See* the UN Declaration on the Elimination of All Forms of Racial Discrimination, *proclaimed* by General Assembly resolution 1904 (XVIII) of 20 Nov. 1963; ILO Convention No. 111 Concerning Discrimination in Respect of Employment and Occupation, *adopted* on 25 June 1958, *entered into force* 15 June 1960; ILO Convention No.100 Concerning Equal Remuneration for Men and Women Workers for Work of Equal Value, *adopted* on 29 June 1951, *entered into force* 23 May 1953; UNESCO Convention against Discrimination in Education, *adopted* on 14 Dec. 1960, *entered into force* 22 May 1962 and the 1962 Protocol; Declaration on the Elimination of Discrimination against Women, *proclaimed* by General Assembly resolution 2263 (XXII) of 7 Nov. 1967; Convention on the Elimination of All Forms of Discrimination against Women, *adopted* by General Assembly resolution 34/180 on 18 Dec. 1979, *entered into force* on 3 Sept. 1981; Declaration on the Elimination of All Forms of Intolerance and of Discrimination Based on Religion or Belief, *proclaimed* by General Assembly resolution 36/55 of 25 Nov. 1981; Declaration on Fundamental Principles concerning the Contribution of the Mass Media to Strengthening Peace and International Understanding to the Promotion of Human Rights and to Countering Racialism, Apartheid and Incitement to War, *proclaimed* by UNESCO on 28 Nov. 1978; and the Declaration on Race and Racial Prejudice, *adopted and proclaimed* by UNESCO on 27 Nov. 1978.

discriminatory rhetoric and treatment of a particular minority, such as in Rwanda, and in a number of republics of the former Yugoslavia, foreshadowed the eventual expression of religious and ethnic hatred in the form of genocide.

Finally 'persecution' should not be treated as if it were a substantive element of an international penal code's competence *ratione materiae*. It would be better to have inserted a provision that guarantees the right against 'persecution on social, political, racial, religious or cultural grounds' as a separate provision in the first part of the 1991 draft Code or even in a redrafted introductory paragraph to Article 21. If set out as a general procedural principle in the first part of the 1991 draft Code, the essential content of 'persecution on social, political, racial, religious or cultural grounds' would relate *generally* to the application of all crimes covered in the draft Code.

- *Deportation or Forcible Transfer of Population*

Deportation or forcible transfer of population, aimed at a particular target group (on the basis of racial, ethnic, cultural, religious or national origin or other such basis) is inherently discriminatory in that it fails to accommodate consideration of the merits of each individual's particular situation.[96] In other words, deportation or forcible transfer of population involves the displacement of a group of persons on the basis of the immutable characteristics of its members, and not according to the particular aspects of each person.

The Nuremberg Charter definitions of 'war crimes' and 'crimes against humanity' include "deportation to slave labour or for any other purpose of civilian population of or in occupied territory" and "deport-

---

[96] The term 'deportation' implies forcible movement of persons (either individually or *en masse*) to a place beyond the territory of the deporting State whereas the term 'forcible transfer of population' implies the forced relocation of persons within the territory of a single State. However, this distinction should not be overemphasized since neither the *lex lata* nor the draft Code provision are based on it. Moreover, the term 'forcible transfer of population' is synonymous with the term 'mass expulsion'. *See* Jean-Marie Henckaerts, Mass Expulsion in Modern International Law and Practice (1995) at 21.

ation, and other inhumane acts committed against any civilian population before or during the war" respectively.[97]

The question of the legal validity of deportation or forcible transfer of population was raised in the Nuremberg Trial case of Hans Frank who, charged with mass deportations contrary to the Nuremberg Charter, and Article 46 of the 1907 Hague Regulations,[98] intended to demonstrate that his Allied accusers were no less legally culpable. In this connection, the defense counsel for Frank pointed out that the Allies had transferred over 10 million ethnic German civilians from Silesia and the Sudetenland to Germany. In fact, pursuant to the Potsdam Agreement of 2 August 1945 concerning the territorial post-World War II settlement, it is estimated that around 16 million ethnic Germans were forcibly transferred from Poland, Czechoslovakia and Hungary, to Germany, and "2 million of them perished during this massive operation which lasted approximately until 1949."[99]

Unfortunately, the Nuremberg Tribunal merely ruled that the Allied forced transfer was irrelevant to the case at hand. Strictly speaking, the Tribunal may have been right, in the sense that its competence under the Nuremberg Charter was to determine individual criminal responsibility of the major Axis war criminals in connection with the Second World War, and not with postwar events. However, as Bassiouni points out,[100] the Nuremberg Tribunal could have entered into the question of the legal validity of population transfer, and the circumstances under which international legal norms prohibit such

---

[97]   Command Paper 6903. His Majesty's Stationery Office (1945). *See* Cherif Bassiouni, Crimes against Humanity in International Criminal Law (1992) at 301-317, which recounts *inter alia* the position of the Allied Powers as regards the Nazi deportations, mass expulsions and forcible transfer of populations during World War II.

[98]   Article 46 of the Hague Regulations respecting the laws and customs of war on land, *adopted* 18 Oct. 1907, provides that: "Family honour and rights, the lives of persons, and private property, as well as religious convictions and practice, must be respected. ... Private property cannot be confiscated."

[99]   Henckaerts, *supra* note 96 at 8. *See further* Alfred de Zayas, *International Law and Mass Populations Transfers*, 16 Harvard International Law Journal (1975) at 228.

[100]   Bassiouni, *supra* note 97 at 310-311.

action, distinguishing between *inter alia*, deportation for purposes of extermination and other serious violations of human rights, and transfer of population in pursuance of the postwar changes in sovereign control over territory. The *lex lata* extant at the time of the Nuremberg Trial supported such a distinction, and thus, would have permitted the Tribunal to differentiate between Nazi deportation in pursuance of the Final Solution and the Allied forcible transfer of ethnic Germans from eastern Europe. Moreover, contemporary international law continues to reflect these distinctions.[101]

Aside from the Nuremberg proceedings, Allied policy makers should not have escaped responsibility for the forcible transfer of ethnic Germans. Allied decision makers knew, or ought to have known, that the forcible transfer of these populations, already on the brink of starvation and suffering from serious diseases exacerbated by years of war, would hasten or directly cause hundreds of thousands of civilian deaths, unless conducted with great care. The inherently perilous character of forcible population transfer requires observance of the highest standard of care.

According to the Fourth Geneva Convention, 1949, which for the first time extended direct humanitarian protection to the civilian population, forcible transfer is only allowable under certain circumstances and for certain purposes. With respect to occupied territories in time of international armed conflict, Article 49 of the Fourth Geneva Convention provides that:

> Individual or mass forcible transfers, as well as deportations of protected persons from occupied territory to the territory of the Occupying Power or to that of any other country, occupied or not, are prohibited, regardless of their motive.

However, Article 49 allows for evacuations to be made, consistent with the main aim of modern international humanitarian law ("to regulate

---

[101]   *Ibid.*

hostilities in order to attenuate their hardships"),[102] by entitling the Occupying Power to:

> undertake total or partial evacuation of a given area if the security of the population or imperative military reasons so demand. Such evacuation may not involve the displacement of protected persons outside the bounds of the occupied territory except when for material reasons it is impossible to avoid such displacement. Persons thus evacuated shall be transferred back to their homes as soon as hostilities in the area in question have ceased.

In addition, an Occupying Power executing a transfer policy, is under an obligation to:

> ensure, to the greatest practicable extent, that proper accommodation is provided to receive the protected persons, that the removals are effected in satisfactory conditions of hygiene, health, safety and nutrition, and that members of the same family are not separated.

Moreover, the Protecting Power is to be informed of any transfers and the Occupying Power is prohibited from detaining protected persons in areas "exposed to the dangers of war" except where the "security of the population or imperative military reasons so demand". Finally, Article 49 also prohibits the occupying Power from deporting or transferring all or part of its own civilian population to territory under its occupation.

Protocol II, which develops and supplements Article 3 common to the four Geneva Conventions, 1949, provides in Article 17, that:

> 1.   The displacement of the civilian population shall not be ordered for reasons related to the conflict unless the security of the civilians involved or imperative

---

[102]   Jean Pictet, Development and Principles of International Humanitarian Law (1985) at 1.

military reasons so demand. Should such displacements have to be carried out, all possible measures shall be taken in order that the civilian population may be received under satisfactory conditions of shelter, hygiene, health, safety and nutrition.

2.   Civilians shall not be compelled to leave their own territory for reasons connected with the conflict.[103]

Parties to the conflict are also prohibited from deportation or forcible transfer of the civilian population for use as 'human shields' to prevent an attack. In this regard, Protocol I provides in Article 51(7), that:

The presence or movements of the civilian population or individual civilians shall not be used to render certain points or areas immune from military operations, in particular in attempts to shield military objectives from attacks or to shield, favour or impede military operations. The Parties to the conflict shall not direct the movement of the civilian population or individual civilians in order to attempt to shield military objectives from attacks or to shield military operations.

The Geneva Conventions, 1949, and 1977 Protocols additional thereto, provide for individual criminal responsibility for deportation or forcible transfer of population in situations of international armed conflict, and perhaps in situations of non-international armed conflict

---

[103]   *See also* Article 35 of the Fourth Geneva Convention, 1949, which provides that: "All protected persons who may desire to leave the territory at the outset of, or during a conflict, shall be entitled to do so, unless their departure is contrary to the national interests of the State. The applications of such persons to leave shall be decided in accordance with regularly established procedures and the decision shall be taken as rapidly as possible. Those persons permitted to leave may provide themselves with the necessary funds for their journey and take with them a reasonable amount of their effects and articles of personal use." Paragraphs 2 and 3 of Article 35 provide for administrative review and the giving of reasons for a decision to refuse application for permission to leave the territory.

as well.[104] Specifically, Article 147 of the Fourth Geneva Convention lists "unlawful deportation or transfer or unlawful confinement of a protected person" as a grave breach of the Conventions giving rise to individual criminal responsibility.

Beyond situations covered by international humanitarian law, no international human rights norm explicitly prohibits deportation or forcible transfer of population. Henckaerts suggests that the Allied Powers' forcible transfer of German populations, following the end of the Second World War, accounts for the fact that neither the Universal Declaration of Human Rights, 1948, nor the European Convention on Human Rights, 1950, address deportation or forcible transfer.[105]

Article 13 of the International Covenant on Civil and Political Rights, 1966, does not address the specific question of mass deportation or forcible transfer of populations, but is nevertheless relevant in providing that:

> An alien lawfully in the territory of a State Party to the present Covenant may be expelled therefrom only in pursuance of a decision reached in accordance with law and shall, except where compelling reasons of national security otherwise require, be allowed to submit the reasons against his expulsion and to have his case reviewed by, and be represented for the purpose before, the competent authority or a person or

---

[104]   See the Preliminary Report of the Independent Commission of Experts established in accordance with Security Council resolution 935: UN Doc. S/1994/1125 of 4 Oct. 1994; and Final Report of the Commission of Experts established pursuant to Security Council resolution 935: UN Doc. S/1994/1405 of 9 Dec. 1994, which consider common Article 3 of the four Geneva Conventions, 1949 and Protocol II additional thereto as providing for individual criminal responsibility, applicable to the situation in Rwanda, which it determined to be a 'non-international armed conflict'. See also Article 4 of the Statute of the International Tribunal for Rwanda, which confers upon the Tribunal "the power to prosecute persons committing or ordering to be committed serious violations of Article 3 common to the Geneva Conventions of 12 August 1949 for the Protection of War Victims, and of Additional Protocol II thereto of 8 June 1977."

[105]   Henckaerts, supra note 96 at 8-9.

persons especially designated by the competent authority.

As Nowak observes, aliens may not be forced to leave their new place of residence where they create a permanent home outside their country of origin. Although the Covenant does not prohibit deportation or forcible transfer, Article 13 establishes procedural guarantees that in effect enjoin a State party from expelling persons *en masse*.[106]

As regards regional human rights guarantees, Article 4 of Protocol No.4, 1963, to the European Convention on Human Rights, 1950, states: "Collective expulsion of aliens is prohibited."[107] Article 22(9) of the American Convention on Human Rights, 1969, provides that: "The collective expulsion of aliens is prohibited." The African Charter of Human and Peoples' Rights, 1981, provides in Article 12(5), that:

> The mass expulsions of non-nationals shall be pro-
> hibited. Mass expulsion shall be that which is aimed at
> national, racial, ethnic or religious groups.

The fact that prohibition of certain kinds of deportation or forcible transfer of population was placed under Article 21 of the 1991 version of the draft Code, which covers serious human rights violations, rather than under Article 22 on war crimes, indicates that the ILC considered deportation or forcible transfer of population, whether committed during war or peace, to entail individual criminal responsibility. For example, it might be extended to prohibit peace-time efforts by State authorities to deport aliens as a means by which

---

[106]   *See* Manfred Nowak, UN Covenant on Civil and Political Rights: CCPR Commentary (1993) at 226: "In its General Comment on the positions of aliens under the Covenant, the Committee went one step further and inferred from the procedural guarantees for the individual that *collective expulsions* of aliens provided by law represent a violation of Art. 13."

[107]   European Convention for the Protection of Human Rights and Fundamental Freedoms securing certain Rights and Freedoms other than Those Already Included in the Convention and in the First Protocol, *adopted* 16 Sept. 1963, *entered into force* 2 May 1968; 58 American Journal of International Law (1964) 334.

to alter the racial or cultural composition of the population in a given territory.[108]

The respective Statutes of the two *ad hoc* international criminal Tribunals contain provisions on deportation. The Statute of the International Criminal Tribunal for the Former Yugoslavia, provides individual criminal responsibility for "unlawful deportation or transfer or unlawful confinement of a civilian" where committed "against persons or property protected under the provisions of the relevant Geneva Convention".[109] Article 5(d) of the same Statute confers upon the Tribunal the power to prosecute persons responsible for deportation directed against any civilian population, regardless of the status of the conflict.

Article 3 of the Statute of the International Criminal Tribunal for Rwanda prohibits deportation as a crime against humanity "when committed as part of a widespread or systematic attack against any civilian population" and adds a further condition, namely, that the attack must be based "on national, political, ethnic, racial or religious grounds". The reference in Article 3 of the Rwanda Tribunal's Statute to 'attack', instead of 'armed conflict' at least appears to lower the threshold of applicability of the norm prohibiting crimes against humanity, although by how much is not clear. It would have been far preferable if the Statute had mentioned neither the condition of the existence of an attack (or the condition of being widespread or systematic) nor 'national, political, ethnic, racial or religious grounds'.

The Commentary to Article 21 of the 1991 draft Code distinguishes between transfer of population to places outside the territory of the State and forcible transfer of population within the territory of a single State.[110] The Commentary also emphasizes that the object of forcible transfer of populations is relevant to determination of culpabil-

---

[108]   *See also* the Commentary to Article 21 in the Draft Report of the International Law Commission on the Work of the Forty-Third Session, Draft Code of Crimes against the Peace and Security of Mankind, 43rd session, (29 Apr.- 19 July 1991), UN Doc. A/CN.4/L.464/Add.4, 15 July 1991 at 29, para. 11.

[109]   *See* Article 2(g) of the Statute.

[110]   *See* Draft Code of Crimes against the Peace and Security of Mankind, A/CN.4/L.464/Add.4 of 15 July 1991, 43rd ILC Session, (Apr. 29 -19 July 1991).

ity. The provision does not contemplate individual criminal responsibility for transfer of population ordered by the authorities on account of natural disasters or to safeguard public health or safety.

In sum, the formula of the 1991 draft Code is to be preferred over those of the pertinent provisions in the two *ad hoc* international criminal Tribunal Statutes, which are unduly narrow.

iii) 1996 Draft Code Provisions on Crimes against Humanity

Article 18 of the 1996 draft Code, as set out below, represents a substantial improvement over Article 21 of the 1991 draft Code:

Crimes against humanity

A crime against humanity means any of the following acts, when committed in a systematic manner or on a large scale and instigated or directed by a government or by any organization or group:

(a) murder;

(b) extermination;

(c) torture;

(d) enslavement;

(e) persecution on political, racial, religious or ethnic grounds;

(f) institutionalized discrimination on racial, ethnic or religious grounds involving the violation of fundamental human rights and freedoms and resulting in seriously disadvantaging a part of the population;

(g) arbitrary deportation or forcible transfer of population;

(h) forced disappearance of persons;

(i) rape, enforced prostitution and other forms of sexual abuse;

(j) other inhumane acts which severely damage physical or mental integrity, health or human dignity, such as mutilation and severe bodily harm.

By replacing the title 'systematic or mass violations of human rights' with 'crimes against humanity', Article 18 implicitly broadens the provision beyond the scope of international human rights law. International human rights law applies primarily in peace-time rather than during armed conflict (except as regards norms from which no exception or derogation is permitted, such as those prohibiting torture which apply even in times of public emergency, including war). Although the application of norms prohibiting crimes against humanity has not always been so broad, it has now become well-established that norms prohibiting crimes against humanity apply equally in situations of peace-time and during armed conflict.

As recounted above in connection with norms on genocide,[111] originally, these norms acquired a legal status with their insertion in the Nuremberg Charter to ensure the Tribunal's competence *ratione materiae* would reach beyond 'crimes against peace' and 'war crimes'. At the drafting stage, the US Government insisted the Nuremberg Charter include the new category of 'crimes against humanity' since norms prohibiting war crimes covered enemy soldiers only and not acts committed by the Government of Germany against its own nationals. Unfortunately, the way the Nuremberg Charter provision on crimes against humanity was drafted, and subsequently amended, made 'crimes against humanity' overlap with 'war crimes' in that an act could only qualify as a 'crime against humanity' if it were factually linked to a 'crime against peace' or a 'war crime' coming within the jurisdiction of the Nuremberg Tribunal.[112]   In other words, the Nuremberg Charter cast the norm prohibiting crimes against humanity as necessarily tied to the events of the Second World War, which thereby restricted the norm in its earlier formulation to acts committed in time of armed conflict, and perhaps only to acts committed in time of international armed conflict.

However, certain developments subsequent to the inception of the Nuremberg Charter loosened this straitjacket and eventually freed the norm from its earlier restrictive interpretation.

The first development in this regard was Control Council Law No. 10 of 20 December 1945, adopted by the Allied Powers' following

---

[111]   *See* Chapter II(1) above.
[112]   *See further*, Sunga, *supra* note 4, Chapter II(4).

Germany's unconditional surrender on 8 May 1945. In Article 2(1c), Control Council Law No. 10 defines 'crimes against humanity' more broadly than Article 6(c) of the Nuremberg Charter, as:

> Atrocities and offenses, including but not limited to murder, extermination, enslavement, deportation, imprisonment, torture, rape, or other inhumane acts committed against any civilian population, or persecutions on political, racial or religious grounds whether or not in violation of the domestic laws of the country where perpetrated.[113]

Not only did Control Council Law No. 10 refer to the enumerated prohibited acts in a non-exhaustive manner, but it omitted any reference to 'armed conflict', thus paving the way for the subsequent expansion of the norm prohibiting crimes against humanity.

Second, since 1954, the International Law Commission's draft Code did not link 'crimes against humanity' with 'before or after the war' which had appeared in Article 6(c) of the Nuremberg Charter nor has the draft Code employed any similar clause.

Third, the meaning of the term 'crimes against humanity' was expanded through its inclusion in multilateral human rights conventions. In particular, the Genocide Convention, 1948, both refers to genocide as a 'crime against humanity' and prohibits acts of genocide whether committed in time of war or peace. Also, the Apartheid Convention, 1973, characterizes apartheid as a 'crime against humanity' and applies both in peace and in war.

These three major developments effectively enlarged the applicability of the norm to cover peace-time situations in addition to its already well-established application to situations of international armed conflict.

It was therefore all the more shocking when the Statute for the International Criminal Tribunal for the Former Yugoslavia made its appearance with a grossly outdated definition of 'crimes against

---

[113] Article 2(3) of Control Council Law No. 10 provides for a list of possible penalties ranging from 'deprivation of some or all civil rights' to 'death'.

humanity', set out in Article 5, as comprising murder, extermination, enslavement, deportation, imprisonment, torture, rape, persecutions on political, racial and religious grounds, and other inhumane acts, "when committed in armed conflict, whether international or internal in character, and directed against any civilian population". This retrograde approach, ignoring a half century of legal development, threatened to set the law back in a giant leap to the past. Fortunately, in the *Dusko Tadic Trial* the Appeals Chambers of the Tribunal ruled against a defense motion to dismiss the case on the grounds the Tribunal lacked jurisdiction *ratione materiae*, holding:

> It is by now a settled rule of customary international law that crimes against humanity do not require a connection to international armed conflict. Indeed, as the Prosecutor points out, customary international law may not require a connection between crimes against humanity and any conflict at all. Thus, by requiring that crimes against humanity be committed in either internal or international armed conflict, the Security Council may have defined the crime in Article 5 more narrowly than necessary under customary international law.[114]

Article 3 of the Statute of the International Criminal Tribunal for Rwanda reflects customary international law more closely in this regard, enumerating as crimes against humanity certain acts "when committed as part of a widespread or systematic attack against any civilian population on national, political, ethnic, racial or religious grounds". Article 3 thus omits any mention of 'armed conflict'. However, it restricts the material scope of the Tribunal to acts committed as part of a 'widespread or systematic attack', thereby distinguishing 'crimes against humanity' from murder, rape, etc. committed as common crimes.

On another point, the 1996 draft Code maintains the phrase 'persecution on political, racial, religious or ethnic grounds'. The

---

[114] The *Prosecutor* v. *Dusko Tadic*, Decision of the Appeals Chamber on the Defense Motion of the Interlocutory Appeal concerning Jurisdiction at 73; Case No. IT-94-1-D, of 2 Oct. 1995.

problem that 'persecution' conceptually should be treated not as a distinct violation of human rights, but as an overarching element to apply to all substantive norms, remains in the 1996 draft Code. In their comments and observations on the 1991 draft Code, the delegates of Australia and the United States underlined this point.[115]

4. WAR CRIMES

i) Background

Individual responsibility for war crimes is provided for in an indirect way in the 1899 and 1907 Hague Conventions concerning the Laws and Customs of War on Land and in the Regulations annexed to each.[116] The main aim of the Hague Regulations in regard to penal enforcement for breaches of laws of war is to oblige States parties to institute proceedings against suspected offenders.[117] Hague Convention IV of 1907 expands the scope of State responsibility for the commission of illegal acts.[118] This codification of customary interna-

---

[115]   *See* Comments and Observations of Governments on the Draft Code of Crimes against the Peace and Security of Mankind adopted on First Reading by the International Law Commission at its 43rd Session, A/CN.4/ 448 of 1 March 1993.

[116]   Article 22 of Hague Convention No. II of 1899 and Hague Convention No. IV, 1907, stipulate that the "right of belligerents to adopt means of injuring the enemy is not unlimited". This stipulation is followed by Article 23 expressly prohibiting certain means of warfare.

[117]   Under Articles 41 of the Regulations to Hague Conventions No. II, 1899, and No. IV, 1907, if an individual acted in a personal capacity in violation of an armistice agreement, the injured State could demand prosecution of the offender and request indemnity for losses sustained. *See* Scott, The Hague Conventions and Declarations of 1899 and 1907 (1915) at 122. Article 56 common to both Regulations provides that seizure, destruction, or intentional damage to historic monuments, works of art and science, is prohibited, and should be made the subject of legal proceedings.

[118]   By Article 3, a "belligerent party which violates the provisions of the said Regulations shall, if the case demands, be liable to pay compensation. It shall be responsible for all acts committed by persons forming part of its armed forces".

tional law maintains the principle that the State, rather than the individual, is responsible under international law for breach of the laws and customs of war.[119]

The Versailles Treaty, 1919,[120] concluded at the end of World War I, stipulates in Articles 228 to 230, that the German Government recognizes the right of the Allied Powers to try persons accused of having committed acts in violation of the laws and customs of war and it obliges the German Government to hand over German suspects to the Allied Powers for prosecution. Similar provisions were inserted in other peace treaties following the end of the World War I.[121]

Development of the legal concept of 'war crimes' was promoted by the London International Assembly, a non-official body whose members were designated by Allied Governments during the Second World War. The Assembly created a Commission which, after lengthy consideration, concluded that the concept of 'war crimes' evolves as the conduct of war changes in mode and method. It recommended that 'war crimes' should be defined through enumeration of specific criminal acts, instead of being understood as 'violations of the laws of war'. This preference for enumeration tended toward a more flexible approach to the definition of 'war crimes' than the alternative definition of 'war crimes' *stricto sensu* which denoted violations of the laws of war more narrowly construed as those limited in application to specific technical methods in the use of weaponry etc. or to specific situations.[122]

The Allied Powers adopted a broad definition of 'war crimes', construed as covering the preparation and waging of a war of aggression, and crimes committed for the purpose of racial or political

---

[119]   *See* G.I.A.D. Draper, *The Modern Pattern of War Criminality*, 6 Israel Yearbook on Human Rights (1976) at 15. The individual was not responsible in a personal capacity except in so far as States had a right at customary law to try enemy personnel for war crimes.

[120]   *Signed* 28 June 1919.

[121]   *See e.g.* 1920 Treaty of Peace Between the Allied Powers and Turkey (Treaty of Sèvres), *signed* at Sèvres 10 Aug. 1920, but never ratified. The Treaty of Sèvres was replaced by the 1923 Treaty of Lausanne which exempted individuals from criminal responsibility.

[122]   *See* History of the UN War Crimes Commission (1948) at 172.

extermination, wherever committed.[123] Article 6(b) of the Nuremberg Charter[124] provides that 'war crimes' include, but shall not be limited to:

> ... murder, ill-treatment or deportation to slave labour or for any other purpose of civilian population of or in occupied territory, murder or ill-treatment of prisoners of war or persons on the seas, killing of hostages, plunder of public or private property, wanton destruction of cities, towns or villages, or devastation not justified by military necessity.

Norms in the Nuremberg Charter prohibiting breach of laws of war differ substantially from those of classic international law. The adoption of a broad definition of 'war crime' over the concept of 'war crimes *stricto sensu*' following World War II allowed for progressive development of the norm prohibiting war crimes.

Norms prohibiting war crimes form the 'hard core' of international criminal law in the sense that they are much more well-established and more clear and specific in meaning compared to most other kinds of acts encompassed by the 1991 draft Code. It is unnecessary to deal at length with the content and legal status of these norms here since norms on murder, ill-treatment, deportation and slavery have already been discussed *in extenso* above. Moreover, these and other

---

[123]   *Ibid.* The Legal Committee of the Commission recommended that "indiscriminate mass arrests for the purpose of terrorizing the population ... and acts violating family honour and rights, the lives of individuals, religious convictions and liberty of worship" should be included in the definition of 'war crimes'. The Legal Committee opined that the legal basis for this inclusion is the de Martens Preamble to Hague Convention No. IV, 1907, which signifies that the concept of 'war crimes' in international law is not limited to acts covered in the Hague Conventions, but is amenable to change and adaptation as circumstances might require.

[124]   Command Paper 6903 His Majesty's Stationery Office (1945).

war crimes have been treated extensively in scholarly literature to which the reader may refer.[125]

ii) 1991 Draft Code Provisions on War Crimes

Article 22(2) of the 1991 draft Code provides that:

> For the purposes of this Code, an exceptionally serious war crime is an exceptionally serious violation of principles and rules of international law applicable in armed conflict consisting of any of the following acts:
>
> a) acts of inhumanity, cruelty or barbarity directed against the life, dignity or

---

[125] *See e.g.* War Crimes in International Law (ed. Dinstein and Tabory) (1996); The Prosecution of International Crimes (ed. Clark and Sann) (1996); John Honnold, International Crimes (1995); Peter Kooijmans, *The Judging of War Criminals: Individual Responsibility and Jurisdiction*, 8(2) Leiden Journal of International Law (1995); Theodor Meron, *International Criminalization of Internal Atrocities*, 89 American Journal of International Law (1995); Olivier Lanotte, Répression des crimes de guerre: espoir ou utopie (1995); War Crimes: Bosnia and Beyond: (a series of articles in 34(2) Virginia Journal of International Law (1994); Theodor Meron, *War Crimes in Yugoslavia and the Development of International Law*, 88(1) American Journal of International Law (1994); Gavan Davis, Prisoners of the Japanese: POWs of World War II in the Pacific (1994); The Laws of War: a Comprehensive Collection of Primary Documents on International Law governing Armed Conflict (ed. Reisman and Antoniou) (1994); Helen Fein, Discriminating Genocide from War Crimes: Vietnam and Afghanistan Reexamined (1993); Howard Levie, Terrorism in War: the Law of War Crimes (1993); Hillary McCoubrey, War Crimes; the Criminal Jurisprudence of Armed Conflicts (1992); Christine van den Wyngaert, The Suppression of War Crimes under Additional Protocol I in the Humanitarian Law of Armed Conflict: Challenges Ahead (ed. Delissen and Tanja) (1991); Donald A. Wells, War Crimes and Laws of War (2nd ed.) (1991); A.P.V. Rogers, War Crimes Trials under the Royal Warrant: British Practice (1990); Ghislaine Doucet, La qualification des infractions graves au droit international humanitaire (1989); and (ed. Norman Tutorow), War Crimes, War Criminals and War Crimes: an Annotated Bibliography and Source Book (1988).

physical or mental integrity of persons [, in particular wilful killing, torture, mutilation, biological experiments, taking of hostages, compelling a protected person to serve in the forces of a hostile power, unjustifiable delay in the repatriation of prisoners of war after the cessation of active hostilities, deportation or transfer of the civilian population and collective punishment];
b) establishment of settlers in an occupied territory and changes to the demographic composition of an occupied territory;
c) use of unlawful weapons;
d) employing methods or means of warfare which are intended or may be expected to cause, widespread, long-term and severe damage to the natural environment;
e) large-scale destruction of civilian property;
f) wilful attacks on property of exceptional religious, historical or cultural value.

Article 22, originally entitled simply 'War Crimes', was the subject of lengthy and heated debate in the ILC 1991 drafting session. Some members of the ILC argued that Article 22 should cover all 'grave breaches' as set out in the Geneva Conventions, 1949, and 1977 Protocols Additional thereto.[126] However, it was strenuously argued by one member that the draft Code should stipulate individual criminal responsibility to cover only the most serious of war crimes. To accommodate this view, Article 22 is entitled 'Exceptionally Serious War Crimes'.

---

[126] *See* the Geneva Conventions, 1949, and the 1977 Protocols additional thereto.

At its 1991 session, the ILC members could not agree as to whether Article 22 should provide a general definition of 'exceptionally serious war crime' or whether it should also enumerate in detail all war crimes coming within the jurisdiction of the proposed international criminal court. Since these conflicting views could not be reconciled, Article 22 incorporates both approaches.

'Exceptionally serious war crimes' - the terminology of the 1991 draft Code - might be understood to cover only 'grave breaches' as provided for under the Geneva Conventions, 1949. 'Grave breaches' are defined in the Geneva Conventions as involving any of the following acts, if committed against persons or property protected by the Convention:

> wilful killing, torture or inhuman treatment, including biological experiments, wilfully causing great suffering or serious injury to body or health, and extensive destruction and appropriation of property, not justified by military necessity and carried out unlawfully and wantonly.

Grave breaches also include compelling a protected person to serve in the forces of a hostile power, depriving a protected person of the guarantee to a fair and regular trial, unlawful confinement of hostages, unlawful deportation or transfer of civilians, and hostage-taking.

By covering "unjustifiable delay in the repatriation of prisoners of war after the cessation of active hostilities" and "employing methods or means of warfare which are intended or may be expected to cause, widespread, long-term and severe damage to the natural environment", Article 22's scope extends beyond the content of 'grave breaches'. On the other hand, Article 22 does not cover the content of the Geneva Conventions 'grave breaches' in their entirety since it omits "deprivation of a protected person of the guarantee to a fair and regular trial' and 'unlawful confinement of hostages".[127]

---

[127]   *See* Arts. 50 of Geneva Convention I, 51 of II, 130 of III, 147 of IV and Art. 85 of 1977 Protocol I. *See generally,* Sandoz, *supra* note 36; and Blishchenko, *supra* note 36.

Article 22 refers to 'armed conflict', rather than to '*international* armed conflict'. Therefore, Article 22 applies to all four categories of armed conflict that appear in the Geneva Conventions, 1949, and the 1977 Protocols Additional thereto.[128] These include: international armed conflicts between States as covered in Article 2 common to the four Geneva Conventions, 1949;[129] non-international armed conflicts according to Article 3 common to the four Geneva Conventions, 1949 as supplemented by Article 1(1) of Protocol II (Relating to the Protection of Victims of Non-International Conflicts);[130] and finally, wars of national liberation (struggles of 'peoples fighting against

---

[128]   *See generally* Veuthey, *Non-International Armed Conflict and Guerilla Warfare* in 1 International Criminal Law (ed. Bassiouni 1986);

[129]   Article 1(3) of 1977 Protocol I relating to the Protection of Victims of International Armed Conflicts covers inter-State armed conflicts by providing that: "This Protocol, which supplements the Geneva Conventions of 12 August 1949 for the protection of war victims, shall apply in the situations referred to in Article 2 common to those Conventions." Article 2 provides that: "... the present Convention shall apply to all cases of declared war or of any other armed conflict which may arise between two or more of the High Contracting Parties, even if the state of war is not recognized by one of them."

[130]   Specifically, the Protocol applies to: "... all armed conflicts which are not covered by Article 1 of the Protocol Additional to the Geneva Conventions of 12 August 1949, and relating to the Protection of Victims of International Armed Conflicts (Protocol I) and which take place in the territory of a High Contracting Party between its armed forces and dissident armed forces or other organized armed groups which, under responsible command, exercise such control over a part of its territory as to enable them to carry out sustained and concerted military operations and to implement this Protocol." Article 1(1) of Protocol II thus 'develops and supplements' common Article 3, but does not modify conditions for its application. Article 1(2) of Protocol II provides that: "This Protocol shall not apply to situations of internal disturbances and tensions, such as riots, isolated and sporadic acts of violence and other acts of a similar nature, not being armed conflicts." *See further*, Rosemary Abi-Saab, *Humanitarian Law and Internal Conflicts: The Evolution of Legal Concern*, in Humanitarian Law of Armed Conflict: Challenges Ahead (ed. Delissen and Tanja) 1991.

colonial domination and alien occupation and against racist regimes in the exercise of their right to self-determination').[131]

iii) 1996 Draft Code

Article 22 of the 1991 draft Code seems too narrow. It would apply only to a class of exceptionally serious war crimes. The term 'exceptionally serious war crimes' implies a hierarchy of war crimes, according to their degree of seriousness: exceptionally serious war crimes; serious war crimes; and war crimes.

To add 'exceptionally serious war crimes' to the already existing categories of 'war crimes *stricto sensu*' (commonly understood to refer to breaches of classic laws of war), the Nuremberg Charter concept of 'war crimes' (broader than 'war crimes *stricto sensu*'), and 'grave breaches' (as defined in the Geneva Conventions, 1949, and 1977 Protocols additional thereto) could only complicate the law further.

Eliminating the words 'exceptionally serious' would have simplified Article 22 without unduly broadening it. Creating finer categories would likely render norms on individual responsibility for war crimes less clear and could eventually diminish their legal status as well. Introduction of a hierarchical categorization of war crimes in international law definitely would be a step backward in efforts to arrive at a coherent system of international criminal law because it would introduce unnecessary complexity into the law without serving a purpose and would represent neither codification nor progressive development.

These concerns were echoed in the comments and observations of Governments on the 1991 draft Code.[132] The Government of Australia remarked that 'exceptionally serious war crimes' would represent a new category of norms, and given that war crimes and grave breaches of the Geneva Conventions, 1949, are serious breaches of laws of war, it was unclear what 'exceptionally serious'

---

[131]   Article 1(4) of Protocol I.

[132]   *See* Comments and Observations of Governments on the Draft Code of Crimes against the Peace and Security of Mankind adopted on First Reading by the International Law Commission at its 43rd Session, A/CN.4/448 of 1 March 1993.

could mean.   The Governments of The Netherlands, Paraguay, Switzerland, the UK and US, voiced similar concerns.[133]

For the 1996 draft Code, the ILC dropped 'exceptionally serious war crimes' as the title from Article 22, and replaced it to read simply 'war crimes'. The Commentary to Article 20 on 'war crimes' in the 1996 draft Code notes that although 'violations of humanitarian law applicable in armed conflict' would have been more precise from a technical standpoint, the Commission preferred the shorter title.

Article 20 on war crimes covers only war crimes 'committed in a systematic manner or on a large-scale' restricting the competence of the proposed international criminal court only to widespread breaches of the laws of war.

Article 20 of the 1996 draft Code is considerably more developed than its 1991 draft Code counterpart. As the Commentary explains, Article 20 implies at least seven main categories of war crimes, as follows:

1)   grave breaches of the Geneva Conventions, 1949;
2)   grave breaches as prohibited in Article 85(3) of 1977 Protocol I additional to the Geneva Conventions, 1949, (concerning death or serious injury to body or health);
3)   grave breaches as prohibited in Article 85(4) of 1977 Protocol I additional to the Geneva Conventions, 1949, (concerning transfer of civilian population or unjustifiable delay in the repatriation of prisoners of war or civilians);
4)   "outrages upon personal dignity in violation of international humanitarian law, in particular humiliating and degrading treatment, rape, enforced prostitution and any form of indecent assault";
5)   serious violations of 1907 Hague Convention No. IV respecting the Laws and Customs of War on Land and the Regulations annexed thereto;
6)   breaches of Article 3 common to the four Geneva Conventions, 1949, applicable in situations of armed conflict not of an international character; and,

---

[133]   *Ibid.*

7)   the employment of 'methods or means of warfare not justified by military necessity with the intent to cause widespread, long-term and severe damage to the natural environment and thereby gravely prejudice the health or survival of the population and such damage occurs.'

One advantage of Article 20 of the 1996 draft Code is that it provides a more comprehensive catalogue of war crimes than does the 1991 draft Code, while conforming more closely to the *lex lata*. However, it appears that some of the provisions overlap unnecessarily with each other; much more economic formulations to simplify interpretation and adjudication could be used.

5. MASS RAPE

i) Background

Although mass rape of women has been perpetrated during armed conflict and in occupied territories since time immemorial, there has been a noticeable paucity of legal provisions specifically prohibiting this crime. Indeed, it is remarkable that the 1991 draft Code makes no express mention of rape.

The lack of specific legal provisions prohibiting rape may stem from a number of factors. First, until the Second World War exposed their outdated character, laws of war were largely premised on the traditional military view that the civilian population was not likely to become the direct object of attack. Second, frequently rape has been considered more as a manifestation of man's uncontrolled natural impulses which might be less amenable to legal regulation than as regards certain other crimes, rather than as a form of brutality akin to assault, torture or inhuman or other degrading treatment. Third, international law doctrine has been developed predominately by males. As women progressively overcome long-established barriers to positions in the higher echelons of political diplomacy and law in countries around the world, rape and other crimes specifically targeting women may be more adequately addressed.

It is somewhat encouraging that the Statutes of the two *ad hoc* criminal Tribunals expressly refer to 'rape' (although the fact that they appear under the heading of 'crimes against humanity' gives cause for concern). In 1996, the ILC hastened to include mass rape in the draft Code[134] and as a result, the 1996 draft Code[135] specifically refers to rape in Articles 18 and 20(d) entitled 'Crimes against Humanity' and 'War Crimes' respectively.

Mass rape continues to be committed frequently in time of armed conflict. In some cases, rape is used to motivate soldiers in combat zones.

> The rape of women, where permitted or systematized as 'booty' of war, is likewise an engine of war: it maintains the morale of soldiers, feeds their hatred and sense of superiority, and keeps them fighting. The Japanese military industrialized the sexual slavery of women in the Second World War: 200,000 to 400,000 mostly Korean, but also Philippine, Chinese, and Dutch women from Indonesia were deceived or disappeared into 'comfort stations', raped repeatedly and moved from battlefield to battlefield to motivate as well as reward the Japanese soldiers. Genocide was not a goal, but it is believed that 70 to 90 percent of these women died in captivity, and among the known survivors, none were subsequently able to bear children. For similar reasons, the United States military in Vietnam raped Vietnamese women and established brothels, relying on dire economic necessity rather than kidnapping to fill them.[136]

---

[134] Article 5(g) of the Statute of the International Criminal Tribunal for the Former Yugoslavia and Article 3(g) of the Statute of the International Criminal Tribunal for Rwanda.

[135] Draft Code of Crimes against the Peace and Security of Mankind; A/CN.4/L.522 of 31 May 1996.

[136] *See* Rhonda Copelon, *Surfacing Gender: Reconceptualizing Crimes against Women in Time of War* in Mass Rape: The War against Women in Bosnia-Herzegovina (ed. Stiglmayer) (1994) at 205-206. *See further* Alexandra Stiglmayer, *The Rapes in Bosnia-Herzegovina*, in the same book

The particularly brutal way in which mass rape is most often perpetrated seems to indicate deep-seated motivations to humiliate not only the female victim, but also the local 'enemy' community. The situation in the former Yugoslavia lends further insight into the use of mass rape, perpetrated in a systematic and widespread manner, as a means to terrorize and drive an ethnic or religious minority civilian population from its territory.[137]   Particularly in Bosnia-Herzegovina, mass rape has been perpetrated systematically to force the Muslim civilian population from certain areas under Serb attack, occupation or control.[138]

> According to reliable information public rapes took place in front of a whole village, designed to terrorize the population and force ethnic groups to flee. .... Thus, the rape of women, has become a weapon of the deliberate destroying of minority groups. ... It has also been stated, that the systematic rape of women, and children as a means of humiliating them had contributed to ethnic cleansing through enforced procreation.[139]

---

at 84.
[137]   *See* General Assembly resolution 50/192 of 23 February 1996 entitled "Rape and Abuse of Women in the Areas of Armed Conflict in the Former Yugoslavia"; UN Doc. A/Res/50/192.
[138]   *See* the Reports of the Secretary-General to the UN Commission on Human Rights on Rape and Abuse of Women in the Territory of the Former Yugoslavia, E/CN.4/1994/5 of 30 June 1993; A/48/858 of 29 Jan. 1994; General Assembly resolution A/Res/49/205 of 6 March 1995; and the Report of the Secretary-General on Rape and Abuse of Women in the Areas of Armed Conflict in the Former Yugoslavia, A/50/329 of 4 Aug. 1995.
[139]   Erica-Irene Daes, *New Types of War Crimes and Crimes against Humanity: Violations of International Humanitarian and Human Rights Law*, International Geneva Yearbook (1993) at 60. Moreover: "[m]any victims have suffered multiple rapes. Many rapes involve sexual torture and sadism: victims have been sexually abused with guns, broken bottles, or truncheons; family members have been forced to assault each other. Some witnesses describe atrocities of a ritualistic nature where, after the rapes, women's breasts are cut off and their stomachs slit open. Other rapes appear to replicate acts portrayed in sadomasochistic material, which survivors say is

Whatever the precise motives for mass rape, women are frequently killed following rape (or in some cases before the act). Those that manage to survive are very likely to suffer severe physical and psychological trauma. In addition, rape victims frequently endure feelings of shame as well as extreme social ostracism from family and community.

The severe effects of mass rape on individual victims, their families, on the local community and where particularly extensive, on regional peace and security, make clear that an effective and coherent system of international criminal law must comprise well-defined legal norms providing for individual criminal responsibility for mass rape. In this regard, it is valuable to examine the *lex lata* on individual criminal responsibility for rape as well as prospects for better enforcement.

Rape committed by soldiers has been considered a serious breach of the code of the men of arms and of knightly honour since the Middle Ages, as evidenced in the 1474 Trial of Peter von Hagenbach, held criminally responsible for, among other serious crimes, murder and rape committed by his subordinates during the attack he led on Breisach in the Upper Rhine.

The Lieber Code (General Orders No. 100) of 24 April 1863, or *Instructions for the Government of Armies of the United States in the Field*, which were to prove influential as a model also for a number of European countries, provides in Article 44 that:

> All wanton violence committed against persons in the invaded country ... all rape, wounding, maiming or killing of such inhabitants, are prohibited under the penalty of death, or such other severe punishment as may seem adequate for the gravity of the offense.
>
> A soldier, officer or private, in the act of committing such violence, and disobeying a superior ordering him to abstain from it, may be lawfully killed on the spot by such superior.

---

pervasive in some of the rape camps." *See* Catherine N. Niarchos, *Women, War and Rape: Challenges Facing the International Tribunal for the Former Yugoslavia,* 17(4) Human Rights Quarterly (1995) at 657.

Article 47 prescribes severe punishment for, *inter alia*, rape.

Following the First World War, the 15-member Commission created by the Allied Powers at the Preliminary Peace Conference in January 1919 to determine responsibility for acts connected to the war, created a list of war crimes that includes 'rape' as well as "abduction of girls and women for the purpose of enforced prostitution".

Article 6(c) of the Nuremberg Charter, without expressly mentioning 'rape', prohibits *inter alia* "enslavement ... and other inhumane acts committed against any civilian population" which can be interpreted to apply to cases of sexual slavery ('enslavement') and rape (as an 'inhumane act') within the Tribunal's competence.[140]

The Nuremberg Tribunal heard evidence on systematic mass rape perpetrated by Axis forces during World War II, but did not specifically address the problem. However, the Judgement of the Tokyo Tribunal indicated that massive rapes were committed by occupying Japanese forces, often in the most sadistic manner. The Tokyo Tribunal charged Admiral Toyoda with, *inter alia*, "[w]illfully and unlawfully disregarding and failing to discharge his duties by ordering, directing, inciting, causing, permitting, ratifying and failing to prevent Japanese Naval personnel of units and organizations under his command, control and supervision to abuse, mistreat, torture, rape, kill and commit other atrocities".[141]

However, international war crimes trials are more notable for their scarcity: perpetrators of war crimes generally, including rape committed in time of armed conflict, almost always have gone unpunished.

> Military histories rarely refer to rape, and military tribunals rarely either charge or sanction it. This is true even where rape and forced prostitution are mass and systematic, as with the rape of women in both theatres

---

[140] *See* the Preparatory Document submitted by Mrs. Linda Chavez on the question of systematic rape, sexual slavery and slavery-like practices during wartime; E/CN.4/Sub.2/1993/44 of 7 Sept. 1993.
[141] *Cited in* C.P.M Cleiren, and M.E.M. Tijssen, *Rape and Other Forms of Sexual Assault in the Armed Conflict in the Former Yugoslavia: Legal, Procedural, and Evidentiary Issues*, 5 Criminal Law Forum (1994) at 481.

of the Second World War, it is even true where the open, mass, and systematic rape has been thought to shock the conscience of the world, such as the 'Rape of Nanking' or the rape of an estimated 200,000 Bengali women during the war of independence from Pakistan. Though discussed in the judgment of the International Military Tribunal in Tokyo, rape was not separately charged against the Japanese commander as a crime. In Bangladesh, amnesty was quietly traded for independence.[142]

Control Council Law No. 10 specifically refers to 'rape', thereby clearly including the prohibition of rape within the definition of 'crimes against humanity'. However, as part of municipal law, the overall effect of Control Council Law No. 10 on international criminal law is limited.

With regard to armed conflicts 'not of an international character', Articles 3(a) and 3(c), common to the four Geneva Conventions, 1949, prohibit:

(a) Violence to life and person, in particular murder of all kinds, mutilation, cruel treatment and torture; ...
(c) Outrages upon personal dignity, in particular humiliating and degrading treatment.

Protocol II of 1977 relating to the Protection of Victims of Non-International Armed Conflicts is more specific. Article 4(2)(e) provides that: "outrages upon personal dignity, in particular humiliating and degrading treatment, rape, enforced prostitution and any form of indecent assault" are "prohibited at any time and in any place whatsoever".

The Fourth Geneva Convention, 1949, relative to the Protection of Civilian Persons in Time of War provides in Article 27 that:

Women shall be especially protected against any attack on their honour, in particular against rape, enforced prostitution, or any form of indecent assault.

---

[142]   Copelon, *supra* note 136 at 197.

Article 11(1) of Protocol I relative to the Protection of Victims of International Armed Conflicts, 1977, provides that:

> The physical or mental health or integrity of persons who are in the power of the adverse Party or who are interned, detained or otherwise deprived of liberty as a result of a situation referred to in Article 1 shall not be endangered by any unjustified act or omission.[143]

Article 11(1) does not explicitly mention rape or sexual assault. However, these acts are implicitly covered as endangering physical or mental health or integrity.[144] Moreover, Article 11 must be read together with Article 76 of Protocol I, which provides that:

> 1. Women shall be the object of special respect and shall be protected in particular against rape, forced prostitution and any other form of indecent assault.
> 2. Pregnant women and mothers having dependent infants who are arrested, detained or interned for reasons related to the armed conflict, shall have their cases considered with the utmost priority.

Article 11(4) makes "Any wilful act or omission which seriously endangers the physical or mental health of any person ... a grave breach of this Protocol" thereby importing individual criminal responsibility therefor.

---

[143] Article 1 of Protocol I refers to situations of international armed conflict as so defined in Article 2 common to the four Geneva Conventions, 1949, as well as "armed conflicts in which peoples are fighting against colonial domination and alien occupation and against racist regimes in the exercise of their right to self-determination".

[144] The intense trauma women experience from rape may be exacerbated by long term illness or death from sexually transmitted disease, including gonorrhoea, syphilis or AIDS, all of which may be more prevalent in war-time.

ii) Considering Mass Rape as a Crime Independent of
'Violations of Honour', 'Genocide' and 'Crimes against Humanity'

In her 1982 ground-breaking work *Dignity and Honour of Women as Basic and Fundamental Human Rights*, Khushalani read into certain provisions of the Hague Regulations respecting the Laws and Customs of War on Land, annexed to the 1899 and 1907 Hague Conventions, the implicit prohibition against rape. For example, Article 46 provides that:

> Family honour and rights, the lives of persons ... as well as religious convictions and practice, must be respected.

As Khushalani argues,[145] family honour may be interpreted to comprise the protection of a woman's honour, which implies the right not to be raped.

On the other hand, the reference to 'honour' in connection with rape strikes some commentators to gloss over, even to contradict, the particularly grave character of rape.

> Where rape is treated as a crime against honour, the honour of women is called into question and virginity or chastity is often a precondition. Honour implies the loss of station or respect; it reinforces the social view, internalized by women, that the raped woman is dishonourable. And while the concept of dignity potentially embraces more profound concerns, standing alone it obfuscates the fact that rape is fundamentally violence against women - violence against a woman's body, autonomy, integrity, selfhood, security, and self-esteem as well as her standing in the community. This failure to recognize rape as violence is critical to the

---

[145] Yougindra Khushalani, Dignity and Honour of Women as Basic and Fundamental Human Rights (1982) at 10.

traditionally lesser or ambiguous status of rape in humanitarian law.[146]

For these reasons, international criminal law should avoid couching provisions on individual criminal responsibility for rape in terms of 'honour' or 'dignity'.

Similarly, while it is important to recognize that mass rape may be employed as an instrument of terror or in a genocidal policy,[147] it does not follow that international legal norms prohibiting rape should be tied to norms prohibiting genocide. This link would unduly narrow developing norms on rape where an international criminal tribunal might feel bound to impose criminal responsibility for rape only in situations involving genocide.[148]

iii) 1996 Draft Code

The inclusion of rape as a 'crime against humanity' in the Statutes of the two *ad hoc* criminal Tribunals illustrates very well the perils of subsuming norms prohibiting mass rape with other more established legal norms. As discussed above, the Statute of the International Criminal Tribunal for the Former Yugoslavia links 'crimes against humanity' with crimes committed in armed conflict, instead of reaffirming that norms prohibiting crimes against humanity apply to all situations of war and peace. Had the grave defects of the provision on crimes against humanity in the Statute not been minimized by the Appeals Chamber in the *Dusko Tadic Trial*, as discussed above, norms prohibiting mass rape would have been left unnecessarily narrow, even before they had a chance to develop fully.

Unfortunately, in Article 18(i) of the 1996 draft Code, 'rape' is listed as a 'crime against humanity', rather than as a crime on its own, meaning the norms prohibiting it are circumscribed by the chapeau to Article 18, which defines 'crimes against humanity' as the listed "acts, when committed in a systematic manner or on a large scale and

---

[146] *See* Copelon, *supra* note 136 at 200-201. *See also* Niarchos, *supra* note 139 at 674 on this point.

[147] *See e.g.* Beverly Allen, Rape Warfare: the Hidden Genocide in Bosnia-Herzegovina and Croatia (1996).

[148] *See* Copelon, *supra* note 136 at 206-207 on this point.

instigated or directed by a government or by any organization or group". However, this danger is somewhat mitigated by Articles 20(d) and 20 (f)(v) of the 1996 draft Code which specifically mention 'rape' as 'war crimes', thereby filling potential gaps in the coverage of norms prohibiting rape.

It would have been more valuable were the International Law Commission to have included an express prohibition of mass rape separate and independent from other violations listed. On the other hand, it is true that only rape committed on a mass or systematic scale, rather than isolated cases that do not reveal such a pattern, should be included in an international penal code, for the same reasons that only murder on a systematic or mass scale is covered in the 1991 draft Code. Isolated cases are already covered as a grave breach of the Geneva Conventions, 1949, and 1977 Protocols additional thereto, in situations of armed conflict and most likely as a serious criminal law violation in the domestic law of the State as well.

As a final point, the International Law Commission should consider revising the draft Code on Crimes against the Peace and Security of Mankind to read 'draft Code on Crimes against the Peace and Security of Humanity' so as to convey a non-sexist i.e. non-discriminatory attitude through its terminology.

CHAPTER III

MERCENARY ACTIVITY, TERRORISM, CRIMES AGAINST UN PERSONNEL, DRUG-TRAFFICKING, AND WILFUL AND SEVERE DAMAGE TO THE NATURAL ENVIRONMENT

1. RECRUITMENT, USE, FINANCING AND TRAINING OF MERCENARIES

i) Background

The use of mercenaries dates at least as far back as ancient Egypt and Mesopotamia. Mercenaries played an important role in securing major conquests in ancient Greece and the Roman Empire. During the Middle Ages, German, Italian and Swiss nationals were hired often as mercenaries to fight in various European campaigns.[1] Large-scale use of mercenaries declined in the 16th and 17th centuries as new European States formed professional armies staffed with paid regulars. However, mercenaries were used increasingly in parts of Africa by local rulers in the 18th and 19th centuries.[2]

Following World War II, mercenaries were used by European Powers to maintain colonial domination over many African peoples. The French Foreign Legion is perhaps the most notorious example.[3]

---

[1]   See Charles C. Bayley, Mercenaries for the Crimea: The German, Swiss and Italian Legions in British Service 1854-1856 (1977) and Michael E. Mallett, Mercenaries and Their Masters: Warfare in Renaissance Italy (1974).

[2]   See E.I. Nwogugu, *Recent Developments in the Law Relating to Mercenaries*, 20 Revue de droit pénal militaire (1981) at 11. *See also* Edward Kwakwa, *The Current Status of Mercenaries in the Law of Armed Conflict*, 14(1) Hastings International and Comparative Law Review (1990).

[3]   See D. Forsythe, Dogs of War (1976), and Burchett and Roebuck, The Whores of War (1977); E. I. Nwogugu, *ibid.;* and Peter, *Mercenaries and International Humanitarian Law*, 24(3) Indian Journal of International Law (1984).

The use of mercenaries escalated during the late 1950's, and early 1960's, as the process of decolonization achieved full force in Africa. By this time, it had become politically unacceptable for colonial Powers to engage their regular armed forces to prevent or hinder the process of decolonization. Many colonial Powers therefore resorted to the covert use of mercenaries as a more feasible means by which to maintain colonial control.

> In Black Africa a mercenary is deemed to be engaged in a sordid and inhuman occupation, and the term is used with opprobrium. This attitude is not accidental, for, apart from the usual antipathy towards a mercenary as a hired assassin, the mercenary represents to the African everything he fights to defeat: namely, racism and colonialism. For the mercenary is almost invariably white and his participation in African liberation struggles inevitably carries racialist overtones. Moreover, the mercenary is seen as the accomplice of powerful colonial interests - those which stand most to gain from maintaining the status quo.[4]

Mercenaries continue to be used in Africa and in other regions against peoples struggling to exercise their right to self-determination.[5]

In classic international law, issues surrounding the legal status of mercenaries focused on State rather than individual responsibility. This should not be surprising since the classic law of international responsibility relates almost exclusively to States rather than to non-

---

[4]   *See* Martin, *Mercenaries and the Rule of Law*, 17 Review of the International Commission of Jurists (1976) at 52.

[5]   *See* "Report on the question of the use of mercenaries as a means of violating human rights and impeding the exercise of the right of peoples to self-determination, submitted by the Special Rapporteur of the Commission on Human Rights", transmitted by the Secretary-General to the General Assembly; A/50/390 of 29 August 1995, which draws attention to the alleged use of mercenaries in the 1990's in, among other places, Nagorno-Karabakh by the Governments of Armenia and Azerbaijan; in Liberia; Sudan; Zaire, as well as numerous other African countries; and in the territory of the former Yugoslavia, particularly in Croatia, Bosnia and Herzegovina.

State entities. However, Grotius referred to two kinds of general State obligations for acts of private individuals. Where the State has not taken adequate measures to prevent a crime from being committed by a private individual against a foreigner (*patienta*), or where the State fails to prosecute or extradite an offender (*receptus*), the State engages international responsibility by reason that it has implicitly condoned, or even complied with, the act of the individual.[6] Publicists since Vitoria in the early 17th century have commented on the status of mercenaries in international law.

A major issue concerns the extent to which obligations in international law are engaged by a neutral State whose nationals act as mercenaries against a foreign power.[7] The 1907 Hague Convention on Neutrality[8] contains some provisions relating to mercenaries which probably reflect customary international law.[9] Article 4 of the Convention provides that: "Corps of combatants cannot be formed nor recruiting agencies opened on the territory of a neutral Power to assist the belligerents."[10]

---

[6]   *See* Hugo Grotius, De Jure belli ac Pacis, Lib.II, cap. XXI. According to Mosler, in *The International Society as a Legal Community*, 140 Hague Recueil (1974) at 177, Grotius' statement still reflects contemporary international law. *But see* Jiménez de Arechaga, *International Law in the Past Third of a Century*, 159 Hague Recueil (1978) at 283, where it is argued that this view, although supported by nineteenth century arbitral jurisprudence and the writings of publicists, is today outdated.

[7]   *See* H. Burmester, *The Recruitment and Use of Mercenaries in Armed Conflicts*, 72 American Journal of International Law (1978) at 41-2.

[8]   Hague Convention respecting the Rights and Duties of Neutral Powers and Persons in Case of War on Land, *adopted* 18 Oct. 1907, in International Committee of the Red Cross, International Law concerning the Conduct of Hostilities: Collection of Hague Conventions and Some Other Treaties (1989) at 144.

[9]   *See* Burmester, *supra* note 7.

[10]   Article 5 prohibits a neutral Power from, *inter alia*, allowing activities enjoined in Article 4 to take place on its territory, but a neutral Power "is not called upon to punish acts in violation of its neutrality unless the said acts have been committed on its own territory." Article 6 provides that: "The responsibility of a neutral Power is not engaged by the fact of persons crossing the frontier separately to offer their services to one of the belligerents." *See* Articles 16-18 of Hague Convention No. IV, 1907, on the status

Aside from General Assembly and Security Council resolutions addressing specific cases,[11] the General Assembly Declaration on Principles of International Law concerning Friendly Relations and Co-operation among States in Accordance with the Charter of the United Nations, 1970,[12] addressed the problem of mercenaries by stating explicitly that "[e]very State has the duty to refrain from organizing or encouraging the organization of irregular forces of armed bands, including mercenaries, for incursion into the territory of another State." General Assembly resolution 3314 on the definition of Aggression prohibits "the sending by or on behalf of a State of armed bands, groups, irregulars or mercenaries".[13]

The Organization of African Unity has adopted several resolutions and a convention on mercenaries, but these instruments bind only Member States of the OAU, and not other States, such as France, Belgium, the United Kingdom or United States whence mercenaries were recruited for action in the Congo, Angola, Sudan

---

of nationals of a neutral State who voluntarily enlist in the ranks of the armed forces of one of the belligerents.

[11] For example, during the Belgian Congo independence struggle, the Province of Katanga attempted to secede from the Belgian Congo with the assistance of mercenaries. On 21 Feb. 1961, the Security Council called for the "immediate withdrawal and evacuation from the Congo of all Belgian and other para-military personnel, political advisers not under the United Nations command and mercenaries". Security Council resolution 161 of 21 Feb. 1961; 16 SCOR S/4741. *See further* Burchett and Roebuck, *supra* note 3. In 1966, Katanga again attempted to secede from the Congo with the help of European and South African mercenaries. *See* Security Council resolution 239 of 10 July 1967; 22 SCOR 13. The use of mercenaries in Angola, and in Guinea, impelled the Security Council and the General Assembly to pass several other resolutions condemning the use of mercenaries against the exercise of the right to self-determination. In addition, two Security Council reports document the use of mercenaries against the political independence of Benin, (Official Records of the Security Council, Thirty-Second Year, Special Supplement No.3, UN Doc. S/12294/Rev.1.) and the Seychelles, Thirty-Seventh Year, Special Supplement No. 2, UN Doc. S/14905/Rev.1, and Special Supplement No. 3 UN Doc. S/15492/Rev.1.

[12] Resolution 2625 of 24 Oct. 1970, *adopted without a vote*, 25 GAOR Supp., (No.28) 121, UN Doc. A/8028 (1970).

[13] Resolution 3314 (XXIX) UN GAOR 29th Session, Supp. No.31.

and elsewhere in Africa.[14]   There has been concern also in other regional fora over the threat to the territorial integrity of small States posed by mercenaries.[15]

International humanitarian law partially addresses the problem of mercenaries in an indirect way.   Article 4(2) of the Third Geneva Convention, 1949,[16] extends prisoner of war status under certain conditions to "[m]embers of other militia and members of other volunteer corps, including those of organized resistance movements" who do not form part of the regular armed forces.   However, Article 4 neither mentions nor describes mercenaries, consequently the Geneva Conventions do not extend prisoner of war status to mercenaries.   By omitting mention of mercenaries, the Third Geneva Convention implicitly recognizes an important distinction between volunteers (whom a Party to the conflict is obliged to treat as prisoners of war if detained) and mercenaries (who are not entitled to such protection). Article 47(1) of Protocol I affirms that: "A mercenary shall not have the right to be a combatant or a prisoner of war".

International efforts to arrive at a definition of 'mercenary' and to develop clear legal rules prohibiting mercenary activity culminated in Article 47(2) of Protocol I,[17] which was subsequently incorporated into the 1989 International Convention against the Recruitment, Use,

---

[14]   *See* the Convention for the Elimination of Mercenarism in Africa, OAU Doc. CM/817 (XXIX) of 12 Dec. 1973.

[15]   *See e.g.* resolution 22/19-P, 'Question of the Security of Small States and the Solidarity of the Islamic Ummah in Safe-Guarding the Sovereignty and Territorial Integrity of Small States from the Threats Posed by Actions of Mercenaries, *adopted* by the Nineteenth Islamic Conference of Foreign Ministers, held at Cairo, Egypt, 31 July - 5 Aug. 1990.

[16]   Geneva Convention Relative to the Treatment of Prisoners of War, *adopted* 12 Aug. 1949.

[17]   The Protocols were adopted at a time when the use of mercenaries in the civil wars of Angola and Rhodesia gained international notoriety. *See* resolution 1990/7 *adopted* by the Commission on Human Rights of 19 Feb. 1990, 'Use of Mercenaries as a Means of Impeding the Exercise of the Right of Peoples to Self-Determination'. *See* G.W. Okoth-Obbo, *Mercenaries and Humanitarian Law, with Particular Reference to Protocol I Additional to the Geneva Conventions of 1949*, Revue de Droit International (1989).

Financing and Training of Mercenaries.[18] Article 1(1) of the 1989 UN Convention on Mercenaries is identical in wording to Article 47(2) of Protocol I, except that the Protocol I requirement that a mercenary is any person who 'does, in fact, take a direct part in the hostilities', was not included in the Convention definition. The 1989 Convention on Mercenaries, and the 1991 draft Code definition of 'mercenary' which follows that of the 1989 Convention, are thus broader than the Protocol I definition; a person recruited to fight in an armed conflict may be counted as a mercenary, regardless as to whether he or she has actually seen action.

ii) 1991 Draft Code Provisions on Mercenaries

Article 1(2) of the UN Convention on Mercenaries is incorporated word-for-word in Article 23(3) of the 1991 draft Code except that the 1991 draft Code refers to 'any individual', whereas both Protocol I and the 1989 UN Convention refer to 'any person'. In the 1991 draft Code definition of 'mercenary', all the constituent elements must be met.[19]

The 1991 draft Code does not make the individual mercenary criminally responsible whereas the 1989 Convention on Mercenaries does. The 1989 Convention stipulates responsibility for the individual mercenary "who participates directly in hostilities or in a concerted act of violence" (thereby incorporating the narrower requirements of the Protocol I definition of 'mercenary' for the purposes of responsibility). Article 3(1) states that a mercenary, as defined in Article 1 of the Convention, "who participates directly in hostilities or in a concerted act of violence, as the case may be, commits an offence for the purposes of the Convention." Article 2 of the Convention provides that "Any person who recruits, uses, finances or trains mercenaries"

---

[18]   *See* Art. 1 of the International Convention against the Recruitment, Use, Financing and Training of Mercenaries, A/Res/44/34 *adopted* by the General Assembly 4 Dec. 1989, 29 International Legal Materials (1990). On 4 Dec. 1980, the General Assembly *adopted* resolution 35/48 establishing the *Ad Hoc* Committee to draft the Convention.

[19]   *See* Article 23 of the Draft Code of Crimes against the Peace and Security of Mankind, A/CN.4/L.464/Add.4 of 15 July 1991, 43rd ILC Session (29 Apr.-19 July 1991) at 11, which forms Annex 1 of the present book.

commits an offence under the Convention. Other provisions prohibit States from engaging in the recruitment, use, financing or training, of mercenaries.[20]

These differences are reflected in the respective approaches to implementation. The UN Convention on Mercenaries provides for individual responsibility, in an indirect way, by obliging States Parties to the Convention to make sure the offenses under the Convention are incorporated in their national laws.[21] In contrast, Article 23 of the 1991 draft Code provides for criminal responsibility in respect of an 'individual who as an agent or representative of a State' commits one of the acts enumerated as offenses. Thus, under the draft Code, private individuals can not be held criminally responsible; there must be a relationship of agency (or representation) of the individual to the State for that individual to come within the coverage of Article 23.

This may seem rather odd since private mercenaries have carried out horrible atrocities against unarmed civilians in numerous armed conflict situations. However, the principal thrust of the draft Code is not to provide individual criminal responsibility for every kind of heinous activity, but to prohibit acts that constitute a threat to the peace and security of mankind. Arguably, private mercenaries pose less of a threat to international peace and security than State-sponsored mercenaries, and their acts should therefore not be considered of sufficient gravity to warrant inclusion in an international penal code. Indeed, some of the most atrocious acts of private mercenaries may be partially covered by other draft Code provisions, such as those prohibiting genocide or murder, which apply to 'anyone', although this coverage is likely to be sketchy at best.

On the other hand, while domestic law is likely to prohibit murder, torture or other serious violations, in situations where mercenaries are conducting their activities it is very likely that law and order within the country have disappeared in which case domestic criminal law may no longer be effective. To cover such cases, it would be better to sweep in private mercenaries within the coverage of an international penal code.

---

[20]   Article 5 of the International Convention against the Recruitment, Use, Financing and Training of Mercenaries 29 International Legal Materials (1990) 89-97.

[21]   Article 5(3).

Another difficulty is that the agency relationship between the individual mercenary and a State is likely to be very difficult to prove in practice.   Covert State sponsorship of mercenaries abroad, calculated to undermine or disrupt a foreign government, may be ordered, and carried out, by elements of the interfering government's executive branch, which may lack transparency or clear public accountability.   In such cases, extensive extra-budgetary financial, logistical and bureaucratic forms of support, which do not figure in public records or accounts, may be provided to mercenary elements. Again, bringing private mercenaries within the competence *ratione personae* of an international criminal court would eliminate the need to prove this agency relationship.

iii) 1996 Draft Code

The 1996 draft Code does not include provisions on mercenary activity. In their comments and observations on the 1991 draft Code,[22] the Governments of Austria, Denmark, Finland, Iceland, The Netherlands, Norway, the UK and the USA, objected to the inclusion of Article 23 in the 1991 draft Code on the grounds that it lacked precision. Many of these Governments expressed their doubts as to whether the problem of mercenaries was sufficiently serious as to warrant the inclusion of provisions seeking to address it, in an international penal code.   The Government of Australia did not specifically object to the inclusion of provisions prohibiting mercenary activity, but observed that the ILC had not explained why the contents of Article 23 varied from the 1989 Mercenaries Convention.

The adoption of the 1989 UN Convention on Mercenaries seems to signal increasing international recognition that mercenaries pose a serious threat to the territorial independence of States and to the legitimate struggle of peoples for self-determination.[23]   As the

---

[22]   Comments and Observations of Governments on the Draft Code of Crimes against the Peace and Security of Mankind adopted on First Reading by the International Law Commission at its 43rd Session, A/CN.4/448 of 1 March 1993.

[23]   *See* Commission on Human Rights resolution 1990/7, 19 Feb. 1990, Report of the Forty-Sixth Session, ECOSOC Official Records, (29 Jan. - 9 Mar. 1990), Supp. No. 2, E/CN.4/1990/94.

Convention becomes more widely ratified and followed in the practice of States, the international community may support progressive development of the international criminal law norms on mercenary activity. However, to this point, western States have consistently opposed the 1991 draft Code's provisions on the mercenary problem, which seems to account for their having been deleted from the 1996 version of the draft Code.

2. INTERNATIONAL TERRORISM

i) Background

To this point, neither treaty law nor customary norms provide for a comprehensive definition of 'terrorism'.[24] Generally speaking, acts of terror frequently involve the premeditated use or threat of violence calculated to create a climate of fear with a view to provoking the Government into overreaction, or to intimidate the Government or a section of the population into changing a particular policy or course of action. In many cases, terrorism is intended to raise the profile of the terrorist organization so as to highlight its political aims and objectives, perhaps in order to generate popular support.[25]

---

[24] One may refer to Louis René Beres, *The Meaning of Terrorism: Jurisprudential and Definitional Clarifications*, 28(2) Vanderbilt Journal of Transnational Law (1995) at 239-240, who says that: "Indeed, judging from the standard definitions of terrorism currently in professional use - definitions that offer no operational benefit for scholars or practitioners - the term has become so broad and so imprecise that it embraces even the most discrepant activities. For example, under certain prevailing definitions of terrorism, adopted by United States Government agencies and some scholars, the United States War for Independence, the Gulf War (Desert Storm), the Contra insurgency for Nicaragua, and the anti-Castro insurgency supported by the United States are all examples of terrorism."

[25] *See also* Robert A. Friedlander, *Reflections on Terrorist Havens*, in 68 Readings on International Law from the Naval War College Review, (ed. Moore and Turner) (1995) at 378, who has put forward certain criteria as minimum elements of terrorism: "Terror violence, either international or transnational, must include at least one of the following elements: (1) the act

During the Cold War, the prevailing East-West tensions were reflected in the struggles of peoples for self-determination and the use of terrorist tactics on both sides of many of these struggles.

> In the shadow of the nuclear balance of terror between the superpowers methods of conventional and proxy war, such as terrorism, became more attractive as instruments of policy for states and sub-state organizations such as national liberation movements. Such methods are low-cost, relatively low-risk, and yet afford the possibilities of high yield in terms of weakening, penetrating or even gaining control through covert means. Moreover, such methods carry far less cost and less risk of escalation than conventional war. State-sponsored international terrorism carries the added attraction for its perpetrators that it can be carried out secretly, and, if suspicions are voiced, plausibly denied.[26]

Unfortunately, many governments have used the term 'terrorist' loosely to condemn not only real terrorists, but legitimate national liberation movements whose political aims they may not share.[27] As Beres states:

---

or series of acts must take place in more than one State; (2) the act or series of acts must involve citizens of more than one State; (3) the act or series of acts must be directed at internationally protected persons; (4) the act or series of acts must occur outside of an exclusively national jurisdiction; (5) the act or series of acts must be directed against internationally protected property. If one or more of these elements is satisfied, then the act or acts in question are no longer merely common criminality but rather international crimes affecting world public order."

[26]   Paul Wilkinson, *Terrorist Targets and Tactics: New Risks to World Order*, in Terrorism and Drug Trafficking in the 1990s, (ed. Jamieson) (1994) at 181.

[27]   *See* Walter Laqueur (ed.), The Terrorism Reader: A Historical Anthology (1978).

The United States characterized any insurgent force
operating against an allegedly pro-Soviet regime as
lawful, regardless of the means used in the insurgency.
Reciprocally, any activity by an insurgent force operating against a pro-United States regime was automati-
cally characterized as terrorism. The Soviet leaders
believed that the United States was using the term
'terrorism' to discredit what the Soviets alleged were
legitimate movements for self-determination and human
rights. Under the Soviet view, insurgency against what
the United States freely called authoritarian regimes -
for example, the regimes in El Salvador, Guatemala,
and Chile - was not terrorism, as the United States had
maintained, but national liberation.[28]

Thus, whether the African National Congress or the Palestinian
Liberation Organization[29] were considered legitimate representatives
of peoples struggling for self-determination, or on the contrary, as
terrorist organizations, depended not so much on the means and
methods they may have employed to reach their objectives, but on
purely political considerations reflecting particular ideological procliv-
ities and self-interests.[30]

However, neither the accession of colonies to independent
status nor the end of the Cold War, have brought about an end to
terrorist violence. Rather, there has been a discernable change in the
pattern of motives, perpetrators and targets of terrorism. Following
the independence of most African and Asian countries, many of the
freshly liberated States became entangled in bitter civil war. In

---

[28]   Beres, *supra* note 24 at 248.

[29]   *See* resolution No.39/19-P, 'Convening an International Conference
under the Auspices of the UN to Define Terrorism and Distinguish it from
Peoples' Struggle for National Liberation', *adopted* by the Nineteenth Islamic
Conference of Foreign Ministers, held at Cairo, Egypt, 31 July - 5 Aug. 1990.
This point was also raised in the Sixth Committee of the UN General
Assembly, 45th Session. *See* UN Doc. A/CN.4/456 of 6 Feb. 1991.

[30]   For an analysis of US policy on terrorist activity, *see* Antonio
Cassese, *The International Community's 'Legal' Response to Terrorism*, 38
International and Comparative Law Quarterly (1989).

numerous cases, these civil wars arose from new movements of self-determination launched by groups claiming to represent a religious, ethnic or linguistic minority that perhaps felt alienated by their new leaders, particularly in cases where independence brought corrupt and bloody dictatorship.[31] Of course, the artificial boundaries which had been imposed by the colonial Powers to further their divide and rule policies, or for mere administrative convenience, meant that the political and cultural integrity of many ethnic groups was disrupted or destroyed.

The end of the Cold War, and the fall of the Soviet Union, have also unleashed ethnic and religious liberation struggles and general political instability in many former Soviet republics, such as Chechnya, Azerbaijan, Nagorno-Karabakh, Armenia and Abkhazia, Georgia. Advances in the technical capacity to produce weapons (including deliverable chemical and biological missiles), the increased availability of nearly undetectable plastic explosives (such as Semtex) as well as perfidious triggering mechanisms,[32] wide mass media coverage of terrorist incidents (perpetuating a strong incentive to terrorists), the lack of effective suppression of international terrorism on the part of many States in times of severe budgetary constraints, and moreover, an abiding regard in democratic countries for the individual's right not to be subject to arbitrary surveillance, search and seizure, seem to guarantee that terrorist incidents will continue to be perpetrated in future.

---

[31]   Wilkinson, *supra* note 26 at 181.

[32]   *See* Elliot Hurwitz, *Terrorists and Chemical / Biological Weapons*; and Stephen Rose, *The Coming Explosion of Silent Weapons*, in 68 Readings on International Law from the Naval War College Review (ed. Moore and Turner: 1995); Graham T. Allison et al., Avoiding Nuclear Anarchy: Containing the Threat of Loose Russian Weapons and Fissile Material (1996); Edward M. Spiers, Chemical and Biological Weapons: A Study of Proliferation (1994); Richard Clutterbuck, Terrorism in an Unstable World (1994); Richard Clutterbuck, *Technology and Civil Liberties*, in Terrorism and Drug Trafficking in the 1990s (ed. Jamieson) (1994); and Leonard J. Hippchen, Terrorism, International Crime and Arms Control (1982).

ii) International Legal Response relative
to Terrorist Acts Committed in Peace-Time

- Multilateral Conventions

Efforts to create an international tribunal to try individuals for terrorism first arose from the international outcry over the assassinations of Yugoslavian King Alexander and French Minister M. Barthou at Marseilles on 9 October 1934. A League of Nations Committee of Experts[33] prepared two draft conventions: one for the repression of terrorism and the other for the creation of an international criminal court. These draft conventions were adopted in November 1937 as the Convention for the Prevention and Punishment of Terrorism and the Convention for the Creation of an International Criminal Court, but both failed to attain sufficient ratifications to enter into force.[34] The former defines 'terrorism' in Article 1(2) as: "criminal acts directed against a State and intended to or calculated to create a state of terror in the minds of particular persons, or a group of persons or the general public".

Since that time, several United Nations conventions have been adopted relative to very specific situations, circumstances or places, which prohibit the following: hijacking,[35] unlawful acts against the safety of civil aviation,[36] crimes against internationally protected per-

---

[33] Resolution *adopted* on 10 Dec. 1934, League of Nations C. 94 M. 47 (1938) V at 183.

[34] *Adopted* 16 Nov. 1937, *see* Proceedings of the International Conference on the Repression of Terrorism, 1937, League of Nations Publication C.94.M.47.V. The Convention for the Creation of an International Criminal Court was signed by 24 States, but ratified only by India.

[35] Tokyo Convention on Offenses and Certain Other Acts Committed on Aircraft, 1963, signed 14 Sept., the 1963 Hague Convention for the Suppression of Unlawful Seizure of Aircraft, *signed* 16 Dec. 1970, *entered into force* 14 Oct. 1971, 106 UNTS 860, 10 International Legal Materials (1971) 133.

[36] *See* the Montreal Convention for the Suppression of Unlawful Acts against the Safety of Civil Aviation 1971, *signed* 23 Sept. 1971, *entered into force* 26 Jan. 1973, 10 International Legal Materials (1971) 1151; and Protocol for the Suppression of Unlawful Acts of Violence at Airports Serving

sons,[37] hostage-taking,[38] unlawful acts against the safety of maritime navigation,[39] and unlawful acts against the safety of fixed platforms at sea (such as oil rigs).[40] On 3 March 1980, the Convention on the Physical Protection of Nuclear Material was adopted in Vienna, followed by the adoption in 1991 of the Convention on the Marking of Plastic Explosives for the Purpose of Detection.[41]

Important regional initiatives to suppress terrorism have been launched under the auspices of the Council of Europe[42] and the Organization of American States.[43]

International Civil Aviation, supplementary to the Convention for the Suppression of Unlawful Acts against the Safety of Civil Aviation, *signed* at Montreal on 24 Feb. 1988.

[37]   UN Convention on the Prevention and Punishment of Crimes against Internationally Protected Persons, *adopted* 14 Dec. 1973, *entered into force* 20 Feb. 1977; 13 International Legal Materials (Jan 1974) 41.

[38]   International Convention against the Taking of Hostages, *adopted* by General Assembly resolution 43/146, 17 Dec. 1979, 18 International Legal Materials (Nov. 1979) 1460.

[39]   *See* the Convention for the Suppression of Unlawful Acts against the Safety of Maritime Navigation, *adopted* in Rome on 10 Mar. 1988; General Assembly resolution 34/146, GAOR, 34th Session, Supp. 46. *See* Malvina Halberstam, *Terrorist Acts against and on Board Ships*, 19 Israel Yearbook on Human Rights (1989); and Christopher C. Joyner, *Suppression of Terrorism on the High Seas: the 1988 IMO Convention on the Safety of Maritime Navigation*, 19 Israel Yearbook on Human Rights (1989).

[40]   *See* the Protocol for the Suppression of Unlawful Acts against the Safety of Fixed Platforms Located on the Continental Shelf, *adopted* at Rome on 10 Mar. 1988.

[41]   *Adopted* on 1 Mar. 1991 in Montreal.

[42]   *See e.g.* the European Convention on the Suppression of Terrorism, *adopted* 10 Nov. 1976, *opened for signature* 27 Jan. 1977, *entered into force*, 24 Aug. 1978, 15 International Legal Materials (Nov. 1976) 1572.

[43]   *See* the OAS Convention to Prevent and Punish Acts of Terrorism Taking the Form of Crimes against Persons and Related Extortion that Are of International Significance, *adopted* on 2 Feb. 1971 in Washington; (UN Doc. A/C.6/418); 10 International Legal Materials (1971) 255, *entered into force* on 16 Oct. 1973.

Mercenary Activity, Terrorism, Crimes
against UN Personnel, Drug-Trafficking,
Wilful and Severe Damage to the Environment

197

- General Assembly Resolutions,
Security Council Action and the Lockerbie Case

Of general significance to norms on terrorism is the General Assembly's Declaration on Principles of International Law concerning Friendly Relations and Co-operation among States in accordance with the Charter of the United Nations,[44] which affirms that: "Every State has the duty to refrain from organizing, instigating, assisting or participating in acts of civil strife or terrorist acts in another State or acquiescing in organized activities within its territory directed towards the commission of such acts". In 1994, the General Assembly adopted resolution 49/60[45] concerning ways to eliminate international terrorism. The resolution's annex, entitled Declaration on Measures to Eliminate International Terrorism, specifically rules out "political, philosophical, ideological, racial, ethnic, religious or any other" grounds as excuses in its denunciation of terrorist acts. On 11 December 1995, the General Assembly adopted resolution 53,[46] entitled 'Measures to Eliminate Terrorism', which refers to the need for further international cooperation to combat terrorism, "*[r]eiterates* that criminal acts intended or calculated to provoke a state of terror in the general public, a group of persons or particular persons for political purposes are in any circumstance unjustifiable, whatever the consider-ations of a political, philosophical, ideological, racial, ethnic, religious or any other nature that may be invoked to justify them", "*urges* all States to strengthen cooperation with one another to ensure that those who participate in terrorist activities, whatever the nature of their participation, find no safe haven anywhere" and "*[r]ecalls* the role of the Security Council in combating international terrorism whenever it poses a threat to international peace and security."

On a number of occasions, the Security Council has adopted resolutions which either prohibit terrorist acts generally or relate specifically to particular terrorist incidents. For example, in 1989, the Security Council passed resolution 635 in reaction to the terrorist attack on a civilian aircraft over the Sahara which claimed the lives of

---

[44] Resolution 2625, *adopted* by the General Assembly on 24 Oct. 1970.
[45] *Adopted* on 9 Dec. 1994.
[46] *See* General Assembly resolution 53 of 29 Jan. 1996, *adopted on* 11 Dec. 1995; A/Res/50/53.

over 400 individuals. A more important case, from the point of view of an international legal response, involves the shooting down of Pan Am 103 over Lockerbie, Scotland. The *Lockerbie Case*[47] is discussed in Chapter V(3)(iii) of the present enquiry in the context of the use of Security Council authority to bring the alleged offender before a domestic court.

iii) International Legal Response relative to Terrorist Acts Committed in Situations of Armed Conflict

Rules on terrorism committed within the specific context of armed conflict are found in international humanitarian law, namely in the four Geneva Conventions, 1949, and the two 1977 Protocols additional thereto. Two basic criteria in the Geneva Conventions and Protocols delimit lawful from unlawful warfare and bear on the prohibition of terrorism:

> The *first criterion* relates to the status of the person committing violence: members of the armed forces of a party to an armed conflict have a right to participate directly in hostilities. No other persons have that right. Should they nevertheless resort to violence, they breach the law. Their deeds may constitute acts of terrorism. ...
>
> The *second criterion* is derived from the rules governing the protection of specific categories of persons and the rules on methods and means of warfare in armed conflicts; to be licit, the use of violence in warfare must respect the restrictions imposed by the law of war. Consequently, even members of the armed forces legitimately entitled to the use of violence may become terrorists if they violate the laws of war.[48]

---

[47] *Questions of Interpretation and Application of the 1971 Montreal Convention arising from the Aerial Incident at Lockerbie* (Libya v. U.K.) 1992 ICJ Reports; and (Libya v. U.S.) 114-217.

[48] Hans-Peter Gasser, *Prohibition of Terrorist Acts in International Humanitarian Law*, International Review of the Red Cross (July-Aug. 1986).

Mercenary Activity, Terrorism, Crimes   199
against UN Personnel, Drug-Trafficking,
Wilful and Severe Damage to the Environment

As regards international armed conflict, Article 33 of the fourth Geneva Convention relative to the protection of civilians in time of war, stipulates that:

> No protected person may be punished for an offence he or she has not personally committed. Collective penalties and likewise all measures of intimidation or of terrorism are prohibited.

Article 33 also prohibits pillage and reprisals against protected persons and their property.[49] Article 34 adds that "[t]he taking of hostages is prohibited."

Updating and supplementing these provisions, Article 51(2) of 1977 Protocol I relating to international armed conflict provides that:

> The civilian population as such, as well as individual civilians, shall not be the object of attack. Acts or threats of violence the primary purpose of which is to spread terror among the civilian population are prohibited.

Peoples exercising their legitimate right to self-determination may resort to any means necessary for them to achieve their struggle, as long as they do not breach rules of international law, in particular, laws of war or international humanitarian law. Moreover, as wars of national liberation are considered international armed conflicts in the 1977 Protocols, this means that "the entire code of international humanitarian law applicable to international conflicts enters into force, along with all its attendant rights and obligations."[50] Thus, rules prohibiting terrorism in the Geneva Conventions and Protocols apply to wars of national liberation.[51]

---

[49] *See also* Article 4 of The Hague Convention of 14 May 1954 for the Protection of Cultural Property in the Event of Armed Conflict.

[50] Gasser, *supra* note 48 at 13.

[51] *See* Elizabeth Chadwick, Self-Determination, Terrorism and the International Humanitarian Law of Armed Conflict (1996).

With respect to non-international armed conflicts, Article 3 common to the four Geneva Conventions in effect outlaws terrorism through its prohibition of:

> ... violence to life and person, in particular murder of all kinds, mutilation, cruel treatment and torture; ... taking of hostages; ... outrages upon personal dignity, in particular, humiliating and degrading treatment ...

thereby establishing a minimum standard of treatment. Protocol II supplementing common Article 3, expressly prohibits 'acts of terrorism' in Article 4(2)(d). Moreover, Article 13(2) of Protocol II repeats Article 51(2) of Protocol I (quoted above); the prohibition of terrorist acts directed against the civilian population therefore applies to all situations of armed conflicts, whether international or non-international in character.

iv) 1991 Draft Code Provisions on Terrorism

Article 24 of the 1991 draft Code provides that:

> An individual who as an agent or representative of a State commits or orders the commission of any of the following acts:
>   - undertaking, organizing, assisting, financing, encouraging or tolerating acts against another State directed at persons or property and of such a nature as to create a state of terror in the minds of public figures, groups of persons or the general public
> shall, on conviction thereof, be sentenced [to...].

Article 24 applies only to agents or representatives of the State and not to private individuals. The presumption implicit in Article 24 is that State-sponsored terrorism poses the greater threat and therefore that only this more serious form should qualify as a 'crime against the peace and security of mankind'. Terrorist organizations which can rely on the support of a State enjoy enhanced capacity to operate on a transnational basis. A State may confer unofficially to a terrorist organization access to false passports to confound police in other countries and to help evade detection. Also, a State may misuse diplomatic status, privileges and immunities by issuing diplomatic passports to agents in order to support terrorist cells abroad.

As indicated by the development of the *lex lata* on terrorism, many States recognize that effective international cooperation is urgently needed to suppress terrorism; every State is vulnerable to the terrorist threat. However, due to the politically charged nature of terrorist activity, many States are reluctant to support the progressive development of individual criminal responsibility in international law for terrorism unless 'terrorism' is defined in legal terms first. As long as there exists no comprehensive multilateral instrument defining 'terrorism', the issue is likely to remain unresolved at the international level.

Despite considerable evidence indicating that terrorism is closely intertwined with international trafficking in illicit narcotic drugs, States have been slow to recognize the need for an international criminal court with competence over terrorism. Consequently, every State continues to rely on its municipal criminal law, which applies on a primarily territorial basis, to deal with terrorist threats despite the ease with which any individual may leave the territory. This leaves the prosecuting State little alternative but to request extradition, or where there is no extradition treaty, to rely on friendly relations and cooperation in the surrender of an alleged offender from the territory of another State. This approach is not likely to meet with success in a great many cases since States often disagree as to what acts committed by whom constitute terrorism.

v) 1996 Draft Code

In their comments and observations on the 1991 draft Code,[52] several Governments observed that Article 24 of the 1991 draft Code

---

[52] *See* Comments and Observations of Governments on the Draft Code of Crimes against the Peace and Security of Mankind adopted on First Reading by the International Law Commission at its 43rd Session, A/CN.4/ 448 of 1 March 1993.

failed to achieve the precision necessary for the purposes of international criminal law. The Government of Australia noted that the definition of 'international terrorism' did not specifically refer to violence, and as such, was overly vague. Conceivably, it could encompass mere propaganda intended to create a state of terror. The Governments of Belarus, Denmark, Finland, Iceland, Norway, Paraguay, Sweden and the UK, argued the provision was too narrow, because it was linked only to the State, whereas private terrorism equally could pose a threat to the peace and security of mankind. The Government of The Netherlands considered the provision too vague for the purposes of international criminal law.

In the 1996 version of the draft Code, 'terrorism' does not constitute a discrete 'crime against the peace and security of mankind' but appears within the rubric of 'war crimes'.[53] This approach by the ILC seems to reflect continuing reluctance on the part of States to admit terrorism within the jurisdiction of the proposed international criminal court. Currently, States appear to be sticking to traditional means of domestic enforcement and limited international cooperation, however inadequate these appear, out of the persistent fear of entrusting enforcement power to an international criminal court on such a politically sensitive matter.

Article 20(f)(iv) of the 1996 draft Code prohibits "acts of terror" under the rubric of 'war crimes' without defining it. The inclusion of 'acts of terror' as a war crime narrows the coverage of the norm prohibiting terrorism only to those acts "committed in a systematic manner or on a large scale". Further, as the chapeau of subparagraph (f) indicates, the provision applies only to acts "committed in violation of international humanitarian law applicable in armed conflict not of an international character". In other words, the 1996 draft Code definition of terrorism applies only to widespread acts of terror which breach that part of humanitarian law applicable in non-international armed conflict.

---

[53]   *See* new Article 20 (f)(iv) of the Draft Code of Crimes against the Peace and Security of Mankind adopted by the International Law Commission at its 48th session (1996); A/CN.4/L.532 of 8 July 1996.

3. CRIMES AGAINST UNITED NATIONS AND ASSOCIATED PERSONNEL

In 1996, the ILC introduced a new provision into the draft Code on crimes against United Nations and associated personnel. Article 19 of the 1996 draft Code provides that "murder, kidnapping or other attack upon the person or liberty of personnel", or "violent attack upon the official premises, the private accommodation or the means of transportation of any such personnel likely to endanger his or her person or liberty" are prohibited "when committed intentionally and in a systematic manner or on a large scale" and "with a view to preventing or impeding that operation from fulfilling its mandate".

Paragraph 2 provides that Article 19 shall not apply to United Nations enforcement action being carried out under Chapter VII of the United Nations Charter "in which any of the personnel are engaged as combatants against organized armed forces and to which the law of international armed conflict applies". Thus Article 19 would apply to any UN civilian operations, such as human rights field operations, elections monitoring or any other missions other than those involving Chapter VII enforcement action.

As the Commentary to Article 19[54] notes, in the last few years, United Nations personnel increasingly have become the target of attack. This may be partially due to the new expanded role of the United Nations since the end of the Cold War. Security Council authority to enforce the peace has been invoked more often. Moreover, the end of the Cold War seems to have resulted in an increased number of situations that involve the phenomenon of the collapsed State; situations where governmental authority has imploded from the outbreak of civil war, perhaps driven by ethnic hatred, or where domestic law and order have disappeared with the sudden withdrawal of superpower support which had buttressed the power of the State from outside. In these kinds of political power vacuum situations, militia groups may seek to raise their international profile by attacking staff or personnel of the United Nations, who may symbolize to them the unwanted hand of foreign interference.

---

[54]   A/CN.4/L.527/Add.10.

Concerned with the increasing number of attacks on UN and associated personnel, on 17 February 1995, the General Assembly adopted resolution 49/59[55] the annex to which is the Convention on the Safety of United Nations and Associated Personnel.   The Convention defines 'United Nations personnel' and 'associated personnel', sets out requirements for the identification of personnel, vehicles, vessels and aircraft of the United Nations, and obliges the host State and the United Nations to conclude an agreement on the status of the operation in question incorporating provisions concerning the privileges and immunities of military and police components of the operation. Article 7 of the Convention imposes upon States Parties a duty to ensure the safety and security of United Nations and associated personnel. Article 8 imposes a duty to release or return such personnel in case they are captured or detained. Article 9 of the Convention, which forms the basis of Article 19 of the 1996 draft Code, provides that:

1.   The intentional commission of:
(a)   A murder, kidnapping or other attack upon the person or liberty of any United Nations or associated personnel;
(b)   A violent attack upon the official premises, the private accommodation or the means of transportation of any United Nations or associated personnel likely to endanger his or her person or liberty;
(c)   A threat to commit any such attack with the objective of compelling a physical or juridical person to do or to refrain from doing any act;
(d)   An attempt to commit any such attack; and
(e)   An act constituting participation as an accomplice in any such attack, or in an attempt to commit such attack, or in

---

[55]   Convention on the Safety of United Nations and Associated Personnel, *adopted unanimously*, 17 Feb. 1995; A/Res/49/59.

           organizing or ordering others to commit
           such attack,
shall be made by each State Party a crime under its
national law.

2.   Each State Party shall make the crimes
           set out in paragraph 1 punishable by
           appropriate penalties which shall take
           into account their grave nature.

Article 14 of the Convention imposes a duty upon the State Party, in whose territory the alleged offender is present, either to prosecute or extradite him or her. Articles 15 and 16 concern extradition. Article 17 provides for the fair treatment of any person "regarding whom investigations or proceedings are being carried out".

Article 19 of the 1996 draft Code is deliberately narrow in scope. It envisages individual criminal responsibility only where the acts set out in Article 19 are committed intentionally "and in a systematic manner or on a large scale" and with a view to preventing or impeding the UN operation involved from fulfilling its mandate. The element of criminal intention is necessary to avoid any suggestion that criminal responsibility should accrue for cases arising from accidents not involving criminal negligence.

However, against the background of the right of the accused to be presumed innocent until proven guilty, and the requirement of the prosecution to prove its case beyond a reasonable doubt, the elements that the acts must be committed on a systematic or large scale, along with the overall motivation of preventing or impeding a UN operation from carrying out its mandate, make the definition of the crime far too narrow, but oddly enough, too vague as well. The terms 'systematic' and 'large-scale' are not sufficiently precise in this context for the purposes of international criminal law because they seem to imply that the murder of one or a few UN personnel might not involve criminal responsibility. Perhaps these conditions should be deleted from Article 19.

4. ILLICIT TRAFFIC IN NARCOTIC DRUGS

i) Background

The illicit traffic in narcotic drugs, particularly of opium, morphine, and heroine (derivatives of the poppy plant), and in recent years, cocaine (a derivative of coca leaves) including crack (a free-base ten times more powerful than cocaine), has managed to circumvent and in some regions even to subordinate law enforcement authorities. In the worst cases, governments and national economies have become dependent upon the illicit drug trade.

The illicit traffic in narcotic drugs has become a problem of international concern, particularly in those cases where it is connected to terrorism or illegal intervention in the domestic affairs of a foreign State. Where the courts or even the executive branch of a State have become compromised by the illicit narcotics trade, or for other reasons are unable to stem or suppress this activity, international criminal law may be valuable to complement domestic law enforcement efforts. In cases where the top levels of the Government are implicated in illicit drug-trafficking, and there seems little likelihood of prosecutions under domestic law, as appears to have been the case in Panama under General Manuel Noriega,[56] international criminal law may play a particularly important role.

- *Opium, Morphine and Heroine*

Narcotic drugs have been used for thousands of years for medicinal properties and in rituals and ceremonies in various cultures and religions. Opium was used as early as 2000 B.C. in Cyprus, Crete and Greece, in India as early as 1000 B.C. and in the Americas by indigenous peoples as early as 200 A.D.[57] In the early 1700's,

---

[56]   However, in this case, the United States unilaterally invaded Panama, and then forcibly apprehended and brought Noriega before the South District of Florida federal courts to face an indictment for illicit drug-trafficking. *See United States* v. *Noriega*, 746 F. Supp., 1506 (S.D. Fla. 1990); and 752 F. Supp., 1032 (S.D. Fla. 1990).

[57]   S.K. Chatterjee, Legal Aspects of International Drug Control (1981) at 3.

opium was traded internationally by Holland and Portugal along with other foodstuffs, such as tea and coffee, condiments and spices, when these countries gained control of Indian Ocean trade from Arab merchants.[58]

However, trafficking in opium assumed much larger dimensions with the extension of the British Empire to Asia. In 1773, the Crown granted the British East India Company the exclusive right to trade opium in Bengal. As the Ming Dynasty came to an end, the Company was able to force into China the importation of Indian opium over the efforts of the Ming and Manchu authorities to halt influx of the addictive substance.[59]

By 1830, the East India Company was successful in establishing an effective system of smuggling Indian opium into China.[60] The financial interests at stake were very high. By the time of the Opium War, China had around 10 million addicts and spent almost all of its total yearly revenue on opium.[61] The opium trade was used as leverage to pry open Asian commercial markets. Taxes collected from opium trade proceeds were used to finance the extension of the British colonial system throughout Asia. The financial and strategic interests of the British Empire were sufficiently engaged in the opium trade that the British Government fought two 'Opium Wars' (1839-1842 and 1856-1858) to maintain control over the highly lucrative enterprise. By 1886, the British were estimated to be "selling 200,000

---

[58]   William L. Smith, Why People Grow Drugs: Narcotics and Development in the Third World (1992) at 6-7.

[59]   William O. Walker, Opium and Foreign Policy: The Anglo-American Search for Order in Asia, 1912-1954 (1991) at 4.

[60]   As Walker, *ibid.* at 8, states: "The carrying of opium into Chinese waters, though legitimate under British laws, troubled consuls in the treaty ports. The ports could not adequately serve their intended purpose of encouraging Anglo-Chinese commerce if distinctions had to be made about what constituted licit trade. To remedy the situation, a system of receiving stations was established at anchorages just outside the ports. British consuls took no official notice of the stations, and the opium trade flourished unimpeded by legal difficulties. Better to serve both sellers and smugglers, the Crown Colony of Hong Kong began operating within a few years as a warehouse and distribution centre."

[61]   *Ibid.* at 5.

cases of opium per year to the Chinese, whose addiction rate rose to over 100 million".[62]

Although prohibited in China since 1800, the influx of opium continued and eventually gave rise to criminal trafficking networks. The migration of Chinese labourers to the Americas, Europe and other parts of Asia, spread opium use to other countries. The problem in China continued until the Communist Revolution in 1949 brought a determined approach to eliminate Chinese opium production, which successfully forced the sudden withdrawal of millions of addicts.[63]

Unfortunately, the Chinese Revolution could not eliminate opium production and trafficking beyond Chinese borders. Criminal gangs merely found other ideal growing areas, namely in the Golden Triangle (that covers parts of Laos, Myanmar and Thailand), and later, in the Golden Crescent (that covers parts of Afghanistan, Iran and Pakistan).

The involvement of France and later on the United States in Southeast Asia, resulted in further exacerbation of what had become an international drug problem by the 1950's and 1960's.

> The complexities of the superpower politics revolving around the war in Vietnam created situations in which first the French colonial government and then the US Central Intelligence Agency (CIA) aided and abetted the Royal Laotian Army and hill tribes, which were actively involved in the heroine trade. Then, in the 1960's, US troops provided a new heroine market and, in 1969, heroine laboratories were introduced into the region, marking an escalation in the productive capacity of Golden Triangle trafficking rings. By 1975, when the last US troops were withdrawn, there was a new Asian market of 500,000 heroine users waiting to be supplied.[64]

---

[62]   Alison Jamieson, *Global Drug Trafficking*, in Terrorism and Drug Trafficking in the 1990s (ed. Jamieson) (1994) at 70.

[63]   Smith, *supra* note 58 at 7-8. Some American companies were also active in the opium trade in the early 1800's, but these could not compete with British control. *See* Walker, *supra* note 59 at 8.

[64]   Smith *supra* note 58 at 10-11.

The consequences were staggering. Estimates by the US State Department indicate that opium production increased from some 400 metric tonnes in 1979, to 2,565 tonnes in 1990, almost all of it produced in Myanmar.[65] In the 1990's, world opium production is estimated to have reached 4000 metric tonnes, which once refined, could produce 400 metric tonnes of heroine.[66]

- Coca, Cocaine and Crack

Coca has been cultivated and traded in the Andes for centuries, but did not figure as a major international commodity until the 1980's.[67] The incentive to produce coca on a large scale finds its roots in post-World War II policies in Bolivia, Colombia and Peru. These policies were designed to control overpopulation and stimulate economic development through resettlement of people inland to produce cash crops. However, for decades, inopportune busts in the commodity markets sabotaged numerous Government attempts to establish viable production of legitimate cash crops. From the mid-1970's, fledgling Colombian cocaine traffickers introduced coca farming in areas where Government agricultural policies had failed.

> With an efficiency unencumbered by government bureaucracy or regulations, they brought in coca seeds, set up demonstration plots, provided venture capital and guaranteed purchase of the harvest. ... From that time and through most of the 1980's, coca acreage grew by 10% a year.[68]

Throughout the 1980's, cocaine production, which hitherto had been only of very marginal significance, expanded to the point that many South American economies now depend heavily on cash earnings from illicit sales of cocaine, primarily to the huge US market.

---

[65] *Ibid.*

[66] Jamieson, *supra* note 62 at 70-71.

[67] Smith, *supra* note 58 at 12. Cocaine was refined for the first time in 1862 by a German scientist.

[68] *Ibid.* at 16.

> The illicit cocaine traffic has increased by 400 per cent in recent years; world seizures have risen over 90 times in the last 15 years ... but even the most optimistic view puts seizures at between 10 and 20 per cent of the real total. European cocaine seizures almost doubled from 3,970 kg in 1987 to 6,994 kg in 1988. ... Importantly, the supply and demand for cocaine have not reduced the demand for heroine but have grown alongside it: in 1987 for the first time European cocaine seizures surpassed those of heroine; the trend became even more pronounced in 1988 ...[69]

The profits from cocaine are immense. It is worth considering that in 1989, a single cocaine seizure was made in Los Angeles of 21.4 metric tonnes with "a street value of around 6 billion dollars - more than the gross national product of 100 sovereign states".[70]

The power of cocaine has compromised law enforcement authorities in a number of countries, particularly in Latin America. In some countries, key public officials, including certain judges and politicians, appear to have found it difficult or impossible to resist the force exerted upon them by powerful drug kingpins through the combination of bribes and threats. The hearings before the United States Senate Subcommittee on Terrorism, Narcotics and International Operations of the Committee on Foreign Relations, conducted in 1987 and 1988, raised a number of very disturbing questions in this regard. The hearings also lent credence to allegations of major involvement even of some elements of the top echelons of the Reagan Administration with known cocaine drug-traffickers (some of whom were under indictment in US federal courts at the time) in order to provide

---

[69]   Jamieson, *supra* note 62 at 71.

[70]   *Ibid.* at 69; and at 100: "[A]n estimated 6 per cent of US citizens are drug addicts; since 1984 there has been a 28-fold increase in hospital admissions involving the smoking of cocaine which is now the prime cause of drug-related death; between 1986 and 1988 the number of babies born with birth defects linked to cocaine abuse tripled; 60 per cent of homicides in Washington D.C. are drug-related. New York police made 90,000 drug arrests in 1988, the equivalent of one every six minutes ...; of all arrests made in the city, only 10 per cent have no trace of drugs in their bodies.."

financial and material support to the Contras' efforts to topple the Sandinista Government of Nicaragua.[71]

Sworn testimony tendered at the Subcommittee hearings revealed that long after the US State Department and the Federal Bureau of Investigation had become aware that Costa Rica based Contra organizations were heavily involved in illicit drug-trafficking operations, the US Justice Department continued to issue statements denying allegations of these connections. Moreover, the State Department paid funds to Contra suppliers through companies that were owned, managed or controlled by known drug-traffickers.

Ultimately, it appears that certain elements of the US Government involved in the Iran / Contra Affair, such as those indicted or convicted on numerous counts related thereto, were at least grossly negligent and perhaps criminally responsible for having supported cocaine trafficking organizations in Latin America with US tax-payer funds in order to meet political ends. This action allowed drug-traffickers to cover their illicit activities with the American support for the Contra movement and to secure new inroads to meet the burgeoning US consumer demand for cocaine.[72]

By the end of 1980's, US market demand was being met and the price of cocaine in the US had plummeted to around US$ 10 per gram. However, South American drug cartels appear to have forged

---

[71]   In 1986, the Subcommittee had intended to investigate allegations of covert US Government involvement or support for illegal arms shipments to the Contras. However, as the evidence mounted, it became clear that a number of US Government agencies had provided financial and material support to Contra organizations, under the cover of humanitarian assistance, through known drug-traffickers in the Bahamas, Costa Rica and Honduras. The Subcommittee therefore expanded its mandate to take into account the broader foreign policy and law enforcement implications of illicit drug-trafficking in Central America. *See* the Subcommittee Hearings testimony of Federal Prisoner George Morales who had been convicted of illicit drug-trafficking in connection with the Contras, in Drugs, Law Enforcement and Foreign Policy: The Cartel, Haiti and Central America, Hearings before the Subcommittee on Terrorism, Narcotics and International Communications of the Committee on Foreign Relations, United States Senate, Part 3, 4-7 April 1988 at 287 *et seq.*

[72]   *See* Peter D. Scott and Jonathan Marshall, Cocaine Politics: Drugs, Armies and the CIA in Central America (1991).

supply networks with criminal organizations in Europe where the price per gram varied from between nine to twenty times the US price (depending on the country), providing drug traffickers with a powerful incentive to expand operations into these new markets.[73]

ii) International Legal Response relative to the Illicit Traffic in Narcotic Drugs

Several conventions on narcotic drugs have been adopted by the League of Nations and United Nations. The earlier conventions were aimed at controlling illicit trade in opium.[74] The first international conference to control the movement of narcotic drugs was held in Shanghai in 1909, and culminated in the International Opium Convention of 1912.[75] This was the first Convention designed to restrict shipments of opium and opium derivatives, leaving open an exception for shipments deemed necessary for medical purposes. Article 5 attempts to bring the problem of opium traffic under legal control by stipulating that "the Contracting Powers shall not allow the import and export of raw opium except by duly authorized persons". Article 6 provides that parties "shall take measures for the gradual and effective suppression of the manufacture of, internal trade in, and use of prepared opium, with due regard to the varying circumstance in each country concerned". Article 7 does the same for 'prepared opium', thereby covering the derivatives of morphine and heroine. Article 13 obliges States parties to the Convention to "use their best endeavours to adopt, or cause to be adopted, measures to ensure that morphine, cocaine, and their respective salts shall not be exported from their countries, possessions, colonies". A number of States were reluctant to sign the Convention and so, in accordance

---

[73]   Jamieson, *supra* note 62 at 71.

[74]   *See* Cherif Bassiouni, *The International Narcotics Scheme* in 1 International Criminal Law (ed. Bassiouni) (1987). *See generally* United Nations, The United Nations and Drug Abuse Control (1989) UN Pub. Sales No. E.90.I.3.

[75]   *Signed* at the Hague 23 Jan. 1912, *entered into force* 11 Feb. 1915, 6 American Journal of International Law 177 (Supp. 1912).

with the Convention, further conferences were convened[76] to encourage States which had not participated in the 1912 opium conference to sign and ratify the Convention.

The end of the First World War and the creation of the League of Nations enhanced efforts at suppressing the illicit traffic in narcotic drugs through international cooperation. Pursuant to Article 23(c) of the Covenant entrusting the League of Nations with "general supervision over the execution of agreements with regard to ... the traffic in opium and other dangerous drugs", the Advisory Committee on Traffic in Opium and Other Dangerous Drugs was established in 1920. This Committee, appointed in 1921, provided advice to the League of Nations Council on matters involving the opium trade, and encouraged the better observance of the 1912 Opium Convention.

In 1925, the International Opium Convention was adopted[77] to tighten the control system created under the 1912 Opium Convention, and in Article 19, provided for the creation of the Permanent Central Narcotics Board. Although the Board did not have investigative powers, it undertook to estimate the world requirement of narcotic drugs for legitimate scientific and medical uses by obtaining information from reports submitted by States working alongside the League's Health Committee. It also attempted to determine the global level of production, manufacture, stock and consumption of opium and coca.[78] The Convention also contained provisions on Indian hemp, thereby extending coverage to a previously unregulated substance. The Permanent Central Narcotics Board was in a position to draw the attention of the League of Nations Council to any situation in which a particular country was involved in the accumulation of illicit narcotic drugs within its territory.

In July 1933, pursuant to Article 5(6) of the 1931 Convention for Limiting the Manufacture and Regulating the Distribution of Narcotic Drugs,[79] a Drug Supervisory Body to oversee the functioning of the international narcotics control system was set up. The

---

[76]   These conferences were held in The Hague in July 1913 and June 1914.
[77]   *Entered into force* 25 Sept. 1928.
[78]   Chatterjee, *supra* note 57 at 89.
[79]   *Entered into force* 9 July 1933, 28 American Journal of International Law (1934).

Supervisory Body endeavoured to enhance international coordination of domestic legislation and enforcement to counter illicit narcotics traffic. It was also authorized to gather information, complementary to that initially provided by States, with a view to coming to precise estimates of world narcotics production and traffic.

The Convention for the Suppression of the Illicit Traffic in Dangerous Drugs,[80] adopted in 1936, obliges ratifying States to ensure that drug traffickers in their respective jurisdictions are severely punished. A Protocol of 1946[81] provided for establishment of the United Nations Commission on Narcotic Drugs, a functional commission of the Economic and Social Council with a mandate to execute functions previously carried out by the League of Nations' Advisory Committee. A 1947 Protocol[82] extended the scope of the international drug control system to cover certain new synthetic drugs. The Opium Protocol for Limiting and Regulating the Cultivation of the Poppy Plant, the Production of, International and Wholesale Trade in and Use of Opium,[83] adopted in 1953, restricted legal opium use to certain medical and scientific uses, and created limits on production and stocks of opium by States.

In 1961, the UN adopted the Single Convention on Narcotic Drugs[84] to supersede and consolidate all of the earlier conventions on drug-trafficking in order to reduce complexity in the *lex lata*.[85] The Single Convention extends international regulatory control over cultivation of the bush and leaves of the coca plant as well as over cannabis. This approach attempts to strike literally at the roots of narcotic drug production by targeting production in its early phases. The four Schedules to the Convention list the substances subject to prohibition and introduce a measure of flexibility into the legal norms on narcotic drugs by seeking to control all substances which exhibit

---

[80]   *Entered into force* 29 Sept. 1939, 31 American Journal of International Law (1937).

[81]   *Entered into force* 10 Oct. 1947.

[82]   *Entered into force* 1 Dec. 1949.

[83]   *Signed* at New York, *entered into force* 8 Mar. 1963.

[84]   *Adopted on* 30 Mar. 1961 *entered into force on* 13 Dec. 1964; UN Doc. E/Conf. 34/22 (1961).

[85]   In addition the Convention created the International Narcotics Board by combining the Drug Supervisory Body and the Permanent Central Board.

addictive properties or engender a propensity for abuse in addition to outlawing the particular substances themselves. Formulated in this way, minor alterations in the molecular structure or innovations in addictive substances which could maintain their addictive properties, may be brought within the ambit of the Convention. Like earlier conventions, the Single Convention aims to suppress only the abuse of narcotic drugs, rather than its therapeutic, medical or beneficial scientific properties, and relies on domestic means of enforcement.

In 1971, the scope of international drug regulation was extended to certain categories of hallucinogens including LSD, mescaline, amphetamines and certain barbiturates through adoption of the UN Convention on Psychotropic Substances.[86] In addition, the Convention provides that the World Health Organization shall be responsible for determining whether a new substance should be listed in one of the Convention's Schedules as a prohibited drug.

A Protocol[87] of 1972 amends the 1961 Single Convention and places greater emphasis on the importance of treatment and drug addict rehabilitation as well as penal law enforcement.

In 1988, the United Nations adopted the Convention against Illicit Traffic in Narcotic Drugs and Psychotropic Substances,[88] which obliges each State Party to establish criminal offenses under its domestic law to cover "production, manufacture, extraction, preparation, offering, offering for sale, distribution, sale, delivery on any terms whatsoever, brokerage, dispatch, dispatch in transit, transport, importation or exportation of any narcotic drug or any psychotropic

---

[86]   *Done* at Vienna, 21 Feb. 1971, *entered into force* 16 Aug. 1976, 10 International Legal Materials (1971).   The Convention maintains the categorization of illicit substances in four groups and prescribes measures for controlling various aspects of manufacture, export and import, stockpiles, and use and possession for scientific and medical purposes.   *See* the four Schedules annexed to the Convention.

[87]   *Adopted on* 25 Mar. 1972 in Geneva, *entered into force*, 8 Aug. 1975, 11 International Legal Materials (1972).

[88]   *Done* at Vienna, Austria, 20 Dec. 1988, *entered into force* 11 Nov. 1990, E/CONF.82/15 of 19 Dec. 1988, 28 International Legal Materials 493 (1989). *See* General Assembly resolution 45/146 of 18 Dec. 1990, calling upon States to ratify and apply the provisions of the 1988 Convention.

substance contrary to the provisions of the 1961 Convention, as amended, or the 1971 Convention".[89]

On 4 December 1989, the UN General Assembly adopted resolution 44/39,[90] requesting the International Law Commission:

> to address the question of establishing an international criminal court or other international criminal trial mechanism with jurisdiction over persons alleged to have committed crimes which may be covered under [the draft Code of Offenses against the Peace and Security of Mankind] including persons engaged in illicit trafficking in narcotic drugs across national frontiers ...

The proliferation of international agreements designed to suppress trafficking in illicit drugs indicates that the international community has recognized the need for international rather than purely domestic solutions to the drug problem.

The substantial increase in the number of births of drug-addicted babies is shocking. In light of the high incidence of drug abuse and of a growing illicit trafficking of narcotic drugs, it can not be said the international narcotic drug control system has been effective. In addition there is the relation between illicit narcotic drug-trafficking, intravenous drug use and the spread of the human immuno-deficiency virus (HIV) and acquired immuno-deficiency syndrome (AIDS). As discussed above, the very security and stability of some Government institutions remain vulnerable to intimidation from 'narco-terrorists'. All these and other perils demand imaginative solutions be taken at the international level and for States to allocate sufficient priority to this problem.

---

[89]   Article 3 prohibits possession, manufacture, financing, conversion of transfer of property and concealment of the use of property used for committing an offence prohibited in the Convention, *ibid.*

[90]   *Adopted* by the General Assembly 4 Dec. 1989, UN Doc. A/44/39.

iii) 1991 Draft Code Provisions on Illicit Drug-Trafficking

Article 25 of the 1991 draft Code provides that:

1.   An individual who commits or orders the commission of any of the following acts:
　　　 - undertaking, organizing, facilitating,
　　　 financing or encouraging illicit traffic in
　　　 narcotic drugs on a large scale, whether
　　　 within the confines of a State or in a
　　　 transboundary context
shall, on conviction thereof, be sentenced [to ...].
2.   For the purpose of paragraph 1, facilitating or
encouraging illicit traffic in narcotic drugs includes the
acquisition, holding, conversion or traffic of property by
an individual who knows that such property is derived
from the crime described in this article in order to
conceal or disguise the illicit origin of the property.
3.   Illicit traffic in narcotic drugs means any production, manufacture, extraction, preparation, offering,
offering for sale, distribution, sale, delivery on any
terms whatsoever, brokerage, dispatch, dispatch in
transit, transport, importation or exportation of any
narcotic drug or any psychotropic substance contrary to
internal or international law.

Article 25 is designed to cover all major aspects of illicit drug-
trafficking. Interestingly, Article 25 applies to illicit traffic within the
confines of a State as well as to transnational traffic. Article 25(2)
would allow for the bringing to trial before an international criminal
court of persons for money laundering.

However, the 1991 draft Code would not extend international
criminal responsibility to the use and possession of narcotic drugs for
individual consumption. First, small-scale use of narcotic drugs is too
insignificant to be considered a 'crime against the peace and security
of mankind'. Second, national laws differ widely in the scale of
punishment prescribed for narcotic drug use. It would be unrealistic

therefore to stipulate individual criminal responsibility on a uniform basis to apply to all States.[91]

It is not clear whether the phrase 'on a large scale' in Article 25(1) refers to the weight or volume of narcotic drugs alleged to have been trafficked or whether it refers to the extent narcotic drugs may be manufactured, processed and distributed by even one individual. In other words, Article 25(1) does not indicate the threshold at which individuals knowingly involved in narcotic drug shipments would become subject to the international criminal court's jurisdiction.

iv) 1996 Draft Code

In their comments and observations on the 1991 draft Code, a number of State representatives indicated strong doubts as to whether illicit traffic in narcotic drugs should be covered by an international penal code.[92] The Australian representative stated that the draft Code should spell out in detail the Code's relation to the existing conventional system of illicit narcotic drug-traffic control, in particular, that provided for in the 1988 Convention against Illicit Traffic in Narcotic Drugs and Psychotropic Substances, as well as with municipal legal control systems. The Government of The Netherlands stated its opposition to the inclusion of the 1991 draft Code's provisions on drug-trafficking and argued that an international criminal court might not be the best means by which to enforce anti-drug-trafficking norms.

The Government of Switzerland, however, supported the inclusion of provisions on illicit trafficking of narcotic drugs, citing what it believed was a clear relation between terrorism and drug-trafficking.

---

[91] In recent years, some countries, such as the Netherlands and Switzerland, have experimented with official toleration of possession and personal use of small amounts of narcotic drugs, whereas many countries of the Middle East and Southeast Asia, tend towards imposition of severe penalties for possession of even trace amounts of certain illicit drugs.

[92] Namely, those of Australia, Austria, The Netherlands, UK, Poland and the US; *see* Comments and Observations of Governments on the Draft Code of Crimes against the Peace and Security of Mankind adopted on First Reading by the International Law Commission at its 43rd Session, A/CN.4/ 448 of 1 March 1993.

The 1996 version of the draft Code does not include provisions on illicit trafficking of narcotic drugs. It appears that, for the time being, many States remain unwilling to recognize the competence of a global international criminal court in this domain. However, should bilateral or regional arrangements prove insufficient to stem the supply and demand for illicit narcotics, it would seem unwise to dismiss lightly possible avenues for more comprehensive prohibition and enforcement at the international level.

Should a global international criminal court not prove a palatable option for States, perhaps the possible creation of a specialized court or courts with specific competence over illicit drug-trafficking cases on a regional basis could gain more support. Specialized regional courts at the international level could serve more closely the needs and interests of the countries of particular regions, while still benefitting from the independence and impartiality conferred by the international character of such a court.

5. WILFUL AND SEVERE DAMAGE
TO THE NATURAL ENVIRONMENT

i) Background

Effective protection of the natural environment demands international cooperation since the effects of pollution do not respect national boundaries. However, it is unclear under what circumstances, if any, should norms of international law impose individual criminal responsibility for damage to the natural environment. In this connection, it is valuable to review the relevant *lex lata* and then to consider the 1991 draft Code provisions on wilful and severe damage to the natural environment.

The *Trail Smelter Case*, which concerned sulphur dioxide gas emissions from a Canadian smelting company that passed to the US side, is often cited for its statement of general principle with respect to cross-boundary pollution. In that case, the International Joint Commission held that:

> ... under the principles of international law, as well as
> of the law of the United States, no State has the right

to use or permit the use of its territory in such a manner as to cause injury by fumes in or to the territory of another or the properties or persons therein, when the case is of serious consequence and the injury is established by clear and convincing evidence.[93]

The holding in the *Lac Lanoux Arbitration* referred tangentially to the issue of cross-boundary pollution. In that case, the Tribunal observed that Spain would have had a stronger case on the merits against France for having diverted water if it "... had been argued that the works would bring about an ultimate pollution of the waters ... or that the returned waters would have a chemical composition or a temperature or some characteristic which could injure Spanish interests".[94]

In another context, the International Court of Justice observed in the *Corfu Channel Case*,[95] that "... every State's obligation not to allow knowingly its territory to be used for acts contrary to the rights of other States" is a well-recognized general principle of international law. This principle, expressed in its classic formulation as *sic utere tuo ut alienum non laedas*, is fundamental also to the doctrine of *abus de droit*: a State is obliged to exercise its rights in such a way as not to cause harm to other States.

Prior to the early 1970's, established international legal norms on the environment were in a disorganized state and few in number. A comprehensive approach to develop norms concerning protection of the natural environment was taken by the United Nations Conference on the Human Environment, held in Stockholm, from 5 to June 1972, which culminated in a report and Declaration of Principles. The Report of the conference sets forth a number of principles which lay the groundwork for more comprehensive international cooperation on the environment.[96] The two more pertinent principles of the Declar-

---

[93]   (US v. Canada) 3 Reports of International Arbitral Awards (1938 and 1941) 1905.

[94]   24 International Law Reports (1957) 101.

[95]   *Corfu Channel Case* (United Kingdom v. Albania) (Merits) 1949 ICJ Reports 4.

[96]   United Nations, Report of the United Nations Conference on the Human Environment, Stockholm, 5-16 June 1972, (New York, 1973).

ation are set out below. Principle 21 of the Stockholm Declaration provides that:

> States have, in accordance with the Charter of the
> United Nations and the principles of international law,
> the sovereign right to exploit their own resources
> pursuant to their own environmental policies, and the
> responsibility to ensure that activities within their
> jurisdiction or control do not cause damage to the
> environment of other States or of areas beyond the
> limits of national jurisdiction.

Principle 22 provides that:

> States shall cooperate to develop further the interna-
> tional law regarding liability and compensation for the
> victims of pollution and other environmental damage
> caused by activities within the jurisdiction or control of
> such States to areas beyond their jurisdiction.

Taken together, Principles 21 and 22 affirm the national sovereignty of the State to decide how to exploit its own resources according to domestic priorities. They also emphasize the State's responsibility to ensure activities conducted within its territory do not cause damage in areas beyond its jurisdiction as well as its obligation to cooperate with other States as regards development of norms on liability and compensation.

Several conventions oblige States to prevent and reduce damage to the marine environment. For example, Part XII of the United Nations Convention on the Law of the Sea, 1982,[97] comprising 47 articles and entitled 'Protection and Preservation of the Marine

---

[97]   *See* the United Nations Convention on the Law of the Sea, *signed* at Montego Bay, 10 Dec. 1982, UN Doc. A/CONF.62/122, 21 International Legal Materials (1982) 1261.

Environment', establishes extensive international obligations concerning pollution of marine areas.[98]

The International Convention Relating to Intervention on the High Seas in Cases of Oil Pollution Casualties, 1969,[99] and the International Convention on Civil Liability for Oil Pollution Damage, 1969,[100] relate specifically to oil pollution, while treaties such as the London Convention on the Prevention of Marine Pollution by Dumping of Wastes and Other Matter, 1972,[101] Oslo Convention for the Prevention of Marine Pollution by Dumping from Ships and Aircraft, 1972,[102] Paris Convention for the Prevention of Pollution from Land-Based Sources, 1974[103] and Convention for the Protection of the Mediterranean Sea against Pollution, 1974,[104] apply to particular kinds of water systems, geographic locations etc.

Specific conventions have been adopted that provide for: international cooperation with respect to protection of waterfowl and migratory birds;[105] prohibition of international trade in endangered species of plants and animals;[106] pertinent international labour standards;[107] limits on nuclear weapons testing,[108] transport[109] and

---

[98]   These provisions cover: global and regional cooperation; technical assistance; monitoring and environmental assessment; the relation of international rules to national legislation to prevent, reduce and control pollution of the marine environment; enforcement; safeguards; protection of ice-covered areas; responsibility and liability; and non-applicability of the provisions of the Convention to "warships, naval auxiliaries, other vessels or aircraft owned or operated by a State and used, for the time being, only on government non-commercial service".

[99]   9 International Legal Materials (1969) 25.

[100]   9 International Legal Materials (1969) 45.

[101]   11 International Legal Materials (1972) 1291.

[102]   11 International Legal Materials (1972) 262.

[103]   13 International Legal Materials (1974) 352.

[104]   15 International Legal Materials (1976) 290.

[105]   Convention on Wetlands of International Importance Especially as Waterfowl Habitat, 1971.

[106]   Convention on International Trade in Endangered Species of Wild Fauna and Flora, 1973.

[107]   *See e.g.* Convention No. 148 (Working Environment: Air Pollution, Noise and Vibration) (and Recommendation No. 156) both of 1977, Convention No. 13, 1921 (white lead painting), Recommendation No. 4, 1919

emplacement of nuclear materials devices;[110] prohibition of use of weapons hostile to the environment;[111] and principles governing activities of States in outer space.[112]

The absence of a clear international legal regime protecting the environment, and the development of 'soft law'[113] guiding States as to what standards of conduct they are expected to observe in the exercise of their rights, have given rise to ILC efforts to progressively develop international legal norms with respect to international liability for injurious consequences arising out of acts not prohibited by international law.[114]

The above-mentioned conventions incorporate notions of risk, harm, liability and the obligation of a State to make reparation or

---

(Lead Poisoning: Women and Children), Convention No. 114, 1960 (Radiation Protection) and Convention No. 136, 1971 (Benzene) (and Recommendation No. 144, 1971).

[108]   *See* the *Nuclear Tests Cases* (Australia v. France); (New Zealand v. France), 1974 ICJ Reports at 457.

[109]   *See e.g.* the Nuclear Test Ban Treaty, 1963, 480 UNTS 43, the Brussels Convention on the Liability of Operators of Nuclear Ships, 1962.

[110]   *See* the Treaty on the Prohibition of the Emplacement of Nuclear Weapons and Other Weapons of Mass Destruction on the Sea-Bed and the Ocean Floor and in the Subsoil Thereof, 1971.

[111]   *See e.g.* Convention on the Prohibition of the Development, Production and Stockpiling of Bacteriological (Biological) and Toxic Weapons and on their Destruction, 1972, and the Convention on the Prohibition of Military or Any Other Hostile Use of Environmental Modification Techniques, 1976.

[112]   *See* Treaty on Principles Governing the Activities of States in the Exploration and Use of Outer Space, including the Moon and Other Celestial Bodies, 1967; 610 UNTS 205.

[113]   *See* Pierre-Marie Dupuy, *Soft Law and the International Law of the Environment*, 12(2) Michigan Journal of International Law (1991).

[114]   *See* the Fifth Report on International Liability for Injurious Consequences arising out of Acts not Prohibited by International Law; [1989 ILC Yearbook; A/CN.4/1989 (Part 2). *See also* Constance O'Keefe, *Transboundary Pollution and the Strict Liability Issue: The Work of the International Law Commission on the Topic of International Liability for Injurious Consequences Arising Out of Acts Not Prohibited by International Law*, 18(2) Denver Journal of International Law and Policy (1990).

compensation in case of a breach, but do not specifically address the issue of individual criminal responsibility.

However, an important step in preventing damage to the environment was taken with the adoption of the Convention on the Prohibition of Military or Any Other Hostile Use of Environmental Modification Techniques.[115] This Convention obliges States parties to refrain from committing acts which are of such scale and character that they cause 'widespread, long-lasting or severe damage'. Particularly illustrative examples of such damage are found in the practice of the superpowers.[116] The testing carried out by many of the nuclear powers are likely to have caused 'widespread, long-lasting or severe' damage to the environment.

ii) 1991 Draft Code Provisions on Environmental Damage

Article 26 of the 1991 draft Code provides that:

An individual who wilfully causes or orders the causing of widespread, long-term and severe damage to the natural environment shall, on conviction thereof, be sentenced [to ...].

Article 26 applies to *any* individual. There does not need to be a colour of official capacity between the person causing the damage and a State to result in a finding of criminal responsibility under Article 26.

As stated in paragraph 4 of the Commentary to Article 26 of the 1991 draft Code:

... Article 2 on the Convention on the Prohibition of Military or Any Other Hostile Use of Environmental Modification Techniques ... defines the expression 'environmental modification technique' as 'any tech-

---

[115] *Adopted* by the General Assembly on 10 Dec. 1976; *entered into force* 5 Oct. 1978. As of 31 Dec. 1995, there were 63 parties and 48 signatories.

[116] Igor P. Blishchenko and Vladimir Ph. Sharov, *The Legal Basis of Claims for Damage to the Environment resulting from Military Action*, 40(1) Austrian Journal of Public and International Law (1989) at 30.

nique for changing - through the deliberate manipulation of natural processes - the dynamics, composition or structure of the earth, including its biota, lithosphere, hydrosphere and atmosphere, or of outer space'.

Thus, the scope of the 1976 Convention would be relevant to an interpretation of the prohibited acts covered by Article 26 of the 1991 draft Code.

The formula of 'widespread, long-term and severe damage to the natural environment' derives from Article 55 of Protocol I Additional to the Geneva Conventions, 1949, relating to the Protection of Victims of International Armed Conflicts which itself borrows from the 1976 Environmental Modification Convention. The first sentence of Article 55 of Protocol I reads: "Care shall be taken in warfare to protect the natural environment against widespread, long-term and severe damage."

The scope of Article 26 of the 1991 draft Code is broader than the Protocol I formula in that it covers both peace-time situations and situations of armed conflict. However, Article 26 is very narrow in that it is meant to cover only wilful rather than negligent damage. Consequently, it is not clear whether this provision could extend to cover gross negligence or failure to supervise an activity that poses a clear threat to the environment.

Determining whether an occurrence is of long-term significance can be problematic. Aside from radioactive leakages, it may be difficult to ascertain whether the damage caused to the natural environment is long-term and severe, except after an appreciable period of time has elapsed. Yet, criminal law must be promptly enforced to be effective. If an international criminal court were obliged to take a 'wait and see' approach to seize jurisdiction with regard to cases of individual criminal responsibility for damage to the natural environment, the court's effectiveness would be undermined in this area. Moreover, fairness requires that criminal cases be tried without undue delay in order to prevent prejudice to the rights of the accused.

iii) 1996 Draft Code

In their comments and observations on the 1991 draft Code,[117] the Governments of Australia, Belgium and Uruguay considered the requisite element of *mens rea* to be too high, arguing that cases of negligence should also come within the scope of Article 26.

The Governments of the Scandinavian countries, the UK and the US, considered the scope of the provision too vague and too broad for the purposes of international criminal law.

Although international cooperation to protect the natural environment is in a rapid stage of development, there is at present a paucity of established international legal norms specifically providing for individual criminal responsibility for damage to the environment.[118] It can not be said yet that effective implementation is already under way. This may account for the inclusion of an overly narrow formula for individual criminal responsibility in Article 26 of the 1991 draft Code. The 1996 draft Code does not include a separate provision on individual criminal responsibility for damage to the environment. However, it at least incorporates such provisions in Article 20(g) under the expanded coverage of 'war crimes'.[119]

---

[117] *See* Comments and Observations of Governments on the Draft Code of Crimes against the Peace and Security of Mankind adopted on First Reading by the International Law Commission at its 43rd Session, A/CN.4/448 of 1 March 1993.

[118] *See* Pierre-Marie Dupuy, *Le droit international de l'environnement et la souveraineté des états. Bilan et perspectives*; Philippe Sand, *Environmental Law in the United Nations Environment Programme*; and Klemm, *Le patrimonie naturel de l'humanité*, all in The Future of the International Law of the Environment: Workshop (ed. Dupuy) (1984).

[119] *See* Titles and Texts of articles on the Draft Code of Crimes against the Peace and Security of Mankind adopted by the International Law Commission at its 48th session (1996); A/CN.4/L.532 of 8 July 1996, which forms the Annex 6 of the present book.

PART 2

DEVELOPMENTS IN IMPLEMENTATION

CHAPTER IV

ADVENT OF NORMATIVE HIERARCHY IN INTERNATIONAL LAW AND ITS RELATION TO INDIVIDUAL CRIMINAL RESPONSIBILITY

In order for criminal law to function as an effective system, there must exist a legal authority capable of enforcing the collective will against the law-breaker. At the municipal level, this authority is the State. The system of international law, in contrast, has developed almost exclusively from the web of bilateral rights and obligations between States that has grown over the centuries. In classic international law, the breach of a legal obligation has entailed the responsibility of the law-breaker State towards the injured State only. More recently, however, there has been growing recognition that certain acts constitute particularly serious violations, and as such, entail a greater level of legal responsibility i.e. greater legal consequences for the law-breaker State. This recognition of a higher level of legal responsibility for certain more serious violations of international law represents a shift away from the classic system of purely bilateral rights, obligations and responsibility, towards a hierarchical system of international legal responsibility. The advent of normative hierarchy in the international law of responsibility, which has become manifest through the emergence of the legal categories of *jus cogens*, obligations *erga omnes* and 'international crimes of State', strengthens the foundation for more effective international criminal law implementation. This Chapter explores these legal categories as they pertain to the principle of individual criminal responsibility in international law.

1. *JUS COGENS*

Generally speaking, the concept of a 'criminal act' presupposes that, in the collective judgement of the community, the act in question violates a norm of special importance. At the international level, fundamental norms recognized to have a superior status over other norms, are referred to as *jus cogens*.

Some publicists trace the origin of *jus cogens* to Roman law, and refer to its role in civil law and common law jurisdictions as a principle establishing that "certain types of contract are, by their very nature, injurious to society and therefore contrary to public policy".[1] Certain others however, argue that linking the concept to a supposed 'international public policy' ignores differences between the international and municipal legal orders.[2] The international legal system is less centralized, less institutionalized and more dependent on the will and consent of individual legal subjects, primarily States.

The concept of *jus cogens* in international law derives primarily from the law of treaties. The World Court has referred explicitly to *jus cogens* on a number of occasions. In the Judgement of the *Oscar Chinn Case*,[3] decided in 1934, Judge Schucking held that:

> The Covenant of the League of Nations, as a whole, and more particularly in Article 20, in which the Members agree not to enter into obligations or understandings *inter se* inconsistent with its provisions, would possess little value unless treaties concluded in violation of that undertaking were to be regarded as absolutely null and void, that is to say, as being automatically void. And I can hardly believe that the League of Nations would have already embarked on the codification of international law if it were not possible, even today, to create a *jus cogens*, the effect of which would be that, once States have agreed on certain rules of law, and have also given an undertaking that these rules may not be altered by some only of their number, any act adopted in contravention of that undertaking would be automatically void.

In his dissenting judgment in the South West Africa Cases (Second Phase) 1966, Judge Tanaka posited that international human rights

---

[1]   *See e.g.* Ian Sinclair, The Vienna Convention on the Law of Treaties (1973) at 110.
[2]   *See e.g.* Sztucki, *Jus Cogens* and the Vienna Convention on the Law of Treaties (1974) at 10.
[3]   1934 PCIJ Ser. A/B No. 63 at 134-136.

law forms part of the *jus cogens*, in contrast to the *jus dispositivum*, which may be changed by agreement between States.[4] In the *North Sea Continental Shelf Cases*, Judge Padilla Nervo held in a separate opinion that:

> ... no right is conferred to make unilateral reservations to articles which are declaratory of established principles of international law. Customary rules belonging to the category of *jus cogens* cannot be subjected to unilateral reservations.[5]

A year later, Judge Ammoun held in a separate opinion to the *Barcelona Traction Case*,[6] that:

> ... through an already lengthy practice of the United Nations, the concept of *jus cogens* obtains a greater degree of effectiveness, by ratifying, as an imperative norm of international law, the principles appearing in the preamble to the Charter.[7]

and referred to:

> ... an action brought in defence of a collective or general interest, the objective being to safeguard legality or the respect due to principles of an interna-

---

[4]   *South West Africa Case* (Second Phase), 1966 ICJ Reports at 298.

[5]   *North Sea Continental Shelf Cases*, 1969 ICJ Reports at 97. Judge Tanaka opined in dissent that: "... if a reservation were concerned with the equidistance principle, it would not necessarily have a negative effect upon the formation of customary international law, because in this case the reservation would in itself be null and void as contrary to an essential principle of the continental shelf institution which must be recognized as *jus cogens*."

[6]   *Barcelona Traction, Light and Power Co. Ltd. Case* (Spain v. Belgium) 1970 ICJ Reports at 304.

[7]   *Ibid.*

tional or humane nature, translated into imperative legal norms (*jus cogens*).[8]

In a number of other cases, the World Court has referred to norms of an 'overriding' or 'fundamental' character without specifically mentioning '*jus cogens*'.

Definitive recognition[9] by the international community of the status of *jus cogens* was clearly expressed in the Vienna Convention on the Law of Treaties, 1969, Article 53 of which provides:

> ... a peremptory norm of general international law is a norm accepted and recognized by the international community of States as a whole as a norm from which no derogation is permitted and which can be modified only by a subsequent norm of general international law having the same character.

According to this formal definition no derogation can be made from obligations prescribed by a peremptory norm.[10] Article 64 of the Convention provides that where a new rule of *jus cogens* emerges, any existing treaty that conflicts with the new norm becomes void and terminates.

Recognition of *jus cogens* in general international law symbolizes the recognition of peremptory interests and values which concern the entire international community. According to Rozakis, one of the changes brought about by the emergence of *jus cogens* is:

> ... the introduction of the notion of objective illegality in the domain of international law. The term objective illegality means the objective recognition of an illegality,

---

[8]   *Ibid.* at 325.

[9]   Schachter concludes that: "Although the concept of *jus cogens* was a subject of controversy among international lawyers for some decades, its inclusion in the Vienna Convention on the Law of Treaties (Article 53) is evidence that it has now been accepted virtually by all States." *See* Oscar Schachter, International Law in Theory and Practice (1991) at 342.

[10]   *See also* Article 71 of the Vienna Convention on the Law of Treaties, 1969.

as such, which can, therefore, be invoked with a view to its extinction by all members of the international community regardless of whether there is a particular damage sustained by the invoking State or States.[11]

Article 53 does not specify or enumerate the specific subject matter of a norm of *jus cogens in concreto*. Some commentators have criticized *jus cogens* as being a purely formal, rather than substantive concept because clear consensus on precisely which norms of international law qualify as *jus cogens* has not yet emerged. However, as Professor Abi-Saab has argued:

> This criticism is simply wrong. ... even as an empty box *jus cogens* is necessary, because if you do not have the box, you cannot put anything in it. Without having the category we cannot have consensus on *which* rules do or can belong to this category.[12]

The normative content of *jus cogens* appears to overlap with that of both obligations *erga omnes* and the concept of 'international crimes of State', namely, norms safeguarding peace and security, the right to self-determination, fundamental human rights such as the norms prohibiting slavery, genocide, apartheid and other gross and systematic violations of human rights and perhaps certain norms protecting the natural environment.

The connection between *jus cogens* and 'international crimes of State', discussed below, raises the issue as to whether a violation of a norm of *jus cogens* implies that collective sanctions may be enforced against the law-breaker State and whether it gives rise to claims by third States not directly affected by the breach.

---

[11] Rozakis, The Concept of *Jus Cogens* in the Law of Treaties (1976) at 24.

[12] *See Discussion*, in Change and Stability in International Law-Making, (ed. Cassese and Weiler) (1988) at 96.

2. OBLIGATIONS *ERGA OMNES*

A possible role for obligations *erga omnes* was opened up by the ICJ in the *Barcelona Traction Case*. However, a quarter century later, this potential role was severely weakened by the Court's holding in the *East Timor Case*. In the *Barcelona Traction Case*, the ICJ made a famous pronouncement on obligations *erga omnes*, perhaps motivated to make amends for its highly criticized *South West Africa* decision of 1966. In order to appreciate fully the significance of the *Barcelona Traction Case*, it is necessary to consider briefly the *South West Africa Cases*.

The *South West Africa Cases* were brought to the International Court of Justice by Ethiopia and Liberia against South Africa. These States claimed South Africa had breached its League of Nations mandate obligations by, *inter alia*, instituting a policy of apartheid instead of promoting the welfare of the inhabitants. The applicant States argued that, as Members of the League of Nations, they had legal standing to bring the dispute before the International Court of Justice. South Africa challenged the jurisdiction of the Court and the legal standing of Ethiopia and Liberia by way of preliminary objection. In 1962, the Court held that it had jurisdiction to consider the merits of the case.[13] However, when considering the merits in 1966, the Court decided in a tie vote which required the President of the Court to break, that the applicants had not established any legal interest or right in the dispute, and that the claim of Ethiopia and Liberia:

> amounts to a plea that the Court should allow the equivalent of an *actio popularis*, or right resident in any member of a community to take legal action in vindication of a public interest. But although a right of this kind may be known to certain municipal systems of law, it is not known to international law as it stands at present: nor is the Court able to regard it as imported by the 'general principles of law' referred to in Article 38, paragraph 1(c), of its Statute.[14]

---

[13]   The Court's vote was eight to seven.
[14]   1966 ICJ Reports at 47.

This decision was met with bitter criticism from many quarters, especially from many countries which had only recently achieved independence from colonial domination. The rigidly positivist stance of the Judgement seemed to play into the hands of the Government of South Africa and fly in the face of the international community's increasingly strong denunciation of the policy of apartheid, which the Government had officially instituted in 1948.

More significantly, by rejecting the claims of Ethiopia and Liberia in this case, the Court also rejected the principle according to which any member of the international community enjoys *locus standi* 'to take legal action in vindication of a public interest'. In effect, the Court reaffirmed the classical two-dimensional notion of the international law of responsibility which is premised on the classic pattern of inter-State relations, rather than taking into account developments affirming the rise of collective values and interests protected on a multilateral basis.

On the occasion of the *Barcelona Traction Case*, it appears that the International Court of Justice went out of its way to enunciate a view much more in line with current mores in order to accommodate the changing values of the international community. In the *Barcelona Traction Case*, the Court opined by way of *obiter dicta*, that:

> ... [A]n essential distinction should be drawn between the obligations of a State towards the international community as a whole, and those arising *vis-à-vis* another State in the field of diplomatic protection. By their very nature the former are the concern of all States. In view of the importance of the rights involved, all States can be held to have a legal interest in their protection; they are obligations *erga omnes*.
>
> Such obligations derive, for example, in contemporary international law, from the outlawing of acts of aggression, and of genocide, as also from the principles and rules concerning the basic rights of the

human person, including protection from slavery and racial discrimination.[15]

An obligation *erga omnes* is an obligation that a State owes towards the international community as a whole in respect of a beneficiary.

However, it is not clear whether the emergence of obligations *erga omnes* implies the right of States to maintain an *actio popularis*. In the *Case concerning East Timor*,[16] Portugal instituted proceedings against Australia claiming that Australia had "failed to observe ... the obligation to respect the duties and powers of [Portugal] as the administering Power [of East Timor] ... and ... the right of the people of East Timor to self-determination and the related rights."[17] The dispute arose in connection with a treaty Australia concluded with Indonesia on behalf of East Timor on 11 December 1989 in relation to the continental shelf located off East Timor.[18] Portugal maintained that:

> ... Australia is bound, in relation to the people of East Timor, to Portugal and to the international community, to cease from all breaches of the rights and international norms ... until such time as the people of East Timor shall have exercised its right to self-determination, under the conditions laid down by the United Nations.

---

[15]   *Barcelona Traction, Light and Power Co. Ltd. Case* (Spain v. Belgium) 1970 ICJ Reports at paras. 33-34.

[16]   *Case concerning East Timor* (Portugal v. Australia) 1995 ICJ Reports 90.

[17]   *Ibid.* quoting from the Application of Portugal filed in the Registry of the Court.

[18]   Portugal requested the Court, *inter alia*: "To adjudge and declare that, first, the rights of the people of East Timor to self-determination, to territorial integrity and unity and to permanent sovereignty over its wealth and natural resources and, secondly, the duties, powers and rights of Portugal as the administering Power of the Territory of East Timor are opposable to Australia, which is under an obligation not to disregard them, but to respect them." *See ibid.* at para. 1.

In effect, Portugal contended that the right of East Timor to self-determination and permanent sovereignty over its natural resources were rights *erga omnes* which Australia owed towards the international community as a whole in respect of East Timor.

For its part, Australia countered by requesting the Court to declare Portugal's claims inadmissible on the grounds that they would require the Court to render judgment on the rights and obligations of Indonesia in spite of the fact that Indonesia was not a party to the proceedings, nor had it signified its consent to be bound by the Court's ruling. Australia, citing the case of *Monetary Gold Removed from Rome in 1943*,[19] as well as numerous cases affirming it, maintained that in the absence of Indonesia's consent to the jurisdiction of the Court, the Court was obliged not to hear the case. On this point, the Court ruled "that one of the fundamental principles of its Statute is that it cannot decide a dispute between States without the consent of those States to its jurisdiction".

To overcome Australia's objection to the jurisdiction of the Court, Portugal argued that the right of peoples to self-determination gives rise to an obligation *erga omnes* on the part of other States to respect it, and as such, Portugal could require Australia to respect the rights of East Timor regardless of the conduct of Indonesia. The Court accepted Portugal's argument that the right to self-determination has an *erga omnes* character, but considered that:

> ... the *erga omnes* character of a norm and the rule of consent to jurisdiction are two different things. Whatever the nature of the obligations invoked, the Court could not rule on the lawfulness of the conduct of a State when its judgment would imply an evaluation of the lawfulness of the conduct of another State which it not a party to the case. Where this is so, the Court cannot act, even if the right in question is a right *erga omnes*.[20]

---

[19] 1954 ICJ Reports 19.
[20] *Ibid.* at para. 29.

Accordingly, the Court refused to exercise jurisdiction over the case, ruling fourteen votes to two in favour of Australia.

In his dissenting opinion, Judge Weeramantry articulated a right *erga omnes* as:

> ... a series of separate rights *erga singulum*, including *inter alia*, a separate right *erga singulum* against Australia, and a separate right *erga singulum* against Indonesia. These rights are in no way dependent one upon the other. With the violation by any State of the obligation so lying upon it, the rights enjoyed *erga omnes* become opposable *erga singulum* to the State so acting.[21]

Judge Weeramantry went on to argue that the Majority Judgment hampers the effective operation of a right *erga omnes*.

> The present case is one where quite clearly the consequences of the *erga omnes* principle follow through to their logical conclusion - that the obligation which is a corollary of the right may well have been contravened. This would lead, in my view, to the grant of judicial relief for the violation of the right.[22]

Furthermore, Judge Weeramantry observed that:

> The *erga omnes* concept has been at the door of this Court for many years. A disregard of *erga omnes* obligations makes a serious tear in the web of international obligations, and the current state of international law requires that violations of the concept be followed through to their logical and legal conclusion.[23]

---

[21]   Dissenting Opinion of Judge Weeramantry, 1995 ICJ Reports at 172.
[22]   *Ibid.* at 216.
[23]   *Ibid.*

At this point, the Court obviously appears unable to recognize the procedural capacity of a third State to bring a claim before it in order to vindicate the breach of an obligation *erga omnes*.

However, it cannot be denied that certain States, in this case Portugal, view the breach of an obligation *erga omnes* as conferring such procedural capacity. It is difficult to tell the extent to which the international community as a whole embraces this view, yet the interests of States appear increasingly to be shared in common. Although the Court's ruling affirms that the rule of consent to jurisdiction cannot be overridden by a claim brought by a third State to vindicate the breach of an obligation *erga omnes*, the ruling neither negates the existence of obligations *erga omnes* as a valid legal category nor its possible role where consent to jurisdiction might not be at stake. Given that judicial decision-making typically lags behind changing social practice, the debate over the procedural implications of obligations *erga omnes* cannot be considered closed.

3. CONCEPT OF 'INTERNATIONAL CRIMES OF STATE'

Were all rules of international law considered equally important, no particular breach of international law would entail any greater degree of legal responsibility than any other. In other words, no matter what kind of breach were involved, the obligation of the law-breaker State would always be the same, specifically, to return matters to the *status quo ante* the breach and to make reparation for damages resulting from the wrong attributable to it. In effect, rules of international legal responsibility would be two-dimensional in the sense that all legal rights and obligations pertaining to international responsibility would operate on the same normative plane.

However, on a political level, States have always recognized certain breaches of international law, such as the launching of a war of aggression, as more serious than lesser sorts of interference. Aggression, and certain other violations which threaten State sovereignty and independence for example, are universally recognized to violate principles fundamental to the international community as a whole.

The concept of 'international crimes of State' is a product of the International Law Commission's codification and progressive development of international law. The law of State responsibility was one of fourteen subjects undertaken by the International Law Commission in 1949. The first report to the ILC on State Responsibility was submitted in 1956 by Garcia-Amador. He distinguished between internationally wrongful acts, and a category of more serious 'punishable' acts that includes, *inter alia*, genocide and crimes against humanity. Garcia-Amador asked the ILC whether the scope of his study should cover these 'punishable acts', but the Commission decided at the time that these lay outside the proper scope of ILC codification.[24]

In 1976 Roberto Ago, who succeeded Garcia-Amador as Special Rapporteur, proposed that the concept of international crimes be incorporated within the codification efforts. Almost all ILC members agreed with this proposal, and in the Sixth Committee of the General Assembly (responsible for consideration of ILC Reports), the socialist countries and developing countries supported the concept of particularly wrongful acts while many western States remained sceptical.[25]

With respect to international responsibility, the ILC has drawn a strict distinction between 'primary rules' and 'secondary rules' of international law. The term 'primary rules' refers to rules of international law that prescribe obligations the breach of which gives rise to international responsibility. 'Secondary rules' are those 'which define the legal consequences of failure to fulfil obligations established by the primary rules',[26] and as such, belong specifically to the domain of the international law of responsibility.[27]

---

[24]   *See* Marina Spinedi, *International Crimes of State: the Legislative History*, in Change and Stability in International Law-Making, (ed. Cassese and Weiler) (1988) at 11.

[25]   *Ibid.* at 51-2.

[26]   2 Yearbook of the ILC (1976) Part 2, at 71 para. 68, UN Doc. A/CN.4/Ser.A/1976/ Add.1 (Pt. 2).

[27]   The distinction between primary and secondary rules is a valuable one. It emphasizes the relation of secondary rules to primary rules while leaving open the question of the precise content of primary rules, thereby freeing the ILC from having to attempt codification of the entire *corpus* of substantive international law.

The ILC draft articles on State responsibility are structured according to this distinction such that Part 1 deals with determination of grounds by which international responsibility may arise, while Part 2 concerns the content, forms and degrees of international responsibility.

Article 19 of Part 1 of the ILC Draft Articles on State responsibility distinguishes between two main categories of internationally wrongful acts: a broad category of wrongs (delicts); and a special category of particularly serious wrongs (international crimes):[28]

ARTICLE 19 - INTERNATIONAL CRIMES AND INTERNATIONAL DELICTS

1.   An act of a State which constitutes a breach of an international obligation is an internationally wrongful act, regardless of the subject-matter of the obligation breached.

2.   An internationally wrongful act which results from the breach by a State of an international obligation so essential for the protection of fundamental interests of the international community that its breach is recognized as a crime by that community as a whole, constitutes an international crime.

3.   Subject to paragraph 2, and on the basis of the rules of international law in force, an international crime may result, *inter alia*, from:

(a) a serious breach of an international obligation of essential importance for the maintenance of international peace and security, such as that prohibiting aggression;

(b) a serious breach of an international obligation of essential importance for safeguarding the right of self-determination of peoples, such as that prohibiting the establishment or maintenance by force of colonial domination;

---

[28]   2 Yearbook of the ILC (1976) Part 2. para. 6 (Commentary to Art. 19), UN Doc. A/CN.4/ Ser.A/1976/ Add.1 (Pt. 2).

(c) a serious breach on a widespread scale of an international obligation of essential importance for safeguarding the human being, such as those prohibiting slavery, genocide and apartheid;

(d) a serious breach of an international obligation of essential importance for the safeguarding and preservation of the human environment, such as those prohibiting massive pollution of the atmosphere or of the seas.

4. Any internationally wrongful act which is not an international crime in accordance with paragraph 2, constitutes an international delict.[29]

It follows logically that the commission of an international crime incurs a set of legal consequences distinct from those that follow from a delict.[30] Elaboration of 'international crimes' alludes to recognition that certain acts are serious enough to warrant *collective* sanctions by the international community as a whole, according to international law.[31]

---

[29]   2 Yearbook of the ILC (1976) Part 2, at 75, UN Doc. A/CN.4/ Ser.A /1976/ Add.1 (Pt. 2).

[30]   The question of the legal consequences of an international crime was taken up by Mr. Riphagen appointed new Special Rapporteur in 1979, in Part 2 of the Draft Articles relating to the degrees, forms and content of responsibility. *See* UN Doc. A/CN.4/330, reproduced in 2 Yearbook of the ILC (1980) Part 1. Article 5(3) of Part 2, provisionally adopted by the Commission at its 37th session, provides that: "'injured State' means, if the internationally wrongful act constitutes an international crime [and in the context of the rights and obligations of States under Articles 14 and 15], all other States". 2 Yearbook of the ILC (1987) Part 2, at 25, UN Doc. A/CN.4/1985/Add.1 (Part 2). This provision establishes that the commission of an international crime entails injury to all other States.

[31]   Article 14 provides that an "international crime entails all the legal consequences of an internationally wrongful act and ... such rights and obligations as are determined by the applicable rules accepted by the international community as a whole." Article 14(2) obliges every other State: a) not to recognize as legal the situation created by such crime; b) not to render aid or assistance to the State that committed the crime in maintaining the illegal situation; and c) to join other States in affording mutual assistance to carry out the duties of non-recognition already specified.

The concept of 'international crime' (which concerns crimes committed by the State) is not to be confused with 'crime under international law' or 'crimes against the peace and security of mankind' (which concern crimes committed by individuals). Article 19 concerns internationally wrongful acts entailing *State* responsibility, not individual responsibility in international law. As Sinclair remarks, Article 19:

> ... does not establish the *criminal* responsibility of States; it simply posits an *aggravated* degree of responsibility for internationally wrongful acts designated, for want of a better term, as 'international crimes'.[32]

The obligation to punish individuals in a personal capacity for wrongs which qualify as international crimes is not a form of international responsibility of the State nor does it necessarily exhaust the State's responsibility.[33] Therefore, there is no *necessary* relation between 'international crimes' and individual criminal responsibility.

However, recognition of international legal norms that provide for heightened State responsibility for especially grave acts does signify recognition of a differentiated system of international responsibility as opposed to a uniform system of norms.[34]

In effect, the United Nations Charter already provides for a three-dimensional system of international State responsibility, i.e. that in which there exists a level over and above the web of bilateral rights and obligations. The chief basis for this argument lies in Chapter VII of the UN Charter. Article 39 of the UN Charter authorizes the

---

[32] Ian Sinclair, *State Responsibility: Lex Ferenda and Crimes of State*, in International Crimes of State (ed. Cassese and Spinedi) (1989) at 242. *Also see* Bernhardt Graefrath, *Responsibility and Damages Caused*, 185 Hague Recueil (1984) at 57.

[33] 2 Yearbook of the ILC (1976) Part 2, at 104. para. 21; UN Doc A/CN.4/ Ser.A /1976/Add.1 (Pt. 2), (Commentary to Art. 19).

[34] Spinedi observes "that of the eighty or so States that have expressed opinions on Draft Article 19, only Sweden took a position entirely incompatible with the idea of drawing a distinction between two categories of internationally wrongful acts". *See* Spinedi, *supra* note 24 at 57.

Security Council to "determine the existence of any threat to the peace, breach of the peace, or act of aggression" and to "make recommendations, or decide what measures shall be taken in accordance with Articles 41 and 42 to maintain or restore international peace and security". Articles 41 and 42 provide the Security Council with the authority to impose collective measures ranging from complete or partial interruption of economic relations to the deployment of military force. Because the decisions of the Council pursuant to Chapter VII of the Charter are binding on all States, any State that commits a 'threat to the peace, breach of the peace, or act of aggression' may become subject to the higher level of legal responsibility, namely, that imposed upon it by the collective will of the international community as a whole.

Of course, this does not imply that single States should be empowered to take whatever action unilaterally they deem appropriate to redress the breach. In this connection, Jiménez de Aréchaga cautions that:

> ... it is important that the dual régime should be implemented with the greatest care. The legal interest which every member of the international community is recognized as possessing if an international crime is committed cannot be permitted to entitle any State to take individual action when it believes that an international crime has been committed.
>
> Such an anarchical system would lead to a repetition of the worst forms of intervention which occurred in international relations in the nineteenth century.[35]

The commission of aggression is probably the only instance where all States may resort to the use of force individually or collectively to exercise their customary right of self-defence or in accord with any

---

[35]   Jiménez de Aréchaga and Tanzi, *International State Responsibility*, in International Law: Achievement and Prospects (ed. Bedjaoui) (1991) at 357.

measures recommended or taken by the Security Council acting pursuant to Chapter VII of the UN Charter.

Professor Abi-Saab has put in a nutshell the significance of the concept of 'international crimes':

> In sum, the 'value-added' of the concept of 'international crimes', in relation to the normal regime of State responsibility, in terms of legal effects, boils down to recognizing two faculties for third parties: a) the possibility of taking reprisals or rather sanctions (countermeasures) in the absence of a 'collective determination'; and b) the possibility of resorting to international adjudication or putting into motion other institutional mechanisms, particularly in view of the fact that in most cases the victim has no or little voice on the international level.[36]

The ILC observed that the subject matters of the two regimes of international responsibility for crimes committed by States, and crimes committed by individuals, coincide to the extent that the international community recognizes both categories to be of 'exceptional importance'.[37] In other words, the ILC's position is that the normative content of 'international crime' relates to individual criminal responsibility only in respect of its subject matter, rather than in relation to the rights and obligations it confers or to the entities it binds.

'International crimes of State' constitute breaches of obligations *erga omnes* i.e. States owe an obligation to the international community as a whole to refrain from committing the breach. However, while the two concepts are related, 'international crime' is not equivalent to obligation *erga omnes*. All international crimes constitute breaches of obligations *erga omnes* but not all breaches of obligations *erga omnes* constitute international crimes. Similarly, 'international crimes of State'

---

[36] *See* Georges M. Abi-Saab, *The Concept of "International Crimes" and its Place in Contemporary International Law*, in International Crimes of State: A Critical Analysis of the ILC's Draft Article 19 on State Responsibility (ed. Weiler, Cassese and Spinedi) (1989) at 150.

[37] *Ibid.*

is not equivalent to '*jus cogens*' although they are related categories as the ILC was careful to emphasize in its Commentary to Article 19.[38]

4. RELATION OF NORMATIVE HIERARCHY IN INTERNATIONAL LAW TO INDIVIDUAL CRIMINAL RESPONSIBILITY

The rising functional significance of *jus cogens* and obligations *erga omnes* as well as the Article 19 concept of 'international crime' amplify individual criminal responsibility in international law through their convergent focus on interests fundamental to the international community as a whole, in particular, the maintenance of international peace and security. International criminal law focuses on the same categories of violations as those subject to heightened State responsibility. For example, the 1996 draft Code provides for individual criminal responsibility for the kinds of violations of international law addressed also by *jus cogens*, obligations *erga omnes* and 'international crimes of State', namely, *inter alia,* aggression, genocide, crimes against humanity and war crimes. International criminal law complements the international law of State responsibility and is thereby related at a very practical level to the fundamental interests of the international community as expressed in obligations *erga omnes* and *jus cogens*. Together, they provide the basis for more effective prevention and deterrence of crimes under international law. In this context, the complementary role of international criminal law has been very dramatically illustrated by the Security Council's decisions to create the International Criminal Tribunals for the Former Yugoslavia and Rwanda, both of whose competence derives from the Council's legal authority pursuant to Chapter VII of the UN Charter. Both Security Council resolution 827 of 25 May 1993 and resolution 955 of 8 November 1994 respectively creating the Tribunals for the former Yugoslavia and Rwanda recognize the link between the prosecution of individuals for crimes under international law and the restoration of peace in the country, i.e. a natural connection between international

---

[38]   *See* 2 Yearbook of the ILC (1976) Part 2. at 119, para. 62; UN Doc. A/CN.4/ Ser.A/1976/Add.1 (Part 2) (Commentary to Art. 19).

criminal law and the maintenance of international peace and security. This connection may be further strengthened and expanded with the apparent willingness on the part of the Security Council to read 'threat to the peace, breach of the peace, or act of aggression' in Article 39 of the UN Charter more broadly than it has done in past decades. Thus, the advent of normative hierarchy in international law, spurred on by a certain level of transformation in the international law of responsibility, supports the emergence of international criminal law as a system.

CHAPTER V

IMPLEMENTATION OF INTERNATIONAL CRIMINAL LAW THROUGH MUNICIPAL JURISDICTION

1. INTRODUCTION

As discussed in Part I of the present enquiry, international legal norms stipulating criminal responsibility for particular kinds of violations have emerged sporadically over the last five centuries. The emergence of such rules reflects a certain level of recognition of the need for international law to prohibit certain categories of offenses. However, it does not necessarily follow from such recognition that States recognize also a need for international as opposed to domestic organs to enforce these rules. In principle, were international criminal law adequately enforced by domestic organs, international mechanisms to pursue the same ends would be unnecessary. For example, if war crimes or slave-trading were prosecuted regularly and systematically by States in whose territory the suspect is found, supplementary mechanisms such as an *ad hoc* or permanent international criminal court would be superfluous.

In fact, international criminal law has been enforced in few instances either by international or domestic organs. Whereas the creation of international criminal tribunals is highly exceptional, municipal legal systems have at their disposal all necessary means for effective enforcement, including regular standing corps of police and military officers, undercover agents for surveillance and detective work, sophisticated technical means of investigation and forensic expertise, highly organized legal procedures governing the initiation and processing of complaints, indictment, prosecution, trial, sentencing, punishment and rehabilitation, all sustained by State-collected tax revenues. In contrast, judging from the very weak start of the International Criminal Tribunals for the Former Yugoslavia and Rwanda, it appears that the institutionalization of investigative and enforcement procedures at the international level are barely at the infant stage.

This Chapter outlines the internationally recognized bases of municipal criminal jurisdiction so as to evaluate the limits of inter-State enforcement, and in particular, whether and to what extent universal jurisdiction provides a firm legal basis for the domestic prosecution of crimes under international law. Second, the problems of acquiring custody over the offender at the domestic level, limitations to the existing extradition system as well as the resort by some States to forcible means of apprehension of the criminal suspect in the territory of another State (i.e. State-sponsored kidnapping), are discussed in light of prospects for the fair and effective implementation of international criminal law.

The present Chapter aims not to provide an exhaustive account of inter-State criminal jurisdiction, but rather to highlight the main issues in existing inter-State implementation and their significance for the emerging system of international criminal law. In this regard, it is unnecessary to consider domestic cases in detail, which only pertain to the present enquiry to the extent crimes under international law are incorporated in the domestic criminal law of the prosecuting State.

2. INTERNATIONALLY RECOGNIZED BASES OF MUNICIPAL CRIMINAL JURISDICTION INCLUDING THE DOCTRINE OF UNIVERSAL JURISDICTION

In order to discern the extent to which municipal enforcement of international criminal law has been regular, systematic and effective, it is necessary first to consider the internationally recognized bases upon which States customarily assert criminal jurisdiction, and in particular, the doctrine of universal jurisdiction as one of these grounds.

Broadly, the pattern of existing municipal criminal law enforcement has developed over time to serve principally the needs and interests of each sovereign State, rather than to address matters of concern common among them. Indeed, the practise relating to universal jurisdiction is so sketchy that at present, as a possible jurisdictional basis, it appears to hold little promise for effective national prosecution of crimes under international law.

In general, the State has exclusive criminal jurisdiction over persons and property to the limits of its territorial sovereignty (and on vessels under its flag in territory *res communis*).

However, territory is not the only basis upon which States customarily exercise jurisdiction. For example, a State may claim the right to prosecute its national for an act committed in the territory of another State even where the act has no other connection to the national State. In other cases, a State may prosecute a foreign national for an act committed abroad where the State considers the act as a threat to its national security interests. Conflicts between or among States therefore may arise where the jurisdictional extent of two or more States overlap in a given instance.

In this connection, it is valuable to consider the Harvard Research Draft Convention on Jurisdiction with Respect to Crime of 1935.[1] States continue to exercise criminal jurisdiction on the bases identified in the Harvard Research Draft Convention, so that although dated, the Draft Convention is still relevant and accurate. The Draft Convention lists five grounds upon which States most often claim criminal jurisdiction: 1) territorial, if the offense was committed within the State's territory; 2) the nationality of the offender; 3) according to the 'protective principle' where the State can show that its national interest has been threatened by the offense; 4) universal jurisdiction for certain offenses in regard to which international law recognizes the right of any State to prosecute the offender; and 5) the passive personality principle referring to the nationality of the person injured by the offence. The authors of the Harvard Research Draft concluded that all States assert criminal jurisdiction on the basis of territory and nationality. The third principle, concerning protection of the national interest, was asserted by some States and not others. Universal jurisdiction was considered by most States to provide a supplementary basis of jurisdiction. As for the passive personality principle, only few States claim a right to exercise criminal jurisdiction on the sole basis that one of their nationals was injured by an offense which otherwise

---

[1]   29 American Journal of International Law Supp. (1935) 443. This research, conducted by several international lawyers of the United States, carries no official status of any kind. Nevertheless, it is valuable because it provides a good comparative synthesis of a considerable body of State practise.

has no connection to the interests of the State. The authors of the Harvard Research Draft therefore felt that the last above-mentioned ground was unnecessary even as an auxiliary jurisdictional basis and therefore omitted it from the Draft Convention.[2]

Of these bases of State jurisdiction, it is significant that the territorial and nationality principles concern the overwhelming majority of crimes prosecuted by States, whereas the protective and universal principles are rarely invoked. In this sense, the classical sovereign principality was always inward looking; particular acts were stigmatized as crimes according to whether they offended the moral code of the local community or threatened the State itself. As such, crimes were defined locally, rather than according to some universal sense of wrong. Thus, the criteria of territoriality and nationality represent connections to the offense more pertinent to localized concerns. However, it is necessary to consider the possibility that universal jurisdiction provides a valuable basis upon which the State may prosecute crimes under international law since this doctrine developed specifically to address certain matters of inter-State concern.

In contrast to the territoriality and nationality bases of jurisdiction, the doctrine of universal jurisdiction finds its roots mainly in the growth of international cooperation. Universal jurisdiction reflects two basic concerns of the international community as a whole. First, one who perpetrates a criminal act in an area beyond the jurisdiction of any State should not be immune from prosecution merely because the place in which the crime was committed may not be covered by the domestic criminal law of any one State. Instead, such acts should be made subject to the criminal jurisdiction of every State equally to increase deterrence without having to recognize the criminal jurisdiction of any particular State as prior to that of any other. Second, certain acts, no matter where committed (whether in territory *res communis omnium* or within the territory of a State or States) are of such gravity that every State should be authorized to exercise criminal jurisdiction over the offender.

---

[2]   *See* Dickinson, Introductory Comment to the Harvard Research Draft Convention on Jurisdiction with Respect to Crime, 29 American Journal of International Law (1935).

As to the first concern, universal jurisdiction serves as a technique for trying to resolve the difficult problem of acquiring custody over an individual who may perpetrate an act in territory *res communis omnium*, that is, in a place where no State has authority to exercise territorial jurisdiction, namely on the high seas (including subsoil beneath it and airspace above it) or in outer space. Recognition for universal jurisdiction to meet this concern came about with international efforts to suppress slavery, slave-trading and piracy, during the Congress of Vienna, held in 1815.

The second concern that spawned recognition for universal jurisdiction arose out of the ancient laws and customs of war and pertained to the commission of war crimes. Ancient customary laws of war provide that certain acts, such as the use of specific prohibited weapons or the subjection of civilians to murder, rape or looting, pose such a serious affront to the honour of the military profession that perpetrators could be tried anywhere, regardless of the *locus delictum* or the nationality of the offender.[3]

In both these contexts, the growing expanse and intricacy of inter-State relations in the modern era have brought about a concomitant reduction in the breadth of matters considered to be 'essentially within the domestic jurisdiction of any State'.[4] In particular, a number of multilateral conventions have been adopted, which provide for universal jurisdiction for specific crimes, namely, aircraft piracy, sabotage, the crime of apartheid, crimes against internationally protected persons, terrorism and hostage-taking.[5] Further recognition of universal jurisdiction could develop in future with regard to 'crimes against the peace and security of mankind' on the basis of the gravity of the acts committed. The doctrine of universal jurisdiction may

---

[3]   *See generally* Maurice H. Keen, The Laws of War in the Late Middle Ages (1965), Chapters II & III.

[4]   Article 2(7) of the United Nations Charter.

[5]   *See* the Hague Convention for the Suppression of Unlawful Seizure of Aircraft, 1970; Montreal Convention for the Suppression for the Unlawful Acts against the Safety of Civil Aviation, 1971; International Convention on the Suppression of the Crime of Apartheid, 1973; Convention on the Prevention and Punishment of Crimes against Internationally Protected Persons, 1973; European Convention to Prevent and Punish the Acts of Terrorism, 1976; and the Convention on the Prevention of the Taking of Hostages, 1979.

therefore appear to provide an avenue for effective implementation of international criminal law by national courts.

However, universal jurisdiction is permissive rather than mandatory and as such does not *require* any particular State to prosecute. Universal jurisdiction has been applied by national courts only on a very sporadic basis. Apart from the controversial *Eichmann Case*,[6] discussed below in the context of State-sponsored kidnapping, there have been few instances in which national courts relied solely on universal jurisdiction to prosecute an individual for crimes in international law, notwithstanding that there have been many serious armed conflicts over the last fifty years in which war crimes, crimes against humanity and genocide were committed.[7] Domestic courts remain reluctant to exercise jurisdiction without a clear connection between the State and the crime.

On the other hand, in future, members of the international community may become less tolerant of a State that knowingly harbours a person suspected of having committed a crime against the peace and security of mankind. The general expectation that such a State either prosecute or extradite the individual without regard to his or her nationality, or the *locus delictum*, may eventually develop into a binding legal obligation. However, pending the further development of State practise on this matter, it appears that the principle advanced by Grotius, that every State is under an obligation either to extradite or to prosecute (*aut dedere aut judicare*), is not yet established firmly. In their Joint Declaration in the *Lockerbie Case*,[8] Judges Evensen, Tarassov, Guillaume, and Aguilar Mawdsley, opined that:

> In so far as general international law is concerned, extradition is a sovereign decision of the requested

---

[6]   *Attorney-General of the Government of Israel* v. *Eichmann* (District Court of Jerusalem) (1961), 36 International Law Reports 5.

[7]   *See* Yves Sandoz, *Penal Aspects of Humanitarian Law* in 1 International Criminal Law: Crimes (ed. Bassiouni)(1986) at 230; and *generally*, Geoff Gilbert, Aspects of Extradition Law (1991) at 213-218.

[8]   *Case concerning Questions of Interpretation and Application of the 1971 Montreal Convention arising from the Aerial Incident at Lockerbie* (Libya v. UK): Request for the Indication of Provisional Measures, Order of 14 April, 1992 ICJ Reports at 24, para. 2 of Joint Declaration.

State, which is never under an obligation to carry it out. Moreover, in general international law there is no obligation to prosecute in default of extradition. Although since the days of Covarruvias and Grotius such a formula has been advocated by some legal scholars, it has never been part of positive law. This being so, every State is at liberty to request extradition and every State is free to refuse it. Should it refuse, a State is not obliged to prosecute.

As Bassiouni and Wise observe:

> No rule of current international law requires states generally to deny a safe haven to those who have committed crimes elsewhere. Thus, arguments in favour of an obligation to extradite (or prosecute) have had to turn instead to the postulate of a communal interest in the repression of at least international offenses. For those who are sceptical about existence of an 'international community' possessing real group authority, this line of argument seems to beg the question. For those who believe in the reality of the 'international community', it is practically self-evident.[9]

Gilbert concludes that:

> ... the better view is that the principle '*aut dedere, aut judicare*' still only applies, at present, when expressly formulated in multilateral conventions on international criminal law.[10]

Thus, it is doubtful that the principle '*aut dedere, aut judicare*' reflects a mandatory obligation of international customary law.

---

[9] Cherif Bassiouni and Edward Wise, Aut Dedere Aut Judicare: The Duty to Extradite or Prosecute in International Law (1995) at 42.

[10] Gilbert, *supra* note 7 at 157.

Although the doctrine of universal jurisdiction shows potential for future development through increasing evidence of *opinio juris*, to this point it remains only a theoretical construct unsupported by general State practice. It does not currently qualify as a rule of international customary law, much less, one of mandatory import; it permits or authorizes a State to prosecute, but does not require the State to do so.

Even were States to exercise universal jurisdiction on a regular basis, a coherent and uniform international criminal law would be unlikely to develop in this way. Significant differences among the criminal laws of States would almost certainly preclude the formation of consistent international criminal law with respect to interpretation, adjudication and sentencing.

In sum, the prosecution of crimes under international law by domestic courts solely on the basis of universal criminal jurisdiction has been practically non-existent. The traditional orientation of State practise in the area of criminal law enforcement naturally involves domestic priorities. Given that the criminal prosecution process is both labour and time intensive, politicians and prosecutors typically have little incentive to commit scarce resources to prosecute crimes that may be only weakly connected to the local community in order to serve the interest of 'the international community as a whole' or 'international public order' or other such seemingly distant value. Moreover, as argued above, a State typically shows interest in prosecuting a crime only where the crime poses a direct threat to that State, in which case other domestic jurisdictional bases are usually available, and it is unnecessary to invoke universal jurisdiction.

3. DOMESTIC EFFORTS TO ACQUIRE CUSTODY OVER THE OFFENDER

The proliferation in the number of States since the end of the Second World War affords criminal suspects vastly greater opportunities to seek safe-haven from a sympathetic sovereign State than ever before and exposes the limits of extradition in the context of the prosecution of the individual for crimes under international law.

It is therefore necessary to consider whether the system of extradition can function effectively as a means of inter-State enforcement of international criminal law. A corollary of the considerable reluctance of States to prosecute crimes beyond the traditional bases of jurisdiction is that no State can be assured that another State, the territory in which the criminal suspect happens to be located, will take measures to prosecute unless it can rely on one of the traditional bases itself. In addition to a lack of interest on the part of the State in cases other than those closely connected to traditional jurisdictional grounds, there may arise practical obstacles to effective prosecution, such as weak access to witness testimony (particularly where witnesses are beyond the reach of a subpoena), or other sources of evidence (such as physical or documentary items), on which the prosecution's case may eventually turn. For these reasons, a State may prefer to acquire custody over the criminal suspect so it can itself prosecute.

i) Limits of Bilateral Extradition Agreements

Paradoxically, both the strengths and weaknesses of the extradition system, as a potentially important tool in the inter-State enforcement of international criminal law, lie in its intricate character. With a view to regularizing the inter-State surrender of criminal suspects, over time, most States have entered into bilateral agreements, and where necessary, have passed appropriate domestic legislation prescribing procedures for the lawful handing over of the alleged offender (or convicted fugitive) to another State for prosecution. The use of extradition dates at least as far back as 1280 B.C. between the Pharaoh Ramses II of Egypt, and Hattushilish III, a prince of the Hittite civilization.[11] However, the modern extradition treaty system arose first between neighbouring countries, mainly in 18th and 19th century Europe, where State sovereignty was most forcefully pronounced.

Generally, the aim of the extradition treaty system is to improve inter-State cooperation in criminal matters in a manner that safeguards the human rights of the individual against the tyranny of Government, in particular, the right to freedom of political opinion and expression and the right to receive a fair trial. The 'political offence exception',

---

[11]   Ian Shearer, Extradition in International law (1971) at 168-9.

found in most extradition treaties, allows the requested State not to comply with a request for extradition where the alleged offence has been qualified as a crime as a result of the requesting State's political persecution of the individual, rather than out of a *bona fide* effort to prosecute the individual for having committed a genuinely criminal act. Where the individual would not likely receive the benefit of a fair trial, compliance with the extradition request would breach the international minimum standard of human rights protection which the requested State owes any individual.

Other procedural norms commonly governing the operation of extradition treaties, such as the 'double criminality rule', or the 'rule of specialty', safeguard primarily the sovereign rights of the requested State, but may also benefit the alleged offender.

The double criminality rule provides that the requested State is obliged to surrender the alleged offender only where the act in question responds to the substantial character of acts defined as crimes in both the requesting State and the requested State. Also, the requesting State must have jurisdiction to prosecute in the first place. The double criminality rule, which reflects the essentially reciprocal character of extradition treaties,[12] may also reduce the chances of an individual being extradited for acts which may be defined as crimes in peculiar or outdated criminal codes, thereby extending some considerations of reasonableness to the alleged offender.

Similarly, the specialty rule limits the requesting State to prosecute or sentence the extradited individual only for the particular crime or crimes forming the subject of the extradition request and not for any other crime.[13] The rule of speciality follows from the principle that the requesting State must exercise good faith in the performance of its applicable treaty obligations to the requested State.[14] As such, it is designed to avoid arbitrariness on the part of the requesting State's criminal law enforcement. The specialty rule also benefits the alleged offender by providing immunity from prosecution for certain

---

[12]   *See* Gilbert, *supra* note 7 at 47-54.

[13]   The rule does not apply in cases where the crime arose from the same set of facts and equally constitutes an extraditable offence, or the individual consents to prosecution on the other crime or crimes.

[14]   Yoram Dinstein, *Some Reflections on Extradition*, 36 German Yearbook of International Law (1993) at 55.

crimes, and also by indicating to him or her precisely the reason for which prosecution is sought.[15]

Extradition law - a highly developed system - remains an indispensable element for the effective inter-State enforcement of international criminal law. Not only do the requesting and requested States benefit from regular avenues facilitating acquisition over the alleged offender so as to enable a State with jurisdiction to prosecute, but the alleged offender benefits as well from numerous procedural safeguards, such as those discussed above, which have developed from domestic criminal law jurisprudence, the treaties themselves, international customary law, as well as 'general principles of law' in the sense of Article 38(1)(c) of the Statute of the International Court of Justice. Moreover, an individual subject to extradition proceedings benefits from the application of pertinent norms of international human rights law, in addition to whatever guarantees exist at the municipal level.[16]

Unfortunately however, these very same procedural safeguards may frustrate the efforts of the requesting State to secure custody, and in practice there may arise substantial disagreement between the States involved as to whether the particular case falls within the scope of the political offence exception and whether the individual is likely to receive a fair trial.

The political offence exception may pose a serious obstacle to the effective implementation of international criminal law through inter-State cooperation, particularly if war crimes, acts of terrorism, or other crimes, are not clearly excluded from the scope of the exception. Since extradition remains a matter of friendly cooperation and of executive discretion, in many cases, the temptation of the requested State to apply subjective political criteria may overwhelm more balanced considerations as to whether the offence allegedly committed is of a political character or not. The purely political offenses

---

[15] In some cases, such precision may reveal to the alleged offender that there are solid grounds for the requested State to invoke the political offense exception, and that an application for asylum to the requested State may be advisable .

[16] *See* Chapter 4 of Gilbert, *supra* note 7 (1991).

of treason, espionage and sedition,[17] are likely to pose little difficulty in this regard. However, 'relative' political offenses i.e. those that may be considered as political where there is a close connection between a criminal act, such as murder, assault or robbery, and a political disturbance,[18] are bound to leave great room for the subjective political discretion of the requested State. Originally introduced in European extradition treaties to protect liberal revolutionaries who sought the overthrow of despotic governments, the political offence exception has since been invoked "in so many different situations that it loses all semblance of coherence, precision or clarity".[19]

The particularly notorious 1956 case of *Artukovic* involved the denial by a US court to a request for extradition on the basis that war crimes constituted political offenses. In that case, Yugoslavia requested the United States to surrender Andrija Artukovic, a former minister in the puppet Nazi Government of the independent State of Croatia, which had been installed in 1941.[20] The basis for Yugoslavia's request was Artukovic's alleged criminal responsibility in the murders of over 700,000 civilians committed in Yugoslav territory between the years 1941-1943. The Court held that the alleged crimes were of a political character and that they therefore fell within the political offence exception. The ruling was vacated by the US Supreme Court, which then remanded the case for a full extradition hearing. However, following a complete extradition hearing, the district court held that, even if there had existed probable cause on a fair reading of the facts, it would have denied Yugoslavia's extradition request.

Courts of the United States in cases involving alleged terrorist acts carried out by members of the Provisional Irish Republican Army have refused to extradite to the United Kingdom individuals against

---

[17]   See the U.S. Federal Court decision of *Eain* v. *Wilkes*, 641 F. 2nd 504 (7th Circuit at 512) (1981).

[18]   See the U.S. case of *Quinn* v. *Robinson*, 783 F. 2nd 776, (89th Circuit) (1986); 107 Supreme Court 271 (1987) which used this test.

[19]   Gilbert, *supra* note 7 at 131.

[20]   *Artukovic* v. *Boyle*; 140 Supp. 245 (S.D. California) (1956); *Karadzole* v. *Artukovic*, 247 F. 2d 198 (9th Circuit) (1957); 355 US 393 (1958), remanded to United States *ex rel Karadzole* v. *Artukovic*, 170 F. Supp. 383 (S.D. California 1959).

whom there has been marshalled strong *prima facie* evidence, on the grounds that these violent acts were political.[21]

Ultimately, the extradition process must be considered cumbersome, and as regards crimes under international law, outdated. The *Artukovic* case symbolizes what may happen where heavily political considerations overtake the original intent of the political offence exception, initially designed to avoid surrender of an individual to his or her homeland, where such surrender could involve a high risk of retaliatory action from an intolerant or autocratic Government. For decades, Cold War distrust made courts in western countries wary to extradite individuals to Eastern Bloc countries where the prospects for fair legal process appeared dim.

To make matters worse, in many instances, there may be no extradition treaty in force between the requesting and requested States. The matter may then be handled in a purely discretionary way. This approach may work sufficiently well in cases where a government feels it has no particular interest in sheltering a person alleged to have committed an act of genocide, terrorism or other such crime. However, in other cases, it may wish to demonstrate its sovereign autonomy by 'standing up' against what it considers to be unwarranted interference in its internal political decision-making. In yet other cases, a government may sympathize with the alleged offender or may wish to adverse political attention or embarrassment, particularly where public opinion may be divided as to the justness of an alleged offender's political cause.

A telling indication of government frustration with the existing means of extradition lies in the increased resort to State-sponsored kidnapping.

---

[21]   *See* Miriam E. Sapiro, *Extradition in an Era of Terrorism: The Need to Abolish the Political Offense Exception*, 61(4) New York University Law Review (1986); and Rena Hozore Reiss, *The Extradition of John Demjanjuk: War Crimes, Universality Jurisdiction, and the Political Offense Doctrine*, 20(2) Cornell International Law Journal (1987).

ii) State-Sponsored Kidnapping of
Criminal Suspects from Foreign Territory

State-sponsored abduction of the criminal suspect from the territory of another State, without the latter State's prior consent, may appear to some States preferable to having to make a regular request for rendition in cases where cooperation between the two States is unsatisfactory to the State seeking to prosecute. This approach dispenses with potentially cumbersome legal and administrative procedures and avoids the long extradition process. Where there exist no formal extradition arrangements in place between the two States involved, and mutual cooperation cannot be relied upon, State-sponsored kidnapping in some cases may appear the only feasible option by which to bring the alleged offender to trial.

In particularly high profile cases, politicians and prosecutors may anticipate significant political returns from a calculated demonstration of bravado in the capture of someone recognized by the public to be an individual *hostis humanis generis*. The full-scale American invasion of Panama on 20 December 1989, *inter alia* to abduct General Manuel Noriega, *de facto* leader of Panama, involved the deployment of more than 26,000 troops and must be considered an extreme case of this kind of approach. At least 240 Panamanians, twenty-three US servicemen and two US civilians were killed. Noriega had been indicted in two Florida courts on twelve counts related to cocaine production, trafficking, money laundering, bribery and complicity in the criminal activities of the Medellín cartel on 4 February 1988.[22] Ultimately, 'Operation Just Cause', as it was dubbed by the Bush Administration, although exceedingly destructive and clumsy, proved effective in bringing about the conviction and incarceration of Noriega in the United States.

---

[22]   *See Indictment, United States* v. *Noriega* No. 88-0079 (Filed on 4 Feb. 1988, S.D. Fla); Nanda, *The Validity of United States Intervention in Panama Under International Law*, 84 American Journal of International Law (1990); *see also* Frances Y.F. Ma, *Noriega's Abduction from Panama: Is Military Invasion an Appropriate Substitute for International Extradition?* 13(4) Loyola of Los Angeles International and Comparative Law Journal (1991).

However, two less extreme cases, the 1961 *Eichmann Case*[23] and the 1992 *Alvarez-Machain Case,*[24] illustrate particularly well the legal, diplomatic and practical issues involved in State-sponsored kidnapping of the criminal suspect from foreign territory where the consent of the territorial State is absent.

- The Eichmann Case

The *Eichmann Case* concerned the prosecution by Israel of Adolph Eichmann, a German national, alleged to have committed war crimes and crimes against humanity in his capacity as Head of the Jewish Office of the Gestapo in the Nazi Government during the Second World War. Following the end of World War II, Eichmann fled Germany, and since 1950, lived in Argentina under the alias of Ricardo Klement. On 11 May 1960, Eichmann was abducted from Buenos Aires, Argentina, and taken to Israel (it seems, by Israeli Secret Service agents). On 23 May, Israel's Prime Minister declared that Eichmann would be tried for his role in the Final Solution, pursuant to the 1950 Nazi and Nazi Collaborators (Punishment) Law for having committed war crimes and crimes against humanity.

The Government of Argentina, which had not been informed in advance of the plans to abduct Eichmann, protested against the Israeli kidnapping as a violation of Argentinean sovereignty and attributed legal responsibility therefor to the State of Israel for having conferred explicit approval upon the operation. The Government of Argentina requested the return of Eichmann as well as the prosecution and punishment of the persons responsible for having violated the law of Argentina. In response to the Argentinean Government's denunciation of Israel's action, the Government of Israel issued a note claiming that the forcible apprehension of Eichmann had been carried out by a 'volunteer group' and expressed regret over any violation of

---

[23]   *Attorney-General of the Government of Israel* v. *Eichmann* (District Court of Jerusalem) *decided* 12 Dec. 1961; 36 International Law Reports, 5-276; Supreme Court, sitting as a Court of Criminal Appeal, *decided* 29 May 1962, 36 International Law Reports (277-350).

[24]   *United States, Petitioner* v. *Humberto Alvarez-Machain, decided* 15 June 1992 (US Supreme Court), No. 91-712, on writ of *certiorari* to the United States Court of Appeals for the Ninth Circuit.

Argentinean sovereignty for which it might have been responsible. The Israeli Prime Minister also expressed similar regrets in a personal letter to the President of Argentina.

This apology did not satisfy the Government of Argentina, which then requested an urgent meeting of the Security Council to deal with the matter. On 23 June 1960, the Security Council passed a resolution[25] declaring "that acts such as that under consideration, which affect the sovereignty of a Member State and therefore cause international friction, may, if repeated, endanger international peace and security", and requested "the Government of Israel to make appropriate reparation in accordance with the Charter of the United Nations and the rules of international law" and finally "expressed the hope that the traditionally friendly relations between Argentina and Israel will be advanced". By 3 August, 1960, the Governments of Argentina and Israel agreed to settle the dispute and issued a joint public statement in which Israel conceded that the forcible apprehension of Eichmann had "infringed the fundamental rights of the State of Argentina", but that both Governments considered the matter closed.

The resolution of the dispute between Argentina and Israel at the diplomatic level did not clarify whether the illegal transfer of Eichmann to Israeli territory vitiated Israeli criminal jurisdiction over Eichmann. The Argentina Government no longer demanded the return of Eichmann to Argentinean territory, indicating that it felt sufficient reparation had been made in the form of satisfaction through Israel's recognition in the joint statement itself of its violation of Argentina's 'fundamental rights'. However, the question of Israeli criminal jurisdiction remained to be resolved by the District Court of Jerusalem before which Eichmann was brought for trial.

At trial, the defense counsel contended that the kidnapping was sponsored by the State of Israel and that its illegality should in no way be condoned by the District Court. More importantly, the defense counsel argued that the abduction of Eichmann from Argentina, in breach of international law, nullified the Court's jurisdiction over the accused.

---

[25]   Security Council resolution S/4349 of 23 June 1960.

In rejecting this argument, the District Court of Jerusalem relied upon the case-law of the United Kingdom, the United States and Israel, finding that:

> It is an established rule of law that a person being tried for an offense against the laws of a State may not oppose his trial by reason of the illegality of his arrest or of the means whereby he was brought within the jurisdiction of that State. The courts in England, the United States and Israel have constantly held that the circumstances of the arrest and the mode of bringing of the accused into the territory of the State have no relevance to his trial, and they have consistently refused in all instances to enter upon an examination of these circumstances.

The Court cited numerous cases, including *Ex parte Susannah Scott*,[26] in which an application for *habeas corpus* pending committal for trial was dismissed, despite the applicant's illegal transfer from Belgium. The Court relied also on *Ex parte Elliott*,[27] in which the application for *habeas corpus* of a British soldier who had deserted and fled to Belgium was denied, though his arrest in Belgium may have contravened Belgian law, on the grounds that the manner of his being brought before the court was irrelevant to the assertion of personal jurisdiction.

Courts in the United States have taken a similar approach. In the landmark 1886 Supreme Court case of *Ker* v. *Illinois*,[28] in which the criminal suspect was forcibly apprehended in Peru, and brought before an Illinois court for larceny, the Court held that "forcible abduction is no sufficient reason why the party should not answer when brought within the jurisdiction of the court which has the right to try him for such an offense, and presents no valid objection to his trial

---

[26] (1829) 9 B.& C. 446; 109 England Reports 106.
[27] (1949) 1 All England Reports 373.
[28] 119 U.S. 436

in such court."[29] In *Frisbie* v. *Collins*,[30] the Supreme Court intoned that:

> This Court has never departed from the rule announced in *Ker* v. *Illinois* that the power of a court to try a person for crime is not impaired by the fact that he had been brought within the court's jurisdiction by reason of 'forcible abduction'. No persuasive reasons are now presented to justify overruling this line of cases. They rest on the sound basis that due process of law is satisfied when one present in court is convicted of crime after having been fairly apprized of the charges against him and after a fair trial in accordance with constitutional procedural safeguards. There is nothing in the Constitution that requires a court to permit a guilty person rightfully convicted to escape justice because he was brought to trial against his will.

Consistent with this approach, US courts have also treated the violation of sovereignty as a political matter between the two States involved to be settled through diplomatic channels.[31] On the other hand, the State whose sovereign rights were infringed by the forcible apprehension and abduction of the criminal suspect, could request the return of the suspect in order to restore the *status quo ante*. While Argentina did not request the return of Eichmann, general rules of international responsibility leave this option open.

Interestingly, Article 16 of the Harvard Research Draft Convention on Jurisdiction With Respect to Crime of 1935,[32] entitled *Apprehension in Violation of International Law*, provides that:

---

[29]   *Ibid.* at 444. The US Supreme Court has applied the *ratio decidendi* in *Ker* v. *Illinois* also to cases of inter-State abduction within the territory of the United States. *See Mahon* v. *Justice* 127 US 700 (1888); *Cook* v. *Hart*, 146 US 183 (1892); *Pettibone* v. *Nichols*, 203 US 192 (1906).

[30]   342 US 519; application for rehearing dismissed, 343 US 397 (1952).

[31]   *See e.g., United States* v. *Unverzagt* (1924), 299 Fed. 1015, concerning the abduction of a US citizen from territory of British Columbia to be tried before a court in the US.

[32]   29 American Journal of International Law 443 Supp. (1935) at 635.

> In exercising jurisdiction under this Convention, no
> State shall prosecute or punish any person who has
> been brought within its territory or a place subject to its
> authority by recourse to measures in violation of
> international law or international convention without first
> obtaining the consent of the State whose rights have
> been violated by such measures.

However, as the District Court observed in the *Eichmann Case*, Article 16 represents a norm *de lege ferenda* and does not represent the established judicial practise of many countries.

In considering Eichmann's appeal, the Supreme Court of Israel affirmed the District Court's ruling that the circumstances by which Eichmann was brought before the Court were irrelevant to the Court's jurisdiction. Moreover, the Supreme Court supported the District Court's holding that the violation of international law concerned the rights of the State of Argentina, not those of the individual suspect, and therefore, the matter had to be resolved at the international level. The *Eichmann Case* thus stands as authority for the maxim *male captus bene detentus*.

- Alvarez-Machain Case

The *Alvarez-Machain* case,[33] which has generated voluminous scholarly comment,[34] involved the abduction of Mr. Alvarez-Machain,

---

[33] *United States, Petitioner* v. *Humberto Alvarez-Machain*, decided 15 June 1992 (US Supreme Court) No. 91-712.

[34] *See e.g.*, Michael J. Glennon, *State-Sponsored Abduction: A Comment on United States* v. *Alvarez-Machain*, 86 American Journal of International Law (1992); Jimmy Gurulé, *Terrorism, Territorial Sovereignty and the Forcible Apprehension of International Criminals Abroad*, 17(3) Hastings International and Comparative Law Review (1994); Malvina Halberstam, *In Defense of the Supreme Court Decision in Alvarez-Machain*, 86 American Journal of International Law (1992); Charles D. Siegal, *Individual Rights under Self-Executing Extradition Treaties: Dr. Alvarez-Machain's Case*, 13(4) Loyola of Los Angeles International and Comparative Law Journal (1990); Andrew L. Strauss, *A Global Paradigm Shattered: The Jurisdictional Nihilism of the Supreme Court's Abduction Decision in Alvarez-*

a citizen and resident of Mexico, from Mexican territory for having allegedly participated in the kidnapping and murder of two officials of the US Drug Enforcement Administration (DEA). Alvarez-Machain, a medical doctor, was alleged to have prolonged one of the DEA agents' lives to enable others to torture and interrogate the agent. On 2 April 1990, two DEA agents captured Alvarez-Machain from his medical office in Guadalajara, Mexico, and forcibly took him by airplane to Texas to be arrested on arrival by DEA authorities. On 18 April 1990, the Government of Mexico requested a full report from the United States Government on its involvement in the abduction. On 16 May and 19 July 1990, the Mexican Government protested strongly to the United States Government in formal diplomatic notes.

As in the *Eichmann Case*, the accused pleaded that the District Court lacked jurisdiction on account of the illegality of his abduction and transfer. However, in *Alvarez-Machain*, the Court accepted the defense argument and therefore Alvarez-Machain had to be repatriated to Mexico. This finding was affirmed by the Court of Appeals on grounds that such abduction violated the purpose (although not the letter) of the extradition treaty.[35] The Court of Appeals confirmed both the repatriation order of the lower court and its dismissal of the indictment.

The United States Government then petitioned the Supreme Court for a writ of *certiorari*. Following a review of the *United States v. Rauscher*,[36] *Ker v. Illinois*, *Frisbie v. Collins* and a number of other cases, the Supreme Court held in regard to the United States-Mexico Extradition Treaty that:

> The history of negotiation and practice under the Treaty ... fails to show that abductions outside of the Treaty constitute a violation of the Treaty. As the Solicitor General notes, the Mexican Government was made aware, as early as 1906, of the *Ker* doctrine, and the

---

Machain, 67(4) Temple Law Review (1994); and Andrew L. Wilder, *The Supreme Court Decision in United States v. Alvarez-Machain*, 32(4) Virginia Journal of International Law (1992).

[35]   Extradition Treaty between United States and Mexico of 4 May 1978; TIAS No. 9656.

[36]   119 U.S. 407 (1886).

United States' position that it applied to forcible abductions made outside the terms of the United States-Mexico extradition treaty. Nonetheless, the current version of the Treaty, signed in 1978, does not attempt to establish a rule that would in any way curtail the effect of *Ker*.

The Court then adverted to Article 16 of the Harvard Research Draft Convention discussed above, arguing that the fact that a new rule had been proposed in 1935 by prominent legal scholars, but had not been adopted in the extradition treaty, implied *a contrario* that the treaty was not intended to prohibit forcible abductions. In response to the accused's contention that the intention of the United States-Mexico Extradition Treaty was to prevent violations of general international law so that a Government would not exercise police enforcement in foreign territory, the Supreme Court replied that:

> There are many actions which could be taken by a nation that would violate this principle, including waging war, but it cannot seriously be contended an invasion of the United States by Mexico would violate the terms of the extradition treaty between the two nations.

The Supreme Court then decided that since the abduction of Alvarez-Machain did not violate the Extradition Treaty, the rule in *Ker* v. *Illinois* applied, and therefore, his abduction from Mexico did not nullify the criminal jurisdiction of the Court.

In a strong dissenting opinion, Justices Blackmun and O'Connor joined with Justice Stevens in observing that:

> It is true, as the Court notes, that there is no express promise by either party to refrain from forcible abductions in the territory of the other Nation. Relying on that omission, the Court, in effect, concludes that the Treaty merely creates an optional method of obtaining jurisdiction over alleged offenders, and that the parties silently reserved the right to resort to self help whenever they deem force more expeditious than legal process. If the United States, for example, thought it

more expedient to torture or simply to execute a person rather than to attempt extradition, these options would be equally available because they, too, were not explicitly prohibited by the Treaty. That, however, is a highly improbable interpretation of a consensual agreement, which on its face appears to have been intended to set forth comprehensive and exclusive rules concerning the subject of extradition.

The dissenting opinion went on to underline the importance of the principle of territorial sovereignty, endorsing Justice Story's view in the *Apollon Case*[37] that:

It would be monstrous to suppose that our revenue officers were authorized to enter into foreign ports and territories, for the purpose of seizing vessels which had offended against our laws. It cannot be presumed that Congress would voluntarily justify such a clear violation of the law of nations.

Moreover, the dissenting opinion pointed out that the Court's judgement does not differentiate between State-sponsored abduction, which incurs international responsibility, and abduction carried out by private persons, which does not necessarily affect the jurisdiction of the Court before which the alleged offender is brought.

The *Eichmann* and *Alvarez-Machain* decisions are myopic. While the individuals responsible for having committed crimes under international law were brought successfully to trial in these two cases, the State-sponsored kidnappings themselves constitute crude violations of the territorial sovereignty of one State by another.

As Abbell argues, the *Alvarez-Machain Case* is likely to diminish the criminal enforcement power of the United States for three principal reasons. The *Alvarez-Machain Case* implies that any State may freely violate the territorial sovereignty of another State in order to capture a criminal suspect whom it seeks to prosecute. Second, while increasing global integration of criminal activity is likely to require

---

[37]   9 Wheaton's Digest 362 at 370-1 (1824).

greater international cooperation and mutual respect on the part of States for each other's sovereign rights under international law, the *Alvarez-Machain* decision signals to other countries that United States criminal law enforcement authorities may have other things in mind, such as plans to unilaterally apprehend the alleged offender. Third, in light of the Supreme Court's reasoning that unless explicitly so prohibited, an extradition treaty must be construed as permitting State-sponsored kidnapping, the United States henceforward may meet with greater difficulty in concluding extradition treaties with other States, unless such treaties expressly prohibit such action.[38]

iii) Use of Security Council Authority to Ensure the Alleged Offender is Properly Tried Before a Domestic Court: The *Lockerbie Case*

The *Lockerbie Case*[39] demonstrates the misuse of Security Council authority to force the surrender of an alleged offender before a domestic court.

The downing of Pan Am flight 103 over Lockerbie, Scotland, on 21 December 1988, took the lives of all 259 persons on board and eleven on the ground. Following investigations by American and Scottish teams, indictments by a District of Columbia grand jury and by the Lord Advocate in Scotland, were issued for the arrest of Lamen Khalifa Flimah and Abdel Basset Ali al-Megrahi, two Libyan nationals (suspected of being Libyan intelligence agents). In November 1991, the UK and the US called on the Government of Libya to surrender the two suspects for trial, to cooperate with criminal investigators, and to pay compensation, even before any factual or legal issues relating to culpability or complicity could be decided by a court of law.

No extradition treaties between Libya and the UK or Libya and the US were in force at the time of the American and British joint

---

[38]   *See* Michael Abbell, *The Need for US Legislation to Curb State-Sponsored Kidnapping*, in The Alleged Transnational Criminal: the Second Biennial International Criminal Law Seminar, (ed. Atkins) (1995) at 90-91.

[39]   *Questions of Interpretation and Application of the 1971 Montreal Convention arising from the Aerial Incident at Lockerbie* (Libya v. United Kingdom), 1992 ICJ Reports 3 of 14 April 1992; and (Libya v. United States) 114-217.

request. However, Libya, the United Kingdom and the United States, were all parties to the 1971 Montreal Convention,[40] which provides that the Convention may be considered a legal basis for surrendering a suspect where there is no extradition treaty between the requesting State and the requested State.

Libya decided not to surrender the two suspects on grounds that the law of Libya did not allow for the extradition of nationals. Instead, the Government of Libya offered to prosecute the two suspects, invited forensic assistance from the United Kingdom and the United States, and offered the opportunity to observe the criminal proceedings to be initiated by Libyan prosecutors.

As argued above, the principle of *aut dedere aut judicare* has not attained the status of customary international law. Therefore, it is doubtful whether the Government of Libya had any mandatory obligation under international law to extradite or prosecute the offenders.

On the other hand, in light of an increasing number of conventions affirming the principle, there exists a strong expectation on the part of States of a certain level of cooperation with respect to particularly serious crimes. In this connection, it must be noted that the Government of Libya had indicated its willingness to prosecute the two suspects (*judicare*), and to cooperate with foreign criminal investigators, more than fulfilling its obligations under international law. However, these offers went unanswered by the Governments of the United Kingdom and the United States. While it may be that the Libyan Government complied with or supported the terrorist act, or that Libyan authorities had no real intention of undertaking a serious prosecution effort, *mala fides* on the part of the Government should not have been assumed in advance of a fair hearing on the facts and law.

However, on 21 January 1992, the Security Council adopted resolution 731[41] which expresses concern "over the results of investigations, which implicate officials of the Libyan Government" in

---

[40]   Montreal Convention for the Suppression of Unlawful Acts against the Safety of Civil Aviation, 1971, *signed* on 23 Sept. 1971, *entered into force* 26 Jan. 1973; 10 International Legal Materials (No. 1971) 1151.

[41]   Resolution 731, *adopted* on 21 Jan. 1992 by the Security Council, S/23574.

connection with the downing of Pan Am 103 (as well as another incident involving an attack carried out against Union de transports aeriens flight 772), "[s]trongly deplores the fact that the Libyan Government has not yet responded effectively to the ... requests to cooperate fully in establishing responsibility" and in paragraph 3, "urges the Libyan Government immediately to provide a full and effective response to [the requests of France, USA and UK] so as to contribute to the elimination of terrorism".

Libya then deposited two applications with the International Court of Justice for provisional measures,[42] arguing that the US and the UK had rejected its offers to cooperate and, *inter alia*, requested the ICJ to enjoin the US and the UK from coercing Libya to surrender the two suspects, or from taking other action that might cause prejudice to the right of Libya to prosecute the alleged offenders according to Libyan law. On 26 and 28 March 1992, the Court heard the issue, but just before the Court could render a ruling, the Security Council invoked Chapter VII of the UN Charter and adopted resolution 748.[43] Resolution 748 expresses deep concern "that the Libyan Government has still not provided a full and effective response to the requests" of the UK and the US, as expressed in resolution 731, and in paragraph 1, "[d]ecides that the Libyan Government must now comply without any further delay with paragraph 3 of resolution 731 (1992)". Further, resolution 748: "[d]ecides also that the Libyan Government must commit itself definitively to cease all forms of terrorist action and all assistance to terrorist groups and that it must promptly, by concrete actions, demonstrate its renunciation of terrorism"; decides that States shall cut off air links with Libya, prohibits the supply of aircraft components, engineering, servicing, insurance, etc. to Libya; and seeks to dry up the sale of weapons, munitions, vehicles and spare parts to Libya. Resolution 748 also requires States, *inter alia*, to "[s]ignificantly reduce the number and the level of the staff of Libyan diplomatic missions and consular posts" in their territory and close Libyan Airline offices. It also establishes a Committee of the Security Council to monitor State compliance with resolution 748.

---

[42]   (Libya v. United Kingdom) 1992 ICJ Reports 3 *et seq.*
[43]   Security Council resolution 748, *adopted* on 31 March 1992.

Ironically, once the crippling effect of the Cold War on Security Council effectiveness had disappeared, the Council chose to exercise its powers in such a way that threatened to undermine the rule of law at the international level. The Security Council's action overtook the process prescribed by the 1971 Montreal Convention, thereby hindering due regard for the system of cooperation the Convention seeks to advance. Worse, as Graefrath has argued:

> It seems that the Security Council by resolution 748 (1992) transformed the terms of settlement recommended by resolution 731 (1992) under Chapter VI into a binding dispute settlement under Chapter VII, a procedure that is not provided for in the Charter. It is not at all convincing that a single act of terrorism could constitute a threat to peace, in particular if compared with other circumstances where the Security Council could not find that a threat to international peace existed. Further, on previous occasions, the Security Council has declined to act even when measures were requested to stop activities which were in clear contempt of an ICJ judgment.[44]

Thus, the Security Council's precipitous 'executive' action struck a severe blow at the judicial independence of the International Court of Justice by preempting its pending order on the question of provisional measures, and threats to hamper the role of the judiciary generally in legal disputes.

Unfortunately, the *Lockerbie Case* indicates not the resolve of the international community to combat terrorism, but the selective and arbitrary use of the enforcement power of the Security Council against a State not proven by any judicial body to have breached international law in the particular instance in question. The preference of the United Kingdom and the United States for coercion over negotiation, cooperation and judicial settlement, against the background of Libya's stated willingness to cooperate with foreign criminal investigators and

---

[44]   Bernard Graefrath, *Leave to the Court What Belongs to the Court: The Libyan Case*, 4(2) European Journal of International Law (1993) at 196.

its pledge to prosecute the two suspects in its custody, indicates how easily some of the more influential States may be provoked into shortsighted overreaction.

CHAPTER VI

IMPLEMENTATION OF INTERNATIONAL CRIMINAL LAW THROUGH INTERNATIONAL CRIMINAL TRIBUNALS

1. INTRODUCTION

The creation of the international criminal tribunals for the former Yugoslavia and Rwanda - a half century after the Nuremberg and Tokyo trials were held - has revived hopes that in the post-Cold War era, crimes under international law can be deterred effectively through international mechanisms.

The need for an international criminal court may be particularly acute in situations where domestic avenues to enforce responsibility for acts which constitute crimes under international law are non-existent or substantially blocked.

In the case of civil war, both perpetrator and victim are likely to be nationals of the State in whose territory the crimes were committed. In this case, normally the territorial State would have jurisdiction to prosecute crimes under international law on a territorial basis and also on grounds that the offender was its own national. Alternatively, the territorial State may assert jurisdiction on grounds its national interest was injured by the offense in question. In other cases, a State may assert jurisdiction on grounds that the victim of the crime was its own national.[1] Despite the fact that there may be several jurisdictional bases for the assertion of domestic criminal enforcement in respect of crimes under international law committed in the context of civil war, an international criminal tribunal may play a very valuable role in the securing of criminal prosecutions, particularly where the territorial Government wishes to prosecute, but cannot. For example, the State may be unable to ensure the rule of law within its

---

[1]   The 'passive personality principle' as a ground for the assertion of domestic criminal jurisdiction has not been as widely recognized as the others grounds, as discussed in Chapter V(2) above.

jurisdiction where its administration of justice has been destroyed or rendered ineffective by war.

Equally, creation of an international criminal tribunal may prove desirable where it is unclear whether the territorial Government wishes to prosecute its own nationals for crimes under international law, for example, as in Croatia,[2] although it may have sufficient capacity to do so. In this regard, it is instructive also to recall the sham Leipzig Trials, described briefly below, which were carried out by the Government of Germany after the First World War, in lieu of surrendering suspects to the Allies for prosecution.

Even in cases where the Government has both the will and the capacity to bring to trial individuals for crimes under international law in conformity with international fair trial standards, an international criminal tribunal may be needed to supplement domestic court jurisdiction. An international criminal tribunal may bring an added sense of objectivity and fairness to the criminal proceedings as well as raise their symbolic profile. Eventually, an international tribunal may prove useful to supplement domestic efforts to acquire custody over the alleged offender where he or she has fled to another country, although to this point, the experience of the International Criminal Tribunal for the Former Yugoslavia has been very disappointing in this regard. In some cases, a government may be more willing to surrender a criminal suspect to an international criminal tribunal for prosecution, rather than to extradite or surrender him or her to the State seeking to prosecute where the chances of fair trial in proceedings conducted by that State may appear slim.

The present Chapter explores the use of the international criminal tribunal as a technique in the implementation of international criminal law. This Chapter intends to provide some background to

---

[2]   In his report to the Security Council of 5 December 1996, the Secretary-General stated that: "According to information received from the Office of the Prosecutor, Croatia's cooperation with the International Tribunal leaves much to be desired". *See also,* Further Report on the Situation of Human Rights in Croatia Pursuant to Security Council resolution 1019 (1995), Part VII of UN Doc. S/1996/1011, and the Periodic Report submitted by Mrs. Rehn, Special Rapporteur of the Commission on Human Rights, pursuant to paragraph 45 of Commission resolution 1996/71, UN. Doc. E/CN.4/1997/9 of 22 October 1996 at para. 35.

those tribunals that have been created to this point, and then to highlight certain procedural or institutional aspects thereof. Finally, some key points concerning the possible creation of a permanent international criminal court are considered in light of the experience gained from the tribunals so far created this century.

2. PRIOR TO WORLD WAR II

Customary international law permits belligerent States to prosecute enemy soldiers in their custody for breach of the laws and customs of war. Such trials may be held before a military court, either domestic or constituted jointly by more than one State (in which case, it would have an international aspect). However, prior to the Second World War, trials through joint military jurisdiction were rare. There are a few ancient cases, which Keen recounts in the *Laws of War*,[3] such as the prosecution and punishment in 1419 of the Seigneur de Barbasan for breach of the medieval laws of war, and the trial of Peter von Hagenbach in 1474, for murder and rape of civilians by soldiers under his command.

Further significant development in the implementation of international criminal law did not occur until around five centuries later, following the end of the First World War.[4] The peace settlement placed an unprecedented focus on the issue of moral and legal responsibility for the outbreak of the war. The Allies went beyond indemnities, territorial concessions, and other measures customarily demanded at peace conferences, to the issue of individual guilt for

---

[3]   Maurice H. Keen, The Laws of War in the Late Middle Ages (1965).

[4]   The First World War had resulted in an estimated nine million casualties, 20 million wounded and over $300 billion dollars in property damage. *See* René Albrecht-Carrié, Europe after 1815 (1959) at 193. On 25 Jan. 1919, the Paris Peace Conference was convened to establish the League of Nations. By 28 June, the First Versailles Treaty was signed between the Allied Powers with Germany and Associated Powers. The League of Nations was officially inaugurated on 10 Jan. 1920 with the entry of force of the Treaty of Versailles. *See* Stephen Duggan et al. (ed.), The League of Nations: The Principle and the Practice (1919).

World War I.[5] Article 227 of the Treaty of Versailles provided that the former Kaiser, Emperor Wilhelm II, would be prosecuted in a personal capacity by a special international tribunal "for a supreme offence against international morality and the sanctity of treaties". However, this provision was never executed. The former Kaiser was admitted to neutral Holland where the Dutch Government refused to prosecute or extradite him.[6]

It seems that Article 227 had been adopted only half-heartedly by Peace Conference delegates in order to mollify international public opinion. The firm decision of the Government of the Netherlands not to extradite Kaiser Wilhelm II had already been taken by the end of December 1918, even prior to the conclusion of the Versailles Treaty. The Dutch Government requested the Kaiser only to refrain from politics during his presence in the Netherlands, a pledge he maintained until his death. Despite the failure of Article 227 to be executed, the provision at least symbolized the possibility that a Head of State might be held personally responsible under international law for launching an aggressive war. That this provision was even put forward, signifies rejection by Conference delegates of the idea that sovereign State immunity exempts political leaders from responsibility for aggression. However, the results of this episode were disappointing and they indicated that, at the time, the international community was not prepared to match words with action.

Perhaps even more disheartening in this affair was the role played by the domestic courts *vis-à-vis* war crimes prosecution. Articles 228-230 of the Treaty of Versailles provided that the German Government recognized the right of the Allied Powers to try persons for war crimes committed against the Allies and obligated the Government to surrender German suspects to the Allied Powers for prosecution. Article 229 provides that:

---

[5]   Article 231 of the Treaty of Versailles, 1919, provides that: "The Allied and associated governments declare, and Germany accepts the responsibility for, all the loss and damage suffered by the Allied and associated governments as a consequence of the war imposed upon them by the aggression of Germany and her allies".

[6]   *See further* Alan W. Palmer, The Kaiser: Warlord of the Second Reich (1978) at 214-215.

Persons guilty of criminal acts against the nationals of one of the Allied and Associated Powers will be brought before the military tribunals of that Power.
Persons guilty of criminal acts against the nationals of more than one of the Allied and Associated Powers will be brought before military tribunals composed of members of the military tribunals of the Powers concerned ...

In December 1919, the Government of Germany, of its own accord, undertook to prosecute its nationals for war crimes, which obviated the need for the Allied Powers to implement Articles 228-230 of the Versailles Treaty. The political climate at the time was such that the Allied Powers had little other option than to provide a list of suspects, which they duly prepared. This list contained the names of 901 war crimes suspects, which the Allies submitted to the Supreme Court of the Reich at Leipzig. However, the few trials that actually were conducted proved to be little more than a sham. There were few convictions and even in those few cases, only very insignificant sentences handed down. The Leipzig Trials indicate that, in certain cases, a government may not be entrusted to enforce the individual criminal responsibility of its own nationals for crimes under international law.[7]

3. NUREMBERG AND TOKYO TRIBUNALS

The Nuremberg and Tokyo Tribunals are commonly regarded as archetypes of modern international criminal law implementation. However, it is important to recognize that these tribunals represent only imperfect examples of such implementation, particularly as regards their international facet.
On the one hand, the Nuremberg and Tokyo Charters specify that the Tribunals shall enforce criminal responsibility for crimes against peace, war crimes and crimes against humanity, thus empowering them to apply international law. Also, the judges were

---

[7]   History of the UN War Crimes Commission (1948) at 48.

drawn from more than one country making them internationally constituted in that sense. The seemingly international character of the Tribunals was further reinforced by Article 2 of the Agreement for the Establishment of an International Military Tribunal which states that the Nuremberg Tribunal was constituted "for the trials of war criminals whose offenses have no particular geographical location".[8] Even their official names - as 'International Military Tribunals' - tend to confirm their international appearance.

However, certain aspects of the Nuremberg and Tokyo Tribunals indicate that these organs more closely resemble products of joint municipal jurisdiction. Concerning Article 2 of the Agreement for the Establishment of an International Military Tribunal, the Nuremberg Tribunal did not in fact need to rely on universal jurisdiction, since a belligerent may conduct war crimes trials on the territory of the defeated State. This right remained undisturbed by Hague Convention IV, 1907, which, along with the other 1899 and 1907 Hague Conventions, were intended 'to revise the laws and general customs of war'. Indeed, the Nuremberg Tribunal represented an exceptional exercise of the territorial jurisdiction of the Allied Powers possible only because Germany was in fact defeated and occupied. The four occupying Powers had the right to exercise "supreme authority with respect to Germany, including all the powers possessed by the German Government, the High Command, and any state, municipal, or local government or authority" according to the declaration of unconditional surrender of the Nazi Government to the Governments of France, the United Kingdom, the United States, and the Union of Soviet Socialist Republics.[9]

Furthermore, while universal jurisdiction authorizes prosecution of certain offenders *regardless of nationality*, the fact that the Nuremberg and Tokyo Tribunals tried soldiers only of enemy countries indicates that the suspect's nationality was a key element in the

---

[8]   5 UNTS 251; 39 American Journal of International Law Supp. (1945) 257.

[9]   Declaration concerning the defeat of Germany and the assumption of supreme authority over Germany by the Governments of the USA, USSR, UK and Provisional Government of the French Republic; 12 Dept. of State Bulletin, 10 June 1945 (1051-1055). On this point, *see generally* Ian Brownlie, Principles of Public International Law, Fourth ed. (1990) at 109.

Prosecutor's selection of persons to be indicted. The expressed intention of the Allies to prosecute enemy individuals, and not their own soldiers or nationals, had been clearly stated in numerous declarations, such as the Declaration of the Moscow Conference, adopted on 1 November 1943, which proclaims that:

> Those German officers and men and members of the Nazi party who have been responsible for, or have taken a consenting part in the ... atrocities, massacres and executions, will be sent back to the countries in which their abominable deeds were done in order that they may be judged and punished according to the laws of these liberated countries and of the free governments which will be created therein ... without prejudice to the case of the major criminals, whose offenses have no particular geographical localization and who will be punished by the joint decision of the Governments of the Allies.[10]

As a matter of principle, nationality would have been entirely irrelevant if universal jurisdiction had been the true basis of the Tribunal's jurisdiction.

Similarly, the Tokyo trials were conducted following unconditional surrender by the Government of Japan to the Allied Powers and Allied occupation of Japanese territory. As in the Nuremberg trials, the Tokyo Tribunal declared its own competence as having derived from the Charter which created it (in this case the Charter of the International Military Tribunal for the Far East).

The Nuremberg and Tokyo Tribunals represent rather equivocal examples of *international* organs and should therefore not be regarded as satisfactory archetypes thereof. In contrast, the International Criminal Tribunals for the Former Yugoslavia and Rwanda establish the beginning of a new pattern in the genuinely international implementation of international criminal law. To appreci-

---

[10]   9 Department of State Bulletin, 6 Nov. 1943 at 311, cited in William B. Simons, *The Jurisdictional Bases of the International Military Tribunal at Nuremberg*, in The Nuremberg Trial and International Law (ed. Ginsburgs and Kudriavtsev) (1990) at 42.

ate the significance of the more recently created tribunals in this regard, it is helpful to review the background and development of each.

4. INTERNATIONAL CRIMINAL TRIBUNAL FOR THE FORMER YUGOSLAVIA

Yugoslavia, created in 1918 from the Kingdoms of Serbia, Montenegro and portions of the defunct Austro-Hungarian empire, was known as the 'State of Serbs, Croats and Slovenes' until it was renamed 'Yugoslavia' in 1929, and in 1974, the 'Socialist Federal Republic of Yugoslavia'. Prior to the Second World War, Yugoslavia was ruled by King Alexander I as a unitarist monarchy. Ethnic divisions were not strongly exhibited in the country.[11]

In 1941, the Axis Powers invaded Yugoslavia, whose army was forced to surrender. From 1941 to 1945, the Axis Powers created a succession of puppet governments to administer various parts of the territory of Yugoslavia. As Dimitrijević observes, the policy of the Axis Powers had far-reaching consequences:

> Those parts of the territory historically claimed by Croats and not annexed by other powers, i.e. Italy, were constituted into 'The Independent State of Croatia'. This territory was governed by a former terrorist movement, whose members came from Italy and Hungary, and who attempted to emulate Hitler's racist policies. In addition to Jews and Gypsies, who were few, their main targets were Serbs, who in that 'independent State' suffered a veritable genocide, with several hundred thousand victims, according to most conservative estimates.[12]

---

[11] *See* Vojin Dimitrijević, *Nationalities and Minorities in the Yugoslav Federation*, The Protection of Minorities and Human Rights (ed. Dinstein and Tabory) (1992).

[12] *Ibid.* at 420-421.

Opposition to the Fascist State of Croatia was taken up first and foremost by Josip Broz Tito, himself a Croat, as leader of the Communist resistance as well as by General Mihailović, leader of the četniks. The četniks were comprised primarily of anti-communist Serbs who were loyal to the monarchist Government of King Peter II, exiled at that time in London.

In 1946, following the victory of Tito's forces and the ascent to power of the Communist Party in Yugoslavia, the monarchy was abolished, and the Federal People's Republic of Yugoslavia was reconstituted as a federation. The component five states of Croatia, Macedonia, Montenegro, Serbia and Slovenia, each contained a majority of the ethnic group as reflected in the name of each state. A sixth province, Bosnia-Herzegovina, whose borders reflected administrative lines drawn by the former Ottoman and Austro-Hungarian empires, was home mainly to Croats, Serbs and Muslims (who had converted to Islam during Ottoman rule). In the 1970's, certain other divisions were created, such as the region of Kosovo and the Province of Vojvodina, autonomous units within the Yugoslav federation.[13]

Tito had suppressed resurgent nationalist ambitions of ethnic groups consistently rule from 1946 until his death in 1980. Not long after Tito's death, however, individual states within Yugoslavia began to agitate for greater autonomy from the central Government.

In a Slovenian referendum on the question of secession from Yugoslavia, held in December 1990, an overwhelming majority of voters opted for independence. A declaration of independence was announced on 8 May 1991, followed by the necessary amendments to the operative constitutional law on 25 June. The secession of Slovenia from the Federal Republic of Yugoslavia opened the door to several other secessionist claims. The resulting disorder and instability in the other Yugoslav republics unleashed many long dormant territorial disputes among the ethnic and religious groups of Yugoslavia and revived the determination on the part of certain groups to settle old scores. The rise in tension expressed itself in armed hostilities, eventually degenerating into full-fledged armed conflict. Arguably, the disintegration of Yugoslavia was exacerbated by

---

[13]   *Ibid.* at 422.

premature recognition on the part of certain influential members of the international community of Slovenia as an independent State.

Serbs living in the Republic of Croatia declared their independence from the rump Federation of Yugoslavia on 16 March 1991. By 1992, Franjo Tudjman was elected President of Croatia.

In Bosnia-Herzegovina, 63% voted for the emergence of an independent Republic, headed by President Alija Izetbegovic. Bosnia-Herzegovina declared itself independent in April 1992.

Within a few days of the declaration of independence of Bosnia-Herzegovina, Serb nationalist militia, including some soldiers from the Yugoslav National Army, invaded parts of Bosnia-Herzegovina. Under Serbian Democratic Party leader Radovan Karadzic[14] the Serb Republic was proclaimed with its administrative centre in Pale. Well-armed Serbian militia were able to occupy, at some points, 70% of Bosnian territory. The Serbian leaders carried out a policy of 'ethnic cleansing' to try to rid the occupied territories of Bosnian Muslims through a systematic policy of widespread massacres and other serious violations of human rights and humanitarian law, including mass deportations of civilian Muslims.

In response to the deteriorating human rights situation in the former Yugoslavia, the UN Commission on Human Rights was called into its first ever special session, during which it adopted resolution 1992/S-1/1 on 14 August 1992, requesting the Chairman of the Commission to appoint a special rapporteur "to investigate first hand the human rights situation in the territory of the former Yugoslavia, in particular within Bosnia and Herzegovina".[15]

The first report[16] of Special Rapporteur Mazowiecki to the Commission on Human Rights concerns, *inter alia*, the policy of ethnic cleansing and other serious human rights violations committed in the territory of the former Yugoslavia. The report states that:

---

[14]   In July 1996, Karadzic was indicted by the International Criminal Tribunal for the Former Yugoslavia.

[15]   *See* Report on the situation of human rights in the territory of the former Yugoslavia submitted by Mr. Tadeusz Mazowiecki, Special Rapporteur of the Commission on Human Rights, pursuant to paragraph 14 of Commission resolution 1992/S-1/1 of 14 Aug. 1992, E/CN.4/1992/S-1/9, 28 Aug. 1992.

[16]   *Ibid.* Chapter I.

The need to prosecute those responsible for mass and flagrant human rights violations and for breaches of international humanitarian law and to deter future violators requires the systematic collection of documentation on such crimes and of personal data concerning those responsible.[17]

The Special Rapporteur then recommended that:

A commission should be created to assess and further investigate specific cases in which prosecution may be warranted.   This information should include data already collected by various entities within the United Nations system, by other intergovernmental organizations and by non-governmental organizations.[18]

Subsequently, a number of reports called for criminal investigation of war crimes and serious violations of humanitarian law as well as the timely collection of information and evidence to support such investigations.[19] Various Governments, international organizations and non-

---

[17]   *Ibid.* at para. 69.

[18]   *Ibid.* at para. 70.

[19]   *See e.g.* E/CN.4/1992/S-1/10 of 27 Oct. 1992 at para 18 as well as Annex II (Statement by Dr. Clyde Snow). *See also* Report of the Special Rapporteur (transmitted by the Secretary-General to the Security Council and General Assembly) A/47/666; S/24809 of 17 Nov. 1992, para. 140, where Mr. Mazowiecki stated: "There is growing evidence that war crimes have been committed. Further investigation is needed to determine the extent of such acts and the identity of those responsible, with a view to their prosecution by an international tribunal, if appropriate". *See further* the later reports of the Special Rapporteur for more details on the human rights situation in the former Yugoslavia: E/CN.4/1993/50 of 10 Feb. 1993; E/CN.4/1994/3 of 5 May 1993; E/CN.4/1994/4 of 19 May 1993; E/CN.4/1994/6 of 26 Aug, 1993; E/CN.4/1994/8 of 6 Sept. 1993; E/CN.4/1994/47 of 17 Nov. 1993; E/CN.4/1994/110 of 21 Feb. 1994; E/CN.4/1995/4 of 10 June 1994; E/CN.4/1995/10 of 4 Aug. 1994; A/49/641-S/1994/1252 of 4 Nov. 1994; E/CN.4/1995/54 of 13 Dec. 1995; E/CN.4/1995/57 of 9 Jan. 1995; E/CN.4/1996/3 of 21 Apr. 1995; and E/CN.4/1996/6 of 5 July 1995.   On 27 July 1995, Mr. Mazowiecki informed the Commission of his decision to resign his mandate.   The

governmental organizations also urged international prosecutions to be carried out.

On 6 October 1992, the Security Council adopted resolution 780[20] which:

> *Requests* the Secretary-General to establish, as a matter of urgency, an impartial Commission of Experts to examine and analyze the information submitted pursuant to resolution 771 (1992) and the present resolution, together with such further information as the Commission of Experts may obtain through its own investigation or efforts, of other persons or bodies pursuant to resolution 771 (1992), with a view to providing the Secretary-General with its conclusions on the evidence of grave breaches of the Geneva Conventions and other violations of international humanitarian law committed in the territory of the former Yugoslavia.

Security Council resolution 771, adopted on 13 August 1992, requires Member States to submit reports on violations of humanitarian law perpetrated in the territory of the former Yugoslavia.

In October 1992, the Secretary-General constituted a five-member independent and impartial Commission of Experts to determine whether there were grave breaches of the Geneva Conventions, 1949.[21] The Commission collected information from various sources, carried out a number of investigations, and submitted three reports to the Secretary-General on serious violations of international humanitarian law in the territory of former Yugoslavia, referring to widespread patterns of 'wilful killing', 'ethnic cleansing',

---

responsibilities of the Special Rapporteur on the former Yugoslavia were taken up by Ms. Elisabeth Rehn of Finland as of Sept. 1995.

[20] *See* S/Res/780 (1992) *adopted* by the Security Council at its 3119th meeting, 6 Oct. 1992. Reprinted in 31 International Legal Materials (1992) 1476.

[21] *See* Report of the Secretary-General on the Establishment of the Commission of Experts pursuant to paragraph 2 of Security Council resolution 780 (1992), UN Doc. S/24657 (1992).

'mass killings, torture, rape, pillage and destruction of civilian property, destruction of cultural and religious property and arbitrary arrests'.[22]

On 22 February 1993, the Security Council unanimously adopted resolution 808, which underlined the Council's intention to create an international tribunal to prosecute individuals responsible for "serious violations of international humanitarian law committed in the territory of former Yugoslavia since 1991" and requested the Secretary-General to report on all aspects of the matter and to make specific proposals on the resolution's implementation.[23] On 3 May 1993, the Secretary-General duly submitted his report to the Security Council as requested.[24] The report explains the legal basis for the tribunal's establishment, its competence and organization, investigation and pre-trial proceedings, trial and post-trial proceedings (including those relating to the rights of the accused, witness protection, judgement and penalties, appeal, review and the enforcement of sentences), and makes provision for cooperation and judicial assistance of States with the Tribunal. The Statute of the International Criminal Tribunal for the Former Yugoslavia, as proposed by the Committee of Experts to the Secretary-General, forms the appendix to the Secretary-General's report.

On 25 May 1993, the Security Council adopted resolution 827 and unanimously approved the report of the Secretary-General,[25] deciding:

> ... to establish an international tribunal for the sole purpose of prosecuting persons responsible for serious violations of international humanitarian law committed in the territory of former Yugoslavia between 1 January 1991 and a date to be determined by the Security Council upon the restoration of peace and to this end to adopt the statute of the International Tribunal annexed to the report of the Secretary-General.

---

[22]   *See* UN Doc. S/25274 of 9 Feb. 1993.
[23]   *See* S/Res/808 of 22 Feb. 1993.
[24]   *See* Report of the Secretary-General Pursuant to paragraph 2 of Security Council resolution 808 (1993), UN Doc. S/25704 of 3 May 1993.
[25]   S/25704 of 3 May 1993 & Add.1 of 17 May 1993.

The Secretary-General's report reiterates the point that the creation of the Tribunal was intended to apply only to the territory of the former Yugoslavia and to persons responsible for serious violations of international humanitarian law committed since 1991, not as a step towards the possible establishment of a permanent international criminal court.[26]

5. INTERNATIONAL CRIMINAL TRIBUNAL FOR RWANDA

Prior to the genocide, the population of Rwanda consisted of an estimated 85% Hutu, 14% Tutsi, and 1% Twa and other.[27]

As far back as the 15th century, the Rwanda-Burundi area was ruled by monarchic clans. Prior to the colonial era, political tensions in Rwanda were not particularly accentuated along ethnic lines. However, as the nineteenth century drew to an end, Germany began to assert indirect colonial rule over Rwanda and Burundi with only a very small presence through the tactic of 'divide and rule'. The reinforcement and manipulation of the ruling elites in Rwanda formed an important element of Germany's colonial policy from 1897 to 1916.[28] During the First World War, Germany lost control over the area to Belgium, which then ruled Rwanda from 1916 to 1962. Belgium administered Rwanda under the League of Nations mandates system, pursuant to Article 22 of the Covenant, and then, following dissolution of the League of Nations on 18 April 1946, as a United Nations Trust Territory.

As Germany had done, Belgium reinforced the centuries-old Tutsi monarchy in Rwanda through a system of patron-client control, favouring the minority Tutsi people as the ruling class, partly on the grounds that the Tutsi people originated from the Nile River region,

---

[26]   *Ibid.* at para. 12.

[27]   The indigenous Twa minority was the first people to populate the area of Rwanda as far back as 2,000 B.C. Around 3,000 years later, a migration of Hutu to the area began. People of Tutsi extraction began to migrate to the area around 1500 A.D. Traditionally, the Hutu have been agrarian and sedentary whereas the Tutsi have been cattle-owners and nomadic.

[28]   *See generally* Alain Destexhe, Rwanda and Genocide (1995).

were somehow 'more European' in character than the Hutu people, and therefore, were supposedly superior as well.[29] Thus, by 1933-34, when the colonial administration carried out a census and introduced a mandatory identity card for every Rwandese citizen indicating his or her ethnic origin, the distinction between Hutu and Tutsi had become a cornerstone of Belgian colonial rule.

After the Second World War ended, Rwandan Hutus pushed for democratic reforms, a goal supported by the Belgian Government. Belgian patronage of the Tutsis continued, but relations became strained. Tutsis not only opposed Belgium's proposed democratic reforms, which threatened to undermine Tutsi positions of privilege and power, but intensified a drive for national independence from Belgium.

Eventually, Belgium was able to institute a number of democratic reforms in Rwanda, over the objections of Tutsi leaders, and pushed through the holding of local and national elections in Rwanda. It was clear that the Hutus stood to gain from democratic elections whereas the Tutsi-dominated Government was likely to be voted out. In November 1959, the heightened resentment between the two groups took the form of open hostilities. Several hundred Tutsis were massacred, which in turn sparked a mass exodus of thousands of Tutsis from Rwanda, mostly to Uganda and Zaire.

On 26 October 1961, Grégoire Kayibanda, leader of Parmehutu (Party for the Emancipation of the Hutu people), was formally elected President of the newly formed Parliament of the Republic of Rwanda, and maintained political control until 1973. In 1961, the Rwandan monarchy, which had existed for centuries, was abolished by overwhelming popular demand through national referendum and replaced by a republican form of Government. On 1 July 1962, Rwanda achieved independence. In the early 1960's, violence was

---

[29]   *See e.g.* Pierre Ryckmans, Dominer pour servir (1931) at 26: "The Batutsi were meant to reign. Their fine presence is in itself enough to give them a great prestige *vis-à-vis* the inferior races which surround ... It is not surprising that those good Bahutu, less intelligent, more simple, more spontaneous, more trusting, have let themselves be enslaved without ever daring to revolt" as quoted in Gérard Prunier, The Rwanda Crisis 1959-1994: History of a Genocide (1995) at 9.

never absent from the scene. Particularly large-scale massacres were perpetrated in 1963 and 1966, mainly against Tutsis.

In July 1973, Juvénal Habyarimana, a Hutu from the north of Rwanda, seized control of the Government, and in 1975, formed the National Revolutionary Movement for Development. Although Habyarimana promised to create a fair balance between the Hutu and Tutsi groups, he banned all opposition political parties except his own, and in 1978, changed the Constitution to make Rwanda officially a one-party State.

Motivated to regain their former position of prestige in the country, and concerned to aid their brothers and sisters in Rwanda from the recurrent violence perpetrated against them, Tutsi paramilitary forces coalesced into the Rwandese Patriotic Front (RPF). The RPF launched small-scale incursions from neighbouring countries into Rwandese territory in order to force Habyarimana towards power-sharing. On 1 October 1990, the insurgent RPF crossed the Ugandan border and carried out several military operations in the north of Rwanda. Out of revenge, Hutu groups killed some 300 Tutsis in the following weeks.[30] By 1992, over 350,000 persons had fled the violence in the northern regions of Rwanda, becoming displaced in the interior of Rwanda.

By 1993, it must have been clear to the Habyarimana Government that the Rwandese Patriotic Front had become an insurgency movement capable of destabilizing Rwanda and that it would be prudent to explore the possibilities of a cease-fire. On the other side, RPF commanders were obliged to negotiate with the Government in order to translate small-scale military victories into longer lasting political success. Negotiations between the Government of Rwanda and the Rwandese Patriotic Front commenced at Arusha, Tanzania, on 10 August 1992. The main issues to be addressed at the Arusha peace negotiations were: the need for multi-party elections and power-sharing in Rwanda; the fostering of peace and respect for the rule of law; and, an end to the RPF insurgency. These negotiations did not bear fruit immediately.

---

[30]   *See generally* François Misser, Vers un nouveau Rwanda? (1995) for a series of interviews conducted with the Vice-President and Minister of Defense of the Government of Rwanda, Major-General Paul Kagame.

However, further meetings were convened in August 1993 and these ended with a political settlement. On 4 August 1993, the Arusha Accords were signed between the Rwandese Patriotic Front and the Government of Rwanda. The Accords, sponsored by the Governments of Tanzania, Belgium and Germany, as well as by the United Nations, were designed to promote respect for basic human rights and the rule of law, broaden power-sharing in Rwanda, and end the RPF insurgency.

In a report of 11 August 1993, the Special Rapporteur of the Commission on Human Rights on extrajudicial, summary or arbitrary executions[31] drew attention to continuing serious human rights violations in Rwanda and raised the question as to whether these violations might qualify as 'genocide'.[32]

On 24 September 1993, the UN Secretary-General laid before the Security Council a plan to empower an international military force to ensure compliance with the Arusha Accords. He recommended that the existing peace-keeping force, dubbed UNOMUR,[33] be folded into a 'United Nations Assistance Mission in Rwanda' (UNAMIR). On 5 October 1993, the Security Council adopted resolution 872 which created UNAMIR for an initial period of six months.

While the Arusha Accords were considered by many as the first sign of effective power-sharing, they also bolstered the accusations made by extremist Hutu elements that the Habyarimana régime was merely a puppet of foreign Tutsi interests who threatened to regain direct control over the Government. In the final months of 1993, these extremist Hutu elements began to plan the elimination of the Tutsi people by training groups of 300 persons, in methods of systematic slaughter.

In early April 1994, President Habyarimana flew to Dar-es-Salaam to attend a meeting with President Ali Hassan Mwinyi of Tanzania, Kenyan Vice-President George Saitoti, Burundian President Cyprien Ntayamira, and President Yoweri Museveni of Uganda, concerning the maintenance of peace and security in the region.

---

[31] See the report of Mr. Bacre Waly Ndiaye on his mission to Rwanda from 8-17 April 1993, E/CN.4/1994/7/Add.1 of 11 August 1993.

[32] *Ibid.* at paras. 78-80.

[33] UNOMUR stands for United Nations Observer Mission Uganda-Rwanda.

On 6 April, following the meeting, the President of Rwanda returned by jet to Kigali accompanied by the President of Burundi who intended to continue on to Bujumbura. As the presidential aircraft circled Kigali airport to land, it was shot down. All those aboard, including Juvénal Habyarimana and Cyprien Ntyamira, several ministers and their entourages, died in the crash.

The downing of the aircraft triggered massacres throughout the country. Within thirty to forty minutes of the aircraft crash, roadblocks were set up in Kigali by Hutu militia, at which identity cards were checked, Tutsis singled out, and murdered on the spot. The immense slaughter plunged Rwanda into total chaos.

On 7 April, Prime Minister Agathe Unwilingiyimana, as well as 10 Belgian peace-keeping soldiers assigned to protect her, were murdered by soldiers of the Rwandese Government. Shocked by these events, and by the rapid and serious deterioration of security in Rwanda, the Government of Belgium decided on 12 April to remove its UNAMIR contingent from Rwanda.[34]

The massacres continued, perpetrated mainly by extremist Hutu militia associated with Habyarimana's political party, the Coalition for the Defense of the Republic, members of the Presidential Guard and regular army forces of the then Government of Rwanda. The slaughter required extensive administrative and logistical planning, evidenced by the chillingly calculated and thorough way in which it was carried out, and by the fact that most of the victims - between 500,000 and 1 million mainly Tutsi persons as well as politically moderate Hutu leaders and their families[35] - were killed over the relatively short period from 6 April through the first three weeks of May 1994.

---

[34] UNAMIR had been vested only with a UN Charter Chapter VI mandate to monitor and assist in the implementation of the Arusha Accords. It had neither the capability nor the mandate to enforce peace that could have been made available to it pursuant to Chapter VII of the Charter. On 21 April, the Security Council adopted resolution 912, which reduced the size of UNAMIR from 2,500 to 270.

[35] See Report on the situation of human rights in Rwanda submitted by R. Dégni-Ségui, Special Rapporteur of the Commission on Human Rights, pursuant to paragraph 20 of Commission resolution E/CN.4/S-3/1 of 25 May 1994, doc. E/CN.4/1995/7 of 28 June 1994, para. 24.

> If we consider that probably around 800,000 people
> were slaughtered during that short period ... the daily
> killing rate was at least five times that of the Nazi death
> camps.[36]

Shortly after the Hutu extremists launched the genocide, the
RPF undertook a military offensive, moving from Uganda into northern
Rwanda. By mid-July 1994, under the leadership of Paul Kagame, the
RPF was able to halt the genocide, force the retreat of the former
Government of Rwanda and associated militia from Kigali, and assert
effective control over the rest of Rwandese territory. Kagame was
elevated to Vice-President and Minister of Defense in the new
Government of Rwanda.

Most of the individuals responsible for carrying out violations
of human rights and humanitarian law fled the country amongst the
over 2 million that sought refuge in the neighbouring countries of
Burundi, Zaire and Tanzania, for fear of possible Tutsi reprisals and
revenge attacks. Numerous criminal suspects fled to francophone
west African countries, as well as to Kenya, and as far away as
Belgium, Canada, France, Switzerland and the United States.[37]

Once the International Criminal Tribunal for the Former
Yugoslavia had been created, it would have appeared patently
discriminatory for the Security Council not to have considered creation
of an international criminal tribunal also for Rwanda. Despite the fact
that many of the Security Council's Members did not consider Rwanda
to be as closely tied to their national interests as the former Yugoslavia, the Security Council nevertheless had to respond in a like
manner.

In response to the massive violations of human rights and
humanitarian law in Rwanda, the Security Council adopted resolution
935 on 1 July 1994, which recalled that "all persons who commit or
authorize the commission of serious violations of international
humanitarian law are individually responsible for those violations and
should be brought to justice" and requested the Secretary-General:

---

[36] Prunier, *supra* note 29 at 261.

[37] *See generally* La justice internationale face au drame rwandais (ed.
Dupaquier) (1996).

... to establish, as a matter of urgency, an impartial Commission of Experts to examine and analyze information submitted pursuant to the present resolution, together with such further information as the Commission of Experts might obtain, through its own investigations or the efforts of other persons or bodies, including the information made available by the Special Rapporteur on Rwanda, with a view to providing the Secretary-General with its conclusions on the evidence of grave violations of international humanitarian law committed in the territory of Rwanda, including the evidence of possible acts of genocide.

Resolution 935 requested the Secretary-General to report to the Security Council within four months of the Commission's establishment.

The Commission of Experts concluded that both sides to the armed conflict in Rwanda during the period 6 April 1994 to 15 July 1994 were responsible:

... for serious breaches of international humanitarian law, in particular of obligations set forth in article 3 common to the four Geneva Conventions of 12 August 1949 and in Protocol II additional to the Geneva Conventions and relating to the protection of victims of non-international armed conflicts, of 8 June 1977.[38]

While the Commission took note of violations committed both by elements associated with the former Government of Rwanda as well as by members of the Rwandese Patriotic Front, it concluded that:

... there exists overwhelming evidence to prove that acts of genocide against the Tutsi group were perpetrated by Hutu elements in a concerted, planned, systematic and methodical way. Abundant evidence

---

[38] *See* Preliminary Report 4 October 1994, part VIII (A); UN Doc. S/1994/1125.

shows that these mass exterminations perpetrated by Hutu elements against the Tutsi group as such, during the period mentioned above, constitute genocide within the meaning of article II of the Convention on the Prevention and Punishment of the Crime of Genocide, adopted on 9 December 1948. To this point, the Commission has not uncovered any evidence to indicate that Tutsi elements perpetrated acts committed with intent to destroy the Hutu ethnic group as such during the said period, within the meaning of the Genocide Convention of 1948.

The Commission therefore recommended international prosecution of the persons responsible for these crimes under international law and that:

... the Security Council amend the Statute of the International Criminal Tribunal for the former Yugoslavia to ensure that its jurisdiction covers crimes under international law committed during the armed conflict in Rwanda that began on 6 April 1994.

On 8 November 1994, the Security Council adopted resolution 955 creating the International Criminal Tribunal for Rwanda, with its Statute as the resolution's annex. Resolution 955 reiterates the Council's "grave concern at the reports indicating that genocide and other systematic, widespread and flagrant violations of international humanitarian law have been committed in Rwanda", determines "that this situation continues to constitute a threat to international peace and security" and resolves "to put an end to such crimes and to take effective measures to bring to justice the persons who are responsible for them". Resolution 955 underlines the Security Council's conviction that prosecution of individuals responsible for serious violations of international humanitarian law are intended to contribute to the process of national reconciliation and the restoration and maintenance of peace.

6. SOME ISSUES CONCERNING THE POSSIBLE ESTABLISHMENT OF A PERMANENT INTERNATIONAL CRIMINAL COURT IN THE LIGHT OF THE EXISTING TWO *AD HOC* INTERNATIONAL CRIMINAL TRIBUNALS

At this juncture, it is worth considering some issues concerning the possible creation of a permanent international criminal court, with a view to promoting regularity and unity in the implementation of international criminal law, keeping in mind the character of the *ad hoc* tribunals for Rwanda and the former Yugoslavia.

i) The Process of Creating the *Ad Hoc* Tribunals and Their Relation to the Security Council

The International Criminal Tribunals for the Former Yugoslavia and Rwanda could have been created through multilateral conventions prepared and put forward by the General Assembly for adoption by States. In principle, this approach would have maximized the legitimacy of the Tribunals through the broadening of political participation in their creation and would have ensured that they were more firmly based on the sovereign will of States.

However, the seeking of consensus through the General Assembly or specially convened diplomatic conference would not likely have met with success on account of the highly sensitive nature of the issue. Probably few States could have been persuaded to lend their approval to an international criminal tribunal without their lengthy and detailed consideration, particularly since such a tribunal might have been viewed as a step towards a permanent international criminal court. Furthermore, it was clear that action had to be taken relatively quickly in the cases of the former Yugoslavia and Rwanda and that substantially more time would have elapsed before a sufficient number of ratifications would be deposited as to enable such a convention to enter into force. Moreover, such a convention put forward for adoption by the General Assembly or conference would probably have reflected the lowest common denominator among States and could have resulted in a heavily compromised tribunal statute.

Even worse, by the time the two *ad hoc* Tribunals could become operational, if ever, political will to make them work may have dissipated. The chances for transforming political will and good intentions into effective implementation may have long disappeared.

In light of these serious disadvantages to proceed by way of multilateral convention, the Secretary-General proposed that the International Criminal Tribunal for the Former Yugoslavia be created on the basis of Chapter VII of the UN Charter. The Tribunal was therefore created as a subsidiary organ of the Security Council, pursuant to Article 29 of the UN Charter, which provides that: "The Security Council may establish such subsidiary organs as it deems necessary for the performance of its functions". This approach, which was repeated with regard to the International Criminal Tribunal for Rwanda, ensured that all States were legally bound to implement the Security Council's decisions in respect of the Tribunals.[39]

As subsidiary organs of the Security Council, a political body, the Tribunals may be criticized for not being wholly independent from the Council or the political influences of the more powerful States. On the other hand, most municipal courts or other judicial organs are also created through political decisions and institutions. Such organs are not *ipso facto* unable to render judgement in a fair and unbiased manner. Indeed, even judicial organs created by other judicial organs ultimately trace their origins to the political process. This is not to posit the absolutely objective character of judicial decision-making, but rather, the possibility of relatively independent adjudication by organs created through the political process.

The Secretary-General's report[40] on the creation of the International Criminal Tribunal for the Former Yugoslavia emphasizes that the tribunal "would, of course, have to perform its functions independently of political considerations; it would not be subject to the authority or control of the Security Council with regard to the performance of its judicial functions". Ultimately, such provisions are unlikely to determine the level of the Tribunal's independence and impartiality. It will be up to each Tribunal to establish its own image of independence and impartiality through the quality of the judgements it renders.

---

[39]   *See* Articles 48 and 49 of the UN Charter in this regard.

[40]   Report of the Secretary-General pursuant to Paragraph 2 of Security Council resolution 808 (1993), including the Statute of the Tribunal, UN. Doc. S/25704 of 3 May 1993 & Add.1 of 17 May 1993.

The *ad hoc* Tribunals remain, in effect, stopgap measures in the absence of a permanent international criminal court. The need for a solid institution capable of serving the high standards of international criminal justice would be better served by a permanent court of international criminal jurisdiction as discussed in Part 3 of the present enquiry.

ii) The Problem of Acquiring Custody over the Offender in the Case of International Criminal Tribunals

- In General

The Nuremberg and Tokyo Trials were conducted in territory occupied by the Allies. The Allies, entitled to occupy Germany and Japan pursuant to the terms of unconditional surrender, were in a position to apprehend and prosecute the offenders on the spot, first and foremost through the Nuremberg and Tokyo Tribunals, with regard to the top leaders, but also through thousands of subsequent trials in the occupied zones.[41]

Article 29 of the Statute of the International Criminal Tribunal for the Former Yugoslavia, corresponding to Article 28 of the Statute of the International Criminal Tribunal for Rwanda, obliges States "to cooperate with the International Tribunal in the investigation and prosecution of persons accused of committing serious violations of international humanitarian law" as well as to comply without delay with any request for assistance or an order coming from the Trial Chamber, as regards, *inter alia*, "the arrest or detention of persons" and "the surrender or the transfer of the accused" to the International Tribunal.

In some cases, such as in Rwanda, the acute interest of the Government in prosecuting the perpetrators of crimes under international law, may coincide with the interests of the international community. In a joint statement delivered on 19 December 1994 to the international press, the Minister of Justice of Rwanda and the

---

[41]   *See* Irina Lediakh, *The Application of the Nuremberg Principles by Other Military Tribunals and National Courts*, in The Nuremberg Trial and International Law (ed. Ginsburgs and Kudriatsev) (1990) 263-283.

Prosecutor of the International Criminal Tribunal for Rwanda, explained that:

> ... the primary focus of [the International Tribunal's] investigation and prosecution would be directed at those who planned and executed the gravest of violations against International Humanitarian Law, including serious allegations of genocide and crimes against humanity. A significant number of those whose participation will be investigated are now residing outside Rwanda.

Rwanda's judiciary, on the other hand, would endeavour to try all those persons responsible for the pertinent crimes under international law other than those indicted by the International Criminal Tribunal for Rwanda.

The work of the International Criminal Tribunals for the Former Yugoslavia and Rwanda cannot be made effective without the cooperation of the Governments in whose territory the crimes were committed, since there is no occupying power (only new territorial settlements or arrangements) and no international force presently deployed that is capable or willing to arrest suspected criminals. In the case of the former Yugoslavia, a government in whose territory war crimes or crimes against humanity were committed may view the Tribunal's work as inimical to its own political interests and may subvert or sabotage the Tribunal's attempts to acquire custody over alleged offenders. In such a case of non-cooperation or obstruction, the Tribunal may be relegated to the prosecution of individuals largely on a random basis, according to its fortunes in gaining custody over the alleged offender.

International political pressure has so far not proven very effective as a means by which to ensure surrender of alleged offenders to the Tribunal. For example, on 9 November 1996, the Government of Serbia responded to international pressure and relieved Mr. Ratko Mladic - a high-profile commander indicted for war crimes before the International Criminal Tribunal for the Former Yugoslavia - from his official responsibilities. However, Mr. Mladic has yet to be apprehended or turned over by the Serb authorities to the Tribunal.

In effect, the absence both of full cooperation from the territorial Government and of political resolve on the part of the international community to forcibly apprehend alleged offenders through an international police force, leaves the Tribunals with few other options. In most cases, political pressure is likely to be a far too blunt and unreliable tool to provide a substitute for regularized mandatory arrest and detention procedures. Each Tribunal therefore is consigned to hoping that individual suspects make the mistake of venturing beyond the protection of their national State into the territory of other States whose governments may be more willing to apprehend and surrender them.

In order to force the surrender of an alleged offender from a recalcitrant State, the Security Council may decide to impose sanctions against the Government. However, the imposition of economic, military or other restrictions for such a purpose, constitutes an inappropriately powerful, imprecise and perhaps ineffective tool. The rationale is that sanctions imposed upon a government may pressure it to comply with its legal obligations. Yet, in many instances, governments may be willing to endure such sanctions without responding. Moreover, the use of sanctions against a government is easily confused in the public mind as a form of collective punishment against the entire population. This kind of misperception may not only hinder efforts to secure cooperation, but may also play inadvertently into the hands of the Government by politicizing the issue. Furthermore, the unfortunate and erroneous impression left with the population that sanctions are meant to punish it, certainly undermines the whole thrust of international criminal law which is to enforce responsibility for crimes under international law on an individual rather than collective basis. The *Lockerbie Case*, discussed in Chapter V(3)(iii) of the present enquiry, illustrates how the imposition of sanctions to force surrender of criminal suspects in some cases may even threaten to undermine the rule of law at the international level, rather than to strengthen it.

In this connection, it should be noted that Rule 39(iii) of the Rules of Procedure and Evidence, common to both the International Criminal Tribunals for the Former Yugoslavia and Rwanda, provides that in the conduct of an investigation, the Prosecutor may seek "the assistance of any State authority concerned, as well as of any relevant international body including the International Criminal Police Organization (INTERPOL)".

INTERPOL, created in 1946, was not specifically designed to assist in *international* prosecutions, but rather "to ensure and promote the widest possible mutual assistance between all criminal police authorities within the limits of the laws existing in the different countries and in the spirit of the Universal Declaration of Human Rights" as per Article 2 of the INTERPOL Constitution. However, nothing in the Constitution prevents INTERPOL from providing assistance to an international criminal tribunal.

In September 1994, the INTERPOL General Assembly decided to extend all possible support to the International Criminal Tribunal for the Former Yugoslavia. Since then, INTERPOL has relayed urgent messages it has received from the Tribunal to its 176 Member States in order to identify and locate suspects. It has also disseminated 'red notices' to all Member States with a view to ensuring the arrest and provisional detention of these suspects. By 31 December 1996, 68 red notices had been published in regard to sixty-eight persons with regard to the International Criminal Tribunal for the Former Yugoslavia. The International Criminal Tribunal for Rwanda, on the other hand, had not requested the dissemination of any red notices by 31 December 1996. Significantly, the INTERPOL General Assembly has invited the INTERPOL General Secretariat to intensify its assistance to the United Nations in general. By General Assembly resolution 1, adopted on 22 October 1996, INTERPOL acquired observer status with the United Nations, thereby regularizing INTERPOL's avenues of cooperation with the United Nations, including the two *ad hoc* international criminal tribunals.

- A Proposed Set of Procedures to Enhance Compliance with Requests and Orders of an International Criminal Tribunal to Acquire Custody over the Alleged Offender

The problem of bringing the alleged offender to trial is bound to be one of the more significant weaknesses of any international criminal tribunal unless practical solutions are advanced in this regard. The following ideas are put forward therefore as points for consideration to this end.

At one level, the upcoming Preparatory Committee on the Establishment of an International Criminal Court could prepare a protocol, to be annexed to the statute creating a permanent international criminal court, that obliges States Parties to surrender alleged offenders to the international criminal court, upon its request, according to procedures prescribed therein. This protocol would help in providing a firm legal basis for the surrender of alleged offenders to a permanent international criminal court if such a court were created and would thereby enhance regular cooperation in this regard. However, this arrangement, based on the voluntary will of States to sign and ratify such a protocol, would not be effective in overcoming the resistance or refusal of less cooperative States.

Another separate set of procedures could be established to deal with the hard cases involving less cooperative States. A supervisory commission could be established through a convention creating a permanent international criminal court. This commission would be comprised of representatives of ten or fifteen of the States Parties to the convention, drawn from the main regions of the globe. The commission would monitor the level of cooperation, judicial assistance and compliance of States with the requests and orders issued by the court, and where necessary, recommend action be taken by the Security Council according to the procedures proposed below.

Where a State has failed to respond or take action in accordance with a request or order of the international criminal court, the supervisory commission would be authorized to request the Government of a State, in whose territory an alleged offender appears or is known to be located, to provide it with information on what measures the State has taken, or plans to take, to apprehend the individual in question. Failing that, the Government may be requested to provide an explanation as to why the order or request of the court has not been accorded satisfactory compliance.

Second, where the Government has failed to respond within three months to the official request of the supervisory commission, the commission would be authorized then to prepare a confidential report, which when completed, is provided to the Government in question. This report would: reiterate the efforts of the court to secure cooperation in the acquisition of custody over the offender, as well as its grounds for believing that the individual is located in the territory of the requested State; record the requests the supervisory commission has made to the Government and any reaction or response from the Government on the case at hand; and, indicate that if no satisfactory response is made to the confidential report within a further one month or other appropriate deadline, the report shall be tabled at a public session of the supervisory commission.

The next step would be that the supervisory commission could recommend further action be taken by the international community, for example, that a high-level delegation composed of three persons drawn either from the commission itself, or appointed from outside, be sent to meet with representatives of the Government in question in order to seek its cooperation on the matter outstanding. Should such a mission not be accepted by the Government, and where it appears that the Government in question remains unwilling to cooperate, the supervisory commission should be authorized then to recommend what further measures, including those of a coercive nature, should be taken by the Security Council.

Finally, upon request by the supervisory commission, the Security Council could consider any of its recommendations and, should the Council approve, decide on whatever measures it deems appropriate according to its own procedures and legal authority, including mandatory measures under Chapter VII of the UN Charter.

These proposed procedures might appear cumbersome or overly bureaucratic, particularly in a time of UN budget-cutting. However, if the international community seriously intends to ensure the effective implementation of international criminal law, there must be a much more concerted effort to ensure the international criminal court has the benefit of regular and effective means by which to acquire custody over alleged offenders. There would be little point in expending large outlays for an elaborate court if the alleged offenders cannot be pursued and apprehended. Thus, the setting up of a supervisory commission might prove well worth the expense were it to remove a major obstacle to the effectiveness of the entire prosecution effort. The set of procedures proposed above would have the advantage of exerting political pressure on a particular Government in stages, rather than to jump from the tribunal's appeal to States for cooperation, to Security Council sanctions. They would allow the Government a fair opportunity to discuss internally how to best deal with the request made and for its members to consider more carefully whether it might not be better to cooperate with the rest of the international community instead of risking further adverse attention. The mere existence of established procedures might even encourage otherwise less cooperative States to comply with the orders and requests of a permanent international criminal court.

It might appear that one possible disadvantage of the supervisory commission, as proposed above, is that it would be inherently political. The members of the commission would be representatives of States. However, the political character of the commission could figure as its strongest asset. Decisions could be made within the supervisory commission, according to a two-thirds majority, to ensure it represents a broad-based international will. This proposed process at least would reflect a much more universal constituency than the narrow one currently represented by the permanent Members of the Security Council, and as such, would thereby enhance the legitimacy of international criminal law implementation.

iii) Exclusive versus Concurrent Jurisdiction

Governments are not likely to support the creation of a permanent international criminal court unless they feel sufficiently assured it will not hamper their domestic criminal jurisdiction. Not only do States remain jealous to guard their national sovereignty, but from a practical point of view, it would be counterproductive to replace domestic criminal law with an untried international system which may prove to function poorly or not at all. However, if carefully designed, a permanent international criminal court could provide a valuable means by which to supplement rather than supplant domestic jurisdiction.

The Report of the Ad Hoc Committee on the Establishment of an International Criminal Court took note of the concerns of States that an international criminal court should be complementary to national criminal justice systems and summarized its reasons as follows:

>   a)   all those involved would be working within the
>   context of an established legal system, including
>   existing bilateral and multilateral arrangements;
>   b)   the applicable law would be more certain and
>   more developed;

c)   the prosecution would be less complicated,
because it would be based on familiar precedents and
rules;
d)   both prosecution and defence were likely to be
less expensive;
e)   evidence and witnesses would normally be more
readily available;
f)   language problems would be minimized;
g)   local courts would apply established means for
obtaining evidence and testimony, including application
of rules relating to perjury; and
h)   penalties would be clearly defined and readily
enforceable.[42]

It was also stressed that the State held a vital interest in remaining
accountable and responsible for the prosecution of violations of its
law. This interest coincides with that of the international community,
inasmuch as national systems enforce adherence to international
standards of behaviour within their own respective jurisdictions.[43]
However, the Report goes on to explain that the principle of
complementarity should not be interpreted in such a way as to
relegate international criminal court jurisdiction as residual only to
domestic criminal jurisdiction.

Many States have raised concerns also that a permanent
international criminal court should cover only those acts clearly
recognized by the international community to constitute crimes.

7. FAIR TRIAL STANDARDS

Full observance of fair trial standards is essential to international criminal law. It is valuable to mention the main sources and
elements of fair trial standards in international law and then to review
briefly these elements in the context of the statutes of international
criminal tribunals created so far this century.

---

[42]   A/50/22 of 6 Sept. 1995 at para. 29.
[43]   *Ibid.* at para. 31.

The right to fair trial is recognized in international law as a fundamental human right. Article 10 of the Universal Declaration of Human Rights, 1948, provides that: "Everyone is entitled in full equality to a fair and public hearing by an independent and impartial tribunal, in the determination of his rights and obligations and of any criminal charge against him". The "right to be presumed innocent until proved guilty according to law in a public trial at which he has had all the guarantees necessary for his defence" is provided for in Article 11(1) of the Declaration.

The basic elements of the right to a fair trial are found in Article 14 of the International Covenant on Civil and Political Rights, 1966. Article 14 provides for the right to equality before the courts, the right to a fair and public hearing, the right to be presumed innocent until proved guilty according to law, the right to be informed of the charge promptly and in detail, the right to prepare adequately a defense (including the right to adequate time, facilities and counsel in this regard), the right to be tried without undue delay, the right to be present at trial and to present a defense in a language of one's own choosing, the right to examine witnesses, to have the benefit of an interpreter where required, the right to remain silent, the right to an appeal, the right to receive compensation in case of a miscarriage of justice, and the principle of *non bis in idem* i.e. the right of the accused not to be tried or punished more than once for an offense for which he or she has been convicted or acquitted. The Covenant also guarantees the right to an effective remedy in case the right to fair trial has been breached.

On 1 September 1989, the United Nations Sub-Commission on Prevention of Discrimination and Protection of Minorities appointed Mr. Stanislav Chernichenko and Mr. William Treat, two of its Special Rapporteurs, to prepare a report on the international legal norms relating to the right to fair trial with a view to recommending which of these norms ought to be made non-derogable. Among the three annexes to the Final Report[44] are the Draft Third Optional Protocol to the International Covenant on Civil and Political Rights and a Draft

---

[44]   The Report is entitled "The Right to a Fair Trial: Current Recognition and Measures Necessary for its Strengthening"; UN Doc. E/CN.4/ Sub.2/ 1994/24 of 3 June 1994.

Body of Principles, both of which spell out in greater detail than does the Covenant the elements of the right to a fair trial and a remedy.[45]

A number of other international human rights conventions also affirm the right to fair trial, for example, the Convention against Torture and Other Cruel, Inhuman or Degrading Treatment or Punishment, 1984, and the Convention on the Rights of the Child, 1989. On 29 November 1985, the General Assembly adopted resolution 40/32, and on 13 December 1985, resolution 40/146, both of which endorse the Basic Principles on the Independence of the Judiciary, which had been adopted by the Seventh United Nations Congress on the Prevention of Crime and the Treatment of Offenders in Milan in August, 1985. On 29 November 1985, the General Assembly also adopted resolution 40/34 entitled the Declaration of Basic Principles of Justice for Victims of Crime and Abuse of Power.

At the regional level, the main international human rights instruments also contain relevant provisions, namely: Articles 6 (fair and public hearing) and 7 (principle of non-retroactivity of criminal law) of the European Convention on Human Rights, 1950; Articles 8 (on fair trial), 9 (on the non-retroactivity of criminal law) and 10 (on the right to compensation in case of a miscarriage of justice) of the American Convention on Human Rights, 1969; and Article 7 (right to fair trial and non-retroactivity of criminal law) of the African Charter on Human and Peoples' Rights, 1981.

The right to fair trial is also expressed in modern international humanitarian law. As regards situations of non-international armed conflict, Article 3 common to the four Geneva Conventions, 1949, prohibits "the passing of sentences and the carrying out of executions without previous judgment pronounced by a regularly constituted court, affording all the judicial guarantees which are recognized as indispensable by civilized peoples". Common Article 3 is supplemented by Article 6 of 1977 Additional Protocol II which applies to "the prosecution and punishment of criminal offenses related to the armed conflict". The Third and Fourth Geneva Conventions prescribes a number of fair trial guarantees applicable to prisoners of war and in

---

[45] On 29 August 1996 the Sub-Commission adopted without a vote resolution 1996/29 which requests that the study be updated and prepared for publication under the auspices of the UN Commission on Human Rights.

occupied territories respectively. In Article 75, Protocol I relating to international armed conflict provides for numerous fair trial standards for persons in the power of a party to the conflict.

i) Nuremberg and Tokyo Tribunals

Although the International Criminal Tribunals for the Former Yugoslavia and Rwanda are more recent, the experience of the Nuremberg and Tokyo Trials as regards standards of fair trial, should not be ignored.

One of the more troublesome aspects of the Nuremberg and Tokyo Trials concerns the issue of conspiracy. During the drafting of the Nuremberg Charter, the Allied Powers could not agree as to whether criminal responsibility should be enforced on a strictly individual basis or whether the Tribunal should be vested also with competence over acts of conspiracy.

On the one hand, the violations committed by the Nazis were so massive and systematic that the Nuremberg Tribunal proceedings risked appearing artificial, even as a mockery of justice, if they were to put on trial the Nazi High Command only, and to ignore the thousands of other perpetrators directly responsible for having committed crimes of extreme barbarity. However, sufficient evidence to meet the strict standards of criminal justice certainly did not exist in many individual cases and was only partial or purely circumstantial in many others. For example, there was naturally a high concentration of war criminals among the members of the organizations, such as the Gestapo[46] (German Secret State Police), or the SS (*Schutz-Staffel*), that masterminded, directed, or carried out many war crimes. The United States representative to the London Conference therefore proposed the indictment of the principal Nazi organizations at the main Nuremberg Trial in order that members of organizations could be prosecuted in proceedings subsequent to the main Trial. This way, it was hoped that Germany could be denazified - a political objective of the Allies - through judicial procedures. The consent of members of criminal organizations to the criminal acts perpetrated was to be

---

[46]   *Gestapo* is an acronym for *Geheime Staatspolizei*.

presumed and the burden would then shift to the defendant to prove the contrary.[47]

On the other hand, the prosecution of persons according to their mere membership in a criminal organization would have constituted a patent violation of the basic presumption of innocence owed to an accused. In the absence of specific evidence to support the charge in each case, one could never be certain that individuals who were not guilty of any crime were being prosecuted, tried and punished, purely on the basis that their names appeared on the membership lists of organizations declared criminal by the Tribunal.[48] Together with the fact that the Nuremberg Tribunal applied law retroactively, the whole idea of conspiracy met with considerable scepticism from some Allied Powers. At the London Conference, the Soviet and the French representatives both viewed the doctrine of conspiracy as unworthy of modern law and inappropriate for insertion into the Charter, particularly since Germans were unfamiliar with the legal concept of conspiracy. The Soviet delegation opposed the American plan, arguing that since major criminal Nazi organizations had already been dissolved by the Allies, there was no longer a need to prosecute them.

Eventually however, the differences between the United States and Soviet delegations were reduced, and the Allies agreed that organizations should be prosecuted, mainly because without the prosecution of organizations, there would be great difficulties in assembling evidence against each and every individual. The result is that conspiracy appears as a crime punishable *per se*. Article 9 of the Nuremberg Charter reads:

> At the trial of any individual member of any group or organization the Tribunal may declare (in connection with any act of which the individual may be convicted) that the group or organization of which the individual was a member was a criminal organization.

---

[47] *See* Stanislaw Pomorski, *Conspiracy and Criminal Organizations*, in The Nuremberg Trial and International Law (ed. Ginsburgs and Kudriavtsev) (1990).

[48] *Ibid.*

> After receipt of the Indictment the Tribunal shall give such notice as it thinks fit that the prosecution intends to ask the Tribunal to make such a declaration and any member of the organization will be entitled to apply to the Tribunal for leave to be heard by the Tribunal upon the question of the criminal character of the organization. The Tribunal shall have the power to allow or reject the application. If the application is allowed, the Tribunal may direct in what manner the applicants shall be represented and heard.

Article 10 provides that once the Nuremberg Tribunal declares a particular group or organization criminal, competent national authorities may prosecute individuals for having been members of such entities, and that in such cases, "the criminal nature of the group or organization is considered proved and shall not be questioned". The result was that six organizations were indicted at the Nuremberg Trial, of which three were declared criminal, namely, the SS, the Gestapo and the Leadership Corps.[49] Prosecutions were then followed up in hundreds of national court trials against members of these criminal organizations or groups.

Interestingly, Article 12 of the Nuremberg Charter provides that:

> The Tribunal shall have the right to take proceedings against a person charged with crimes set out in Article 6 of this Charter in his absence, if he has not been found or if the Tribunal, for any reason, finds it necessary, in the interest of justice, to conduct the hearing in his absence.

Article 12, permitting trial *in absentia*, must be seen as a radical violation of the basic right to fair trial. It should go without saying that the right to prepare a defense and to be heard are completely negated in the case of a trial *in absentia*. However, trial *in absentia* should not

---

[49]   The High Command, the Reich Cabinet and the SA were not declared to be criminal organizations. The SA (*Sturm Abteilungen*) which had a million and a half members, was prominent in the early stages of Nazism, but had little role in the war itself. *Ibid.* at 238.

be confused with the situation where, in the interests of justice, the accused is ordered to leave the courtroom on account of his or her attempts to obstruct or disrupt the proceedings.

Aside from the issues surrounding the Tribunal's competence over cases of criminal conspiracy, and the possibility of trial *in absentia*, Article 13 of the Nuremberg Charter provides that the Tribunal "shall draw up rules for its procedure". Pursuant to these rules, the accused were afforded a minimum of thirty days to prepare their defence prior to the commencement of the trial as well as the opportunity to have access to documents and witnesses. The accused were also provided with the right to legal assistance, the right to be informed of the charges against them in their own language (the indictment was translated into German), and to follow the proceedings in their own language (through simultaneous interpretation). The defense had a right to cross-examine prosecution witnesses and to adduce evidence.[50]

In the Tokyo Trials, similar arguments were raised as to the ambiguity and injustice of indicting an individual on grounds of conspiracy. It is to be noted that one of the many grounds upon which the Indian Justice on the Tokyo Tribunal registered his dissent was that the legal concept of conspiracy derived from Anglo-Saxon law and was foreign to Asia. In Justice Pal's view, it was not acceptable for a court to arrive at a conspiracy theory as a conclusion of guilt and then to work backwards to construct the involvement of the accused in it.[51]

More generally, aside from the trial process itself, larger questions of procedural fairness arise from the fact that the entire Nuremberg and Tokyo processes smack of victor's justice, as discussed above.[52]

---

[50]   *See* Quincy Wright, *The Law of the Nuremberg Trial* 41 American Journal of International Law (1947).

[51]   *See further* Elizabeth S. Kopelman, *Ideology and International Law: the Dissent of the Indian Justice at the Tokyo War Crimes Trial*, 23(2) New York University Journal of International Law and Politics (1991).

[52]   While the Statutes for the International Criminal Tribunals for the Former Yugoslavia and Rwanda do not contain any general provisions that sweep in criminal responsibility for conspiracy, as a crime in and of itself, both Statutes prohibit 'conspiracy to commit genocide'. The material

ii) International Criminal Tribunals for the Former Yugoslavia and Rwanda

Article 20 of the Statute for the International Criminal Tribunal for the Former Yugoslavia (corresponding to Article 19 of the Statute for the Rwanda Tribunal), concerning commencement and conduct of trial proceedings, provides that the Trial Chambers shall ensure the trial:

> ... is fair and expeditious and that proceedings are conducted in accordance with the rules of procedure and evidence, with full respect for the rights of the accused and due regard for the protection of victims and witnesses.

A person who has been indicted by the Tribunal "shall, pursuant to an order or an arrest warrant of the International Tribunal, be taken into custody, immediately informed of the charges against him and transferred to the International Tribunal". The Trial Chamber is then obliged to read the indictment and "satisfy itself that the rights of the accused are respected, confirm that the accused understands the indictment, and instruct the accused to enter a plea". A trial date is then set. Article 20(4) provides that the hearings shall be public unless the Trial Chamber decides to close the proceedings in accordance with the Rules of Procedure and Evidence,[53] as discussed below.

---

competence of each Tribunal over conspiracy to commit genocide may be a useful means by which to reach the planners and organizers of the genocidal policies carried out in those countries. However, the presumption of innocence must not be treated lightly. It is important that at trial, membership in criminal organizations, in and of itself, should not shift the burden of proof to the accused to prove he or she did not participate in the genocide.

[53] The Rules of Procedure and Evidence, adopted pursuant to Article 15 of the Statute of the International Criminal Tribunal for the Former Yugoslavia, apply also to the Tribunal for Rwanda, by virtue of Article 14 of the latter's Statute. The Rules of Procedure have Nine Parts entitled as follows: General Provisions; Primacy of the Tribunal; Organization of the Tribunal; Investigations and Rights of Suspects; Pre-Trial Procedures; Proceedings Before Trial Chambers; Appellate Proceedings; Review Proceedings; and

Article 21 of the Statute for the International Criminal Tribunal for the Former Yugoslavia, which corresponds, *mutatis mutandis* to Article 20 of the Statute for the Rwanda Tribunal, incorporates the provisions of Article 14 of the International Covenant on Civil and Political Rights, 1966 (see Annexes 2 and 3). As regards the protection of victims and witnesses, Article 22 of the Yugoslavia Statute, corresponding to Article 21 of the Rwanda Statute, provides as follows:

> The International Tribunal shall provide in its rules of procedure and evidence for the protection of victims and witnesses. Such protection measures shall include, but shall not be limited to, the conduct of *in camera* proceedings and the protection of the victim's identity.

Rule 3(A) provides that the working languages of the Tribunal shall be English and French. Rule 3(B) provides that: "An accused shall have the right to use his or her own language". Equally, any other person appearing before the Tribunal, in case of insufficient knowledge of either English or French, may use his or her own language. Interestingly, Rule 3(D) provides that:

> counsel for an accused may apply to the Presiding Judge of a Chamber for leave to use a language other than the two working ones or the language of the accused. If such leave is granted, the expenses of interpretation and translation shall be borne by the Tribunal to the extent, if any, determined by the President, taking into account the rights of the defence and the interests of justice.

Article 14(f) of the International Covenant on Civil and Political Rights, 1966, provides that everyone shall be entitled, in full equality, to have the free assistance of an interpreter, but does not provide the right of counsel to apply for leave to use a language in court other than its

---

Pardon and Commutation of Sentence.

working language or languages. Thus, as regards language, the
Rules of Procedure appear to be more generous than the Covenant.
    Part Six of the Rules of Procedure provides for, *inter alia*, the
right of each party to the proceedings to call witnesses and to present
evidence. Both parties have the right to conduct examination-in-chief,
cross-examination and re-examination. Rule 85(C) provides that "[t]he
accused, may, if he so desires, appear as a witness in his own
defence". Rule 86 provides for the right to make closing arguments.
    Rule 75(A) concerning the protection of victims and witnesses
provides that:

> A Judge or a Chamber may, *proprio motu*, or at the
> request of either party, or of the victim or witnesses
> concerned, order appropriate measures for the privacy
> and protection of victims and witnesses, provided that
> the measures are consistent with the rights of the
> accused.

Rule 75 provides that in order to protect a victim or witness, a judge
or a Chamber may allow the "giving of testimony through image- or
voice-altering devices or closed circuit television" as well as to take
other measures in order to prevent the disclosure of the identity of
victim or witness to the public. Similarly, one-way closed circuit
television may be used to facilitate the testimony of vulnerable victims
and witnesses.[54]
    In certain cases, the prevention of disclosure "to the public or
the media of the identity or whereabouts of a victim or a witness, or
of persons related to or associated with" the accused might possibly
restrict an unforeseen opportunity of the defence to prove he or she
was not at the scene of the crime. There may be cases where a
member of the public, informed through media reports of the trial that
a certain witness has been called to testify for the prosecution,
decides to come forward with evidence showing such witness could

---

[54]   It is important to note that Rule 75 does not provide victims or
witnesses the right to give testimony anonymously or to have his or her
identity concealed from the accused. While the protection of victims and
witnesses is essential, an accused has a right to know the source of the
accusations in order to afford a fair opportunity to counter them effectively.

not possibly have witnessed the particular crime in question. However, Rule 75 strikes a balance between the right of the accused and the rights of victims and witnesses. Rule 75 seeks to protect the victim or witness from the risk of substantial harm, for example, at the hands of former militia or other elements in the local community who may attempt to exact revenge, once the victim or witness returns. While Rule 75 may reduce the chance that, in certain cases, the defence argument may be aided by unexpected evidence coming from a member of the public who is previously unknown to the accused, and therefore could not be called by the defence without such witness voluntarily coming forward, such circumstances would be entirely hypothetical and fortuitous, whereas the need for the victim or witness to benefit from protection is both more certain and immediate.

Rule 89(D), concerning the rules of evidence to be applied by the Tribunals, provides that: "A Chamber may exclude evidence if its probative value is substantially outweighed by the need to ensure a fair trial".

As for confessions, Rule 92 provides that: "A confession by the accused given during questioning by the Prosecutor shall, provided the requirements of Rule 63 were strictly complied with, be presumed to have been free and voluntary unless the contrary is proved". Rule 63 stipulates that the Prosecutor shall not question the accused "unless his counsel is present and the questioning is tape-recorded or video-recorded in accordance with the procedure provided for in Rule 43". The Prosecutor is obliged to caution the accused, at the outset of the questioning, that he or she "is not obliged to say anything unless he wishes to do so but that whatever he says may be given in evidence". Rule 43 provides for certain technical requirements and procedures to be followed in the tape or video recording of questioning of suspects to ensure the integrity of such recordings.

The public character of the proceedings effectively ensures that the right to fair trial is fully respected. The principle that trials shall be held openly protects both the prosecution and the defence, as well as the legitimacy of the Tribunal itself as a whole. People may disagree as to whether the process or result in any given case was fair or just, however, through openness, ill-founded suspicion or rumour as to what went on, is eliminated. For this reason, closed proceedings may be ordered only in exceptional cases. According to Rule 79, the Trial Chamber may order that the press and the public be excluded from all or part of the proceedings on the grounds of 'public order or morality', 'safety, security or non-disclosure of the identity of a victim or witness', or 'the protection of the interests of justice'. As Morris and Scharf explain:[55]

> Although the Statute only envisioned conducting closed proceedings to protect victims and witnesses, it expressly authorized the judges to address the question of closed proceedings in adopting the Rules. The provisions adopted are consistent with the relevant international standards. The reasons for closing the proceedings may appear to be somewhat vague. This could give rise to the possibility for abuse. However, the Trial Chamber is required to issue a public order to close the proceedings and to state the reasons therefor. Furthermore, the public and the press should be permitted to attend the remainder of the proceedings when the reasons for closure no longer apply.

In recent years, there has been a long awaited recognition in the legislatures and courts of some countries that cases of sexual assault require certain special procedures. Numerous studies have found consistently that cases of ordinary criminal cases of rape or sexual assault are vastly under-reported. In cases of mass rape perpetrated in time of armed conflict in which hostilities may target the civilian population, the problem of under-reporting is likely to be much greater. As discussed in Chapter II(5) above, rape victims characteristically suffer from intense shock, trauma, as well as shame from being ostracized by their own communities, in essence, blamed for the violations perpetrated against them. Frequently, women are unwilling to disclose the crimes to which they were subjected, let alone to provide detailed testimony before a court of law. In other cases, victims or witnesses may fear that, should their identity become known in the context of criminal proceedings, they will be targeted for reprisals once they return home to their communities.

---

[55] Virginia Morris and Michael P. Scharf, 1 An Insider's Guide to the International Criminal Tribunal for the Former Yugoslavia (1995) at 255.

Rule 96 provides that in cases of sexual assault, "no corroboration of the victim's testimony shall be required", "consent shall not be allowed as a defence" where the victim either "has been subjected to or threatened with or has had reason to fear violence, duress, detention or psychological oppression" or "reasonably believed that if she did not submit, another might be so subjected, threatened or put in fear". As Morris and Scharf record:

> The initial proposal for this provision contained a detailed description of the situations in which a victim could not possibly have freely consented to the act in question and the defence counsel was therefore precluded from raising the defence of consent. In an attempt to simplify the proposal, the judges adopted a rule under which the defense counsel was prevented from raising consent as a defense to the crime, particularly in cross-examining the victim, but could argue nonetheless that the prosecution had failed to meet its burden of proving force or coercion as an element of the crime of rape or sexual assault. In response to criticism by governments and nongovernmental organizations of this sweeping approach, the judges decided to return to the original approach by amending the rule to identify the inherently threatening or coercive situations which preclude the possibility of consent by the victim and, consequently, the possibility of the defense counsel raising this issue at trial.[56]

Furthermore, the "prior sexual conduct of the victim shall not be admitted in evidence". In cases where violence or the threat of violence accompanied the rape, Rule 96 prevents the defence from seeking to adduce through cross-examination the promiscuous character of the victim in making the argument that she was not a victim at all, but a willing participant in a mutually consensual act.

The Rules of Procedure and Evidence for the two international criminal tribunals largely incorporate the fair trial standards set out in

---

[56]   *Ibid.* at 263.

the International Covenant on Civil and Political Rights. However, as the Special Rapporteurs on the right to fair trial for the Sub-Commission on Prevention of Discrimination and Protection of Minorities observed in their Final Report,[57] the Rules of Procedure and Evidence make no mention of the treatment of detainees prior to the trial, such as the right not to be subjected to torture or other cruel, inhuman or degrading treatment or punishment. Should a statute for a permanent international criminal court be adopted in future, it ought to incorporate explicitly the most comprehensive and up-to-date human rights guarantees relating to conditions of detention.

---

[57]   *See* "The Right to a Fair Trial: Current Recognition and Measures Necessary for its Strengthening"; UN Doc. E/CN.4/Sub.2/1994/24, para. 83, of 3 June 1994.

PART 3

FUTURE PROSPECTS

CHAPTER VII

THE EMERGENCE OF A SYSTEM
OF INTERNATIONAL CRIMINAL LAW

1. INTRODUCTION

The foregoing Chapters explored the main elements of international criminal law norms and means of implementation. Using the 1991 and 1996 versions of the ILC draft Code of Crimes against the Peace and Security of Mankind as reference points, Part 1 of the present enquiry examined the areas in which international criminal law norms are more established, as well as areas of potential future growth. Part 2 considered the main institutional aspects of international criminal law implementation at both the inter-State and international levels, taking account of increasing normative hierarchy in general international law. However, to this point, the present enquiry's focus on the various elements of norms and implementation could only describe and evaluate the component parts of international criminal law, without comprehending fully the aspects of this field that could possibly qualify it as a normative and institutional subsystem of general international law. How the elements eventually may form the basic parts of a system of international criminal law remains to be considered.

This final Chapter evaluates prospects for the emergence of a unified system of international criminal law, characterized by broad and coherent material coverage, as well as fair and effective institutional implementation. In order for international criminal law to emerge as a system with these qualities, it must first become:

- guided by a clearly defined purpose or set of purposes;
- continuous over time;
- stable yet adaptable; and,
- relatively autonomous from other normative systems.

These properties, which are interlinked, even intertwined, are discussed below. Finally, this Chapter locates international criminal law within the main historical dynamics of international law in general, before commenting on the prospects for the emergence of a good system of international criminal law.

2. PURPOSES OF A SYSTEM OF INTERNATIONAL CRIMINAL LAW

Although perfect agreement is not necessary, international criminal law must have at least a generally recognized purpose or set of purposes. International criminal law should be designed so as to:

- wherever possible, end ongoing crimes from being committed through the arrest of the criminal suspect;
- deter crimes from being committed in future through effective enforcement;
- bring to trial, sentence and punish the criminal according to recognized norms of international law and justice, with due regard to ensuring witness protection;
- where appropriate, ensure compensation for the victim or victims;
- foster rehabilitation of the criminal; and
- contribute, through a transparently fair and effective prosecution process, to a just reckoning of individual criminal responsibility for the criminal acts committed as well as promote the rule of law.

Volumes have been written on the broad purposes criminal law serves or ought to serve, and on what interests it actually accommodates. This grand debate, entwined with larger moral, political and philosophical issues, cannot possibly be explored within the scope of the present enquiry.

However, one issue must be touched upon here, if only briefly. That is, whether international criminal law should serve, first and foremost, the goal of providing satisfaction to the party or parties most directly injured by the crime or whether international criminal law should rather have other aims among its primary purposes.

Rationales centred around retribution tend to rely on a circular argument to justify the infliction of punishment of the person found guilty. Typically, such rationales are based on such ideas that 'Those who commit crimes ought not to go unpunished', or 'Criminals deserve to be punished' or 'The guilty should suffer' or 'Justice requires punishment' etc.[1] Such arguments seem to derive from an intuitive sense that there should be 'An eye for an eye and a tooth for a tooth'. These arguments, which imply that retaliation is an intrinsic good, are tautological in which at least part of the conclusion is contained in the premise of the argument.

It cannot be doubted that the infliction of suffering upon the criminal through the imposition of lawfully sanctioned punishment may go some length towards satisfying the victim's drive for revenge, which may be extremely strong in many cases. In this century, there have been numerous armed conflicts in which soldiers or militia force an individual to witness the torture, rape or murder of his or her own family members or is even forced to take part in such violations. Perhaps few affected by such trauma could free themselves from the impulse to exact revenge for such crimes.

However, as a societally-based normative system, international criminal law must serve broader purposes for the community at large, on a constructive and prospective basis, whether built on the foundations of utilitarianism,[2] a 'social engineering approach',[3] the theories

---

[1]   *See* Stanley I. Benn, and Richard S. Peters, Social Principles and the Democratic State (1959) Chapter 8; and H.L.A. Hart, Law, Liberty and Morality (1963) Chapter 3 for a discussion of these issues.

[2]   *See e.g.* Jeremy Bentham, An Introduction to the Principles of Morals and Legislation (ed. Burns and Hart) (1970), Of Laws in General (ed. Hart) (1970); or John Stuart Mill's On Liberty (1974) at 163.

[3]   *See e.g.* Rudolph von Jhering, Law as a Means to an End (trans. I. Husik) (1924); Max Weber, Economy and Society (ed. Rheinstein); Max Weber in Economy and Society (1954); Eugene Ehrlich, Fundamental Principles of the Sociology of Law (trans. Moll) (1936); Roscoe Pound,

of Kelsen[4] or Hart[5] or one of the many other important jurisprudential bases that have gained ground in recent decades.

Utilitarian theories, for example, maintain that criminal law should serve purposes extrinsic to the narrow axioms of retributive justice. According to Bentham, punishment may be employed as a valuable form of social control to achieve at least three important goals: prevention of similar crimes by the same offender; deterrence of other individuals from similar crimes by way of example; and reform of the individual offender.[6]

In order to perform an effective role in preventing crimes, international criminal law would benefit from an established standing international police force with the authority and capability to intervene quickly in threatening situations. The timely deployment of a sufficient presence of international civilian police officers in some cases could help to prevent a further deterioration in security as well as to lower the incidence of crimes under international law. International civilian police could only be deployed valuably in cases of armed conflict against the background of a substantial presence of peace-keeping troops, as in the case of United Nations missions in Haiti,[7] the former Yugoslavia[8] and Cambodia.

Outlines of Jurisprudence (1943); and Richard Quinney, The Social Reality of Crime (1970).

[4]   *See* Hans Kelsen, *The Pure Theory of Law and Analytical Jurisprudence*, 55 Harvard Law Review (1941).

[5]   *See* H.L.A. Hart, The Concept of Law (1961).

[6]   *See generally* Benn and Peters, *supra* note 1 at 179 *et seq*. Perhaps the sharpest differences on this question have arisen between the positions of natural law and those of utilitarianism or positivist legal theory. *See also* H.L.A. Hart, Law, Liberty and Morality (1963); and Patrick Devlin, The Enforcement of Morals (1965).

[7]   The deployment of 567 United Nations Police Monitors was authorized by para. 2 of Security Council resolution 867 of 23 Sept. 1993 to complement the deployment of United Nations military personnel in the United Nations Mission in Haiti (UNMIH). The level of military personnel was eventually authorized by Security Council resolution 940 of 31 July 1994 to reach the level of 6,000.

[8]   In UNPROFOR, deployed in Mar. 1992 until Dec. 1995, there were 727 civilian police as compared to 38,130 military troops.

However, a standing international police force does not currently exist[9] and it seems unlikely many States would agree to the creation of such a force unless its powers were very narrowly defined. An international police force would naturally be more effective if it were not obliged to seek the consent of the host Government, but most governments would be wary to cede criminal enforcement jurisdiction to a force with such a right of independent initiative, particularly since it would entail a high risk of undue intervention from the more powerful States.

One alternative would be to vest in international civilian police deployed by the United Nations on an *ad hoc* basis in the context of peace-keeping operations the powers of criminal investigation, arrest, detention and search and seizure in cases where: the host Government or *de facto* authority agrees to the deployment of such police with these powers; the Security Council has decided to take enforcement action under Chapter VII of the UN Charter and there exists a permanent or *ad hoc* international criminal court or a domestic court capable of trying the alleged offender fairly and without delay; or there exists no State or *de facto* authority in the territory, but a criminal court or tribunal at the international level with competence over the alleged offender.[10]

As regards deterrence, it is not very controversial that, in principle, the individual should be deterred from committing crimes harmful to others and to the community (such as murder or assault). However, in certain kinds of cases, it is unclear what deterrent effect, if any, legal norms could possibly have without a credible threat of punishment. International legal norms prohibiting torture or war

---

[9]   Arrangements such as INTERPOL improve mutual State coordination and cooperation of domestic criminal law enforcement efforts, but are not specifically designed for the prevention of crimes under international law.

[10]   The United Nations Transitional Authority in Cambodia (UNTAC) was created pursuant to Security Council resolution 745 of 28 Feb. 1992, comprising 22,000 military and civilian personnel. On 6 Jan. 1993, the Head of Mission (Special Representative of the Secretary-General Yasushi Akashi) issued a directive which laid out procedures for the prosecution of individuals for serious human rights violations and authorized the 3,600 police monitors deployed as part of UNTAC to exercise powers of arrest and detention for the purposes of these prosecutions.

crimes may have very little effect in respect of armed militia who may be under instructions to commit violations, and moreover, may also ardently believe in their cause. For example, in Nazi Germany, Rwanda and the former Yugoslavia, hate propaganda was used effectively to stir up hatred on the part of militia, as well as everyday civilians sympathetic to the cause, which cleared the way for a policy of genocide to be put in effect. In each case, target groups were stigmatized as threats to society and their members as less than human.

In such situations, neither the rationalist precepts of international criminal law norms, nor the seemingly distant risk that they may be enforced, are likely to appear of any consequence to the potential perpetrator. Sheer ignorance on the part of the potential perpetrator that there even exists international criminal responsibility would negate any possible deterrent value. In other cases, potential perpetrators may be aware of the possibility of international criminal prosecution, but may feel that it poses such a negligible risk of sanction as to be ignorable altogether.

However, it must be admitted that even in extreme cases, international criminal law may have a strong deterrent effect. First, international criminal law, although presently weak, could and should be strengthened so that it symbolizes in a credible way the rule of law and the real likelihood of enforcement. In other words, the present lack of enforcement capabilities provides an argument for strengthening and supporting the further development of international criminal law, rather than looking elsewhere for solutions that may provide for easier but less complete substitutes in the shorter term.

Second, even if international criminal law enforcement mechanisms seem capable of prosecuting only few individuals, this lack of capacity does not wholly undermine their effect. Were a select number of individuals in positions of top governmental authority prosecuted, international criminal law may yet provide some disincentive to precisely those would-be planners and organizers in key posts of future State administrations who might be tempted to instigate crimes on a systematic and widespread basis. In this regard, the deterrent value of international criminal law naturally would be enhanced through wide dissemination of its principles and scope of application and above all, through success in the prosecution of at least these leaders.

With respect to rehabilitation, it is very important that every effort be made to ensure persons found guilty of crimes under international law are rehabilitated. Without genuine efforts at rehabilitation, which not only foster respect for the rights of the detainee as a human being, but also that of society for itself, international criminal justice may be misinterpreted as an means intended to exact revenge upon the vanquished, rather than to protect the international community from crimes under international law. Sincere efforts to rehabilitate the offender would emphasize the positive, curative goals of international criminal justice, rather to portray punishment as a form of revenge.

International criminal trials may provide a society which has been torn by ethnic conflict and has become plagued by deep embitterment, suspicion and distrust, a mirror by which to view itself. If this mirror presents not too distorted a reflection, all elements of society may be brought to a better recognition of the character and scale of the violations committed and the responsibilities involved. To avoid the festering of superficially covered wounds, a fair acknowledgement of responsibilities may afford society a chance to begin a process of healing. Where two ethnic groups have been at war, for example, it will become clear that not every individual of each side committed crimes. The road to reconciliation might be rendered navigable once the guilty are duly tried, punished, and to the extent possible, rehabilitated. In certain situations, truth commissions may provide a valuable alternative to the more adversarial process of international criminal prosecutions and may thus lead more directly to national reconciliation. However, the price for the pursuit of truth through the voluntary rendering of confessions may be amnesties for criminals, and the signal that impunity still reigns for massive crimes.

3. THE NEED FOR A PERMANENT INTERNATIONAL CRIMINAL COURT

Crimes under international law strike at the basic interests of the State and the international community as a whole. They hinder the maintenance of international peace and security and fuel political instability. Where left unchecked, they can exacerbate and escalate deep-rooted grievances into armed hostilities and even war.

International criminal law cannot be effective unless enforced systematically. The two *ad hoc* international criminal tribunals for the former Yugoslavia and Rwanda, although important steps along the road to the possible establishment of a permanent international criminal court, do not in themselves form *a system of international criminal law*.

In the five centuries from the Middle Ages to the Second World War, there had been only a few international war crimes trials which hold little relevance for today. Half a century more passed between the time the international military trials were held in Nuremberg and Tokyo and the creation of the two *ad hoc* tribunals for the former Yugoslavia and Rwanda.

The main elements determining the creation of international criminal tribunals in the 20th century have been the international balance of power, prevailing level of international cooperation, and the character and outcome of the particular armed conflict in question. Such factors may always affect the practical success or failure of implementation efforts in a given situation. However, these ephemeral elements are completely irrelevant to the principle that an individual who commits a crime under international law ought to be held responsible for it, regardless of his or her nationality, religion or beliefs, ethnic origin or other such characteristics.

The fundamental principle that any individual who has committed, or ordered to be committed, a crime under international law, shall be tried, sentenced and punished according to universally accepted norms of international criminal law and justice, must take precedence over any other considerations, whether of politics, administrative convenience or historical accident. The establishment of a permanent international criminal court with universal competence is an essential precondition for full observance of this principle. A permanent international criminal court would best ensure that international criminal law functions not only to punish the guilty on a non-discriminatory basis, but to deter crimes under international law from being committed in future anywhere in the world.

The lack of a permanent international criminal court leaves the international community few viable alternatives by which to ensure the enforcement of criminal responsibility for crimes under international law. Without a permanent international criminal court, the international community is faced with the option to urge the territorial Government to bring to an end crimes under international law being committed in its territory and to prosecute crimes already committed. However, the Government may not be willing to undertake prosecutions and the courts may be subordinate to the tyranny of the Executive. In other situations, there may be sufficient willingness to prosecute, but the administration of justice does not exist or function. In principle, courts in other countries could prosecute crimes under international law where there exist the necessary jurisdictional grounds, but as discussed in Chapter V, courts rarely assert jurisdiction over criminal cases lacking a clear connection to the State or local community.

Ad hoc tribunals, such as those created for the former Yugoslavia and Rwanda, cannot suffice. They are created only after the violations have already been committed and their competence is limited to a particular situation and time-frame. In effect, they are basically retrospective. As such, they symbolize to potential violators in other countries only the *possibility* that another *ad hoc* tribunal might be created in future to deal with a situation after it has arisen. The creation of a permanent court would avoid the Security Council having to act selectively on a case-by-case basis, an inherently discriminatory approach. That there is an International Criminal Tribunal for Rwanda, but not an International Criminal Tribunal for Burundi, an International Criminal Tribunal for the Former Yugoslavia, but none for crimes committed in neighbouring conflict areas, is untenable from a legal point of view.

The creation of a permanent court would also symbolize the international community's determination to enforce criminal responsibility for crimes under international law *universally* and on a *prospective* basis. In addition, it could strengthen enforcement where Governments are more willing to surrender an alleged offender in their custody to a permanent international criminal court rather than to a State where international norms governing pre-trial detention and fair trial may not be respected.

The need for a permanent international criminal court to deter crimes under international law is as universal as the potential for human conflict.[11] The fact that genocide - perhaps the greatest cruelty humanity can inflict upon itself - in this century alone has been perpetrated in Armenia, Cambodia, Germany, Kurdistan, Rwanda, the former Yugoslavia and elsewhere, should be more than sufficient to prove the urgency of the task before us.

4. STABILITY YET ADAPTABILITY

The normative and institutional structures of international criminal law must be sufficiently static and stable as to be recognizable as a system. International criminal law cannot be applied effectively, consistently and universally, unless it exhibits sufficient stability in character and effect. It is therefore essential that permanent administrative structures be created and adequately supported by qualified staff and material resources.

With respect to the flexibility and adaptability of norms, the system of international criminal law benefits, and is also constrained by, the elements of change and stability that apply as regards other norms of international law. The interplay among treaty, custom, general principles of law, the writings of publicists, and the decisions of judicial bodies, provides the mainstay for normative consistency in international criminal law.

Equally, the institutions of international criminal law must be fully vested with the authority to respond flexibly and pragmatically to new events that may have been unanticipated at the time such institutions were created. One problem with *ad hoc* tribunals in this regard, is the difficulty in broadening or narrowing their competence as new events or circumstances arise, such as the commission of crimes in neighbouring territories not originally contemplated or covered by the tribunal's statute. Such flexibility would be enhanced more by a permanent court vested with competence over the entire globe as

---

[11]   As Sigmund Freud envisioned in Civilization and Its Discontents (1961) at 42: "The final outcome should be a rule of law to which all ... have contributed by a sacrifice of their instincts, and which leaves no one ... at the mercy of brute force."

opposed to *ad hoc* international criminal tribunals with limited temporal and territorial competence, as argued above.

As an institutional system, international criminal law must also be capable of maintaining a certain existential equilibrium. Unless its institutionalized organs are funded through stable and long-term contributions from governments, international criminal law will not be able to grow from within as necessary. Whether funded from the general pool of regular assessed contributions provided by United Nations Member States, or from a particular budget such as that for peace-keeping, it is imperative that the administrative organs of international criminal law not be exposed to the political manipulation of any particular State or States. Some States may wish to make payment of funds conditional upon fulfilment of one or other of their own domestic policy interests. Such conditional funding arrangements could severely hamper the impartiality and independence of a permanent international criminal court.

5. RELATIVE AUTONOMY FROM OTHER NORMATIVE SYSTEMS

As a system, international criminal law ought to be relatively autonomous from other normative systems. On the one hand, no legal system can or should be completely isolated or insulated from morals, religion or politics, particularly since the values extant in these systems express a sense universal to the entire human community which infuses also law and procedure. On the other hand, wide variations among cultures with regard to the definition of particular crimes, the scale of punishment, and the need to rehabilitate the offender, should not be ignored.

However, were international criminal law to develop, at least in its initial stages, around the prohibition of the 'hard core violations', such as those primarily featured in the 1996 draft Code, the level of cultural and ideological disagreement over specific meanings of norms and the procedural consequences for their breach, would be minimized. In other words, substantial agreement on the crimes to be prosecuted by an international criminal court would likely minimize procedural disagreements. Governments would probably quibble less over a court's procedural aspects if its competence were limited to acts well-recognized to constitute crimes.

Since there exists no culturally neutral criminal law, a permanent international criminal court should draw its principles, to the maximum extent possible, from the major legal traditions of the world, while avoiding domination by only one or other of these legal traditions. To this end, it is highly important that judges and staff be drawn from a diversity of geographic, religious, national, cultural and ideological backgrounds, which would not only enrich the quality of the institution, but symbolize the universality of international criminal law.

It is essential also that the contribution of personnel by particular governments to an international criminal court, whether permanent or *ad hoc*, be done only to meet short-term needs for highly specialized experts whose services cannot be obtained in any better way. Personnel, contributed *gratis* by governments, may be needed as a stopgap measure where budgeted resources for the tribunal are inadequate. However, the employment of personnel whose salaries, benefits and emoluments, are provided by a particular government directly, may seriously undermine the impartiality and independence of the tribunal from within. Frequently, contributed personnel maintain a strong professional loyalty to their government, which has arranged for their contract and which provides them their pay and benefits. Such loyalty may overshadow the impartiality required of them in their functions as international civil servants. Moreover, personnel contributed by governments may be seconded or contributed to work for an insufficient period of time to provide meaningful benefit to the effective workings of international criminal justice. Furthermore, usually only very few governments have sufficient resources to provide personnel, a factor which may result in substantial over-representation of one or other country's nationals in the ranks of tribunal staff.

International criminal law should become relatively autonomous from other fields of general international law. While international criminal law cannot emerge without the sustenance provided to it from the well springs of ancient laws of war, humanitarian law, human rights law, law of international responsibility, and many other pertinent fields of international law, it must become recognizable as a coherent and relatively self-contained system with a discrete set of purposes, means, methods and procedures. Without a certain level of specialization and autonomy from other fields of international law, international criminal law norms and implementation will remain confused and disorganized. Moreover, without a certain autonomy, international criminal law will always be constrained by the particularities of norms derived from other fields.

6. SYNTHESIS

Prospects for the emergence of a unified system of international criminal law, characterized by broad and coherent material coverage, as well as fair and effective institutional implementation, have never been greater. To understand how and why this is so, it is necessary to relate the historical origins of international law and cooperation to the emergence of international criminal law.

A certain minimum level of international cooperation through international law is a basic precondition for the rise of a system of international criminal law. The year 1648 marks the end of the Thirty Years' War (1618-1648), the fracture of the Holy Roman Empire, the emergence of sovereign States in Europe and the rise of international law applicable between them. However, it was not until 1815 that the first steps towards international cooperation were taken within the framework of the Congress of Vienna. Consequently, in the period 1648 to 1815, there were few significant developments in international criminal law: although there existed a functioning system of international law, this system served the interests of States merely to coexist peacefully, rather than to pursue goals of international cooperation.[12]

The peace treaties of Münster and Ösnabruck, signed in 1648 by almost all parties to the bloody Thirty Years' War,[13] ushered in the Peace of Westphalia. In addition to establishing the secular character of international law through their recognition of Protestantism on an international basis and thus formalizing the decline of the Holy Roman

---

[12]   *See generally* Wolfgang G. Friedmann, The Changing Structure of International Law 1964.

[13]   The treaties were signed by all belligerents except France and Spain which continued fighting until 1659.

Empire,[14] members of the Holy Roman Empire, numbering around three hundred entities, were granted the right to enter into alliances and to wage war, provided only that such alliances or war were not directed against the Empire, public peace or the treaties themselves.

Every State, recognized as a legal entity separate and independent from the Church, could pursue its own self-interests, and even resort to war, purely according to national priorities. Eventually, as the Holy Roman Empire faded,[15] monarchs began to wield almost absolute power within their respective realms. Indeed, the doctrine of exclusive State sovereignty and the principle that each State shall refrain from interference in the affairs of every other State, was originally asserted by monarchs to ensure freedom from Papal interference. The shift in political legitimacy to make law, from supremacy of God to supremacy of the State and institutionally, from the authority of the Church to the authority of Government, cleared the way for sovereign independence from Papal authority, the magnification of princely power and the rise, first, of the monarchical assertion of the divine right to rule, and later on, of the absolute power of the State.

In political and legal philosophy, the State became reified and deified. In Hobbes' *Leviathan*, the power of the State as abstract legal person was considered to be absolute. In this view, it followed that international law was not really law at all, but a series of moral obligations only.[16] International law was considered to operate only

---

[14] The prince was recognized as having the authority to dictate the religion of his people according to the principle of *Cuius regio, eius religio* established by the Peace of Augsburg, 1555 originally recognized to extend a measure of toleration to Lutherans. By such recognition, the German Diet in asserted the monarchical power of princes to take precedence over the monarchical power of the Emperor in the Holy Roman Empire.

[15] The Holy Roman Empire was formally dissolved on August 6, 1806 by the Habsburg Emperor Francis. It had been replaced in July 1806 by the Confederation of the Rhine, which had put Bavaria, Baden, Hesse-Darmstadt and Württemburg effectively under the control of Napoleon following the defeat of Austria by France on 2 Dec. 1805 at the Battle of Austerlitz.

[16] Hobbes' empirical concept of law formed the basis of legal positivism, later elaborated by Bentham, Mill and Austin, who viewed the State as the sole source of law. The term 'international law' itself was first coined by

on the plane of international relations, while each State maintained absolute sovereignty within its jurisdiction.[17] By the early 19th century, Hegel identified the State as a God on Earth,[18] implicit in the cunning and coming of Reason, and immanent in the laws of History.[19]

The rules of international law typical of the period 1648 to 1815 require essentially that States, always potentially hostile entities, remain peacefully apart. As such, classic international law consists primarily of passive obligations not to interfere with the rights of other States, rather than to impose upon each State the obligation to undertake positive action cooperatively with other States in pursuit of common goals.

International criminal law could have only a very limited role in a system where State sovereignty took pre-eminence, inter-State contact was occasional and international cooperation nil. Aside from a few narrow rules prohibiting certain means and methods of war, norms of international criminal law could not arise before there existed a certain level of solidarity, community and cooperation on the international plane. International criminal law could not possibly be effective where State action remained largely unfettered and unregulated. Not only was the State largely free to do as it wished, but the

---

Bentham in 1780 to describe law as law between States.

[17]   The positivist theory that the State, rather than God or human nature, is the supreme source of law, prevailed over natural law philosophy. Along with medieval asceticism, Locke rejected the idea that kingship was a natural institution ordained by God. *See* Locke's arguments in his First Treatise of Government, in Two Treatises of Government, (ed. Laslett)(1960). Locke's arguments were an attack on Sir Robert Filmer's Patriarcha or a Defence of the National Power of Kings against the Unnatural Liberty of the People, published in 1680.

[18]   The original German phrase in Hegel's Philosophy of Right para. 331 (trans. T.M. Knox) (1942), is quoted in Shlomo Avineri, Hegel's Theory of the Modern State (1972), as "Es ist der Gang Gottes in der Welt, dass derr Staat ist".

[19]   According to Hegel as expressed in his *Philosophy of Right*: "The nation as State is mind in its substantive rationality and immediate actuality and is therefore the absolute power on earth. It follows that every State is sovereign and autonomous against its neighbours. It is entitled in the first place and without qualification to be sovereign from their point of view, ie. to be recognized by them as sovereign". Hegel, *ibid.* at 200.

individual, acting as organ of the State, was shielded from sanction by the privileges and immunities that stem from the basic doctrines of State sovereignty, equality and independence.

The Congress of Vienna, 1815,[20] beyond formalizing the new international balance of power following the defeat of Napoleon's armies by Austria, Britain, Prussia and Russia, represents a first in international cooperation to maintain the peace through a collective security arrangement. More significantly for the development of international criminal law, it was also the first time action was taken jointly by States to prohibit slave-trading and piracy perpetrated on the high seas - the first major additions to the rubric of international criminal law since the Middle Ages. The pertinent provisions of the Final Act impose individual criminal responsibility under international law for slave-trading and piracy indirectly, by obliging States to prosecute the alleged offender under their own criminal law.[21]

In the period of the League of Nations, it is significant also that international criminal law norms and implementation could not become more effective than the rest of the institutionalized system of international cooperation of the time. Like the collective security organs of the League of Nations, which could do little more than denounce an aggressor without taking more effective action, Articles 227-230 of the Versailles Treaty, 1919, imposing individual criminal responsibility upon Kaiser Wilhelm II and soldiers under his command, could have symbolic effect only, as discussed in Chapter VI(2).

In the United Nations era, there is greater cause for optimism. Particularly since the end of the Cold War, genuine international cooperation, a precondition for the emergence of a system of international criminal law, operates on a regular basis. In the last few years, a tendency towards unification of the norms of international criminal law has become manifest. The recent codification and

---

[20]   *See generally* C.K. Webster, The Congress of Vienna (1963) at 79; and Harold Nicholson, The Congress of Vienna: A Study in Allied Unity: 1812-1822 (1946).

[21]   The norms were further developed at a number of international conferences held under the auspices of the Concert of Europe, namely, the Congress of Aix-La-Chapelle in 1818, Congress of Troppau in 1820 (moved to Laibach in 1821), Congress of Verona in 1822, Congress of Paris in 1856 and the Congress of Berlin, 1885.

progressive development efforts of the International Law Commission, particularly that of the 1996 draft Code, indicate a trend towards simplicity, unity, economy and clarity in international criminal law norms.

The more established substantive norms of international criminal law concern aggression, genocide, torture, slavery, deportation or forcible transfer of population, mass rape, war crimes, crimes against humanity and grave breaches of the Geneva Conventions, 1949, and 1977 Protocols additional thereto. A second, softer layer of norms, which were embodied in the 1991 draft Code, but dropped from the 1996 draft Code, may eventually come within the *corpus* of international criminal law, namely, the norms *de lege ferenda* relating to colonial domination, apartheid, persecution on social, political, racial, religious or cultural grounds, mercenaries, illicit drug-trafficking, and wilful and severe damage to the natural environment. These norms either have become established only recently or are rapidly becoming established in general international law, but lack the precision required for international criminal law implementation. Further out on the periphery are norms concerning the threat of aggression, intervention and terrorism, which appear too vaguely defined even in general international law to be considered as serious candidates for international criminal law.

As regards international criminal law implementation, unification has been promoted through the creation of the *ad hoc* international criminal tribunals for the former Yugoslavia and Rwanda, which although not wholly consolidated, at least share certain basic institutional organs and procedural ways and means. Moreover, there is the work of the ILC on a draft statute for a permanent international criminal court, and more significantly, preparations are currently under way in the United Nations to convene a conference of plenipotentiaries with a view to establishing a permanent international criminal court. Thus, the raw materials for broad and coherent material coverage, capable of being implemented by a unified system, appear to be present.

As for fairness in prosecutions, international criminal law benefits from a well-developed body of international human rights law that comprises clear standards governing arrest of the alleged offender, surrender or extradition, prosecution and trial, sentencing, punishment and rehabilitation.

However, whether international criminal law will emerge as an effective system remains to be seen. The track record of the International Criminal Tribunal for the Former Yugoslavia has not been very encouraging because of the Tribunal's failure to acquire custody over high-level alleged offenders. On the other hand, the International Criminal Tribunal for Rwanda appears to have a better chance because of the cooperation of the territorial Government.

While the blossoming of international cooperation in the United Nations era has brought about transformation from the lattice structure of the system of bilateral State relations, to a more multilateral system in which the international community acts cooperatively and collectively to reach common goals, every State remains highly prone to the same sovereign reflex that dominated the international political climate of Westphalia. While sovereign States find it increasingly advantageous to bring their domestic and foreign policies in line with certain basic values held by the international community at large, States still act primarily in their own self-interests, even where this course may be at odds with the rest of the international community. Ultimately, the effectiveness of international criminal law at any particular point in time is, and will continue to be, a function of the equilibrium between the centrifugal forces of State autonomy, sovereignty and independence, and centripetal forces arising from the need to pursue international cooperation to serve common interests, values and goals.

* * *

I. TEXT OF THE DRAFT CODE ADOPTED BY THE COMMISSION ON FIRST READING

PART I

CHAPTER 1. DEFINITION AND CHARACTERIZATION

Article 1
Definition

The crimes [under international law] defined in this Code constitute crimes against the peace and security of mankind.

Article 2
Characterization

The characterization of an act or omission as a crime against the peace and security of mankind is independent of internal law. The fact that an act or omission is or is not punishable under internal law does not affect this characterization.

CHAPTER 2. GENERAL PRINCIPLES

Article 3
Responsibility and punishment

1. An individual who commits a crime against the peace and security of mankind is responsible therefor and is liable to punishment.
2. An individual who aids, abets or provides the means for the commission of a crime against the peace and security of mankind or conspires in or directly incites the commission of such a crime is responsible therefor and is liable to punishment.

3.   An individual who commits an act constituting an attempt to commit a crime against the peace and security of mankind [as set out in articles .....] is responsible therefor and is liable to punishment. Attempt means any commencement of execution of a crime that failed or was halted only because of circumstances independent of the perpetrator's intention.

Article 4
Motives

Responsibility for a crime against the peace and security of mankind is not affected by any motives invoked by the accused which are not covered by the definition of the crime.

Article 5
Responsibility of States

Prosecution of an individual for a crime against the peace and security of mankind does not relieve a State of any responsibility under international law for an act or omission attributable to it.

Article 6[2]
Obligation to try or extradite

1.   A State in whose territory an individual alleged to have committed a crime against the peace and security of mankind is present shall either try or extradite him.
2.   If extradition is requested by several States, special consideration shall be given to the request of the State in whose territory the crime was committed.
3.   The provisions of paragraphs 1 and 2 do not prejudge the establishment and the jurisdiction of an international criminal court.

Article 7
Non-applicability of statutory limitations

No statutory limitation shall apply to crimes against the peace and security of mankind.

Article 8
Judicial guarantees

An individual charged with a crime against the peace and security of mankind shall be entitled without discrimination to the minimum guarantees due to all human beings with regard to the law and the facts. In particular, he shall have the right to be presumed innocent until proved guilty and have the rights:

(a)   in the determination of any charge against him, to have a fair and public hearing by a competent, independent and impartial tribunal duly established by law or by treaty;

(b)   to be informed promptly and in detail in a language which he understands of the nature and cause of the charge against him;

(c)   to have adequate time and facilities for the preparation of his defence and to communicate with counsel of his own choosing;

(d)   to be tried without undue delay;

(e)   to be tried in his presence, and to defend himself in person or through legal assistance of his own choosing; to be informed, if he does not have legal assistance, of this right; and to have legal assistance assigned to him and without payment by him in any such case if he does not have sufficient means to pay for it;

(f)   to examine, or have examined, the witnesses against him and to obtain the attendance and examination of witnesses on his behalf under the same conditions as witnesses against him;

(g)   to have the free assistance of an interpreter if he cannot understand or speak the language used in court;

(h)   not to be compelled to testify against himself or to confess guilt.

Article 9
Non bis in idem

1.   No one shall be tried or punished for a crime under this Code for which he has already been finally convicted or acquitted by an international criminal court.[3]
2.   Subject to paragraphs 3, 4 and 5, no one shall be tried or punished for a crime under this Code in respect of an act for which he has already been finally convicted or acquitted by a national court, provided that, if a punishment was imposed, it has been enforced or is in the process of being enforced.
3.   Notwithstanding the provisions of paragraph 2, an individual may be tried and punished by an international criminal court or by a national court for a crime under this Code if the act which was the subject of a trial and judgement as an ordinary crime corresponds to one of the crimes characterized in this Code.[4]
4.   Notwithstanding the provisions of paragraph 2, an individual may be tried and punished by a national court of another State for a crime under this Code:
    (a)   if the act which was the subject of the previous judgement took place in the territory of that State; or
    (b)   if that State has been the main victim of the crime.
5.   In the case of a subsequent conviction under this Code, the court, in passing sentence, shall deduct any penalty imposed and implemented as a result of a previous conviction for the same act.

Article 10
Non-retroactivity

1.   No one shall be convicted under this Code for acts committed before its entry into force.
2.   Nothing in this article shall preclude the trial and punishment of anyone for any act which, at the time when it was committed, was criminal in accordance with international law or domestic law applicable in conformity with international law.

Article 11
Order of a Government or a superior

The fact that an individual charged with a crime against the peace and security of mankind acted pursuant to an order of a Government or a superior does not relieve him of criminal responsibility if, in the circumstances at the time, it was possible for him not to comply with that order.

Article 12
Responsibility of the superior

The fact that a crime against the peace and security of mankind was committed by a subordinate does not relieve his superiors of criminal responsibility, if they knew or had information enabling them to conclude, in the circumstances at the time, that the subordinate was committing or was going to commit such a crime and if they did not take all feasible measures within their power to prevent or repress the crime.

Article 13
Official position and responsibility

The official position of an individual who commits a crime against the peace and security of mankind, and particularly the fact he acts as head of State or Government, does not relieve him of criminal responsibility.

Article 14
Defences and extenuating circumstances

1. The competent court shall determine the admissibility of defences under the general principles of law, in the light of the character of each crime.
2. In passing sentence, the court shall, where appropriate, take into account extenuating circumstances.

PART II

CRIMES AGAINST THE PEACE AND
SECURITY OF MANKIND

Article 15
Aggression

1.	An individual who as leader or organizer plans, commits or orders the commission of an act of aggression shall, on conviction thereof, be sentenced [to ...].

2.	Aggression is the use of armed force by a State against the sovereignty, territorial integrity or political independence of another State, or in any other manner inconsistent with the Charter of the United Nations.

3.	The first use of armed force by a State in contravention of the Charter shall constitute prima facie evidence of an act of aggression, although the Security Council may, in conformity with the Charter, conclude that a determination that an act of aggression has been committed would not be justified in the light of other relevant circumstances, including the fact that the acts concerned or their consequences are not of sufficient gravity.

4.	Any of the following acts, regardless of a declaration of war, constitutes an act of aggression, due regard being paid to paragraphs 2 and 3:

	(a)	the invasion or attack by the armed forces of a State of the territory of another State, or any military occupa-tion, however temporary, resulting from such invasion or attack, or any annexation by the use of force of the territory of another State or part thereof;

	(b)	bombardment by the armed forces of a State against the territory of another State or the use of any weapons by a State against the territory of another State;

	(c)	the blockade of the ports or coasts of a State by the armed forces of another State;

(d)   an attack by the armed forces of a State on the land, sea or air forces, or marine and air fleets of another State;

(e)   the use of armed forces of one State which are within the territory of another State with the agreement of the receiving State, in contravention of the conditions provided for in the agreement, or any extension of their presence in such territory beyond the termination of the agreement;

(f)   the action of a State in allowing its territory, which it has placed at the disposal of another State, to be used by that other State for perpetrating an act of aggression against a third State;

(g)   the sending by or on behalf of a State of armed bands, groups, irregulars or mercenaries, which carry out acts of armed force against another State of such gravity as to amount to the acts listed above, or its substantial involvement therein;

(h)   any other acts determined by the Security Council as constituting acts of aggression under the provisions of the Charter.

[5.   Any determination by the Security Council as to the existence of an act of aggression is binding on national courts].

6.   Nothing in this article shall be interpreted as in any way enlarging or diminishing the scope of the Charter of the United Nations including its provisions concerning cases in which the use of force is lawful.

7.   Nothing in this article could in any way prejudice the right to self-determination, freedom and independence, as derived from the Charter, of peoples forcibly deprived of that right and referred to in the Declaration on Principles of International Law concerning Friendly Relations and Cooperation among States in accordance with the Charter of the United Nations, particularly peoples under colonial and racist regimes or other forms of alien domination; nor the right of these peoples to struggle to that end and to seek and receive support, in accordance with the principles of the Charter and in conformity with the above-mentioned Declaration.

Article 16
Threats of aggression

1.   An individual who as leader or organizer commits or orders the commission of a threat of aggression shall, on conviction thereof, be sentenced [to ...].
2.   Threat of aggression consists of declarations, communications, demonstrations of force or any other measures which would give good reason to the Government of a State to believe that aggression is being seriously contemplated against that State.

Article 17
Intervention

1.   An individual who as leader or organizer commits or orders the commission of an act of intervention in the internal or external affairs of a State shall, on conviction thereof, be sentenced [to...].
2.   Intervention in the internal or external affairs of a State consists of fomenting [armed] subversive or terrorist activities or by organizing, assisting or financing such activities, or supplying arms for the purpose of such activities, thereby [seriously] undermining the free exercise by that State of its sovereign rights.
3.   Nothing in this article shall in any way prejudice the right of peoples to self-determination as enshrined in the Charter of the United Nations.

Article 18
Colonial domination and other forms of alien domination

An individual who as leader or organizer establishes or maintains by force or orders the establishment or maintenance by force of colonial domination or any other form of alien domination contrary to the right of peoples to self-determination as enshrined in the Charter of the United Nations shall, on conviction thereof, be sentenced [to ...].

Article 19
Genocide

1.   An individual who commits or orders the commission of an act of genocide shall, on conviction thereof, be sentenced [to ...].
2.   Genocide means any of the following acts committed with intent to destroy, in whole or in part, a national, ethnic, racial or religious group as such:
   - (a)   killing members of the group;
   - (b)   causing serious bodily or mental harm to members of the group;
   - (c)   deliberately inflicting on the group conditions of life calculated to bring about its physical destruction in whole or in part;
   - (d)   imposing measures intended to prevent births within the group; (e) forcibly transferring children of the group to another group.

Article 20
Apartheid

1.   An individual who as leader or organizer commits or orders the commission of the crime of apartheid shall, on conviction thereof, be sentenced [to ...].
2.   Apartheid consists of any of the following acts based on policies and practices of racial segregation and discrimination committed for the purpose of establishing or maintaining domination by one racial group over any other racial group and systematically oppressing it:
   - (a)   denial to a member or members of a racial group of the right to life and liberty of person;
   - (b)   deliberate imposition on a racial group of living conditions calculated to cause its physical destruction in whole or in part;
   - (c)   any legislative measures and other measures calculated to prevent a racial group from participating in the political, social, economic and cultural life of the country and the deliberate creation of conditions preventing the full development of such a group;

(d)   any measures, including legislative measures, designed to divide the population along racial lines, in particular by the creation of separate reserves and ghettos for the members of a racial group, the prohibition of marriages among members of various racial groups or the expropriation of landed property belonging to a racial group or to members thereof;

(e)   exploitation of the labour of the members of a racial group, in particular by submitting them to forced labour;

(f)   persecution of organizations and persons, by depriving them of fundamental rights and freedoms, because they oppose apartheid.

Article 21
Systematic or mass violations of human rights

An individual who commits or orders the commission of any of the following violations of human rights:

-    murder
-    torture
-    establishing or maintaining over persons a status of slavery, servitude or forced labour
-    persecution on social, political, racial, religious or cultural grounds in a systematic manner or on a mass scale; or
-    deportation of forcible transfer of population

shall, on conviction thereof, be sentenced [to ...].

Article 22
Exceptionally serious war crimes

1.   An individual who commits or orders the commission of an exceptionally serious war crime shall, on conviction thereof, be sentenced [to...].

2.   For the purposes of this Code, an exceptionally serious war crime is an exceptionally serious violation of principles and rules of international law applicable in armed conflict consisting of any of the following acts:

(a)   acts of inhumanity, cruelty or barbarity directed against
        the life, dignity or physical or mental integrity of per-
        sons [, in particular wilful killing, torture, mutilation,
        biological experiments, taking of hostages, compelling
        a protected person to serve in the forces of a hostile
        power, unjustifiable delay in the repatriation of
        prisoners of war after the cessation of active hostilities,
        deportation or transfer of the civilian population and
        collective punishment];

(b)   establishment of settlers in an occupied territory and
        changes to the demographic composition of an
        occupied territory;

(c)   use of unlawful weapons;

(d)   employing methods or means of warfare which are
        intended or may be expected to cause widespread,
        long-term and severe damage to the natural environ-
        ment;

(e)   large-scale destruction of civilian property;

(f)   wilful attacks on property of exceptional religious,
        historical or cultural value.

Article 23
Recruitment, use, financing and training of mercenaries

1.   An individual who as an agent or representative of a State
      commits or orders the commission of any of the following acts:

      -     recruitment, use, financing or training of mercenaries
            for activities directed against another State or for the
            purpose of opposing the legitimate exercise of the
            inalienable right of peoples to self-determination as
            recognized under international law

      shall, on conviction thereof, be sentenced [to...].

2.   A mercenary is any individual, who:

      (a)   is specially recruited locally or abroad in order to fight
              in an armed conflict;

      (b)   is motivated to take part in the hostilities essentially by
              the desire for private gain and, in fact, is promised, by
              or on behalf of a party to the conflict, material compen-
              sation substantially in excess of that promised or paid

to combatants of similar rank and functions in the armed forces of that party;

(c)   is neither a national of a party to the conflict nor a resident of territory controlled by a party to the conflict;

(d)   is not a member of the armed forces of a party to the conflict; and

(e)   has not been sent by a State which is not a party to the conflict on official duty as a member of its armed forces.

3.   A mercenary is also any individual who, in any other situation:

(a)   is specially recruited locally or abroad for the purpose of participating in a concerted act of violence aimed at:

(i)   overthrowing a Government or otherwise undermining the constitutional order of a State; or

(ii)   undermining the territorial integrity of a State;

(b)   is motivated to take part therein essentially by the desire for significant private gain and is prompted by the promise or payment of material compensation;

(c)   is neither a national nor a resident of the State against which such an act is directed;

(d)   has not been sent by a State on official duty; and

(e)   is not a member of the armed forces of the State in whose territory the act is undertaken.

Article 24
International terrorism

An individual who as an agent or representative of a State commits or orders the commission of any of the following acts:

-    undertaking, organizing, assisting, financing, encouraging or tolerating acts against another State directed at persons or property and of such a nature as to create a state of terror in the minds of public figures, groups of persons or the general public shall, on conviction thereof, be sentenced [to ...].

Article 25
Illicit traffic in narcotic drugs

1.   An individual who commits or orders the commission of any of the following acts:

  -      undertaking, organizing, facilitating, financing or encouraging illicit traffic in narcotic drugs on a large scale, whether within the confines of a State or in a transboundary context shall, on conviction thereof, be sentenced [to ...].

2.   For the purposes of paragraph 1, facilitating or encouraging illicit traffic in narcotic drugs includes the acquisition, holding, conversion or transfer of property by an individual who knows that such property is derived from the crime described in this article in order to conceal or disguise the illicit origin of the property.

3.   Illicit traffic in narcotic drugs means any production, manufacture, extraction, preparation, offering, offering for sale, distribution, sale, delivery on any terms whatsoever, brokerage, dispatch, dispatch in transit, transport, importation or exportation of any narcotic drug or any psychotropic substance contrary to internal or international law.

Article 26
Wilful and severe damage to the environment

An individual who wilfully causes or orders the causing of widespread, long term and severe damage to the natural environment shall, on conviction thereof, be sentenced [to ...].

ANNEX 2 - 1993 Statute of the International Criminal Tribunal for the Former Yugoslavia

**(Annex to the Report of the Secretary-General;
UN Doc. S/25704 of 3 May 1993; approved by Security Council
resolution 827, adopted on 25 May 1993)**

Having been established by the Security Council acting under Chapter VII of the Charter of the United Nations, the International Tribunal for the Prosecution of Persons Responsible for Serious Violations of International Humanitarian Law Committed in the Territory of the Former Yugoslavia since 1991 (hereinafter referred to as "the International Tribunal") shall function in accordance with the provisions of the present Statute.

Article 1
Competence of the International Tribunal

The International Tribunal shall have the power to prosecute persons responsible for serious violations of international humanitarian law committed in the territory of the former Yugoslavia since 1991 in accordance with the provisions of the present Statute.

Article 2
Grave breaches of the Geneva Conventions of 1949

The International Tribunal shall have the power to prosecute persons committing or ordering to be committed grave breaches of the Geneva Conventions of 12 August 1949, namely the following acts against persons or property protected under the provisions of the relevant Geneva Convention:

(a)   wilful killing;
(b)   torture or inhuman treatment, including biological experiments;

(c)   wilfully causing great suffering or serious injury to body or health;

(d)   extensive destruction and appropriation of property, not justified by military necessity and carried out unlawfully and wantonly;

(e)   compelling a prisoner of war or a civilian to serve in the forces of a hostile power;

(f)   wilfully depriving a prisoner of war or a civilian of the rights of fair and regular trial;

(g)   unlawful deportation or transfer or unlawful confinement of a civilian;

(h)   taking civilians as hostages.

Article 3
Violations of the laws or customs of war

The International Tribunal shall have the power to prosecute persons violating the laws or customs of war. Such violations shall include, but not be limited to:

(a)   employment of poisonous weapons or other weapons calculated to cause unnecessary suffering;

(b)   wanton destruction of cities, towns or villages, or devastation not justified by military necessity;

(c)   attack, or bombardment, by whatever means, of undefended towns, villages, dwellings, or buildings;

(d)   seizure of, destruction or wilful damage done to institutions dedicated to religion, charity and education, the arts and sciences, historic monuments and works of art and science;

(e)   plunder of public or private property.

Article 4
Genocide

1.   The International Tribunal shall have the power to prosecute persons committing genocide as defined in paragraph 2 of this article or of committing any of the other acts enumerated in paragraph 3 of this article.

2.   Genocide means any of the following acts committed
with intent to destroy, in whole or in part, a national, ethnical, racial or
religious group, as such:
  (a)   killing members of the group;
  (b)   causing serious bodily or mental harm to members of
           the group;
  (c)   deliberately inflicting on the group conditions of life
           calculated to bring about its physical destruction in
           whole or in part;
  (d)   imposing measures intended to prevent births within
           the group;
  (e)   forcibly transferring children of the group to another
           group.
3.   The following acts shall be punishable:
  (a)   genocide;
  (b)   conspiracy to commit genocide;
  (c)   direct and public incitement to commit genocide;
  (d)   attempt to commit genocide;
  (e)   complicity in genocide.

Article 5
Crimes against humanity

The International Tribunal shall have the power to prosecute
persons responsible for the following crimes when committed in armed
conflict, whether international or internal in character, and directed
against any civilian population:
  (a)   murder;
  (b)   extermination;
  (c)   enslavement;
  (d)   deportation;
  (e)   imprisonment;
  (f)   torture;
  (g)   rape;
  (h)   persecutions on political, racial and religious grounds;
  (i)   other inhumane acts.

Article 6
Personal jurisdiction

The International Tribunal shall have jurisdiction over natural persons pursuant to the provisions of the present Statute.

Article 7
Individual criminal responsibility

1.   A person who planned, instigated, ordered, committed or otherwise aided and abetted in the planning, preparation or execution of a crime referred to in articles 2 to 5 of the present Statute, shall be individually responsible for the crime.

2.   The official position of any accused person, whether as Head of State or Government or as a responsible Government official, shall not relieve such person of criminal responsibility nor mitigate punishment.

3.   The fact that any of the acts referred to in articles 2 to 5 of the present Statute was committed by a subordinate does not relieve his superior of criminal responsibility if he knew or had reason to know that the subordinate was about to commit such acts or had done so and the superior failed to take the necessary and reasonable measures to prevent such acts or to punish the perpetrators thereof.

4.   The fact that an accused person acted pursuant to an order of a Government or of a superior shall not relieve him of criminal responsibility, but may be considered in mitigation of punishment if the International Tribunal determines that justice so requires.

Article 8
Territorial and temporal jurisdiction

The territorial jurisdiction of the International Tribunal shall extend to the territory of the former Socialist Federal Republic of Yugoslavia, including its land surface, airspace and territorial waters. The temporal jurisdiction of the International Tribunal shall extend to a period beginning on 1 January 1991.

Article 9
Concurrent jurisdiction

1.   The International Tribunal and national courts shall have concurrent jurisdiction to prosecute persons for serious violations of international humanitarian law committed in the territory of the former Yugoslavia since 1 January 1991.

2.   The International Tribunal shall have primacy over national courts. At any stage of the procedure, the International Tribunal may formally request national courts to defer to the competence of the International Tribunal in accordance with the present Statute and the Rules of Procedure and Evidence of the International Tribunal.

Article 10
Non-bis-in-idem

1.   No person shall be tried before a national court for acts constituting serious violations of international humanitarian law under the present Statute, for which he or she has already been tried by the International Tribunal.

2.   A person who has been tried by a national court for acts constituting serious violations of international humanitarian law may be subsequently tried by the International Tribunal only if:

    (a)   the act for which he or she was tried was characterized as an ordinary crime; or

    (b)   the national court proceedings were not impartial or independent, were designed to shield the accused from international criminal responsibility, or the case was not diligently prosecuted.

3.   In considering the penalty to be imposed on a person convicted of a crime under the present Statute, the International Tribunal shall take into account the extent to which any penalty imposed by a national court on the same person for the same act has already been served.

Article 11
Organization of the International Tribunal

The International Tribunal shall consist of the following organs:
(a)   The Chambers, comprising two Trial Chambers and an Appeals Chamber;
(b)   The Prosecutor; and
(c)   A Registry, servicing both the Chambers and the Prosecutor.

Article 12
Composition of the Chambers

The Chambers shall be composed of eleven independent judges, no two of whom may be nationals of the same State, who shall serve as follows:
(a)   Three judges shall serve in each of the Trial Chambers;
(b)   Five judges shall serve in the Appeals Chamber.

Article 13
Qualifications and election of judges

1.   The judges shall be persons of high moral character, impartiality and integrity who possess the qualifications required in their respective countries for appointment to the highest judicial offices. In the overall composition of the Chambers due account shall be taken of the experience of the judges in criminal law, international law, including international humanitarian law and human rights law.
2.   The judges of the International Tribunal shall be elected by the General Assembly from a list submitted by the Security Council, in the following manner:
(a)   The Secretary-General shall invite nominations for judges of the International Tribunal from States Members of the United Nations and non-member States maintaining permanent observer missions at United Nations Headquarters;
(b)   Within sixty days of the date of the invitation of the Secretary-General, each State may nominate up to two candidates meeting the qualifications set out in para-

graph 1 above, no two of whom shall be of the same nationality;

(c)   The Secretary-General shall forward the nominations received to the Security Council. From the nominations received the Security Council shall establish a list of not less than twenty-two and not more than thirty-three candidates, taking due account of the adequate representation of the principal legal systems of the world;

(d)   The President of the Security Council shall transmit the list of candidates to the President of the General Assembly. From that list the General Assembly shall elect the eleven judges of the International Tribunal. The candidates who receive an absolute majority of the votes of the States Members of the United Nations and of the non-Member States maintaining permanent observer missions at United Nations Headquarters, shall be declared elected. Should two candidates of the same nationality obtain the required majority vote, the one who received the higher number of votes shall be considered elected.

3.   In the event of a vacancy in the Chambers, after consultation with the Presidents of the Security Council and of the General Assembly, the Secretary-General shall appoint a person meeting the qualifications of paragraph 1 above, for the remainder of the term of office concerned.

4.   The judges shall be elected for a term of four years. The terms and conditions of service shall be those of the judges of the International Court of Justice. They shall be eligible for re-election.

Article 14
Officers and members of the Chambers

1.   The judges of the International Tribunal shall elect a President.

2.   The President of the International Tribunal shall be a member of the Appeals Chamber and shall preside over its proceedings.

3.   After consultation with the judges of the International Tribunal, the President shall assign the judges to the Appeals

Chamber and to the Trial Chambers. A judge shall serve only in the Chamber to which he or she was assigned.

4. The judges of each Trial Chamber shall elect a Presiding Judge, who shall conduct all of the proceedings of the Trial Chamber as a whole.

Article 15
Rules of procedure and evidence

The judges of the International Tribunal shall adopt rules of procedure and evidence for the conduct of the pre-trial phase of the proceedings, trials and appeals, the admission of evidence, the protection of victims and witnesses and other appropriate matters.

Article 16
The Prosecutor

1. The Prosecutor shall be responsible for the investigation and prosecution of persons responsible for serious violations of international humanitarian law committed in the territory of the former Yugoslavia since 1 January 1991.

2. The Prosecutor shall act independently as a separate organ of the International Tribunal. He or she shall not seek or receive instructions from any Government or from any other source.

3. The Office of the Prosecutor shall be composed of a Prosecutor and such other qualified staff as may be required.

4. The Prosecutor shall be appointed by the Security Council on nomination by the Secretary-General. He or she shall be of high moral character and possess the highest level of competence and experience in the conduct of investigations and prosecutions of criminal cases. The Prosecutor shall serve for a four-year term and be eligible for reappointment. The terms and conditions of service of the Prosecutor shall be those of an Under-Secretary-General of the United Nations.

5. The staff of the Office of the Prosecutor shall be appointed by the Secretary-General on the recommendation of the Prosecutor.

Article 17
The Registry

1.   The Registry shall be responsible for the administration and servicing of the International Tribunal.

2.   The Registry shall consist of a Registrar and such other staff as may be required.

3.   The Registrar shall be appointed by the Secretary-General after consultation with the President of the International Tribunal. He or she shall serve for a four-year term and be eligible for reappointment. The terms and conditions of service of the Registrar shall be those of an Assistant Secretary-General of the United Nations.

4.   The staff of the Registry shall be appointed by the Secretary-General on the recommendation of the Registrar.

Article 18
Investigation and preparation of indictment

1.   The Prosecutor shall initiate investigations ex-officio or on the basis of information obtained from any source, particularly from Governments, United Nations organs, intergovernmental and non-governmental organizations. The Prosecutor shall assess the information received or obtained and decide whether there is sufficient basis to proceed.

2.   The Prosecutor shall have the power to question suspects, victims and witnesses, to collect evidence and to conduct on-site investigations. In carrying out these tasks, the Prosecutor may, as appropriate, seek the assistance of the State authorities concerned.

3.   If questioned, the suspect shall be entitled to be assisted by counsel of his own choice, including the right to have legal assistance assigned to him without payment by him in any such case if he does not have sufficient means to pay for it, as well as to necessary translation into and from a language he speaks and understands.

4.   Upon a determination that a prima facie case exists, the Prosecutor shall prepare an indictment containing a concise statement of the facts and the crime or crimes with which the accused is charged

under the Statute. The indictment shall be transmitted to a judge of the Trial Chamber.

Article 19
Review of the indictment

1.   The judge of the Trial Chamber to whom the indictment has been transmitted shall review it. If satisfied that a prima facie case has been established by the Prosecutor, he shall confirm the indictment. If not so satisfied, the indictment shall be dismissed.

2.   Upon confirmation of an indictment, the judge may, at the request of the Prosecutor, issue such orders and warrants for the arrest, detention, surrender or transfer of persons, and any other orders as may be required for the conduct of the trial.

Article 20
Commencement and conduct of trial proceedings

1.   The Trial Chambers shall ensure that a trial is fair and expeditious and that proceedings are conducted in accordance with the rules of procedure and evidence, with full respect for the rights of the accused and due regard for the protection of victims and witnesses.

2.   A person against whom an indictment has been confirmed shall, pursuant to an order or an arrest warrant of the International Tribunal, be taken into custody, immediately informed of the charges against him and transferred to the International Tribunal.

3.   The Trial Chamber shall read the indictment, satisfy itself that the rights of the accused are respected, confirm that the accused understands the indictment, and instruct the accused to enter a plea. The Trial Chamber shall then set the date for trial.

4.   The hearings shall be public unless the Trial Chamber decides to close the proceedings in accordance with its rules of procedure and evidence.

Article 21
Rights of the accused

1.   All persons shall be equal before the International Tribunal.

2.   In the determination of charges against him, the accused shall be entitled to a fair and public hearing, subject to article 22 of the Statute.

3.   The accused shall be presumed innocent until proved guilty according to the provisions of the present Statute.

4.   In the determination of any charge against the accused pursuant to the present Statute, the accused shall be entitled to the following minimum guarantees, in full equality:

(a)   to be informed promptly and in detail in a language which he understands of the nature and cause of the charge against him;

(b)   to have adequate time and facilities for the preparation of his defence and to communicate with counsel of his own choosing;

(c)   to be tried without undue delay;

(d)   to be tried in his presence, and to defend himself in person or through legal assistance of his own choosing; to be informed, if he does not have legal assistance, of this right; and to have legal assistance assigned to him, in any case where the interests of justice so require, and without payment by him in any such case if he does not have sufficient means to pay for it;

(e)   to examine, or have examined, the witnesses against him and to obtain the attendance and examination of witnesses on his behalf under the same conditions as witnesses against him;

(f)   to have the free assistance of an interpreter if he cannot understand or speak the language used in the International Tribunal;

(g)   not to be compelled to testify against himself or to confess guilt.

Annex 2

Article 22
Protection of victims and witnesses

The International Tribunal shall provide in its rules of procedure and evidence for the protection of victims and witnesses. Such protection measures shall include, but shall not be limited to, the conduct of *in camera* proceedings and the protection of the victim's identity.

Article 23
Judgement

1.   The Trial Chambers shall pronounce judgements and impose sentences and penalties on persons convicted of serious violations of international humanitarian law.

2.   The judgement shall be rendered by a majority of the judges of the Trial Chamber, and shall be delivered by the Trial Chamber in public. It shall be accompanied by a reasoned opinion in writing, to which separate or dissenting opinions may be appended.

Article 24
Penalties

1.   The penalty imposed by the Trial Chamber shall be limited to imprisonment. In determining the terms of imprisonment, the Trial Chambers shall have recourse to the general practice regarding prison sentences in the courts of the former Yugoslavia.

2.   In imposing the sentences, the Trial Chambers should take into account such factors as the gravity of the offence and the individual circumstances of the convicted person.

3.   In addition to imprisonment, the Trial Chambers may order the return of any property and proceeds acquired by criminal conduct, including by means of duress, to their rightful owners.

Article 25
Appellate proceedings

1.   The Appeals Chamber shall hear appeals from persons convicted by the Trial Chambers or from the Prosecutor on the following grounds:

    (a)   an error on a question of law invalidating the decision; or

    (b)   an error of fact which has occasioned a miscarriage of justice.

2.   The Appeals Chamber may affirm, reverse or revise the decisions taken by the Trial Chambers.

Article 26
Review proceedings

Where a new fact has been discovered which was not known at the time of the proceedings before the Trial Chambers or the Appeals Chamber and which could have been a decisive factor in reaching the decision, the convicted person or the Prosecutor may submit to the International Tribunal an application for review of the judgement.

Article 27
Enforcement of sentences

Imprisonment shall be served in a State designated by the International Tribunal from a list of States which have indicated to the Security Council their willingness to accept convicted persons. Such imprisonment shall be in accordance with the applicable law of the State concerned, subject to the supervision of the International Tribunal.

Article 28
Pardon or commutation of sentences

If, pursuant to the applicable law of the State in which the convicted person is imprisoned, he or she is eligible for pardon or commutation of sentence, the State concerned shall notify the

International Tribunal accordingly. The President of the International Tribunal, in consultation with the judges, shall decide the matter on the basis of the interests of justice and the general principles of law.

Article 29
Cooperation and judicial assistance

1.   States shall cooperate with the International Tribunal in the investigation and prosecution of persons accused of committing serious violations of international humanitarian law.

2.   States shall comply without undue delay with any request for assistance or an order issued by a Trial Chamber, including, but not limited to:

(a)   the identification and location of persons;
(b)   the taking of testimony and the production of evidence;
(c)   the service of documents;
(d)   the arrest or detention of persons;
(e)   the surrender or the transfer of the accused to the International Tribunal.

Article 30
The status, privileges and immunities
of the International Tribunal

1.   The Convention on the Privileges and Immunities of the United Nations of 13 February 1946 shall apply to the International Tribunal, the judges, the Prosecutor and his staff, and the Registrar and his staff.

2.   The judges, the Prosecutor and the Registrar shall enjoy the privileges and immunities, exemptions and facilities accorded to diplomatic envoys, in accordance with international law.

3.   The staff of the Prosecutor and of the Registrar shall enjoy the privileges and immunities accorded to officials of the United Nations under articles V and VII of the Convention referred to in paragraph 1 of this article.

4.   Other persons, including the accused, required at the seat of the International Tribunal shall be accorded such treatment as is necessary for the proper functioning of the International Tribunal.

Article 31
Seat of the International Tribunal

The International Tribunal shall have its seat at The Hague.

Article 32
Expenses of the International Tribunal

The expenses of the International Tribunal shall be borne by the regular budget of the United Nations in accordance with Article 17 of the Charter of the United Nations.

Article 33
Working languages

The working languages of the International Tribunal shall be English and French.

Article 34
Annual report

The President of the International Tribunal shall submit an annual report of the International Tribunal to the Security Council and to the General Assembly.

ANNEX 3 - 1994 Statute of the International Criminal Tribunal for Rwanda

Having been established by the Security Council acting under Chapter VII of the Charter of the United Nations, the International Criminal Tribunal for the Prosecution of Persons Responsible for Genocide and Other Serious Violations of International Humanitarian Law Committed in the Territory of Rwanda and Rwandan citizens responsible for genocide and other such violations committed in the territory of neighbouring States, between 1 January 1994 and 31 December 1994 (hereinafter referred to as "the International Tribunal for Rwanda") shall function in accordance with the provisions of the present Statute.

Article 1
Competence of the International Tribunal for Rwanda

The International Tribunal for Rwanda shall have the power to prosecute persons responsible for serious violations of international humanitarian law committed in the territory of Rwanda and Rwandan citizens responsible for such violations committed in the territory of neighbouring States, between 1 January 1994 and 31 December 1994, in accordance with the provisions of the present Statute.

Article 2
Genocide

1.   The International Tribunal for Rwanda shall have the power to prosecute persons committing genocide as defined in paragraph 2 of this article or of committing any of the other acts enumerated in paragraph 3 of this article.

2.   Genocide means any of the following acts committed with intent to destroy, in whole or in part, a national, ethnical, racial or religious group, as such:
        (a)   Killing members of the group;

(b)   Causing serious bodily or mental harm to members of the group;

(c)   Deliberately inflicting on the group conditions of life calculated to bring about its physical destruction in whole or in part;

(d)   Imposing measures intended to prevent births within the group;

(e)   Forcibly transferring children of the group to another group.

3.   The following acts shall be punishable:

(a)   Genocide;

(b)   Conspiracy to commit genocide;

(c)   Direct and public incitement to commit genocide;

(d)   Attempt to commit genocide;

(e)   Complicity in genocide.

Article 3
Crimes against humanity

The International Tribunal for Rwanda shall have the power to prosecute persons responsible for the following crimes when committed as part of a widespread or systematic attack against any civilian population on national, political, ethnic, racial or religious grounds:

(a)   Murder;

(b)   Extermination;

(c)   Enslavement;

(d)   Deportation;

(e)   Imprisonment;

(f)   Torture;

(g)   Rape;

(h)   Persecutions on political, racial and religious grounds;

(i)   Other inhumane acts.

Article 4
Violations of Article 3 common to the Geneva Conventions and of Additional Protocol II

The International Tribunal for Rwanda shall have the power to prosecute persons committing or ordering to be committed serious violations of Article 3 common to the Geneva Conventions of 12 August 1949 for the Protection of War Victims, and of Additional Protocol II thereto of 8 June 1977. These violations shall include, but shall not be limited to:

(a)   Violence to life, health and physical or mental well-being of persons, in particular murder as well as cruel treatment such as torture, mutilation or any form of corporal punishment;

(b)   Collective punishments;

(c)   Taking of hostages;

(d)   Acts of terrorism;

(e)   Outrages upon personal dignity, in particular humiliating and degrading treatment, rape, enforced prostitution and any form of indecent assault;

(f)   Pillage;

(g)   The passing of sentences and the carrying out of executions without previous judgement pronounced by a regularly constituted court, affording all the judicial guarantees which are recognized as indispensable by civilized peoples;

(h)   Threats to commit any of the foregoing acts.

Article 5
Personal jurisdiction

The International Tribunal for Rwanda shall have jurisdiction over natural persons pursuant to the provisions of the present Statute.

Article 6
Individual criminal responsibility

1.   A person who planned, instigated, ordered, committed or otherwise aided and abetted in the planning, preparation or execution of a crime referred to in articles 2 to 4 of the present Statute, shall be individually responsible for the crime.

2.   The official position of any accused person, whether as Head of State or Government or as a responsible Government official, shall not relieve such person of criminal responsibility nor mitigate punishment.

3.   The fact that any of the acts referred to in articles 2 to 4 of the present Statute was committed by a subordinate does not relieve his or her superior of criminal responsibility if he or she knew or had reason to know that the subordinate was about to commit such acts or had done so and the superior failed to take the necessary and reasonable measures to prevent such acts or to punish the perpetrators thereof.

4.   The fact that an accused person acted pursuant to an order of a Government or of a superior shall not relieve him or her of criminal responsibility, but may be considered in mitigation of punishment if the International Tribunal for Rwanda determines that justice so requires.

Article 7
Territorial and temporal jurisdiction

The territorial jurisdiction of the International Tribunal for Rwanda shall extend to the territory of Rwanda including its land surface and airspace as well as to the territory of neighbouring States in respect of serious violations of international humanitarian law committed by Rwandan citizens. The temporal jurisdiction of the International Tribunal for Rwanda shall extend to a period beginning on 1 January 1994 and ending on 31 December 1994.

Article 8
Concurrent jurisdiction

1.   The International Tribunal for Rwanda and national courts shall have concurrent jurisdiction to prosecute persons for serious violations of international humanitarian law committed in the territory of Rwanda and Rwandan citizens for such violations committed in the territory of neighbouring States, between 1 January 1994 and 31 December 1994.

2.   The International Tribunal for Rwanda shall have primacy over the national courts of all States. At any stage of the procedure, the International Tribunal for Rwanda may formally request national courts to defer to its competence in accordance with the present Statute and the Rules of Procedure and Evidence of the International Tribunal for Rwanda.

Article 9
Non bis in idem

1.   No person shall be tried before a national court for acts constituting serious violations of international humanitarian law under the present Statute, for which he or she has already been tried by the International Tribunal for Rwanda.

2.   A person who has been tried by a national court for acts constituting serious violations of international humanitarian law may be subsequently tried by the International Tribunal for Rwanda only if:

(a)   The act for which he or she was tried was characterized as an ordinary crime; or

(b)   The national court proceedings were not impartial or independent, were designed to shield the accused from international criminal responsibility, or the case was not diligently prosecuted.

3.   In considering the penalty to be imposed on a person convicted of a crime under the present Statute, the International Tribunal for Rwanda shall take into account the extent to which any penalty imposed by a national court on the same person for the same act has already been served.

Article 10
Organization of the International Tribunal for Rwanda

The International Tribunal for Rwanda shall consist of the following organs:

(a)   The Chambers, comprising two Trial Chambers and an Appeals Chamber;

(b)   The Prosecutor; and

(c)   A Registry.

Article 11
Composition of the Chambers

The Chambers shall be composed of eleven independent judges, no two of whom may be nationals of the same State, who shall serve as follows:

(a)   Three judges shall serve in each of the Trial Chambers;

(b)   Five judges shall serve in the Appeals Chamber.

Article 12
Qualification and election of judges

1.   The judges shall be persons of high moral character, impartiality and integrity who possess the qualifications required in their respective countries for appointment to the highest judicial offices. In the overall composition of the Chambers due account shall be taken of the experience of the judges in criminal law, international law, including international humanitarian law and human rights law.

2.   The members of the Appeals Chamber of the International Tribunal for the Prosecution of Persons Responsible for Serious Violations of International Law Committed in the Territory of the Former Yugoslavia since 1991 (hereinafter referred to as "the International Tribunal for the Former Yugoslavia") shall also serve as the members of the Appeals Chamber of the International Tribunal for Rwanda.

3.   The judges of the Trial Chambers of the International Tribunal for Rwanda shall be elected by the General Assembly from a list submitted by the Security Council, in the following manner:

(a)   The Secretary-General shall invite nominations for judges of the Trial Chambers from States Members of the United Nations and non-member States maintaining permanent observer missions at United Nations Headquarters;

(b)   Within thirty days of the date of the invitation of the Secretary-General, each State may nominate up to two candidates meeting the qualifications set out in paragraph 1 above, no two of whom shall be of the same nationality and neither of whom shall be of the same nationality as any judge on the Appeals Chamber;

(c)   The Secretary-General shall forward the nominations received to the Security Council. From the nominations received the Security Council shall establish a list of not less than twelve and not more than eighteen candidates, taking due account of adequate representation on the International Tribunal for Rwanda of the principal legal systems of the world;

(d)   The President of the Security Council shall transmit the list of candidates to the President of the General Assembly. From that list the General Assembly shall elect the six judges of the Trial Chambers. The candidates who receive an absolute majority of the votes of the States Members of the United Nations and of the non-Member States maintaining permanent observer missions at United Nations Headquarters, shall be declared elected. Should two candidates of the same nationality obtain the required majority vote, the one who received the higher number of votes shall be considered elected.

4.   In the event of a vacancy in the Trial Chambers, after consultation with the Presidents of the Security Council and of the General Assembly, the Secretary-General shall appoint a person meeting the qualifications of paragraph 1 above, for the remainder of the term of office concerned.

5.   The judges of the Trial Chambers shall be elected for a term of four years. The terms and conditions of service shall be those of the judges of the International Tribunal for the Former Yugoslavia. They shall be eligible for re-election.

Article 13
Officers and members of the Chambers

1.   The judges of the International Tribunal for Rwanda shall elect a President.

2.   After consultation with the judges of the International Tribunal for Rwanda, the President shall assign the judges to the Trial Chambers. A judge shall serve only in the Chamber to which he or she was assigned.

3.   The judges of each Trial Chamber shall elect a Presiding Judge, who shall conduct all of the proceedings of that Trial Chamber as a whole.

Article 14
Rules of procedure and evidence

The judges of the International Tribunal for Rwanda shall adopt, for the purpose of proceedings before the International Tribunal for Rwanda, the rules of procedure and evidence for the conduct of the pre-trial phase of the proceedings, trials and appeals, the admission of evidence, the protection of victims and witnesses and other appropriate matters of the International Tribunal for the Former Yugoslavia with such changes as they deem necessary.

Article 15
The Prosecutor

1.   The Prosecutor shall be responsible for the investigation and prosecution of persons responsible for serious violations of international humanitarian law committed in the territory of Rwanda and Rwandan citizens responsible for such violations committed in the territory of neighbouring States, between 1 January 1994 and 31 December 1994.

2.   The Prosecutor shall act independently as a separate organ of the International Tribunal for Rwanda. He or she shall not seek or receive instructions from any Government or from any other source.

3.   The Prosecutor of the International Tribunal for the Former Yugoslavia shall also serve as the Prosecutor of the International Tribunal for Rwanda. He or she shall have additional staff, including an additional Deputy Prosecutor, to assist with prosecutions before the International Tribunal for Rwanda. Such staff shall be appointed by the Secretary-General on the recommendation of the Prosecutor.

Article 16
The Registry

1.   The Registry shall be responsible for the administration and servicing of the International Tribunal for Rwanda.

2.   The Registry shall consist of a Registrar and such other staff as may be required.

3.   The Registrar shall be appointed by the Secretary-
-General after consultation with the President of the International
Tribunal for Rwanda. He or she shall serve for a four-year term and
be eligible for reappointment. The terms and conditions of service of
the Registrar shall be those of an Assistant Secretary-General of the
United Nations.

4.   The staff of the Registry shall be appointed by the
Secretary-General on the recommendation of the Registrar.

Article 17
Investigation and preparation of indictment

1.   The Prosecutor shall initiate investigations ex-officio or
on the basis of information obtained from any source, particularly from
Governments, United Nations organs, intergovernmental and non--
governmental organizations. The Prosecutor shall assess the
information received or obtained and decide whether there is sufficient
basis to proceed.

2.   The Prosecutor shall have the power to question
suspects, victims and witnesses, to collect evidence and to conduct
on-site investigations. In carrying out these tasks, the Prosecutor
may, as appropriate, seek the assistance of the State authorities
concerned.

3.   If questioned, the suspect shall be entitled to be
assisted by counsel of his or her own choice, including the right to
have legal assistance assigned to the suspect without payment by him
or her in any such case if he or she does not have sufficient means
to pay for it, as well as to necessary translation into and from a
language he or she speaks and understands.

4.   Upon a determination that a prima facie case exists, the
Prosecutor shall prepare an indictment containing a concise statement
of the facts and the crime or crimes with which the accused is charged
under the Statute. The indictment shall be transmitted to a judge of
the Trial Chamber.

Article 18
Review of the indictment

1.　　The judge of the Trial Chamber to whom the indictment has been transmitted shall review it. If satisfied that a prima facie case has been established by the Prosecutor, he or she shall confirm the indictment. If not so satisfied, the indictment shall be dismissed.

2.　　Upon confirmation of an indictment, the judge may, at the request of the Prosecutor, issue such orders and warrants for the arrest, detention, surrender or transfer of persons, and any other orders as may be required for the conduct of the trial.

Article 19
Commencement and conduct of trial proceedings

1.　　The Trial Chambers shall ensure that a trial is fair and expeditious and that proceedings are conducted in accordance with the rules of procedure and evidence, with full respect for the rights of the accused and due regard for the protection of victims and witnesses.

2.　　A person against whom an indictment has been confirmed shall, pursuant to an order or an arrest warrant of the International Tribunal for Rwanda, be taken into custody, immediately informed of the charges against him or her and transferred to the International Tribunal for Rwanda.

3.　　The Trial Chamber shall read the indictment, satisfy itself that the rights of the accused are respected, confirm that the accused understands the indictment, and instruct the accused to enter a plea. The Trial Chamber shall then set the date for trial.

4.　　The hearings shall be public unless the Trial Chamber decides to close the proceedings in accordance with its rules of procedure and evidence.

Article 20
Rights of the accused

1.　　All persons shall be equal before the International Tribunal for Rwanda.

2.   In the determination of charges against him or her, the accused shall be entitled to a fair and public hearing, subject to article 21 of the Statute.

3.   The accused shall be presumed innocent until proved guilty according to the provisions of the present Statute.

4.   In the determination of any charge against the accused pursuant to the present Statute, the accused shall be entitled to the following minimum guarantees, in full equality:

(a)   To be informed promptly and in detail in a language which he or she understands of the nature and cause of the charge against him or her;

(b)   To have adequate time and facilities for the preparation of his or her defence and to communicate with counsel of his or her own choosing;

(c)   To be tried without undue delay;

(d)   To be tried in his or her presence, and to defend himself or herself in person or through legal assistance of his or her own choosing; to be informed, if he or she does not have legal assistance, of this right; and to have legal assistance assigned to him or her, in any case where the interests of justice so require, and without payment by him or her in any such case if he or she does not have sufficient means to pay for it;

(e)   To examine, or have examined, the witnesses against him or her and to obtain the attendance and examination of witnesses on his or her behalf under the same conditions as witnesses against him or her;

(f)   To have the free assistance of an interpreter if he or she cannot understand or speak the language used in the International Tribunal for Rwanda;

(g)   Not to be compelled to testify against himself or herself or to confess guilt.

Article 21
Protection of victims and witnesses

The International Tribunal for Rwanda shall provide in its rules of procedure and evidence for the protection of victims and witnesses. Such protection measures shall include, but shall not be limited to, the conduct of in camera proceedings and the protection of the victim's identity.

Article 22
Judgement

1.	The Trial Chambers shall pronounce judgements and impose sentences and penalties on persons convicted of serious violations of international humanitarian law.

2.	The judgement shall be rendered by a majority of the judges of the Trial Chamber, and shall be delivered by the Trial Chamber in public. It shall be accompanied by a reasoned opinion in writing, to which separate or dissenting opinions may be appended.

Article 23
Penalties

1.	The penalty imposed by the Trial Chamber shall be limited to imprisonment. In determining the terms of imprisonment, the Trial Chambers shall have recourse to the general practice regarding prison sentences in the courts of Rwanda.

2.	In imposing the sentences, the Trial Chambers should take into account such factors as the gravity of the offence and the individual circumstances of the convicted person.

3.	In addition to imprisonment, the Trial Chambers may order the return of any property and proceeds acquired by criminal conduct, including by means of duress, to their rightful owners.

Article 24
Appellate proceedings

1.	The Appeals Chamber shall hear appeals from persons convicted by the Trial Chambers or from the Prosecutor on the following grounds:
	(a)	An error on a question of law invalidating the decision; or
	(b)	An error of fact which has occasioned a miscarriage of justice.

2.   The Appeals Chamber may affirm, reverse or revise the decisions taken by the Trial Chambers.

Article 25
Review proceedings

Where a new fact has been discovered which was not known at the time of the proceedings before the Trial Chambers or the Appeals Chamber and which could have been a decisive factor in reaching the decision, the convicted person or the Prosecutor may submit to the International Tribunal for Rwanda an application for review of the judgement.

Article 26
Enforcement of sentences

Imprisonment shall be served in Rwanda or any of the States on a list of States which have indicated to the Security Council their willingness to accept convicted persons, as designated by the International Tribunal for Rwanda. Such imprisonment shall be in accordance with the applicable law of the State concerned, subject to the supervision of the International Tribunal for Rwanda.

Article 27
Pardon or commutation of sentences

If, pursuant to the applicable law of the State in which the convicted person is imprisoned, he or she is eligible for pardon or commutation of sentence, the State concerned shall notify the International Tribunal for Rwanda accordingly. There shall only be pardon or commutation of sentence if the President of the International Tribunal for Rwanda, in consultation with the judges, so decides on the basis of the interests of justice and the general principles of law.

Article 28
Cooperation and judicial assistance

1.   States shall cooperate with the International Tribunal for Rwanda in the investigation and prosecution of persons accused of committing serious violations of international humanitarian law.

2.   States shall comply without undue delay with any request for assistance or an order issued by a Trial Chamber, including, but not limited to:

(a)   The identification and location of persons;

(b)   The taking of testimony and the production of evidence;

(c)   The service of documents;

(d)   The arrest or detention of persons;

(e)   The surrender or the transfer of the accused to the International Tribunal for Rwanda.

Article 29
The status, privileges and immunities of the International Tribunal for Rwanda

1.   The Convention on the Privileges and Immunities of the United Nations of 13 February 1946 shall apply to the International Tribunal for Rwanda, the judges, the Prosecutor and his or her staff, and the Registrar and his or her staff.

2.   The judges, the Prosecutor and the Registrar shall enjoy the privileges and immunities, exemptions and facilities accorded to diplomatic envoys, in accordance with international law.

3.   The staff of the Prosecutor and of the Registrar shall enjoy the privileges and immunities accorded to officials of the United Nations under articles V and VII of the Convention referred to in paragraph 1 of this article.

4.   Other persons, including the accused, required at the seat or meeting place of the International Tribunal for Rwanda shall be accorded such treatment as is necessary for the proper functioning of the International Tribunal for Rwanda.

Article 30
Expenses of the International Tribunal for Rwanda

The expenses of the International Tribunal for Rwanda shall be expenses of the Organization in accordance with Article 17 of the Charter of the United Nations.

Article 31
Working languages

The working languages of the International Tribunal shall be English and French.

Article 32
Annual report

The President of the International Tribunal for Rwanda shall submit an annual report of the International Tribunal for Rwanda to the Security Council and to the General Assembly.

- - -

ANNEX 4 - 1994 ILC Draft Statute for an International Criminal Court

(A/CN.4/L.491/Rev.1 of 8 July 1994)

WORKING GROUP ON A DRAFT STATUTE FOR AN INTERNATIONAL CRIMINAL COURT

Report of the Working Group

CONTENTS

A. INTRODUCTION

1.   Pursuant to the decision taken by the International Law Commission at its 2331st and 2332nd meetings held on 5 May 1994 to reconvene the Working Group on a draft statute for an international

criminal court,[1] the Working Group held 25 meetings between 10 May and 7 July 1994.

2.   The mandate given by the Commission to the Working Group was in accordance with paragraphs 4, 5 and 6 of General Assembly resolution 48/31 of December 1993.   In those paragraphs, the Assembly had taken note with appreciation of chapter 11 of the report of the International Law Commission, entitled "Draft Code of Crimes against the Peace and Security of Mankind" which was devoted to the question of a draft statute for an international criminal court; invited States to submit to the Secretary-General by 15 February 1994, as requested by the International Law Commission, written comments on the draft articles proposed by the Working Group on a draft statute for an international criminal court and requested the International Law Commission to continue its work as a matter of priority on this question with a view to elaborating a draft statute if possible at its forty-sixth session in 1994, taking into account the views expressed during the debate in the Sixth Committee as well as any written comments received from States.

3.   In performing its mandate, the Working Group had before it the report of the Working Group on the question of an international criminal jurisdiction included in the Commission's report at its forty-fourth (1992) session (A/47/10, Annex); the report of the Working Group on a draft statute for an international criminal court included in the Commission's report at its previous (1993) session (A/48/10, Annex); the eleventh report on the topic "Draft Code of Crimes against the Peace and Security of Mankind" presented by the Special Rapporteur, Mr. Doudou Thiam at the previous session (A/CN.4/449 and Corr.1, English only); the comments of Governments on the report of the Working Group on the question of an international criminal jurisdiction (document A/CN.4/458 and Adds. 1 to 5); chapter B of the

---

[1]   The composition of the Working Group was as follows: Mr. Crawford, Chairman, Mr. Thiam, ex officio member as Special Rapporteur on the Draft Code of Crimes against the Peace and Security of Mankind, Mr. Kabatsi, *ex officio* as General Rapporteur, Mr. Al-Baharna, Mr. Al-Khasawneh, Mr. Arangio-Ruiz, Mr. Bennouna, Mr. Bowett, Mr. de Saram, Mr. Eiriksson, Mr. Elaraby, Mr. Fomba, Mr. Guney, Mr. He, Mr. Idris, Mr. Rao, Mr. Razafindralambo, Mr. Robinson, Mr. Rosenstock, Mr. Tomuschat, Mr. Vereshchetin, Mr. Villagran-Kramer, Mr. Yankov.

topical summary prepared by the Secretariat of the discussion held in the Sixth Committee of the General Assembly during the forty-eighth session, on the report of the International Law Commission on the work of its forty-fifth session (A/CN.4/446); the report of the Secretary-General pursuant to paragraph 2 of Security Council resolution 808 (1993) (document S/25704); the rules of procedure and evidence adopted by the International Tribunal for the Prosecution of Persons Responsible for Serious Violations of International Humanitarian Law Committed in the Territory of Former Yugoslavia since 1991 (document IT/32 of 14 March 1994) as well as the following informal documents prepared by the Secretariat of the Working Group: (a) a compilation of draft statutes for an international criminal court elaborated in the past either within the framework of United Nations or by other public or private entities;

(b) a compilation of conventions or relevant provisions of conventions relative to the possible subject-matter jurisdiction of an international criminal court and (c) a study on possible ways whereby an international criminal court might enter into relationship with the United Nations.

4.   The Working Group proceeded to a re-examination chapter by chapter, and article by article of the preliminary draft statute for an international criminal court annexed to the Commission's report at the preceding session [2] bearing in mind, *inter alia*, (a) the need to streamline and simplify the articles concerning the subject matter jurisdiction of the Court, while better determining the extent of such jurisdiction; (b) the fact that the Court's system should be conceived as complementary with national systems which function on the basis of existing mechanisms for international cooperation and judicial assistance and (c) the need for coordinating the common articles to be found in the draft statute for an international criminal court and in the draft code of crimes against the peace and security of mankind.

5.   In reshaping the provisions concerning the subject-matter jurisdiction of the Court, the Working Group abandoned the two-strand approach contained in articles 22 and 26 of the draft statute elaborated at the Commission's previous session, and specifically spelled out, under the Court's jurisdiction, a number of crimes under general

---

[2]   A/48/10, Annex.

international law, in addition to the Court's jurisdiction over certain crimes arising from or pursuant to a number of multilateral treaties, which were listed in an annex to the draft statute.

6.   The draft statute prepared by the Working Group is divided into eight main parts: Part 1 on Establishment of the Court; Part 2 on Composition and Administration of the Court; Part 3 on Jurisdiction of the Court; Part 4 on Investigation and Prosecution; Part 5 on the Trial; Part 6 on Appeal and Review; Part 7 on International Cooperation and Judicial Assistance; and Part 8 on Enforcement.

7.   The commentaries to the draft articles explain the special concerns which the Working Group has addressed in considering a provision on a given subject matter and the various views to which it gave rise or the reservations which it aroused.

8.   In drafting the statute, the Working Group did not purport to adjust itself to any specific criminal legal system but rather, to amalgamate into a coherent whole the most appropriate elements for the goals envisaged, having regard to existing treaties, earlier proposals for an international court or tribunals and relevant provisions in national criminal justice systems within the different legal traditions.

9.   Careful note was also taken of the various provisions regulating the International Tribunal for the Prosecution of Persons Responsible for Serious Violations of International Humanitarian Law Committed in the Territory of Former Yugoslavia since 1991.

10.   It is also to be noted that the Working Group has conceived the statute for an international criminal court as an attachment to a future international convention on the matter and has drafted the statute's provisions accordingly.

11.   The Working Group prepared a preliminary version of the revised draft statute which was included in its report of 17 June 1994 to the Commission (document A/CN.4/L.491 and Corr.1 (French only) and Corr.2 (Chinese only)).

12.   The Commission considered the above-mentioned report at its 2356th to 2361st meetings held from 24 June to 5 July 1994.

13.   At the six meetings it held between 28 June and 7 July 1994, the Working Group re-examined its preliminary version of the revised draft statute, bearing in mind the comments and observations made in plenary.

14.   Following is the revised draft statute for an international criminal court, with commentaries thereto, prepared by the Working Group.

Annex 4

B. REVISED DRAFT STATUTE FOR AN
INTERNATIONAL CRIMINAL COURT

Table of Contents

STATUTE OF THE INTERNATIONAL CRIMINAL COURT

The States parties to this Statute,

Desiring to further international cooperation to enhance the effective suppression and prosecution of crimes of international concern, and for that purpose to establish an international criminal court;

Emphasizing that such a court is intended to exercise jurisdiction only over the most serious crimes of concern to the international community as a whole;

Emphasizing further that such a court is intended to be complementary to national criminal justice systems in cases where such trial procedures may not be available or may be ineffective;

Have agreed as follows:

PART 1. ESTABLISHMENT OF THE COURT

Article 1
The Court

There is established an International Criminal Court ("the Court"), whose jurisdiction and functioning shall be governed by the provisions of this Statute.

Article 2
Relationship of the Court to the United Nations

The President, with the approval of the States parties to this Statute ("States parties"), may conclude an agreement establishing an appropriate relationship between the Court and the United Nations.

Article 3
Seat of the Court

1.   The seat of the Court shall be established at ... in ... ("the host State").

2.   The President, with the approval of the States parties, may conclude an agreement with the host State establishing the relationship between that State and the Court.

3.   The Court may exercise its powers and functions on the territory of any State party and, by special agreement, on the territory of any other State.

Article 4
Status and legal capacity

1.   The Court is a permanent institution open to States parties in accordance with this Statute. It shall act when required to consider a case submitted to it.

2.   The Court shall enjoy in the territory of each State party such legal capacity as may be necessary for the exercise of its functions and the fulfilment of its purposes.

PART 2. COMPOSITION AND ADMINISTRATION OF THE COURT

Article 5
Organs of the Court

The Court consists of the following organs:
- (a)   a Presidency, as provided in article 8;
- (b)   an Appeals Chamber, Trial Chambers and other chambers, as provided in article 9;
- (c)   a Procuracy, as provided in article 12; and
- (d)   a Registry, as provided in article 13.

Article 6
Qualification and election of judges

1.   The judges of the Court shall be persons of high moral character, impartiality and integrity who possess the qualifications required in their respective countries for appointment to the highest judicial offices, and have, in addition: ·
   (a)   criminal trial experience;
   (b)   recognized competence in international
           law.
2.   Each State party may nominate for election not more than two persons, of different nationality, who possess the qualification specified in paragraph 1 (a) or that specified in paragraph 1 (b), and who are willing to serve as may be required on the Court.
3.   Eighteen judges shall be elected, in accordance with the Rules, by an absolute majority vote of the States parties by secret ballot. Ten judges shall first be elected, from among the persons nominated as having the qualification referred to in paragraph 1 (a). Eight judges shall then be elected, by secret ballot, from among the persons nominated as having the qualification referred to in paragraph 1 (b).
4.   No two judges may be nationals of the same State.
5.   States parties should bear in mind in the election of the judges that the representation of the principal legal systems of the world should be assured.
6.   Judges hold office for a term of nine years and, subject to paragraph 7 and article 7 (2), are not eligible for re-election. A judge shall, however, continue in office in order to complete any case the hearing of which has commenced.
7.   At the first election, six judges chosen by lot shall serve for a term of three years and are eligible for re-election; six judges chosen by lot shall serve for a term of six years, and the remainder shall serve for a term of nine years.
8.   Judges nominated as having the qualification referred to in paragraph 1 (a) or 1 (b), as the case may be shall be replaced by persons nominated as having the same qualification.

Article 7
Judicial vacancies

1.   In the event of a vacancy, a replacement judge shall be elected in accordance with article 6.
2.   A judge elected to fill a vacancy shall serve for the remainder of the predecessor's term, and if that period is less than five years is eligible for re-election for a further term.

Article 8
The Presidency

1.   The President, the first and second Vice-Presidents and two alternate Vice-Presidents shall be elected by an absolute majority of the judges. They shall serve for a term of three years or until the end of their term of office as judges, whichever is earlier.
2.   The first or second Vice-President, as the case may be, may act in place of the President on any occasion where the President is unavailable or disqualified. An alternate Vice-President may act in place of either Vice-President as required.
3.   The President and the Vice-Presidents shall constitute the Presidency which shall be responsible for:
         (a)   the due administration of the Court; and
         (b)   the other functions conferred on it by this Statute.
4.   Unless otherwise indicated, pre-trial and other procedural functions conferred under this Statute on the Court may be exercised by the Presidency in any case where a chamber of the Court is not seized of the matter.
5.   The Presidency may, in accordance with the Rules, delegate to one or more judges the exercise of a power vested in it under articles 26 (3), 27 (4), 28, 29 or 30 (3) in relation to a case, during the period before a Trial Chamber is established for that case.

Article 9
Chambers

1.   As soon as possible after each election of judges to the Court, the Presidency shall in accordance with the Rules constitute an

Appeals Chamber consisting of the President and six other judges, of whom at least three shall be judges elected from persons nominated as having the qualification referred to in article 5 (1) (b). The President shall preside over the Appeals Chamber.

2.   The Appeals Chamber shall be constituted for a term of three years. Members of the Appeals Chamber shall continue to sit on the Chamber after that term in order to complete hearing any case.

3.   Judges may be renewed as members of the Appeals Chamber for a second or subsequent term.

4.   Judges not members of the Appeals Chamber shall be available to serve on Trial Chambers and other chambers required by this Statute, and to act as substitute members of the Appeals Chamber in case a member of that Chamber is unavailable or disqualified.

5.   The Presidency shall nominate in accordance with the Rules five such judges to be members of the Trial Chamber for a given case. A Trial Chamber shall include at least three judges elected from persons nominated as having the qualifications referred to in article 5 (1) (a).

6.   The Rules may provide for alternate judges to be nominated to attend a trial and to act as judges in the event that a judge dies or becomes unavailable during the course of the trial.

7.   No judge who is a national of a complainant State or of a State of which the accused is a national shall be a member of a chamber dealing with the case.

Article 10
Independence of the judges

1.   In performing their functions, the judges shall be independent.

2.   Judges shall not engage in any activity which is likely to interfere with their judicial functions or to affect confidence in their independence. In particular, they shall not while holding the office of judge be a member of the legislative or executive branches of the Government of a State, or of a body responsible for the investigation or prosecution of crimes.

3.   Any question as to the application of paragraph 2 shall be decided by the Presidency.

4.   On the recommendation of the Presidency, the States parties may by two-thirds majority decide that the work-load of the Court requires that the judges should serve on a full-time basis. In that case:

   (a)   existing judges who elect to serve on a
          full-time basis shall not hold any other
          office or employment; and
   (b)   judges subsequently elected shall not
          hold any other office or employment.

Article 11
Excusing and disqualification of judges

1.   The Presidency at the request of a judge may excuse that judge from the exercise of a function under this Statute.
2.   Judges shall not participate in any case in which they have previously been involved in any capacity or in which their impartiality might reasonably be doubted on any ground, including an actual, apparent or potential conflict of interest.
3.   The Prosecutor or the accused may request the disqualification of a judge under paragraph 2.
4.   Any question as to the disqualification of a judge shall be decided by an absolute majority of the Chamber concerned. The challenged judge shall not take part in the decision.

Article 12
The Procuracy

1.   The Procuracy is an independent organ of the Court responsible for the investigation of complaints made in accordance with this Statute and for the conduct of prosecutions. A member of the Procuracy shall not seek or act on instructions from any external source.
2.   The Procuracy shall be headed by the Prosecutor, assisted by one or more Deputy Prosecutors, who may act in place of the Prosecutor in case of the latter's unavailability. The Prosecutor and the Deputy Prosecutors must be of different nationalities. The Prosecutor may appoint such other qualified staff as may be required.

3.   The Prosecutor and Deputy Prosecutors shall be of high moral character and possess high competence and experience in the prosecution of criminal cases. They shall be elected by secret ballot by an absolute majority of the States parties, from among candidates nominated by them. Unless a shorter term is otherwise decided on at the time of their election, they shall hold office for a term of five years and are eligible for re-election.

4.   The States parties may elect the Prosecutor or a Deputy Prosecutor on the basis of availability to serve as required.

5.   The Prosecutor and Deputy Prosecutors shall not act in relation to a complaint involving a person of their own nationality.

6.   The Presidency may excuse the Prosecutor or Deputy Prosecutor at their request from acting in a particular case, and shall decide any question raised in a particular case as to the disqualification of the Prosecutor or a Deputy Prosecutor.

7.   The staff of the Procuracy shall be subject to Staff Regulations drawn up by the Prosecutor so far as possible in conformity with the United Nations Staff Regulations and Staff Rules, and approved by the Presidency.

Article 13
The Registry

1.   On the proposal of the Presidency, the judges by an absolute majority and by secret ballot shall elect a Registrar, who shall be the principal administrative officer of the Court. They may in the same manner elect a Deputy Registrar.

2.   The Registrar shall hold office for a term of five years, is eligible for re-election, and shall be available on a full-time basis. The Deputy Registrar shall hold office for a term of five years or such shorter term as may be decided on, and may be elected on the basis of availability to serve as required.

3.   The Presidency may appoint or authorize the Registrar to appoint such other staff of the Registry as may be necessary.

4.   The staff of the Registry shall be subject to Staff Regulations drawn up by the Registrar so far as possible in conformity with the United Nations Staff Regulations and Staff Rules, and approved by the Presidency.

Article 14
Solemn undertaking

Before first exercising their functions under this Statute, judges and other officers of the Court shall make a public and solemn undertaking to do so impartially and conscientiously.

Article 15
Loss of office

1.   A judge, the Prosecutor or other officer of the Court who is found to have committed misconduct or a serious breach of this Statute, or to be unable to perform the functions required by this Statute because of long-term illness or disability, shall cease to hold office.
2.   A decision as to the loss of office under paragraph 1 shall be made by secret ballot:
    (a)   in the case of the Prosecutor, by an absolute majority of States parties;
    (b)   in any other case, by a two-thirds majority of the judges.
4.   The judge, the Prosecutor or other officer whose conduct or fitness for office is impugned shall have full opportunity to present evidence and to make submissions but shall not otherwise participate in the discussion of the question.

Article 16
Privileges and immunities

1.   The judges, the Prosecutor, the Deputy Prosecutors and the staff of the Procuracy, the Registrar and the Deputy Registrar shall enjoy the privileges, immunities and facilities of a diplomatic agent within the meaning of the Vienna Convention on Diplomatic Relations of 16 April 1961.
2.   The staff of the Registry shall enjoy the privileges, immunities and facilities necessary to the performance of their functions.
3.   Counsel, experts and witnesses before the Court shall enjoy the privileges and immunities necessary to the independent exercise of their duties.

4.   The judges may by an absolute majority decide to revoke a privilege or waive an immunity conferred by this article, other than an immunity of a judge, the Prosecutor or Registrar as such. In the case of other officers and staff of the Procuracy or Registry, they may do so only on the recommendation of the Prosecutor or Registrar, as the case may be.

Article 17
Allowances and expenses

1.   The President shall receive an annual allowance.
2.   The Vice-Presidents shall receive a special allowance for each day they exercise the functions of the President.
3.   Subject to paragraph 4, the judges shall receive a daily allowance during the period in which they exercise their functions. They may continue to receive a salary payable in respect of another position occupied by them consistently with article 10.
4.   If it is decided under article 10 (4) that judges shall thereafter serve on a full-time basis, existing judges who elect to serve on a full-time basis, and all judges subsequently elected, shall be paid a salary.

Article 18
Working languages

The working languages of the Court shall be English and French.

Article 19
Rules of the Court

1.   Subject to paragraph 2, the judges may by an absolute majority make rules for the functioning of the Court in accordance with this Statute, including rules regulating:
   (a)   the conduct of investigations;
   (b)   the procedure to be followed and the
            rules of evidence to be applied;
   (c)   any other matter which is necessary for
            the implementation of this Statute.

2.   The initial Rules of the Court shall be drafted by the judges within six months of the first elections for the Court, and submitted to a conference of States parties for approval. The judges may decide that a rule subsequently made under paragraph 1 should also be submitted to a conference of States parties for approval.

3.   In any case to which paragraph 2 does not apply, rules made under paragraph 1 shall be transmitted to States parties and may be confirmed by the Presidency unless, within six months after transmission, a majority of States parties have communicated in writing their objections.

4.   A rule may provide for its provisional application in the period prior to its approval or confirmation. A rule not approved or confirmed shall lapse.

PART 3. JURISDICTION OF THE COURT

Article 20
Crimes within the jurisdiction of the Court

The Court has jurisdiction in accordance with this Statute with respect to the following crimes:

(a)   the crime of genocide;

(b)   the crime of aggression;

(c)   serious violations of the laws and customs applicable in armed conflict;

(d)   crimes against humanity;

(e)   crimes, established under or pursuant to the treaty provisions listed in the Annex, which, having regard to the conduct alleged, constitute exceptionally serious crimes of international concern.

Article 21
Preconditions to the exercise of jurisdiction

1.   The Court may exercise its jurisdiction over a person in respect of a crime under article 20 if:

(a)   in a case of genocide, a complaint is
       brought under article 25 (1);
(b)   in any other case, a complaint is brought
       under article 25 (2) and the jurisdiction
       of the Court in respect of the crime is
       accepted under article 22.
       (i)   by the State which has custody of the suspect
               in respect of the crime (the custodial State),
               and
       (ii)   by the State on whose territory the act or
               omission in question occurred.

2.   If, with respect to a crime to which paragraph 1 (b) applies, the
custodial State has received, under an international agreement, a
request from another State to surrender a suspect for the purposes of
prosecution, then, unless the request is rejected, the acceptance by
the requesting State of the Court's jurisdiction with respect of the
crime is also required.

3.   If a State party whose acceptance is required under paragraph
1 [b] [i] has not accepted the jurisdiction of the Court but is a party to
the treaty in question, that State shall, as applicable, take all necessary steps to extradite the suspect to a requesting State for the
purpose of prosecution or to submit the case to its own prosecution
authorities for that purpose.

Article 22
Acceptance of the jurisdiction of the
Court for the purposes of article 21

1.   A State party to this Statute may:
(a)   at the time it expresses its consent to be
       bound by the Statute, by declaration
       lodged with the depositary; or
(b)   at a later time, by declaration lodged
       with the Registrar;
accept the jurisdiction of the Court with respect to such of the crimes
referred to in article 20 as it specifies in the declaration.

2.   A declaration may be of general application, or may be limited to particular conduct or to conduct committed during a particular period of time.

3.   A declaration may be made for a specified period, in which case it may not be withdrawn before the end of that period, or for an unspecified period, in which case it may be withdrawn only upon giving six months' notice of withdrawal to the Registrar. Withdrawal does not affect proceedings already commenced under this Statute.

4.   If under article 21 the acceptance of a State which is not a party to this Statute is required, that State may, by declaration lodged with the Registrar, consent to the Court exercising jurisdiction with respect to the crime.

Article 23
Action by the Security Council

1.   Notwithstanding article 21, the Court has jurisdiction in accordance with this Statute in respect of crimes referred to in Article 20 as a consequence of the referral of a matter to the Court by the Security Council acting under Chapter VII of the Charter of the United Nations.

2.   A complaint of or directly related to an act of aggression may not be brought under this Statute unless the Security Council has first determined that a State has committed the act of aggression which is the subject of the complaint.

3.   No prosecution may be commenced under this Statute arising from a situation which is being dealt with by the Security Council as a threat to or breach of the peace or an act of aggression under Chapter VII of the Charter, unless the Security Council otherwise decides.

Article 24
Duty of the Court as to jurisdiction

The Court shall satisfy itself that it has jurisdiction in any case brought before it.

PART 4. INVESTIGATION AND PROSECUTION

Article 25
Complaint

1.   A State party which is also a Contracting Party to the Convention on the Prevention and Punishment of the Crime of Genocide of 9 December 1948 may lodge a complaint with the Prosecutor alleging that a crime of genocide appears to have been committed.

2.   A State party which accepts the jurisdiction of the Court under article 22 with respect to a crime may lodge a complaint with the Prosecutor alleging that such a crime appears to have been committed.

3.   As far as possible a complaint shall specify the circumstances of the alleged crime and the identity and whereabouts of any suspect, and be accompanied by such supporting documentation as is available to the complainant State.

4.   In any case to which article 23 (1) applies, a complaint is not required for the initiation of an investigation.

Article 26
Investigation of alleged crimes

1.   On receiving a complaint or upon notification of a decision of the Security Council referred to in article 23 (1), the Prosecutor shall initiate an investigation unless the Prosecutor decides that there is no possible basis for a prosecution under this Statute, in which case the Prosecutor shall so inform the Presidency.

2.   The Prosecutor may:
- (a)   request the presence of and question suspects, victims and witnesses;
- (b)   collect documentary and other evidence;
- (c)   conduct on-site investigations;
- (d)   take necessary measures to ensure the confidentiality of information or the protection of any person;
- (e)   as appropriate, seek the cooperation of any State or of the United Nations.

3.   The Presidency may, at the request of the Prosecutor, issue such subpoenas and warrants as may be required for the purposes of an investigation, including a warrant under article 28 for the provisional arrest of a suspect.

4.   If, upon investigation and having regard *inter alia* to the matters referred to in article 35, the Prosecutor concludes that there is no sufficient basis for a prosecution under this Statute, the Prosecutor shall so inform the Presidency giving details of the nature and basis of the complaint and of the reasons for not filing an indictment.

5.   At the request of a complainant State or, in a case to which article 23 applies, the Security Council, the Presidency shall review a decision of the Prosecutor not to initiate an investigation or not to file an indictment, and may request the Prosecutor to reconsider the decision.

6.   A person suspected of a crime under this Statute shall:

    (a)   prior to being questioned, be informed that the person is a suspect and of the rights:

        (i)   to remain silent, without such silence being a consideration in the determination of guilt or innocence; and

        (ii)   to have the assistance of counsel of the suspect's choice or, if the suspect lacks the means to retain counsel, to have legal assistance assigned by the Court;

    (b)   not be compelled to testify or to confess guilt; and

    (c)   if questioned in a language other than a language the suspect understands and speaks, be provided with competent interpretation services and with a translation of any document on which the suspect is to be questioned.

Article 27
Commencement of prosecution

1.   If upon investigation the Prosecutor concludes that there is a prima facie case, the Prosecutor shall file with the Registrar an indictment containing a concise statement of the allegations of fact and of the crime or crimes with which the suspect is charged.

2.   The Presidency shall examine the indictment and any supporting material and determine:

  (a)   whether a prima facie case exists with respect to a crime within the jurisdiction of the Court; and

  (b)   whether, having regard, *inter alia*, to the matters referred to in article 35, the case should on the information available be heard by the Court.

If so, it shall confirm the indictment and establish a trial chamber in accordance with article 9.

3.   If after any adjournment that may be necessary to allow additional material to be produced, the Presidency decides not to confirm the indictment, it shall so inform the complainant State and shall order the release of any suspect who has been provisionally arrested under article 28 (1).

4.   The Presidency may at the request of the Prosecutor amend the indictment, in which case it shall make any necessary orders to ensure that the accused is notified of the amendment and has adequate time to prepare a defence.

5.   The Presidency may make any further orders required for the conduct of the trial, including an order:

  (a)   determining the language or languages to be used during the trial;

  (b)   requiring the disclosure to the defence, within a sufficient time before the trial to enable the preparation of the defence, of documentary or other evidence available to the Prosecutor, whether or not the Prosecutor intends to rely on that evidence;

(c)   providing for the exchange of information between the Prosecutor and the defence, so that both parties are sufficiently aware of the issues to be decided at the trial;

(d)   providing for the protection of the accused, victims, witnesses and confidential information.

Article 28

Arrest

1.   At any time after an investigation has been initiated, the Presidency may at the request of the Prosecutor issue a warrant for the provisional arrest of a suspect if:

(a)   there is probable cause to believe that the suspect may have committed a crime within the jurisdiction of the Court; and

(b)   the suspect may not be available to stand trial unless provisionally arrested.

2.   A suspect who has been provisionally arrested is entitled to release from arrest if the indictment has not been confirmed within 90 days of the arrest, or such longer time as the Presidency may allow.

3.   As soon as practicable after the confirmation of the indictment, the Prosecutor shall seek from the Presidency a warrant for the arrest and transfer of the accused. The Presidency shall issue such a warrant unless it is satisfied that:

(a)   the accused will voluntarily appear for trial; or

(b)   there are special circumstances making it unnecessary for the time being to issue the warrant.

4.   A person arrested shall be informed at the time of arrest of the reasons for the arrest and shall be promptly informed of any charges.

Article 29
Pre-trial detention or release

1.   A person arrested shall be brought promptly before a judicial officer of the State where the arrest occurred. The judicial officer shall determine, in accordance with the procedures applicable in that State, that the warrant has been duly served and that the rights of the accused have been respected.

2.   A person arrested may apply to the Presidency for release pending trial. The Presidency may release the person unconditionally or on bail if it is satisfied that the accused will appear at the trial.

3.   A person arrested may apply to the Presidency for a determination of the lawfulness under this Statute of the arrest or detention. If the Presidency decides that the arrest or detention were unlawful, it shall order the release of the accused, and may award compensation.

4.   A person arrested shall be held, pending trial or release on bail, in an appropriate place of detention in the arresting State, in the State in which the trial is to be held, or, if necessary, in the host State.

Article 30
Notification of the indictment

1.   The Prosecutor shall ensure that a person who has been arrested is personally served, as soon as possible after being taken into custody, with certified copies of the following documents, in a language understood by that person:

    (a)   in the case of a suspect provisionally arrested, a statement of the grounds for the arrest;

    (b)   in any other case, the confirmed indictment;

    (c)   a statement of the accused's rights under this Statute.

2.   In any case to which paragraph (1) (a) applies, the indictment shall be served on the accused as soon as possible after it has been confirmed.

3.   If, 60 days after the indictment has been confirmed, the accused is not in custody pursuant to article 28 (3), or for some

reason the requirements of paragraph 1 cannot be complied with, the Presidency may on the application of the Prosecutor prescribe some other manner of bringing the indictment to the attention of the accused.

Article 31
Designation of persons to assist in a prosecution

1.   A State party may, at the request of the Prosecutor, designate persons to assist in a prosecution.
2.   Such persons should be available for the duration of the prosecution, unless otherwise agreed. They shall serve at the direction of the Prosecutor, and shall not seek or receive instructions from any Government or source other than the Prosecutor in relation to their exercise of functions under this article.
3.   The terms and conditions on which persons may be designated under this article shall be approved by the Presidency on the recommendation of the Prosecutor.

PART 5. THE TRIAL

Article 32
Place of trial

1.   Unless otherwise decided by the Presidency, the place of the trial will be the seat of the Court.

Article 33
Applicable law

The Court shall apply:
(a)   this Statute;
(b)   applicable treaties and the principles and rules of general international law; and
(c)   to the extent applicable, any rule of national law.

Article 34
Challenges to jurisdiction

Challenges to the jurisdiction of the Court may be made, in accordance with the Rules:

(a)   prior to or at the commencement of the hearing, by an accused or any interested State; and

(b)   at any later stage of the trial, by an accused.

Article 35
Issues of admissibility

The Court may, on application by the accused or at the request of an interested State at any time prior to the commencement of the trial, or of its own motion, decide, having regard to the purposes of this Statute set out in the preamble, that a case before it is inadmissible on the ground that the crime in question:

(a)   has been duly investigated by a State with jurisdiction over it, and its decision not to proceed to a prosecution is apparently well-founded;

(b)   is under investigation by a State which has or may have jurisdiction over it, and there is no reason for the Court to take any further action for the time being with respect to the crime; or

(c)   is not of such gravity to justify further action by the Court.

Article 36
Procedure under articles 34 and 35

1.   In a proceeding under articles 34 and 35, the accused and the complainant State have the right to be heard.

2.   Proceedings under articles 34 and 35 shall be decided by the Trial Chamber, unless it considers, having regard to the importance

of the issues involved, that the matter should be referred to the Appeals Chamber.

Article 37
Trial in the presence of the accused

1.   As a general rule, the accused should be present during the trial.

2.   The Trial Chamber may order that the trial proceed in the absence of the accused if:

    (a)   the accused is in custody, or has been released pending trial, and for reasons of security or the ill-health of the accused it is undesirable for the accused to be present;

    (b)   the accused is continuing to disrupt the trial; or

    (c)   the accused has escaped from lawful custody under this Statute or has broken bail.

3.   The Chamber shall, if it makes an order under paragraph 2, ensure that the rights of the accused under this Statute are respected, and in particular:

    (a)   that all reasonable steps have been taken to inform the accused of the charge; and

    (b)   that the accused is legally represented, if necessary by a lawyer appointed by the Court.

4.   The Rules may make provision for:

    (a)   a public hearing of an Indictment Chamber which may be created for the purpose of:

        (i)   recording the evidence;

        (ii)   considering whether the evidence against an accused whose absence is deliberate constitutes a prima facie case.

    (b)   giving appropriate publicity to the finding of the Chamber.

5.   At a subsequent trial of the accused:
(a)   the record of evidence before the Indict-
        ment Chamber shall be admissible;
(b)   members of the Indictment Chamber
        may not serve on the Trial Chamber.

Article 38
Functions and powers of the Trial Chamber

1.   At the commencement of the trial, the Chamber shall:
(a)   have the indictment read;
(b)   ensure that articles 27 (4) (b) and 30
        have been complied with sufficiently in
        advance of the trial to enable adequate
        preparation of the defence;
(c)   satisfy itself that the other rights of the
        accused under this Statute have been
        respected; and
(d)   allow the accused to enter a plea of
        guilty or not guilty.

2.   The Chamber shall ensure that a trial is fair and expeditious,
and is conducted in accordance with this Statute and the Rules, with
full respect for the rights of the accused and due regard for the
protection of victims and witnesses.

3.   The Chamber may, subject to the Rules, hear charges against
more than one accused arising out of the same factual situation.

4.   The trial shall be held in public, unless the Chamber determines that certain proceedings be in closed session in accordance
with article 43, or for the purpose of protecting confidential or sensitive
information which is to be given in evidence.

5.   The Chamber shall, subject to this Statute and the Rules have,
inter alia, the power on the application of a party or of its own motion,
to:
(a)   issue a warrant for the arrest and trans-
        fer of an accused who is not already in
        the custody of the Court;
(b)   require the attendance and testimony of
        witnesses;

(c)   require the production of documentary and other evidentiary materials;

(d)   rule on the admissibility or relevance of evidence;

(e)   protect confidential information; and

(f)   maintain order in the course of a hearing.

7.   The Chamber shall ensure that a complete record of the trial, which accurately reflects the proceedings, is maintained and preserved by the Registrar.

Article 39
Principle of legality (*nullum crimen sine lege*)

An accused shall not be held guilty:

(a)   in the case of a prosecution under article 20 (a)-(d), unless the act or omission in question constituted a crime under international law;

(b)   in the case of a prosecution under article 20 (e), unless the treaty in question was applicable to the conduct of the accused;

at the time the act or omission occurred.

Article 40
Presumption of innocence

An accused shall be presumed innocent until proved guilty in accordance with law. The onus is on the Prosecutor to establish the guilt of the accused beyond reasonable doubt.

Article 41
Rights of the accused

1.   In the determination of any charge under this Statute, the accused is entitled to a fair and public hearing, subject to article 43, and to the following minimum guarantees:

(a)   to be informed promptly and in detail, in a language which the accused understands, of the nature and cause of the charge;

(b)   to have adequate time and facilities for the preparation of the defence, and to communicate with counsel of the accused's choosing;

(c)   to be tried without undue delay;

(d)   subject to article 37 (2), to be present at the trial, to conduct the defence in person or through legal assistance of the accused's own choosing, to be informed, if the accused does not have legal assistance, of this right and to have legal assistance assigned by the Court, without payment if the accused lacks sufficient means to pay for such assistance;

(e)   to examine, or have examined, the prosecution witnesses and to obtain the attendance and examination of witnesses for the defence under the same conditions as witnesses for the prosecution;

(f)   if any of the proceedings of or documents presented to the Court are not in a language the accused understands and speaks, to have, free of any cost, the assistance of a competent interpreter and such translations as are necessary to meet the requirements of fairness;

(g)   not to be compelled to testify or to confess guilt.

2.   Exculpatory evidence that becomes available to the Procuracy prior to the conclusion of the trial shall be made available to the defence. In case of doubt as to the application of this paragraph or as to the admissibility of the evidence, the Trial Chamber shall decide.

Article 42
Non bis in idem

1.   No person shall be tried before any other court for acts constituting a crime of the kind referred to in article 20 for which that person has already been tried by the Court.

2.   A person who has been tried by another court for acts constituting a crime of the kind referred to in article 20 may be tried under this Statute only if:

  (a)   the acts in question were characterized by that court as an ordinary crime and not as a crime which is within the jurisdiction of the Court; or

  (b)   the proceedings in the other court were not impartial or independent, or were designed to shield the accused from international criminal responsibility or the case was not diligently prosecuted.

3.   In considering the penalty to be imposed on a person convicted under this Statute, the Court shall take into account the extent to which a penalty imposed by another court on the same person for the same act has already been served.

Article 43
Protection of the accused, victims and witnesses

The Court shall take necessary measures available to it to protect the accused victims and witnesses and may to that end conduct closed proceedings or allow the presentation of evidence by electronic or other special means.

Article 44
Evidence

1.   Before testifying, each witness shall, in accordance with the Rules, give an undertaking as to the truthfulness of the evidence to be given by that witness.

2.   States parties shall extend their laws of perjury to cover evidence given under this Statute by their nationals, and shall

cooperate with the Court in investigating and where appropriate prosecuting any case of suspected perjury.

3.   The Court may require to be informed of the nature of any evidence before it is offered so that it may rule on its relevance or admissibility.

4.   The Court shall not require proof of facts of common knowledge but may take judicial notice of them.

5.   Evidence obtained by means of a serious violation of this Statute or of other rules of international law shall not be admissible.

Article 45
Quorum and judgment

1.   At least four members of the Trial Chamber must be present at each stage of the trial.

2.   The decisions of the Trial Chamber shall be taken by a majority of the judges. At least three judges must concur in a decision as to conviction or acquittal and as to the sentence to be imposed.

3.   If after sufficient time for deliberation a Chamber which has been reduced to four judges is unable to agree on a decision, it may order a new trial.

4.   The deliberations of the Court shall be and remain secret.

5.   The judgment shall be in writing and shall contain a full and reasoned statement of the findings and conclusions. It shall be the sole judgment issued, and shall be delivered in open court.

Article 46
Sentencing

1.   In the event of a conviction, the Trial Chamber shall hold a further hearing to hear any evidence relevant to sentence, to allow the Prosecutor and the defence to make submissions, and to consider the appropriate sentence to be imposed.

2.   In imposing sentence, the Trial Chamber should take into account such factors as the gravity of the crime and the individual circumstances of the convicted person.

Article 47
Applicable penalties

1.   The Court may impose on a person convicted of a crime under this Statute one or more of the following penalties:

    (a)   a term of life imprisonment, or of imprisonment for a specified number of years;

    (b)   a fine.

2.   In determining the length of a term of imprisonment or the amount of a fine to be imposed, the Court may have regard to the penalties provided for by the law of:

    (a)   the State of which the convicted person is a national;

    (b)   the State where the crime was committed; and

    (c)   the State which had custody of and jurisdiction over the accused.

3.   Fines paid may be transferred, by order of the Court, to one or more of the following:

    (a)   the Registrar, to defray the costs of the trial;

    (b)   a State the nationals of which were the victims of the crime;

    (c)   a trust fund established by the Secretary-General of the United Nations for the benefit of victims of crime.

PART 6. APPEAL AND REVIEW

Article 48
Appeal against judgment or sentence

1.   The Prosecutor and the convicted person may, in accordance with the Rules, appeal against a decision under articles 45 or 47 on grounds of procedural unfairness, error of fact or of law, or disproportion between the crime and the sentence.

2.   Unless the Trial Chamber otherwise orders, a convicted person shall remain in custody pending an appeal.

Article 49
Proceedings on appeal

1.   The Appeals Chamber has all the powers of the Trial Chamber.
2.   If the Chamber finds that the proceedings appealed from were unfair or that the decision is vitiated by error of fact or law, it may:

      (a)   if the appeal is brought by the convicted person, reverse or amend the decision, or, if necessary, order a new trial;

      (b)   if the appeal is brought by the Prosecutor, against an acquittal order a new trial.

3.   If in an appeal against sentence the Chamber finds that the sentence is manifestly disproportionate to the crime, it may vary the sentence in accordance with article 47.
4.   The decision of the Chamber shall be taken by a majority of the judges, and shall be delivered in open court. Six judges constitute a quorum.
5.   Subject to article 50, the decision of an Appeals Chamber shall be final.

Article 50
Revision

1.   The convicted person or the Prosecutor may, in accordance with the Rules, apply to the Presidency for revision of a conviction on the ground that evidence has been discovered which was not available to the applicant at the time the conviction was pronounced or affirmed and which could have been a decisive factor in the conviction.
2.   The Presidency shall request the Prosecutor or the convicted person, as the case may be, to present written observations on whether the application should be accepted.
3.   If the Presidency is of the view that the now evidence could lead to the revision of the conviction, it may:

      (a)   reconvene the Trial Chamber;

(b)   constitute a new Trial Chamber; or

(c)   refer the matter to the Appeals Chamber;

with a view to the Chamber determining, after hearing the parties, whether the new evidence should lead to a revision of the conviction.

PART 7. INTERNATIONAL COOPERATION AND JUDICIAL ASSISTANCE

Article 51
Cooperation and judicial assistance

1.   States parties shall cooperate with the Court in connection with criminal investigations and proceedings under this Statute.

2.   The Registrar may transmit to any State a request for cooperation and judicial assistance with respect to a crime, including, but not limited to:

(a)   the identification and location of persons;

(b)   the taking of testimony and the production of evidence;

(c)   the service of documents;

(d)   the arrest or detention of persons; and

(e)   any other request which may facilitate the administration of justice, including provisional measures as required.

3.   Upon receipt of a request under paragraph 1:

(a)   in a case covered by article 20 (1) (a), all States parties;

(b)   in any other case, States parties which have accepted the jurisdiction of the Court with respect to the crime in question;

shall respond without undue delay to the request.

Article 52
Provisional measures

1.   In case of need, the Court may request a State to take
necessary provisional measures, including the following:
    (a)   to provisionally arrest a suspect;
    (b)   to seize documents or other evidence;
        or
    (c)   to prevent injury to or the intimidation of
        a witness or the destruction of evidence.

2.   The Court shall follow up a request under paragraph 1 by
providing, as soon as possible and in any case within 28 days, a
formal request for assistance complying with article 57.

Article 53
Transfer of an accused to the Court

1.   The Registrar shall transmit to any State on whose territory the
accused may be found a warrant for the arrest and transfer of an
accused issued under article 28, and shall request the cooperation of
that State in the arrest and transfer of the accused.

2.   Upon receipt of a request under paragraph 1:
    (a)   all States parties:
        (i)   in a case covered by article 20 (1) (a), or
        (ii)   which have accepted the jurisdiction of the
            Court with respect to the crime in question;
    shall, subject to paragraphs 5 and 6, take immediate
    steps to arrest and transfer the accused to the Court;
    (b)   in the case of a crime to which article 20
        (e) applies, a State party which is a
        party to the treaty in question but which
        has not accepted the Court's jurisdiction
        with respect to that crime shall, if it
        decides not to transfer the accused to
        the Court, forthwith refer the case to its
        competent authorities for the purpose of
        prosecution or take all necessary steps

to extradite the accused to a requesting
State;

(c)   in any other case, a State party shall
consider whether it can, in accordance
with its legal procedures, take steps to
arrest and transfer the accused to the
Court, or whether it should refer the
matter to its competent authorities for
the purpose of prosecution or of extradition to a requesting State.

3.   The transfer of an accused to the Court constitutes, as
between States parties which accept the jurisdiction of the Court with
respect to the crime, sufficient compliance with a provision of any
treaty requiring that a suspect be extradited or the case submitted to
its competent authorities for the purpose of prosecution.

4.   A State party which accepts the jurisdiction of the Court with
respect to the crime shall, as far as possible, give priority to a request
under paragraph 1 over requests for extradition from other States.

5.   A State party may delay complying with paragraph 2 if the
accused is in its custody or control and is being proceeded against for
a serious crime, or serving a sentence imposed by a court for a crime.
It shall within 45 days of receiving the request inform the Registrar of
the reasons for the delay. In such cases, the requested State:

(a)   may agree to the temporary transfer of
the accused for the purpose of standing
trial under this Statute; or

(b)   shall comply with paragraph 2 after the
prosecution has been completed or
abandoned or the sentence has been
served, as the case may be.

6.   A State party may, within 45 days of receiving a request under
paragraph 1, file a written application with the Registrar requesting the
Court to set aside the request on specified grounds. Pending a
decision of the Court on the application, the State concerned may
delay complying with paragraph 2, but shall take any provisional
measures requested by the Court.

Article 54
Obligation to extradite or prosecute

In a case arising under article 20 (e), a custodial State party to this Statute which is a party to the treaty in question but which has not accepted the Court's jurisdiction with respect to the crime for the purposes of article 21 (1) (b) (i) shall either refer the case to its competent authorities for the purpose of prosecution or take all necessary steps to extradite the suspect to a requesting State.

Article 55
Rule of speciality

1.   A person delivered to the Court under article 53 shall not be subject to prosecution or punishment for any crime other than that for which the person was transferred.

2.   Evidence provided under this Part shall not, if the State when providing it so requests, be used as evidence for any purpose other than that for which it was provided, unless this is necessary to preserve the right of an accused under article 41 (2).

3.   The Court may request the State concerned to waive the requirements of paragraphs 1 or 2, for the reasons and purposes specified in the request.

Article 56
Cooperation with States not parties to this Statute

States not parties to this Statute may assist in relation to the matters referred to in this Part on the basis of comity, a unilateral declaration, an ad hoc arrangement or other agreement with the Court.

Article 57
Communications and documentation

1.   Requests under this Part shall be in writing, or be forthwith reduced to writing, and shall be between the competent national authority and the Registrar. States parties shall inform the Registrar of the name and address of their national authority for this purpose.

2.   When appropriate, communications may also be made through the International Criminal Police Organization.

3.   A request under this Part shall include the following, as applicable:

(a)   a brief statement of the purpose of the request and of the assistance sought, including the legal basis and grounds for the request;

(b)   information concerning the person who is the subject of the request on the evidence sought, in sufficient detail to enable identification;

(c)   a brief description of the essential facts underlying the request; and

(d)   information concerning the complaint or charge to which the request relates and of the basis for the Court's jurisdiction.

4.   A requested State which considers the information provided insufficient to enable the request to be complied with may seek further particulars.

PART 8. ENFORCEMENT

Article 58
Recognition of judgments

States parties undertake to recognize the judgments of the Court.

Article 59
Enforcement of sentences

1.   A sentence of imprisonment shall be served in a State designated by the Court from a list of States which have indicated to the Court their willingness to accept convicted persons.

2.   If no State is designated under paragraph 1, the sentence of imprisonment shall be served in a prison facility made available by the host State.

3.   A sentence of imprisonment shall be subject to the supervision of the Court in accordance with the Rules.

Article 60
Pardon, parole and commutation of sentences

1.   If, under a generally applicable law of the State of imprisonment, a person in the same circumstances who had been convicted for the same conduct by a court of that State would be eligible for pardon, parole or commutation of sentence, the State shall so notify the Court.

2.   If a notification has been given under paragraph 1, the prisoner may apply to the Court in accordance with the Rules, seeking an order for pardon, parole or commutation of the sentence.

3.   If the Presidency decides that an application under paragraph 2 is apparently well-founded, it shall convene a Chamber of five judges to consider and decide whether in the interests of justice the person convicted should be pardoned or paroled, or whether the sentence should be commuted, and on what basis.

4.   When imposing a sentence of imprisonment, a Chamber may stipulate that the sentence is to be served in accordance with specified laws as to pardon, parole or commutation of the State which, under article 59, is responsible for implementing the sentence. The consent of the Court is not required to subsequent action by that State in conformity with those laws, but the Court shall be given at least 45 days' notice of any decision which might materially affect the terms or extent of the imprisonment.

5.   Except as provided in paragraphs 3 and 4, a person serving a sentence imposed by the Court is not to be released before the expiry of the sentence.

Annex (see Article 20 (e))

1.   Grave breaches of:
        (i)   the Geneva Convention for the Amelioration of the
                 Condition of the Wounded and Sick in Armed Forces in
                 the Field of 12 August 1949, as defined by Article 50 of
                 that Convention;
        (ii)   the Geneva Convention for the Amelioration of the
                 Condition of Wounded, Sick and Shipwrecked Members
                 of Armed Forces at Sea of 12 August 1949, as defined
                 by Article 51 of that Convention;
        (iii)   the Geneva Convention relative to the Treatment of
                 Prisoners of War of 12 August 1949, as defined by
                 Article 130 of that Convention;
        (iv)   the Geneva Convention relative to the Protection of
                 Civilian Persons in Time of War of 12 August 1949, as
                 defined by Article 147 of that Convention;
        (v)   Protocol I Additional to the Geneva Conventions of 12
                 August 1949 and relating to the Protection of Victims of
                 International Armed Conflicts of 8 June 1977, as
                 defined by Article 85 of that Protocol.
2.   The unlawful seizure of aircraft as defined by Article 1 of the
Hague Convention for the Suppression of Unlawful Seizure of Aircraft
of 16 December 1970.
3.   The crimes defined by Article 1 of the Montreal Convention for
the Suppression of Unlawful Acts against the Safety of Civil Aviation
of 23 September 1971.
4.   Apartheid and related crimes as defined by Article II of the
International Convention on the Suppression and Punishment of the
Crime of Apartheid of 30 November 1973.
5.   The crimes defined by Article 2 of the Convention on the
Prevention and Punishment of Crimes against Internationally Protected
Persons, including Diplomatic Agents of 14 December 1973.
6.   Hostage-taking and related crimes as defined by Article 1 of
the International Convention against the Taking of Hostages of 17
December 1979.
7.   The crime of torture made punishable pursuant to Article 4 of
the Convention against Torture and Other Cruel, Inhuman or Degrading Treatment or Punishment of 10 December 1984.

8.   The crimes defined by Article 3 of the Convention for the Suppression of Unlawful Acts against the Safety of Maritime navigation of 10 March 1988 and by Article 2 of the Protocol for the Suppression of Unlawful Acts against the Safety of Fixed Platforms Located on the Continental Shelf of 10 May 1988.

9.   Crimes involving illicit traffic in narcotic drugs and psychotropic substances as envisaged by Article 3 (1) of the United Nations Convention against Illicit Traffic in Narcotic Drugs and Psychotropic Substances of 20 December 1988 which, having regard to Article 2 of the Convention, are crimes with an international dimension.

ANNEX 5 - 1995 UN General Assembly Resolution A/50/46 Creating a Preparatory Committee on the Establishment of an International Criminal Court

RESOLUTION ADOPTED BY THE GENERAL ASSEMBLY ON THE REPORT OF THE SIXTH COMMITTEE (A/50/639 and Corr.1)

General Assembly resolution 50/46 on the establishment of an international criminal court, adopted at its 87th Plenary Meeting on 11 December 1995.

The General Assembly,

Recalling its resolution 47/33 of 25 November 1992, in which it requested the International Law Commission to undertake the elaboration of a draft statute for an international criminal court,

Recalling also its resolution 48/31 of 9 December 1993, in which it requested the International Law Commission to continue its work on the question of the draft statute for an international criminal court, with a view to elaborating a draft statute for such a court, if possible at the Commission's forty-sixth session in 1994,

Recalling further that the International Law Commission adopted a draft statute for an international criminal court [1] at its forty-sixth session and decided to recommend that an international conference of plenipotentiaries be convened to study the draft statute and to conclude a convention on the establishment of an international criminal court, [2]

Recalling its resolution 49/53 of 9 December 1994, in which it decided to establish an ad hoc committee, open to all States Members of the United Nations or members of specialized agencies, to review the major substantive and administrative issues arising out of the draft statute prepared by the International Law Commission and, in the light of that review, to consider arrangements for the convening of an international conference of plenipotentiaries,

---

[1]   Official Records of the General Assembly, Forty-ninth Session, Supplement No. 10 (A/49/10), para. 91.

[2]   *Ibid.*, para. 90.

Noting that the Ad Hoc Committee on the Establishment of an International Criminal Court has made considerable progress during its sessions on the review of the major substantive and administrative issues arising out of the draft statute prepared by the International Law Commission,

Noting also that the States participating in the Ad Hoc Committee still have different views on major substantive and administrative issues arising out of the draft statute prepared by the International Law Commission and that, therefore, further discussions are needed for reaching consensus on the above issues in the future,

Noting further that the Ad Hoc Committee is of the opinion that issues can be addressed most effectively by combining further discussions with the drafting of texts, with a view to preparing a consolidated text of a convention for an international criminal court as a next step towards consideration by a conference of plenipotentiaries,

Noting that the Ad Hoc Committee recommends that the General Assembly take up the organization of future work with a view to its early completion, given the interest of the international community in the establishment of an international criminal court,

Noting also that the Ad Hoc Committee encourages participation by the largest number of States in its future work in order to promote universality,

Expressing deep appreciation for the renewed offer of the Government of Italy to host a conference on the establishment of an international criminal court,

1.   *Takes note* of the report of the Ad Hoc Committee on the Establishment of an International Criminal Court, [3] including the recommendations contained therein, and expresses its appreciation to the Ad Hoc Committee for the useful work done;

2.   *Decides* to establish a preparatory committee open to all States Members of the United Nations or members of specialized agencies or of the International Atomic Energy Agency, to discuss further the major substantive and administrative issues arising out of the draft statute prepared by the International Law Commission and, taking into account the different views expressed during the meetings, to draft texts, with a view to preparing a widely acceptable consoli-

---

[3]   *Ibid.*, Fiftieth Session, Supplement No. 22 (A/50/22).

dated text of a convention for an international criminal court as a next step towards consideration by a conference of plenipotentiaries, and also decides that the work of the Preparatory Committee should be based on the draft statute prepared by the International Law Commission and should take into account the report of the Ad Hoc Committee and the written comments submitted by States to the Secretary-General on the draft statute for an international criminal court pursuant to paragraph 4 of General Assembly resolution 49/53 [4] and, as appropriate, contributions of relevant organizations;

3.   *Also decides* that the Preparatory Committee will meet from 25 March to 12 April and from 12 to 30 August 1996 and submit its report to the General Assembly at the beginning of its fifty-first session, and requests the Secretary-General to provide the Preparatory Committee with the necessary facilities for the performance of its work;

4.   *Urges* participation in the Preparatory Committee by the largest number of States in order to promote universal support for an international criminal court;

5.   *Decides* to include in the provisional agenda of its fifty-first session an item entitled "Establishment of an international criminal court", in order to study the report of the Preparatory Committee and, in the light of that report, to decide on the convening of an international conference of plenipotentiaries to finalize and adopt a convention on the establishment of an international criminal court, including on the timing and the duration of the conference.

- - -

---

[4]   A/AC.244/1 and Add.1-4.

ANNEX 6 - 1996 ILC Draft Code on Crimes against the Peace and Security of Mankind

(A/CN.4/L.532 of 8 July 1996)

Titles and texts of articles on the Draft Code of Crimes against the Peace and Security of Mankind adopted by the International Law Commission at its forty-eighth session (1996)

PART I. GENERAL PROVISIONS

Article 1
Scope and application of the present Code

1. The present Code applies to the crimes against the peace and security of mankind set out in Part II.
2. Crimes against the peace and security of mankind are crimes under international law and punishable as such, whether or not they are punishable under national law.

Article 2
Individual responsibility

1. A crime against the peace and security of mankind entails individual responsibility.
2. An individual shall be responsible for the crime of aggression in accordance with article 16.
3. An individual shall be responsible for a crime set out in article 17, 18, 19 or 20 if that individual:
    (a) intentionally commits such a crime;
    (b) orders the commission of such a crime which in fact occurs or is attempted;
    (c) fails to prevent or repress the commission of such a crime in the circumstances set out in article 6;

(d)   knowingly aids, abets or otherwise assists, directly and substantially, in the commission of such a crime, including providing the means for its commission;

(e)   directly participates in planning or conspiring to commit such a crime which in fact occurs;

(f)   directly and publicly incites another individual to commit such a crime which in fact occurs;

(g)   attempts to commit such a crime by taking action commencing the execution of a crime which does not in fact occur because of circumstances independent of his intentions.

Article 3
Punishment

An individual who is responsible for a crime against the peace and security of mankind shall be liable to punishment. The punishment shall be commensurate with the character and gravity of the crime.

Article 4
Responsibility of States

The fact that the present Code provides for the responsibility of individuals for crimes against the peace and security of mankind is without prejudice to any question of the responsibility of States under international law.

Article 5
Order of a Government or a superior

The fact that an individual charged with a crime against the peace and security of mankind acted pursuant to an order of a Government or a superior does not relieve him of criminal responsibility, but may be considered in mitigation of punishment if justice so requires.

Article 6
Responsibility of the superior

The fact that a crime against the peace and security of mankind was committed by a subordinate does not relieve his superiors of criminal responsibility, if they knew or had reason to know, in the circumstances at the time, that the subordinate was committing or was going to commit such a crime and if they did not take all necessary measures within their power to prevent or repress the crime.

Article 7
Official position and responsibility

The official position of an individual who commits a crime against the peace and security of mankind, even if he acted as head of State or Government, does not relieve him of criminal responsibility or mitigate punishment.

Article 8
Establishment of jurisdiction

Without prejudice to the jurisdiction of an international criminal court, each State Party shall take such measures as may be necessary to establish its jurisdiction over the crimes set out in articles 17, 18, 19 and 20, irrespective of where or by whom those crimes were committed. Jurisdiction over the crime set out in article 15 shall rest with an international criminal court. However, a State referred to in article 16 is not precluded from trying its nationals for the crime set out in that article.

Article 9
Obligation to extradite or prosecute

Without prejudice to the jurisdiction of an international criminal court, the State Party in the territory of which an individual alleged to have committed a crime set out in article 17, 18, 19 or 20 is found shall extradite or prosecute that individual.

Article 10
Extradition of alleged offenders

1. To the extent that the crimes set out in articles 17, 18, 19 and 20 are not extraditable offenses in any extradition treaty existing between States Parties, they shall be deemed to be included as such therein. States Parties undertake to include those crimes as extraditable offenses in every extradition treaty to be concluded between them.

2. If a State Party which makes extradition conditional on the existence of a treaty receives a request for extradition from another State Party with which it has no extradition treaty, it may at its option consider the present Code as the legal basis for extradition in respect of those crimes. Extradition shall be subject to the conditions provided in the law of the requested State.

3. States Parties which do not make extradition conditional on the existence of a treaty shall recognize those crimes as extraditable offenses between themselves subject to the conditions provided in the law of the requested State.

4. Each of those crimes shall be treated, for the purpose of extradition between States Parties, as if it had been committed not only in the place in which it occurred but also in the territory of any other State Party.

Article 11
Judicial guarantees

1. An individual charged with a crime against the peace and security of mankind shall be presumed innocent until proved guilty and shall be entitled without discrimination to the minimum guarantees due to all human beings with regard to the law and the facts and shall have the rights:

    (a) in the determination of any charge against him, to have a fair and public hearing by a competent, independent and impartial tribunal duly established by law;

    (b) to be informed promptly and in detail in a language which he understands of the nature and cause of the charge against him;

(c)   to have adequate time and facilities for the preparation of his defence and to communicate with counsel of his own choosing;

(d)   to be tried without undue delay;

(e)   to be tried in his presence, and to defend himself in person or through legal assistance of his own choosing; to be informed, if he does not have legal assistance, of this right; and to have legal assistance assigned to him and without payment by him if he does not have sufficient means to pay for it;

(f)   to examine, or have examined, the witnesses against him and to obtain the attendance and examination of witnesses on his behalf under the same conditions as witnesses against him;

(g)   to have the free assistance of an interpreter if he cannot understand or speak the language used in court;

(h)   not to be compelled to testify against himself or to confess guilt.

2.   An individual convicted of a crime shall have the right to his conviction and sentence being reviewed according to law.

Article 12
Non bis in idem

1.   No one shall be tried for a crime against the peace and security of mankind of which he has already been finally convicted or acquitted by an international criminal court.

2.   An individual may not be tried again for a crime of which he has been finally convicted or acquitted by a national court except in the following cases:

(a)   by an international criminal court, if:

(i)   the act which was the subject of the judgment in the national court was characterized by that court as an ordinary crime and not as a crime against the peace and security of mankind; or

(ii)   the national court proceedings were not impartial or independent or were designed to shield the accused from international criminal respon-

sibility or the case was not diligently prosecuted;
(b)   by a national court of another State, if:
    (i)   the act which was the subject of the previous
judgment took place in the territory of that
State; or
    (ii)   that State was the main victim of the crime.
3.   In the case of a subsequent conviction under the present
Code, the court, in passing sentence, shall take into account the
extent to which any penalty imposed by a national court on the same
person for the same act has already been served.

Article 13
Non-retroactivity

1.   No one shall be convicted under the present Code for acts
committed before its entry into force.
2.   Nothing in this article precludes the trial of anyone for any act
which, at the time when it was committed, was criminal in accordance
with international law or national law.

Article 14
Defenses

The competent court shall determine the admissibility of
defenses in accordance with the general principles of law, in the light
of the character of each crime.

Article 15
Extenuating circumstances

In passing sentence, the court shall, where appropriate, take
into account extenuating circumstances in accordance with the general
principles of law.

PART II. CRIMES AGAINST THE
PEACE AND SECURITY OF MANKIND

Article 16
Crime of aggression

An individual, who, as leader or organizer, actively participates in or orders the planning, preparation, initiation or waging of aggression committed by a State, shall be responsible for a crime of aggression.

Article 17
Crime of Genocide

A crime of genocide means any of the following acts committed with intent to destroy, in whole or in part, a national, ethnic, racial or religious group, as such:

(a)   killing members of the group;
(b)   causing serious bodily or mental harm to members of the group;
(c)   deliberately inflicting on the group conditions of life calculated to bring about its physical destruction in whole or in part;
(d)   imposing measures intended to prevent births within the group;
(e)   forcibly transferring children of the group to another group.

Article 18
Crimes against humanity

A crime against humanity means any of the following acts, when committed in a systematic manner or on a large scale and instigated or directed by a government or by any organization or group:

(a)   murder;
(b)   extermination;
(c)   torture;
(d)   enslavement;

(e)   persecution on political, racial, religious or ethnic grounds;

(f)   institutionalized discrimination on racial, ethnic or religious grounds involving the violation of fundamental human rights and freedoms and resulting in seriously disadvantaging a part of the population;

(g)   arbitrary deportation or forcible transfer of population;

(h)   arbitrary imprisonment;

(i)   forced disappearance of persons;

(j)   rape, enforced prostitution and other forms of sexual abuse;

(k)   other inhumane acts which severely damage physical or mental integrity, health or human dignity, such as mutilation and severe bodily harm.

Article 19
Crimes against United Nations and associated personnel

1.   The following crimes constitute crimes against the peace and security of mankind when committed intentionally and in a systematic manner or on a large scale against United Nations and associated personnel involved in a United Nations operation with a view to preventing or impeding that operation from fulfilling its mandate:

(a)   murder, kidnapping or other attack upon the person or liberty of personnel;

(b)   violent attack upon the official premises, the private accommodation or the means of transportation of any such personnel likely to endanger his or her person or liberty.

2.   This article shall not apply to a United Nations operation authorized by the Security Council as an enforcement action under Chapter VII of the Charter of the United Nations in which any of the personnel are engaged as combatants against organized armed forces and to which the law of international armed conflict applies.

Article 20
War crimes

Any of the following war crimes constitutes a crime against the peace and security of mankind when committed in a systematic manner or on a large scale:

(a) any of the following acts committed in violation of international humanitarian law:

(i) wilful killing;

(ii) torture or inhuman treatment, including biological experiments;

(iii) wilfully causing great suffering or serious injury to body or health;

(iv) extensive destruction and appropriation of property, not justified by military necessity and carried out unlawfully and wantonly;

(v) compelling a prisoner of war or other protected person to serve in the forces of a hostile Power;

(vi) wilfully depriving a prisoner of war or other protected person of the rights of fair and regular trial;

(vii) unlawful deportation or transfer or unlawful confinement of protected persons;

(viii) taking of hostages;

(b) any of the following acts committed wilfully in violation of international humanitarian law and causing death or serious injury to body or health:

(i) making the civilian population or individual civilians the object of attack;

(ii) launching an indiscriminate attack affecting the civilian population or civilian objects in the knowledge that such attack will cause excessive loss of life, injury to civilians or damage to civilian objects;

(iii) launching an attack against works or installations containing dangerous forces in the knowledge that such attack will cause excessive loss of life, injury to civilians or damage to civilian objects;

        (iv)   making a person the object of attack in the knowledge that he is *hors de combat*;

        (v)   the perfidious use of the distinctive emblem of the red cross, red crescent or red lion and sun or of other recognized protective signs;

(c)   any of the following acts committed wilfully in violation of international humanitarian law:

        (i)   the transfer by the Occupying Power of parts of its own civilian population into the territory it occupies;

        (ii)   unjustifiable delay in the repatriation of prisoners of war or civilians;

(d)   outrages upon personal dignity in violation of international humanitarian law, in particular humiliating and degrading treatment, rape, enforced prostitution and any form of indecent assault;

(e)   any of the following acts committed in violation of the laws or customs of war:

        (i)   employment of poisonous weapons or other weapons calculated to cause unnecessary suffering;

        (ii)   wanton destruction of cities, towns or villages, or devastation not justified by military necessity;

        (iii)   attack, or bombardment, by whatever means, of undefended towns, villages, dwellings or buildings or of demilitarized zones;

        (iv)   seizure of, destruction of or wilful damage done to institutions dedicated to religion, charity and education, the arts and sciences, historic monuments and works of art and science;

        (v)   plunder of public or private property;

(f)   any of the following acts committed in violation of international humanitarian law applicable in armed conflict not of an international character:

        (i)   violence to the life, health and physical or mental well-being of persons, in particular murder as well as cruel treatment such as torture, mutilation or any form of corporal punishment;

        (ii)   collective punishments;

(iii)   taking of hostages;
(iv)   acts of terrorism;
(v)   outrages upon personal dignity, in particular
         humiliating and degrading treatment, rape,
         enforced prostitution and any form of indecent
         assault;
(vi)   pillage;
(vii)   the passing of sentences and the carrying out
         of executions without previous judgment pro-
         nounced by a regularly constituted court, affor-
         ding all the judicial guarantees which are gen-
         erally recognized as indispensable;
(g)   in the case of armed conflict, using methods or means
      of warfare not justified by military necessity with the
      intent to cause widespread, long-term and severe
      damage to the natural environment and thereby gravely
      prejudice the health or survival of the population and
      such damage occurs.

* * *

BIBLIOGRAPHY

A. DOCUMENTS

Anti-Slavery International, Forced Prostitution in Turkey: Women in the Genelevs (1993).

ASEAN Secretariat, ASEAN Plan of Action on Drug Abuse Control: including ASEAN Declaration of Principles to Combat the Abuse of Narcotic Drugs, adopted on 26 June 1976 in Manila and the ASEAN Foreign Ministers Joint Statement on the International Problem of Drug Abuse and Trafficking, adopted on 9 July 1985 in Kuala Lumpur (1995).

Boutros-Ghali, Boutros. An Agenda for Peace: Second Edition with the New Supplement and Related UN Documents. New York: United Nations (1995).

Boutros-Ghali, Boutros. Building Peace and Development: Report on the Work of the Organization from the Forty-eighth to the Forty-Ninth Session of the General Assembly: United Nations (1994).

Boutros-Ghali, Boutros. Report on the Work of the Organization from the forty-seventh to the forty-eighth session of the General Assembly: United Nations (1993).

Boutros-Ghali, Boutros. Supplement to An Agenda for Peace: Position Paper of the Secretary-General on the Occasion of the Fiftieth Anniversary of the United Nations; UN Doc. A/50/60-S/1995/1 of 3 January 1995.

Comments and Observations of Governments on the Draft Code of Crimes against the Peace and Security of Mankind adopted on First Reading by the International Law Commission at its 43rd Session, A/CN.4/448 of 1 March 1993.

Draft Code of Crimes against the Peace and Security of Mankind, adopted by the Drafting Committee on Second Reading at its 47th and 48th sessions; A/CN.4/L.522 of 31 May 1996.

Draft Convention for the Prevention and Punishment of Genocide (Doc. A/AC.10/42), 6 June 1947.

Final Report of the Commission of Experts established pursuant to Security Council resolution 935 (1994): UN Doc. S/1994/1405 of 9 Dec. 1994.

Lawyers for Human Rights and Legal Aid, The Flesh Trade: the Trafficking of Women and Children in Pakistan (1993).

International Law concerning the Conduct of Hostilities: Collection of Hague Conventions and Some Other Treaties Geneva: International Committee of the Red Cross (1989).

International Military Tribunal (Nuremberg): Judgment and Sentences, 1 October 1946, 41 American Journal of International Law January (1947): 172-333.

Mazowiecki, Tadeusz. Report on the situation of human rights in the territory of the former Yugoslavia submitted by Mr. Tadeusz Mazowiecki, Special Rapporteur of the Commission on Human Rights, pursuant to Commission resolution 1992/S-1/1 of 14 August 1992: Commission on Human Rights (1993).

Netherlands Advisory Committee on Public International Law. Recommendations concerning the International Law Commission's Report on a Draft Statute for a Permanent International Criminal Court. *Netherlands International Law Review* XLII (1995): 225-247.

Preliminary Report of the Independent Commission of Experts established in accordance with Security Council resolution 935 (1994): UN Doc. S/1994/1125 of 4 Oct. 1994.

Report of Article XIX (The International Centre against Censorship) Broadcasting Genocide: Censorship, Propaganda & State-Sponsored Violence in Rwanda 1990-1994 (1996).

Report of the Ad Hoc Committee on the Establishment of an International Criminal Court: UN Doc. A/50/22 Supp.22: UN General Assembly (1995).

Report of the International Law Commission on the work of its forty-sixth session: 2 May-22 July 1994, UN Doc. A/49/10 Supp. 10: UN General Assembly (1994).

Report of the Secretary-General pursuant to Paragraph 2 of Security Council Resolution 808 (1993), including the Statute of the Tribunal, UN.Doc. S/25704 of 3 May 1993 & Add.1 of 17 May 1993.

Report of the Working Group on Slavery on its First Session; E/CN.4/Sub.2/AC.2/3 of 28 Aug. 1975.

Titles and Texts of articles on the Draft Code of Crimes against the
Peace and Security of Mankind adopted by the International
Law Commission at its 48th session (1996); A/CN.4/L.532 of
8 July 1996.
United States Institute of Peace. Rwanda: Accountability for War
Crimes and Genocide (1995).
Updating of the Report on Slavery Submitted to the Sub-Commission
in 1966: Report by Mr. Benjamin Whitaker, Special Rapporteur;
E/CN.4/Sub.2/1982/20 of 5 July 1982 and Add.1 of 7 July
1982.

B.   BOOKS

Akehurst, Michael. *A Modern Introduction to International Law*, Sixth
ed. London: Routledge (1970).
Allen, Beverly. *Rape Warfare: the Hidden Genocide in
Bosnia-Herzegovina and Croatia*, London: Univ. of Minnesota
Press (1996).
Andreopoulos, George J., (ed.) *Genocide: Conceptual and Historical
Dimensions*, Philadelphia: Univ. of Pennsylvania Press (1994).
Atkins, Richard D., (ed.) *The Alleged Transnational Criminal: the
Second Biennial International Criminal Law Seminar*, The
Hague: Martinus Nijhoff (1995).
Bailey, Sydney. *The UN Security Council and Human Rights*, New
York: St. Martin's Press (1994).
Bassiouni, Cherif. *Crimes against Humanity in International Criminal
Law*, Dordrecht: Martinus Nijhoff (1992).
Bassiouni, Cherif, and Edward Wise. *Aut Dedere Aut Judicare: The
Duty to Extradite or Prosecute in International Law*, Dord-
recht: Martinus Nijhoff (1995).
Bedjaoui, Mohammed. *International Law: Achievements and Pros-
pects,* Dordrecht: Martinus Nijhoff (1991).
Benn, S.I., and R.S. Peters. *Social Principles and the Democratic
State*, London: Allen & Unwin (1959).
Bory, Françoise. *Origin and Development of International Humanitar-
ian Law*, Geneva: International Committee of the Red Cross
(1982).

Bothe, McAlister-Smith, Kurzidem, ed. *National Implementation of International Humanitarian Law*, Dordrecht: Martinus Nijhoff (1990).

Brownlie, Ian. *Principles of Public International Law*, Fourth ed. Oxford: Clarendon Press (1990).

Burgers, J. Herman, and Hans Danelius. *The United Nations Convention against Torture: A Handbook on the Convention against Torture and Other Cruel, Inhuman or Degrading Treatment or Punishment*, Dordrecht: Martinus Nijhoff (1988).

Cassese, Antonio. *International Law in a Divided World*, Oxford: Clarendon Press (1986).

Cassese, Antonio (ed). *The New Humanitarian Law of Armed Conflict*, Napoli: Editoriale scientifica s.r.l. (1979).

Cassese, Antonio. *Terrorism, Politics and Law: the Achille Lauro Affair*, Cambridge: Polity Press (1989).

Cassese, Antonio ed. *The International Fight against Torture*, Baden-Baden: Nomos (1991).

Chadwick, Elizabeth. *Self-Determination, Terrorism and the International Humanitarian Law of Armed Conflict*, The Hague: Martinus Nijhoff (1996).

Chatterjee, S.K. *Drug Abuse and Drug Related Crimes: Some Unresolved Legal Problems*, Dordrecht: Martinus Nijhoff (1989).

Chatterjee, S.K. *Legal Aspects of International Drug Control*, The Hague: Martinus Nijhoff (1981).

Crawford, James. *The Rights of Peoples*, Oxford: Clarendon Press (1988).

Delissen, Astrid, and Gerard Tanja (ed.), *Humanitarian Law of Armed Conflict: Challenges Ahead*, Dordrecht: Martinus Nijhoff (1991).

Devlin, Patrick. *The Enforcement of Morals*, London: Oxford Univ. Press (1965).

Diez Sanchez, Juan José. *El derecho penal internacional: ambito especial de la ley penal*, Madrid: Editorial Colex (1990).

Dinstein, Yoram (ed.) *International Law in a Time of Perplexity*, Dordrecht: Martinus Nijhoff (1989).

Dinstein, Yoram. *War, Aggression and Self-Defence*, New York: Cambridge Univ. Press (1988).

Dinstein, Yoram, and Mala Tabory (ed.), *The Protection of Minorities and Human Rights*, Dordrecht: Martinus Nijhoff (1992).

Duggan, Stephen et al. (ed.), *The League of Nations: The Principle and the Practice*, Boston:The Atlantic Monthly Press (1919).

Dworkin, Ronald. *Taking Rights Seriously*, Cambridge: Harvard Univ. Press (1977).

Elagab, Omer Yousif. *International Law Documents Relating to Terrorism*, London: Cavendish (1995).

Freud, Sigmund. *Civilization and its Discontents*, New York: Norton (1961).

Fuller, Lon. *The Morality of Law*, Princeton: Yale Univ. Press (1964).

Gilbert, Geoff. *Aspects of Extradition Law*, Dordrecht: Martinus Nijhoff (1991).

Ginsburgs, George, and Vladimir Nikolaevich Kudriavtsev (ed.) *The Nuremberg Trial and International Law*, Dordrecht: Martinus Nijhoff (1990).

Han, Henry H. (ed.), *Terrorism and Possibilities of Legal Control*, New York: Oceana (1991).

Harris, D.J. *Cases and Materials on International Law*, Fourth ed. London: Sweet and Maxwell (1991).

Hart, H.L.A. *The Concept of Law*, Oxford: Clarendon (1961).

Hart, H.L.A. *Law, Liberty and Morality*, London: Oxford Univ. Press (1963).

Henckaerts, Jean-Marie. *Mass Expulsion in Modern International Law and Practice*, The Hague: Martinus Nijhoff (1995).

Hicks, George. *The Comfort Women: Sex Slaves of the Japanese Imperial Forces*, London: Souvenir Press (1995).

Jamieson, Alison (ed.). Terrorism and Drug Trafficking in the 1990s, Aldershot: Dartmouth (1994).

Kalshoven, Frits. *Constraints on the Waging of War,* Geneva: International Committee of the Red Cross (1987).

Kalshoven, Frits, and Yves Sandoz (eds.) *Implementation of International Humanitarian Law*, Dordrecht: Martinus Nijhoff (1991).

Khushalani, Yougindra. *Dignity and Honour of Women as Basic and Fundamental Human Rights*, Dordrecht: Martinus Nijhoff (1982).

Kwakwa, Edward. *The International Law of Armed Conflict: Personal and Material Fields of Application*, Dordrecht: Martinus Nijhoff (1992).

Leblanc, Lawrence. *The United States and the Genocide Convention,* Durham, N.C: Duke University Press (1991).

Lemarchand, René, and David Martin. *Selective Genocide in Burundi*, London: Minority Rights Group (1974).

Lemkin, Raphael. *Axis Rule in Occupied Europe*, Washington: Carnegie Endowment for International Peace: Division of International Law Publications (1944).

Lenin, Vladimir. *The Awakening of Asia*, New York: International Publishers (1963).

Lescure, Karine, and Florence Trintignac. *International Justice for Former Yugoslavia: the Working of the International Criminal Tribunal of The Hague,* The Hague: Kluwer (1996).

Lloyd, Dennis. *The Idea of Law*, London: Penguin (1964).

Maclean, Fitzroy. *Josip Broz Tito: A Pictorial Biography*, London: McGraw-Hill (1980).

Malekian, Farhad. *The Concept of Islamic International Criminal Law: a Comparative Study*, Dordrecht: Kluwer (1994).

Meron, Theodor. *Human Rights in Internal Strife: Their International Protection*, Cambridge: Grotius Publications (1987).

Mill, John Stuart. *On Liberty*, Bungay: Pelican (1974).

Morris, Virginia, and Michael P. Scharf. *An Insider's Guide to the International Criminal Tribunal for the Former Yugoslavia*, Irvington-on-Hudson: Transnational Publishers (1995) 2 vols.

Nowak, Manfred. *U.N. Covenant on Civil and Political Rights: CCPR Commentary*, Kehl: N.P. Engel (1993).

Nyiri, Nicolas. *The United Nations' Search for a Definition of Aggression*, New York: Lang (1989).

Pablo, Ramella. *Crimenes contra la humanidad*, Buenos Aires: Ediciones Depalma (1986).

Packer, John, and Kristian Myntti (eds.) *The Protection of Ethnic and Linguistic Minorities in Europe*, Abo / Turku: Institute for Human Rights (1993).

Pictet, Jean. *Development and Principles of International Humanitarian Law*, Dordrecht and Geneva: Martinus Nijhoff and Henry Dunant Institute (1985).

Polak, H.S.L, H.N. Brailsford, and Lord Pethick-Lawrence. *Mahatma Gandhi*, London: Odhams Press (1949).

Popper, Karl R. *The Open Society and Its Enemies*, Princeton: Princeton Univ. Press (1962) Vol. 1.

Power, Samantha. *Breakdown in the Balkans: A Chronicle of Events (January, 1989 to May, 1993),* Carnegie Endowment for International Peace (1993).

Prunier, Gerard, *The Rwanda Crisis 1959-1994,* London: Hurst and Co. (1995).

Rifaat, Ahmed M. *International Aggression: A Study of the Legal Concept - Its Development and Definition in International Law,* Stockholm, Sweden: Almqvist & Wiksell (1979).

Robinson, Nehemiah. *The Genocide Convention: a Commentary,* New York: World Jewish Congress (1960).

Schachter, Oscar. *International Law in Theory and Practice,* Dordrecht: Martinus Nijhoff (1991).

Scott, Peter D., and Jonathan Marshall. *Cocaine Politics: Drugs, Armies and the CIA in Central America,* Oxford: Univ. of California Press (1991).

Smith, William L. *Why People Grow Drugs: Narcotics and Development in the Third World,* London: Panos (1992).

Starke, J.G. *Introduction to International Law,* Tenth ed. London: Butterworths (1989).

Stettinius, Edward R. *Roosevelt and the Russians: The Yalta Conference,* London: Jonathan Cape (1950).

Stiglmayer, Alexandra (ed.). *Mass Rape: The War against Women in Bosnia-Herzegovina,* London: Univ. of Nebraska Press (1994).

Sunga, Lyal S. *Individual Responsibility in International Law for Serious Human Rights Violations,* Dordrecht: Martinus Nijhoff (1992).

Tanca, Antonio. *Foreign Armed Intervention in Internal Conflict,* Dordrecht: Martinus Nijhoff (1993).

Teson, Fernando. *Humanitarian Intervention: An Inquiry into Law and Morality,* Dobbs Ferry, New York: Transnational Publishers Inc. (1988).

Tomuschat, Christian (ed.) *Modern Law of Self-Determination,* Dordrecht: Martinus Nijhoff (1993).

United Nations, *United Nations and Rwanda: 1993-1996,* New York: United Nations (1996).

Walker, William O. *Opium and Foreign Policy: The Anglo-American Search for Order in Asia, 1912-1954,* London: Univ. of North Carolina Press (1991).

Williams, Paul R. *Treatment of Detainees: Examination of Issues Relevant to Detention by the United Nations Human Rights Committee*, Geneva: Henry Dunant Institute (1990).

C.   ARTICLES

Abbell, Michael. *The Need for US Legislation to Curb State-Sponsored Kidnapping*, in The Alleged Transnational Criminal: the Second Biennial International Criminal Law Seminar (ed. Atkins) The Hague: Martinus Nijhoff (1995) 87-113.

Abbell, M. *Obtaining Evidence in the US in Criminal Cases through Use of Compulsory Process,* in The Alleged Transnational Criminal: the Second Biennial International Criminal Law Seminar (ed. Atkins) The Hague: Martinus Nijhoff (1995) 293-301.

Abi-Saab, Georges. *Wars of National Liberation in the Geneva Conventions and Protocols*, 165 Hague Recueil des Cours: The Hague: Martinus Nijhoff (1979) 353-445.

Abi-Saab, Georges. *A 'New World Order'? Some Preliminary Reflections,* 7 Hague Yearbook of International Law (1994): 87-93.

Abi-Saab, Rosemary. *The 'General Principles' of Humanitarian Law according to the International Court of Justice,* 259 International Review of the Red Cross (July - Aug. 1987): 367-375.

Abramovsky, Abraham. *Extraterritorial Jurisdiction: the United States Unwarranted Attempt to Alter International Law in* United States v. Yunis, 15(1) Yale Journal of International Law (1990): 121-161.

Aldrich, George. *Jurisdiction of the International Criminal Tribunal for the Former Yugoslavia,* 90 American Journal of International Law (1996): 64-69.

Alexidze, Levan. *Legal Nature of Jus Cogens in Contemporary International Law,* 172 Hague Recueil (1981): 221-270.

Alland, Denis. *International Responsibility and Sanctions: Self-Defence and Countermeasures in the ILC Codification of Rules Governing International Responsibility,* in United Nations Codification of State Responsibility (eds. Spinedi and Simma), New York: Oceana Publications (1987) 143-195.

Alston, Philip. *The Security Council and Human Rights: Lessons to be Learned from the Iraq-Kuwait Crisis and Its Aftermath,* 13 Australian Yearbook of International Law (1992): 107-176.

Anaya, James. *The Capacity of International Law to Advance Ethnic or Nationality Rights Claims,* 13(3) Human Rights Quarterly (1991): 403-411.

Aubert, Maurice. *The Question of Superior Orders and the Responsibility of Commanding Officers in the Protocol additional to the Geneva Conventions of 12 August 1949 and relating to the protection of victims of international armed conflicts (Protocol I) of 8 June 1977,* 263 International Review of the Red Cross (Mar.-Apr. 1988): 105-120.

Baker, Stuart G. *Comparing the 1993 Airstrike on Iraq to the 1986 Bombing of Libya: the New Interpretation of Article 51,* 24(1) Georgia Journal of International and Comparative Law (1994): 99-116.

Barboza, Julio. *International Liability for the Injurious Consequences of Acts not Prohibited by International Law and Protection of the Environment,* 247 Hague Recueil des Cours, The Hague: (1994) 295-405.

Barsotti, Roberto. *Armed Reprisals,* in The New Humanitarian Law of Armed Conflict (ed. Cassese), Napoli: Editoriale scientifica (1979) 79-110.

Bassiouni, Cherif. *The Commission of Experts Established pursuant to Security Council Resolution 780: Investigating Violations of International Humanitarian Law in the Former Yugoslavia,* 5 Criminal Law Forum (1994): 279-240.

Bassiouni, Cherif. *Enslavement as an International Crime,* 23(2) New York University Journal of International Law and Politics (1991): 445-517.

Bassiouni, Cherif. *The History of the Draft Code of Crimes against the Peace and Security of Mankind,* 27(1) Israel Law Review (1993): 247-267.

Bassiouni, Cherif. *The United Nations Commission of Experts Established Pursuant to Security Council Resolution 780 (1992),* 88 American Journal of International Law (1994): 784-805.

Bassiouni, Cherif, and Benjamin Ferencz. *The Crime against Peace,* in International Criminal Law (ed. Bassiouni) Dobbs Ferry, New York: Transnational Publishers (1986).

Bennouna, Mohammed. *La création d'une juridiction pénale internationale et la souveraineté des états*, 36 Annuaire français de droit international (1990): 299-306.

Beres, Louis René. *Genocide: State and Self*, 18(1) Denver Journal of International Law and Policy (1989): 37-57.

Beres, Louis René. *International Law: Personhood and the Prevention of Genocide*, 11(1) Loyola of Los Angeles International and Comparative Law Journal (1989): 25-65.

Beres, Louis René. *The Meaning of Terrorism: Jurisprudential and Definitional Clarifications*, 28(2) Vanderbilt Journal of Transnational Law (1995): 239-249.

Blakesley, Christopher, and Otto Lagodny. *Finding Harmony amidst Disagreement over Extradition, Jurisdiction, the Role of Human Rights, and Issues of Extraterritoriality under International Criminal Law*, 24(1) Vanderbilt Journal of Transnational Law (1991): 1-73.

Boresz Pike, M. *'Terrorism' and the Political Offence Exception*, in The Alleged Transnational Criminal: the Second Biennial International Criminal Law Seminar (ed. Atkins), The Hague: Martinus Nijhoff (1995) 401-431.

Bothe, Michael. *Les limites des pouvoirs du Conseil de Securité*, in Peace-Keeping and Peace-Building: The Development of the Role of the Security Council (ed. Dupuy) Dordrecht: Martinus Nijhoff (1993) 67-81.

Bottigliero, Ilaria. *Il rapporto della Commissione di Esperti sul Ruanda e l'istituzione di un tribunale internazionale penale*, 49(4) La Comunità Internazionale (1994): 760-768.

Bouvier, Antoine. Protection of the Natural Environment in Time of Armed Conflict, 285 International Review of the Red Cross (1991): 567-578.

Bouvier, Antoine. *Recent Studies on the Protection of the Environment in Time of Armed Conflict*, 291 International Review of the Red Cross (1992): 554-566.

Bowett, Derek. *The Use of Force for the Protection of Nationals Abroad*, in The New Humanitarian Law of Armed Conflict. Napoli: Editoriale scientifica (1979) 39-55.

Bridge, John W. *The Case for an International Court of Criminal Justice and the Formulation of International Criminal Law*, 13 International Law and Comparative Quarterly (1964): 1255-1281.

Brownlie, Ian. *Politics and Principle in Major International Settlements*, in International Law in Transition (Pathak and Dhokalia), Dordrecht: Martinus Nijhoff (1992) 11-20.

Brownlie, Ian. *The United Nations Charter and the Use of Force, 1945-1985*, in The New Humanitarian Law of Armed Conflict (ed. Cassese) Napoli: Editoriale scientifica (1979) 491-504.

Brownmiller, Susan. *Making Female Bodies the Battlefield*, in Mass Rape: The War against Women in Bosnia-Herzegovina, London: Univ. of Nebraska Press (1994) 180-182.

Bryant, Bunyan. *The United States and the 1948 Genocide Convention*, 16(3) Harvard International Law Journal (1975): 683-704.

Buchanan, Allen. *Self-Determination and the Right to Secede*, 45(2) Journal of International Affairs (1992): 347-365.

Burns, Peter. *An International Criminal Tribunal: The Difficult Union of Principle and Politics*, 5 Criminal Law Forum (1994): 341-380.

Campbell, Andrew. *The Ker-Frisbie Doctrine: A Jurisdictional Weapon in the War on Drugs*, 23(2) Vanderbilt Journal of Transnational Law (1990): 385-432.

Caron, David D. *The Legitimacy of the Collective Authority of the Security Council*, 87 American Journal of International Law (1993): 552-588.

Cassese, Antonio. *A New Approach to Human Rights: the European Convention for the Prevention of Torture*, 83(1) American Journal of International Law (1989): 128-153.

Cassese, Antonio. *Return to Westphalia? Considerations on the Gradual Erosion of the Charter System*, in The New Humanitarian Law of Armed Conflict (ed. Cassese), Napoli: Editoriale scientifica (1979) 505-523.

Castillo, Maria. *La compétence du tribunal pénal pour la Yougoslavie*, 98(1) Revue génerale de droit international public (1994): 61-87.

Chowdhury, S. *The Status and Norms of Self-Determination in Contemporary International Law*, in Third World Attitudes towards International Law (ed. Snyder and Sathirithai) Dordrecht: Martinus Nijhoff (1987) 87-99.

Christenson, Gordon A. Jus Cogens: *Guarding Interests Fundamental to International Society*, 28(3) Virginia Journal of International Law (1988): 585-648.

Christol, Carl Q. *Judge Manfred Lachs and the Principle of* Jus Cogens, 22 Journal of Space Law (1994): 33-45.

Churchill, Ward. *Genocide: Toward a Functional Definition*, Alternatives: 11(3) Social Transformation and Human Governance (1986): 403-430.

Cleiren, C.P.M., and M.E.M. Tijssen. *Rape and Other Forms of Sexual Assault in the Armed Conflict in the Former Yugoslavia: Legal, Procedural, and Evidentiary Issues*, 5 Criminal Law Forum (1994): 471-506.

Clergerie, J-L. *La notion de crime contre l'humanité*, 5 Revue du droit public et de la science politique en France et à l'étranger (1988): 1251-1262.

Clutterbuck, Richard, Alison Jamieson, and Juliet Lodge. *Technology and Civil Liberties, 'The Italian Experience' and 'Frontier Problems and the Single Market*, in Terrorism and Drug Trafficking in the 1990s (ed. Jamieson), Aldershot: Dartmouth (1994) 1-30.

Coccia, Massimo. *A Controversial Declaration on the U.N. Convention on Torture*, 1 European Journal of International Law (1990): 314-327.

Combacau, Jean. *The Exception of Self-Defense in UN Practise*, in The New Humanitarian Law of Armed Conflict (ed. Cassese), Napoli: Editoriale scientifica (1979) 9-38.

Conforti, Benedetto. *Le pouvoir discrétionnaire du Conseil de Sécurité en matière de constatation d'une menace contre la paix, d'une rupture de la paix ou d'un acte d'agression*, in Peace-Keeping and Peace-Building: The Development of the Role of the Security Council (ed. Dupuy) Dordrecht: Martinus Nijhoff (1993) 51-60.

Conforti, Benedetto. *The Principle of Non-Intervention*, in International Law: Achievements and Prospects (ed. Bedjaoui & UNESCO) Dordrecht: Martinus Nijhoff (1991) 467-482.

Copelon, Rhonda. *Surfacing Gender: Reconceptualizing Crimes against Women in Time of War*, in Mass Rape: The War against Women in Bosnia-Herzegovina (ed. Stiglmayer), London: Univ. of Nebraska Press (1994) 197-218.

Corell, Hans. *International War Crimes Inquiry and Tribunal*, in The Alleged Transnational Criminal: the Second Biennial International Criminal Law Seminar (ed. Atkins) The Hague: Martinus Nijhoff (1995) 1-7.

Crawford, James. *The ILC Adopts a Statute for an International Criminal Court*, 89 American Journal of International Law (1995): 404-416.

Crawford, James. *The ILC's Draft Statute for an International Criminal Tribunal*, 88(1) American Journal of International Law (1994): 140-152.

Daes, Erica-Irene. *New Types of War Crimes and Crimes against Humanity: Violations of International Humanitarian and Human Rights Law*, 7 International Geneva Yearbook (1993): 55-78.

Damrosch, Lori F. *Politics across Borders: Non-Intervention and Non-Forcible Influence over Domestic Affairs*, 83 American Journal of International Law (1989): 1-50.

David, Erin. *Le tribunal international pénal pour l'ex-Yougoslavie*, 25(2) Revue Belge de droit international (1992): 565-598.

Decocq, André. *Le droit et la notion de crime contre l'humanité*, 147(3) Revue des sciences morales et politiques (1992): 357-372.

Desous, Georges. *Reflexions sur le régime juridique des crimes contre l'humanité*, Revue de science criminelle et de droit pénal comparé (1984): 655-684.

Dhokalia, R.P. *Reflections on International Law-Making and Its Progressive Development in the Contemporary Era of Transition*, in International Law in Transition: Essays in Memory of Judge Nagendra Singh (ed. Pathak and Dhokalia), Dordrecht: Martinus Nijhoff (1992) 203-229.

DiMento, Joseph F. *Criminal Enforcement of Environmental Law*, Annals of the American Academy of Political and Social Science (1993): 134-146.

Dinstein, Yoram. *Some Reflections on Extradition*, 36 German Yearbook of International Law (1993): 46-59.

Dolenc, Pavel. *A Slovenian Perspective on the Statute and Rules of the International Tribunal for the Former Yugoslavia*, 5 Criminal Law Forum (1994): 451-469.

Dolgopol, Ustinia, and Snehal Paranjape. *Comfort Women: an Unfinished Ordeal:* Geneva: International Commission of Jurists (1994).

Doswald-Beck, Louise. *The Legal Validity of Military Intervention by Invitation of the Government*, 55 British Yearbook of International Law (1985): 189-252.

Downing, R. *The Domestic and International Legal Implications of the Abduction from Foreign Soil*, 26(2) Stanford Journal of International Law (1990): 573-599.

Draper, G.I.A.D. *The Implementation and Enforcement of the Geneva Conventions of 1949 and of the Two Additional Protocols of 1978* (sic), 164 Hague Recueil des Cours, The Hague: Martinus Nijhoff (1979).

Dupuy, Pierre-Marie. *Soft Law and the International Law of the Environment*, 12(2) Michigan Journal of International Law (1991): 421-435.

Durand, André. *The International Committee of the Red Cross*, International Review of the Red Cross (1981): 1-68.

Dutli, Maria Teresa. *Captured Child Combatants*, 278 International Review of the Red Cross (1990): 421-434.

Enloe, Cynthia. *Have the Bosnian Rapes Opened a New Era of Feminist Consciousness?* in Mass Rape: The War against Women in Bosnia-Herzegovina (ed. Stiglmayer), London: Univ. of Nebraska Press (1994): 219-230.

Etzioni, Amitai. *The Evils of Self-Determination*, 89 Foreign Policy (1992-1993): 21-35.

Evans, Malcolm, and Rod Morgan. *The European Convention for the Prevention of Torture: Operational Practice*, 41(3) International and Comparative Law Quarterly (1992): 590-614.

Farrell, William R. *Military Involvement in Domestic Terror Incidents*, in 68 Readings on International Law from the Naval War College Review (ed. Moore and Turner) Newport: Naval War College (1995): 411-426.

Farrell, William R. *Responding to Terrorism: What, Why and When?* in 68 Readings on International Law from the Naval War College Review (ed. Moore and Turner) Newport: Naval War College (1995): 449-454.

Farrell, William R. *Terrorism is ...?* in 68 Readings on International Law from the Naval War College Review (ed. Moore and Turner) Newport: Naval War College (1995). 401-410.

Ferencz, Benjamin. *An International Criminal Code and Court: Where They Stand and Where They're Going*, 30(2) Columbia Journal of Transnational Law (1992): 375-399.

Finch, George. *The Nuremberg Trial and International Law*, 41 American Journal of International Law (1947): 20-37.

Flynn, Stephen. *Worldwide Drug Scourge: the Expanding Trade in Illicit Drugs*, 11(1) Brookings Review (1993): 6-11.

Folnegovic-Smalc, Vera. *Psychiatric Aspects of the Rapes in the War against the Republics of Croatia and Bosnia-Herzegovina*, in Mass Rape: The War against Women in Bosnia-Herzegovina (ed. Stiglmayer) London: Univ. of Nebraska Press (1994): 174-179.

Forsythe, David. *Legal Management of Internal War: the 1977 Protocol on Non-International Armed Conflicts*, 72 American Journal of International Law (1978): 272-295.

Forsythe, David. *Politics and the International Tribunal for the Former Yugoslavia*, 5 Criminal Law Forum (1994): 401-422.

Fox, Hazel. *An International Tribunal for War Crimes: Will the U.N. Succeed where Nuremberg Failed?* 49(10) World Today (1993): 194-197.

Franck, Thomas M. *The Emerging Right to Democratic Governance*, 86 American Journal of International Law (1992): 46-91.

Franck, Thomas M. *The Security Council and 'Threats to the Peace': Some Remarks on Remarkable Recent Developments*, in Peace-Keeping and Peace-Building: The Development of the Role of the Security Council (ed. Dupuy), Dordrecht: Martinus Nijhoff (1993): 83-110.

Franck, Thomas M., and Faiza Patel. *U.N. Police Action in Lieu of War: 'The Old Order Changeth'*, 85 American Journal of International Law (1991): 63-74.

Frankowska, Maria. *The United States should withdraw its Reservations to the Genocide Convention: A Response to Professor Paust's Proposal*, 12(1) Michigan Journal of International Law (1990): 141-149.

Friedlander, Robert A. *Reflections on Terrorist Havens*, in 68 Readings on International Law from the Naval War College Review (ed. Moore and Turner) Newport: Naval War College (1995) 377-386.

Gaines, Stanford E. *International Principles for Transnational Environmental Liability: Can Developments in Municipal Law Help Break the Impasse?* 30(2) Harvard International Law Journal (1989): 311-349.

Gaines, Stanford E. *Taking Responsibility for Transboundary Environmental Effects*, 14(4) Hastings International and Comparative Law Review (1991): 781-809.

Gaja, Giorgio. Jus Cogens*: Beyond the Vienna Convention*, Hague Recueil des Cours, The Hague: Martinus Nijhoff (1981). 271-316.

Gallant, Kenneth. *Securing the Presence of Defendants before the International Tribunal for the Former Yugoslavia: Breaking with Tradition*, 5 Criminal Law Forum (1994): 557-588.

Gasser, Hans-Peter. *Prohibition of Terrorist Acts in International Humanitarian Law*, International Review of the Red Cross (1986): 1-16.

Gayim, Eyassu. *Reflections on the Draft Articles of the International Law Commission on State Responsibility: Articles 14, 15, 19 in the Context of the Contemporary International Law of Self-Determination*, 54 Nordisk Tiddskrift for International Ret (1985): 85-110.

George, Alexander. *Genocide in East Timor*, 249 Contemporary Review (1986): 119-123.

Gianaris, William. *The New World Order and the Need for an International Criminal Court*, 16(1) Fordham International Law Journal (1992-93): 88-119.

Gibney, Mark. *The Implementation of Human Rights as an International Concern: the Case of Argentine General Suarez-Mason and Lessons for the World Community*, 24(2) Case Western Reserve Journal of International Law (1992): 165-198.

Gilbert, Geoff. *The 'Law' and 'Transnational Terrorism'*, 26 Netherlands Yearbook of International Law (1995): 3-32.

Gill, T.D. *Legal and Some Political Limitations on the Power of the UN Security Council to Exercise its Enforcement Powers Under Chapter VII of the Charter*, 26 Netherlands Yearbook of International Law (1995): 33-138.

Gilmore, William C. *International Action against Drug-Trafficking: Trends in United Kingdom Law and Practice*, 24(2) The International Lawyer (1990): 365-392.

Glennon, Michael J. *State-Sponsored Abduction: A Comment on United States v. Alvarez-Machain*, 86 American Journal of International Law (1992): 746-756.

Goldie, L.F.E. *Combating International Terrorism: the United Nations Developments*, in 68 Readings on International Law from the Naval War College Review (ed. Moore and Turner) Newport: Naval War College (1995): 387-399.

Gonzalez, Felix Miguel. *Current Developments: the Work of the Sixth Committee at the Forty-Ninth Session of the UNGA*, 89 American Journal of International Law (1995): 607-649.

Goulding, Marrack. *The Evolution of United Nations Peace-Keeping*, 69(3) International Affairs (1993): 451-464.

Gowlland-Debbas, Vera. *The Relationship between the International Court of Justice and the Security Council in the Light of the Lockerbie Case*, 88(4) American Journal of International Law (1994): 643-677.

Gowlland-Debbas, Vera. *Security Council Enforcement Action and Issues of State Responsibility*, 43(1) International and Comparative Law Quarterly (1994): 55-98.

Graefrath, Bernhard. *Leave to the Court What Belongs to the Court: The Libyan Case*, 4(2) European Journal of International Law (1993): 184-205.

Bernhardt Graefrath, *Responsibility and Damages Caused*, 185 Hague Recueil (1984)

Graefrath, Bernhard. *Universal Criminal Jurisdiction and an International Criminal Court*, 1 European Journal of International Law (1990): 86-108.

Gray, Christine. *Self-Determination and the Breakup of the Soviet Union*, 12 Yearbook of European Law (1992): 465-503.

Greenwood, Christopher. *The International Tribunal for Former Yugoslavia*, 69(4) International Affairs (1993): 641-655.

Grilli, Andrea. *Preventing Billions from being Washed Off-Shore: A Growing Approach to Stopping International Drug-Trafficking*, 14 Syracuse Journal of International Law and Commerce (1987): 65-88.

Gully-Hart, Paul. *How to Obtain Evidence in the Civil Law System (Continental Europe)*, in The Alleged Transnational Criminal: the Second Biennial International Criminal Law Seminar (ed. Atkins) The Hague: Martinus Nijhoff (1995) 277-291.

Gundling, Lothar. *Our Responsibility to Future Generations*, 84 American Journal of International Law (1990): 207-212.

Gurulé, Jimmy. *Terrorism, Territorial Sovereignty and the Forcible Apprehension of International Criminals Abroad*, 17(3) Hastings International and Comparative Law Review (1994): 457-495.

Haggenmacher, Peter. *Just War and Regular War in Sixteenth Century Spanish Doctrine*, 290 International Review of the Red Cross (1992): 434-445.

Halberstam, Malvina. *In Defense of the Supreme Court Decision in Alvarez-Machain*, 86 American Journal of International Law (1992): 736-746.

Halberstam, Malvina. *Terrorist Acts against and on Board Ships*, 19 Israel Yearbook on Human Rights (1989): 331-342.

Handl, Gunther. *State Liability for Accidental Transnational Environmental Damage by Private Persons*, 74(3) American Journal of International Law (1980): 525-565.

Hassan, Farooq. *The Theoretical Basis of Punishment in International Criminal Law*, 15(1) Case Western Journal of International Law (1983): 39-60.

Helton, Arthur C. *The Case of Zhang Zhenhai: Reconciling the International Responsibilities of Punishing Air Hijacking and Protecting Refugees*, 13(4) Loyola of Los Angeles International and Comparative Law Journal (1991): 841-849.

Herdegen, Matthias J. *The 'Constitutionalization' of the U.N. Security System*, 27(1) Vanderbilt Journal of Transnational Law (1994): 135-159.

Higgins, Rosalyn. *The New United Nations and Former Yugoslavia*, 3 International Affairs (1993): 465-483.

Hollander, N. *Criminal Justice in the US: Some Thoughts, Concerns and Expectations for the Future*, in The Alleged Transnational Criminal: the Second Biennial International Criminal Law Seminar (ed. Atkins) The Hague: Martinus Nijhoff (1995): 303-314.

Hurwitz, *Elliot. Terrorists and Chemical/Biological Weapons*, in 68 Readings on International Law from the Naval War College Review (ed. Moore and Turner) Newport: Naval War College (1995): 411-426.

Isabirye, David Magadu. *State Responsibility for Nationals who Serve ad Mercenaries in Armed Conflicts*, 26 Indian Journal of International Law (1986): 405-424.

Jamieson, Alison. *Global Drug Trafficking*, in Terrorism and Drug Trafficking in the 1990s (ed. Jamieson) Aldershot: Dartmouth (1994): 69-110.

Jamieson, Alison. *Drug Trafficking after 1992*, in Terrorism and Drug Trafficking in the 1990s (ed. Jamieson) Aldershot: Dartmouth (1994): 111-148.

Jamieson, Alison. *The Modern Mafia: Its Role and Record*, in Terrorism and Drug Trafficking in the 1990s (ed. Jamieson) Aldershot: Dartmouth (1994): 31-68.

Joyner, Christopher C. *Offshore Maritime Terrorism: International Implications and the Legal Response*, in 68 Readings on International Law from the Naval War College Review (ed. Moore and Turner) Newport: Naval War College (1995): 433-447.

Joyner, Christopher C. *Suppression of Terrorism on the High Seas: the 1988 IMO Convention on the Safety of Maritime Navigation*, 19 Israel Yearbook on Human Rights (1989): 343-369.

Kennedy, Robert F. Libya v. United States: *the International Court of Justice and the Power of Judicial Review*, 33(4) Virginia Journal of International Law (1993): 899-925.

Kiss, Alexandre. *The Peoples Right to Self-Determination*, 7 Human Rights Law Journal (1986): 165-175.

Kolodkin, Roman. *An Ad Hoc International Tribunal for the Prosecution of Serious Violations of International Humanitarian Law in the Former Yugoslavia*, 5 Criminal Law Forum (1994): 381-399.

Kooijmans, Peter H. *The Ban on Torture: Legal and Socio-Political Problems*, in The Prohibition of Torture and Freedom of Religion and Conscience: Comparative Aspects (ed. Matscher) Kehl-Am-Rhein: N.P. Engel Verlag (1990) 93-108.

Kooijmans, Peter H. *The Enlargement of the Concept 'Threat to the Peace'*, in Peace-Keeping and Peace-Building: The Development of the Role of the Security Council (ed. Dupuy) Dordrecht: Martinus Nijhoff (1993): 111-138.

Kopelman, Elizabeth S. *Ideology and International Law: the Dissent of the Indian Justice at the Tokyo War Crimes Trial*, 23(2) New York University Journal of International Law and Politics (1991): 373-444.

Krass, Caroline. *Bringing the Perpetrators of Rape in the Balkans to Justice: Time for an International Criminal Court*, 22 Denver Journal of International Law and Policy (1994): 317-374.

Krill, Françoise. *ICRC Action in Aid of Refugees*, 265 International Review of the Red Cross (1988): 328-350.

Krill, Françoise. *The International Fact-Finding Commission: the ICRC's Role*, International Review of the Red Cross (1991): 190-205.

Kunz, Joseph. *The United Nations Convention on Genocide*, 43 American Journal of International Law (1949): 738-746.

Kwakwa, Edward. *The Current Status of Mercenaries in the Law of Armed Conflict*, 14(1) Hastings International and Comparative Law Review (1990): 67-92.

Laing, Edward A. *The Norm of Self-Determination, 1941-1991*, 22(2) California Western International Law Journal (1991-92): 209-308.

Lamberti Zanardi, Pierluigi. *Indirect Military Aggression*, in The New Humanitarian Law of Armed Conflict (ed. Cassese) Napoli: Editoriale scientifica (1979) 111-119.

Lassen, Nina. *Slavery and Slavery-Like Practices: United Nations Standards and Implementation*, 57(2) Nordic Journal of International Law (1988): 197-227.

Leblanc, Lawrence. *The Intent to Destroy Groups in the Genocide Convention: Proposed U.S. Understanding*, 78 The American Journal of International Law (1984): 369-385.

Leigh, Kathy. *Liability for Damage to the Global Commons*, 14 Australian Yearbook of International Law (1992): 129-156.

Levie, Howard. *The Rise and Fall of an International Codified Denial of the Defense of Superior Orders*, 30 Revue de droit militaire et de droit de la guerre (1991): 183-209.

Lillich, Richard B. *Humanitarian Intervention through the United Nations: Towards the Development of Criteria*, 53(3) Heidelberg Journal of International Law (1993): 557-575.

Lukashuk, Igor I. *The Nuremberg and Tokyo Trials: 50 Years Later*, 20(2) Review of Central and East European Law (1994): 207-216.

Ma, Frances Y.F. *Noriega's Abduction from Panama: Is Military Invasion an Appropriate Substitute for International Extradition?* 13(4) Loyola of Los Angeles International and Comparative Law Journal (1991): 925-953.

MacDonald, R. St.-J. *Fundamental Norms in Contemporary International Law*, 25 Canadian Yearbook of International Law (1987): 115-149.

MacKinnon, Catharine A. *Rape, Genocide, and Women's Human Rights*, in Mass Rape: The War against Women in Bosnia--Herzegovina (ed. Stiglmayer) London: Univ. of Nebraska Press (1994) 183-196.

MacKinnon, Catharine A. *Turning Rape into Pornography: Postmodern Genocide*, in Mass Rape: The War against Women in Bosnia-Herzegovina (ed. Stiglmayer) London: Univ. of Nebraska Press (1994) 73-81.

Major, Marie-France. *Mercenaries and International Law*, 22(1) Georgia Journal of International and Comparative Law (1992): 103-150.

Malinverni, Giorgio. *The Settlement of Disputes within International Organizations*, in International Law: Achievements and Prospects (ed. Bedjaoui and UNESCO) Dordrecht: Martinus Nijhoff (1991) 545-587.

Mann, F.A. *Reflections on the Prosecution of Persons Abducted in Breach of International Law*, in International Law at a Time of Perplexity (ed. Dinstein) Dordrecht: Martinus Nijhoff (1989) 407-420.

Marchildon, Gregory, and Edward Maxwell. *Quebec's Right to Secession under Canadian and International Law*, 32(3) Virginia Journal of International Law (1992): 583-623.

McCaffrey, Stephen C. *The Work of the International Law Commission relating to Transfrontier Environmental Harm*, 20(3) New York University Journal of International Law and Politics (1988): 715-731.

McCormack, Timothy, and Gerry Simpson. *The International Law Commission's Draft Code of Crimes against the Peace and Security of Mankind: an Appraisal of the Substantive Provisions*, 5 Criminal Law Forum (1994): 1-55.

McCormack, Timothy, and Gerry Simpson. *A New International Criminal Law Regime?* XLII Netherlands International Law Review (1995): 177-206.

McCorquodale, Robert. *Self-Determination beyond the Colonial Context and its Potential Impact on Africa*, 4(3) African Journal of International and Comparative Law (1992): 592-608.

McCoubrey, Hillaire. *The Armed Conflict in Bosnia and Proposed War Crimes Trials*, 11(5) International Relations (1993): 411-433.

McGinley, Gerald P. *The I.C.J.'s Decision in the Lockerbie Cases*, 22(3) Georgia Journal of International and Comparative Law (1992): 577-607.

Meindersma, Christa. *Violations of Common Article 3 of the Geneva Conventions as Violations of the Laws or Customs of War under Article 3 of the Statute of the International Criminal Tribunal for the Former Yugoslavia*, XLII Netherlands International Law Review (1995): 375-397.

Merle, Marcel. *La sanction des atteintes au droits humanitaires commises dans l'ex-Yougoslavie*, Transnational associations (1994): 119-120.

Meron, Theodor. *International Criminalization of Internal Atrocities*, 89 American Journal of International Law (1995): 554-577.

Meron, Theodor. *Rape as a Crime Under International Humanitarian Law*, 87 American Journal of International Law (1993): 424-428.

Meron, Theodor. *War Crimes in Yugoslavia and the Development of International Law*, 88(1) American Journal of International Law (1994): 78-87.

Meron, Theodor. *The Yugoslav Tribunal: Use of Unnamed Witnesses against Accused*, 90 American Journal of International Law (1996): 235-249.

Meyrowitz, Henri. *The Principle of Superfluous Injury or Unnecessary Suffering*, 299 International Review of the Red Cross (1994): 98-122.

Mohr, Manfred. *The ILC's Distinction between 'International Crimes' and "International Delicts' and its Implications'*, in United Nations Codification of State Responsibility (ed. Spinedi and Simma) New York: Oceana Publications (1987) 115-141.

Morris, Virginia. *Protection of the Environment in Wartime: the United Nations General Assembly Considers the Need for a New Convention*, 27(3) The International Lawyer (1993): 775-782.

Müller, Peter Michael. *Suggested Role and Tools of the Defence before an International Criminal Tribunal*, in The Alleged Transnational Criminal: the Second Biennial International Criminal Law Seminar (ed. Atkins) The Hague: Martinus Nijhoff (1995): 51-58.

Murphy, John F. *Commentary on Intervention to Combat Terrorism and Drug-Trafficking*, in Law and Force in the New International Order (eds. Damrosch and Scheffer) Boulder, Colorado: Westview Press (1991): 241-243.

Muther, Thomas. *The Extradition of International Criminals: A Changing Perspective*, 24(1) Denver Journal of International Law and Policy (1995): 221-228.

Nadelmann, Ethan A. *The Evolution of United States Involvement in the International Rendition of Fugitive Criminals*, 25(4) New York University Journal of International Law and Policy (1993): 813-885.

Nadelmann, Ethan A. *The Role of the United States in the International Enforcement of Criminal Law*, 31(1) Harvard International Law Journal (1990): 37-76.

Nafziger, James A.R. *Self-Determination and Humanitarian Intervention in a Community of Power*, 20(1) Denver Journal of International Law and Policy (1991): 9-39.

Nahlik, Stanislaw. *A Brief Outline of International Humanitarian Law*, Review of the International Committee of the Red Cross (1984): 48.

Nahlik, Stanislaw E. *From Reprisals to Individual Penal Responsibility*, in Humanitarian Law of Armed Conflict: Challenges Ahead (eds. Delissen and Tanja) Dordrecht: Martinus Nijhoff (1991): 165-177.

Naidu, Arjuna. *The Right to be Free from Slavery, Servitude and Forced Labour*, 20(1) Comparative and International Law Journal of Southern Africa (1987): 108-113.

Niarchos, Catherine N. *Women, War and Rape: Challenges Facing the International Tribunal for the Former Yugoslavia*, 17(4) Human Rights Quarterly (1995): 649-690.

Nsereko, Daniel. *Rules of Procedure and Evidence of the International Tribunal for the Former Yugoslavia*, 5 Criminal Law Forum (1994): 507-556.

O'Brien, J.C. *The International Tribunal for Violations of International Humanitarian Law in the Former Yugoslavia*, 87(4) American Journal of International Law (1993): 639-659.

O'Brien, William. *The Nuremberg Precedent and the Gulf War*, 31(3) Virginia Journal of International Law (1991): 391-401.

O'Keefe, Constance. *Transboundary Pollution and the Strict Liability Issue: The Work of the International Law Commission on the Topic of International Liability for Injurious Consequences Arising Out of Acts Not Prohibited by International Law*, 18(2) Denver Journal of International Law and Policy (1990): 145-208.

Okolo, Julius Emeka. *Nigerian Politics and the Dikko Kidnap Affair*, 9(4) Terrorism (1987): 313-339.

Okoth-Obbo, G.W. *Mercenaries and Humanitarian Law, with Particular Reference to Protocol I Additional to the Geneva Conventions of 1949*, Revue de Droit International (1989): 31-56.

Orie, Alfons M.M. *Problems with the Effective Use of Prisoner Transfer Treaties*, in The Alleged Transnational Criminal: the Second Biennial International Criminal Law Seminar (ed. Atkins) The Hague: Martinus Nijhoff (1995) 59-67.

Orrego Vicuna, Francisco. *The Settlement of Diputes and Conflict Resolution in the Context of the Revitalized Role for the United Nations Security Council*, in Peace-Keeping and Peace-Building: The Development of the Role of the Security Council (ed. Dupuy) Dordrecht: Martinus, Nijhoff (1993) 41-50.

Otera, Steven Y. *International Extradition and the Medellin Cocaine Cartel: Surgical Removal of Columbian Cocaine Traffickers for Trial in the United States*, 13(4) Loyola of Los Angeles International and Comparative Law Journal (1991): 955-1008.

Palwankar, Umesh. *Measures Available to States for Fulfilling their Obligation to Ensure Respect for International Humanitarian Law*, 298 International Review of the Red Cross (1994): 9-25.

Parin, Paul. *Open Wounds: Ethnopsychoanalytic Reflections on the Wars in the Former Yugoslavia*, in Mass Rape: The War against Women in Bosnia-Herzegovina (ed. Stiglmayer), London: Univ. of Nebraska Press (1994): 35-53.

Parker, Karen, and Jennifer Chew. *Compensation for Japan's World War II War-Rape Victims*, 17(3) Hastings International and Comparative Law Review (1994): 497-549.

Patel, Faiza. *Crime without Frontiers: A Proposal for an International Narcotics Court*, 22(4) New York University Journal of International Law and Politics (1990): 709-747.

Pellet, Alain. *Le tribunal criminel international pour l'ex-Yougoslavie*, 98(1) Revue génerale du droit international public (1994): 7-41.

Picco, Giandomenico. *The U.N and the Use of Force: Leave the Secretary-General Out of It*, 73 Foreign Affairs (1994): 14-18.

Pomorski, Stanislaw. *Conspiracy and Criminal Organization* The Nuremberg Trial and International Law (ed. Ginsburgs and Kudriavtsev) Dordrecht: Martinus Nijhoff (1990): 213-248.

Prakash, Sanjeev. *The Right to the Environment: Emerging Implications in Theory and Praxis*, 4 Netherlands Quarterly of Human Rights (1995): 363-433.

Quigley, John. *Government Vigilantes at Large: The Danger to Human Rights of Kidnapping of Suspected Terrorists*, 10(2) Human Rights Quarterly (1988): 193-213.

Reisman, Michael. *Coercion and Self-Determination: Construing Charter Article 2(4)*, 78 American Journal of International Law (1984): 642-645.

Reisman, W. Michael. *The Constitutional Crisis in the United Nations*, in Peace-Keeping and Peace-Building: The Security Council and the United Nations System (ed. Dupuy) Dordrecht: Martinus Nijhoff (1993): 399-423.

Reiss, Rena Hozore. *The Extradition of John Demjanjuk: War Crimes, Universality Jurisdiction, and the Political Offense Doctrine*, 20(2) Cornell International Law Journal (1987): 281-315.

Rest, Alfred. *New Tendencies in Environmental Responsibility / Liability Law: The Work of the UN / ECE Task Force on Responsibility and Liability regarding Transboundary Water Pollution*, 21 Environmental Policy and Law (1991): 135-140.

Roberts, Adam. *Humanitarian War: Military Intervention and Human Rights*, 69(3) International Affairs (1993): 429-449.

Rocca, James V. *Superior Orders as a Qualified Defense in International Law*, in *Ius Humanitatis*: Festschrift fur A. Verdross. Berlin: Duncker and Humboldt (1980): 607-630.

Roling, Bert. *The Ban on the Use of Force and the UN Charter*, in The New Humanitarian Law of Armed Conflict (ed. Cassese) Napoli: Editoriale scientifica (1979): 3-8.

Ronzitti, Natalino. *Use of Force, Jus Cogens and State Consent*, in The New Humanitarian Law of Armed Conflict (ed. Cassese) Napoli: Editoriale scientifica (1979): 147-166.

Rose, Stephen. *The Coming Explosion of Silent Weapons*, in 68 Readings on International Law from the Naval War College Review (ed. Moore and Turner) Newport: Naval War College (1995): 501-532.

Rubin, Alfred P. *Current Legal Approaches to International Terrorism*, 14 Terrorism (1990): 277-297.

Rubino, Paolo. *Colonialism and the Use of Force by States*, in The New Humanitarian Law of Armed Conflict (ed. Cassese) Napoli: Editoriale scientifica (1979): 133-145.

Sahovic, Milan. *Le développement récent du role du Conseil de Sécurité et la Charte des Nations Unies*, in Peace-Keeping and Peace-Building: The Security Council and the United Nations System (ed. Dupuy) Dordrecht: Martinus Nijhoff (1993): 339-347.

Sanders, Ronald. *The Drug Problem: Social and Economic Effects - Policy Options for the Caribbean*, 3(3) Caribbean Affairs (1990): 18-28.

Sapiro, Miriam E. *Extradition in an Era of Terrorism: The Need to Abolish the Political Offense Exception*, 61(4) New York University Law Review (1986): 654-702.

Schachter, Oscar. *The Emergence of International Environmental Law*, 44(2) Journal of International Affairs (1991): 457-493.

Schachter, Oscar. *The Legality of Pro-Democratic Invasion*, 78 American Journal of International Law (1984): 645-650.

Schachter, Oscar. *Self-Defense and the Rule of Law*, 83 American Journal of International Law (1989): 259-277.

Schick, F.B. *The Nuremberg Trial and the International Law of the Future*, 41 American Journal of International Law (1947): 770-794.

Schindler, Dietrich. *The Different Types of Armed Conflicts according to the Geneva Conventions and Protocols*, 165 Hague Recueil des Cours. The Hague: Martinus Nijhoff (1979) 119-163.

Schutte, Julian. *Legal and Practical Implications, from the Perspective of the Host Country, Relating to the Establishment of the International Tribunal for the Former Yugoslavia*, 5 Criminal Law Forum (1994): 423-450.

Schwabach, Aaron, and S.A. Patchett. *Doctrine or Dictum: the Ker-Frisbie Doctrine and Official Abductions which Breach International Law*, 25(1) University of Miami Inter-American Law Review (1993): 19-56.

Seifert, Ruth. *War and Rape: A Preliminary Analysis*, in Mass Rape: The War against Women in Bosnia-Herzegovina (ed. Stiglmayer) London: Univ. of Nebraska Press (1994): 54-72.

Selleck, Kathryn. *Jurisdiction after International Kidnapping: a Comparative Study*, 8(1) Boston College International and Comparative Law Review (1985): 237-265.

Sharara, Mohammed. *The Development of the Role of the Security Council: Peace-Building, Peace-Making, Peace-Keeping*, in Peace-Keeping and Peace-Building: The Development of the Role of the Security Council (ed. Dupuy) Dordrecht: Martinus Nijhoff (1993): 61-66.

Siegal, Charles D. *Individual Rights under Self-Executing Extradition Treaties: Dr. Alvarez-Machain's Case*, 13(4) Loyola of Los Angeles International and Comparative Law Journal (1990): 765-798.

Simma, Bruno, and Philip Alston. *The Sources of Human Rights Law: Custom, Jus Cogens, and General Principles*, 12 Australian Yearbook of International Law (1992): 82-108.

Simon, T., and R.D. Atkins. *Prisoner Transfer Treaties: Crucial Time Ahead*, in The Alleged Transnational Criminal: the Second Biennial International Criminal Law Seminar (ed. Atkins) The Hague: Martinus Nijhoff (1995): 69-86.

Simons, B. *The Use of International Human Rights Conventions in Criminal Cases: a Practical Response*, in The Alleged Transnational Criminal: the Second Biennial International Criminal Law Seminar (ed. Atkins) The Hague: Martinus Nijhoff (1995): 433-439.

Simpson, Gerry, J. *Judging the East Timor Dispute: Self--Determination at the International Court of Justice*, 17(2) Hastings International and Comparative Law Review (1994): 323-347.

Sohn, Louis B. *Modernizing the Structure and Procedure of the Security Council*, in Peace-Keeping and Peace-Building: The Security Council and the United Nations System (ed. Dupuy) Dordrecht: Martinus Nijhoff (1993): 385-397.

Solomon, G.B.H. and R. M. Jenkins. *The Impact of EC 1992 on Terrorism and Drug-Trafficking in Europe: U.S. Concerns*, 13(1) Terrorism (1990): 15-22.

Sproule, D.W. and Paul St.-Denis. *The UN Drug-Trafficking Convention: An Ambitious Step*, 27 Canadian Yearbook of International Law 27 (1989): 263-293.

St. John Macdonald, Ronald. *The Use of Force by States in International Law*, in International Law: Achievements and Prospects (ed. Bedjaoui and UNESCO) Dordrecht: Martinus Nijhoff (1991): 717-741.

Stewart, David P. *Internationalizing the War on Drugs: The U.N. Convention Illicit Traffic in Narcotic Drugs and Psychotropic Substances*, 18(3) Denver Journal of International Law and Policy (1990): 387-404.

Stiglmayer, Alexandra. *The Rapes in Bosnia-Herzegovina*, in Mass Rape: The War against Women in Bosnia-Herzegovina (ed. Stiglmayer) London: Univ. of Nebraska Press (1994): 82-169.

Stiglmayer, Alexandra. *The War in the Former Yugoslavia*, in Mass Rape: The War against Women in Bosnia-Herzegovina (ed. Stiglmayer) London: Univ. of Nebraska Press (1994): 1-34.

Strauss, Andrew L. *Beyond National Law: The Neglected Role of the International Law of Personal Jurisdiction in Domestic Courts*, 36(2) Harvard International Law Journal (1995): 373-424.

Strauss, Andrew L. *A Global Paradigm Shattered: The Jurisdictional Nihilism of the Supreme Court's Abduction Decision in Alvarez-Machain*, 67(4) Temple Law Review (1994): 1209-1257.

Stromseth, Jane. *Commentary on the Use of Force against Terrorism and Drug-Trafficking*, in Law and Force in the New International Order (ed. Damrosch and Scheffer) Boulder, Colorado: Westview Press (1991): 237-239.

Sunga, Lyal S. *The Commission of Experts on Rwanda and the Creation of the International Criminal Tribunal for Rwanda / A Note*, 16 Human Rights Law Journal (1995): 121-124.

Sur, Serge. *Sécurité collective et rétablissement de la paix: la résolution 687 (3 avril 1991) dans l'Affaire du Golfe*, in Peace-Keeping and Peace-Building: The Development of the Role of the Security Council (ed. Dupuy) Dordrecht: Martinus Nijhoff (1993): 13-40.

Szaz, Paul. *The Proposed War Crimes Tribunal for Ex-Yugoslavia*, 25(2) New York University Journal of International Law and Politics (1993): 405-488.

Tardu, Maxime E. *The United Nations Convention against Torture and Other Cruel and Inhuman or Degrading Treatment or Punishment*, 56(4) Nordic Journal of International Law (1987): 303-321.

Taulbee, James L. *Myths, Mercenaries and Contemporary International Law*, 15(2) California Western International Law Journal (1985): 339-363.

Terry, James P. *An Appraisal of Lawful Military Response to State-Sponsored Terrorism*, in 68 Readings on International Law from the Naval War College Review (ed. Moore and Turner) Newport: Naval War College (1995): 455-464.

Tomuschat, Christian. *International Criminal Prosecution: The Precedent of Nuremberg Confirmed*, 5 Criminal Law Forum (1994): 237-247.

Tomuschat, Christian. *The Lockerbie Case before the International Court of Justice*, 48 The I.C.J. Review (1992): 38-48.

Tomuschat, Christian. *A System of International Criminal Prosecution is Taking Shape*, 50 The ICJ Review (1993): 56-70.

Treves, Tullio. *La convention de 1989 sur les mercenaires*, 36 Annuaire français de droit international (1990): 520-535.

Verhoeven, Joe. *Le Crime de Génocide: Originalité et Ambiguité*, 24(1) Revue Belge de droit international (1991): 5-26.

Verwey, Wil. *Humanitarian Intervention*, in The New Humanitarian Law of Armed Conflict (ed. Cassese) Napoli: Editoriale scientifica (1979): 57-78.

Vesti, Peter, and Ole Espersen. *Torture: the Need for an International Tribunal to Investigate Individual Doctors Who May Have Been Involved*, 2(4) International Journal of Refugee Law (1990): 611-619.

Viada, Gerardo. *La Lucha Contra Los Delitos Ecologicos y la Protección Juridica del Medio Ambiente en España*, in The Alleged Transnational Criminal: the Second Biennial International Criminal Law Seminar (ed. Atkins) The Hague: Martinus Nijhoff (1995): 441-448.

Wagner, J. Martin. U.S. *Prosecution of Past and Future War Criminals and Criminals against Humanity: Proposals for Reform based on the Canadian and Australian Experience*, 29(4) Virginia Journal of International Law (1989): 887-936.

Wallensteen, Peter. *Representing the World: A Security Council for the 21st Century*, 25(1) Security Dialogue (1994): 63-75.

Webb, John. *Genocide Treaty: Ethnic Cleansing, Substantive and Procedural Hurdles in the Application of the Genocide Convention to Alleged Crimes in the Former Yugoslavia*, 23(2) Georgia Journal of International and Comparative Law (1993): 377-408.

Wegner, Adam W. *Extraterritorial Jurisdiction under International Law: the Yunis Decision as a Model for the Prosecution of Terrorists in U.S. Courts*, 22(2) Law and Policy in International Business (1991): 409-440.

Wetherell, J. *Effective Use by the Defence of International Private Investigative Agencies*, in The Alleged Transnational Criminal: the Second Biennial International Criminal Law Seminar (ed. Atkins) The Hague: Martinus Nijhoff (1995): 269-276.

Whelan, Anthony. *Wilsonian Self-Determination and the Versailles Settlement*, 43 International and Comparative Law Quarterly (1994): 99-115.

Wilder, Andrew L. *The Supreme Court Decision in United States v. Alvarez-Machain*, 32(4) Virginia Journal of International Law (1992): 979-995.

Wilkinson, Paul. *The Lessons of Lockerbie*, in Terrorism and Drug Trafficking in the 1990s (ed. Jamieson) Aldershot: Dartmouth (1994): 149-178.

Wilkinson, Paul. *Terrorist Targets and Tactics: New Risks to World Order*, in Terrorism and Drug Trafficking in the 1990s (ed. Jamieson) Aldershot: Dartmouth (1994): 179-200.

Williams, Sharon. *Extradition to a State that Imposes the Death Penalty*, 28 Canadian Yearbook of International Law (1990): 117-168.

Woltring, H. and J. Greig. *State-Sponsored Kidnapping of Fugitives: an Alternative to Extradition?* in The Alleged Transnational Criminal: the Second Biennial International Criminal Law Seminar (ed. Atkins) The Hague: Martinus Nijhoff (1995): 115-125.

Wright, Quincy. *The Law of the Nuremberg Trial*, 41 American Journal of International Law (1947): 38-72.

Wright, Quincy. *War Criminals*, 39 American Journal of International Law (1945): 257-285.

Wyngaert, Van den. *Applying the European Convention on Human Rights to Extradition: Opening Pandora's Box?* 39(4) International and Comparative Law Quarterly (1990): 757-779.

Zagaris, Bruce. *The Emergence of an International Anti-Money Laundering Regime: Implications for Counselling Businesses*, in The Alleged Transnational Criminal: the Second Biennial International Criminal Law Seminar (ed. Atkins) The Hague: Martinus Nijhoff (1995): 127-217.

Zagaris, Bruce. *International Tax and Related Crimes: Gathering Evidence, Comparative Ethics and Related Matters*, in The Alleged Transnational Criminal: the Second Biennial International Criminal Law Seminar (ed. Atkins) The Hague: Martinus Nijhoff (1995): 315-399.

Zagaris, Bruce. *War Crimes Tribunal in Former Yugoslavia*, in The Alleged Transnational Criminal: the Second Biennial International Criminal Law Seminar (ed. Atkins) The Hague: Martinus Nijhoff (1995): 9-50.

Zagaris-Papavizas. *Using the Organization of American States to Control International Narcotics Trafficking and Money-Laundering*, 57 Revue internationale de droit pénal (1986): 119-132.

Zalihic-Kaurin, Azra. *The Muslim Woman*, in Mass Rape: The War against Women in Bosnia-Herzegovina (ed. Stiglmayer) London: Univ. of Nebraska Press (1994): 170-173.

Zoglin, Kathryn. *United Nations Action against Slavery: A Critical Evaluation*, 8(2) Human Rights Quarterly ((1986): 306-339.

Zoller, Elizabeth. *La définition des crimes contre l'humanité*, 120(3) Journal du droit international (1993): 549-568.

INDEX